The Influence of
Tennessee Williams

The Influence of Tennessee Williams

Essays on Fifteen American Playwrights

*Edited and with
an Introduction by*
Philip C. Kolin

McFarland & Company, Inc., Publishers

Jefferson, North Carolina, and London

Shannon, Sandra G., *From Lorraine Hansberry to August Wilson: An Interview with Lloyd Richards*, 14:1 (1991), pgs. 125, 131, Callaloo ©The Johns Hopkins University Press. Reprinted with permission of The Johns Hopkins University Press.

LIBRARY OF CONGRESS CATALOGUING-IN-PUBLICATION DATA

The influence of Tennessee Willliams :
essays on fifteen American playwrights /
edited and with an introduction by Philip C. Kolin.
p.   cm.
Includes bibliographical references and index.

ISBN 978-0-7864-3475-6
softcover : 50# alkaline paper ∞

1. American drama — 20th century — History and criticism.
2. Williams, Tennessee, 1911–1983 — Influence.
3. Influence (Literary, artistic, etc.)   I. Kolin, Philip C.
PS352.I54 2008   812'.54 — dc22   2008028798

British Library cataloguing data are available

On the cover: (inset) Tennessee Williams, circa 1950s (Photofest);
chairs on stage ©2008 Shutterstock; rose ©2008 iStockphoto
Front cover by TG Design

Manufactured in the United States of America

*McFarland & Company, Inc., Publishers
Box 611, Jefferson, North Carolina 28640
www.mcfarlandpub.com*

To my wonderful grandson,
Evan Philip

Acknowledgments

No one edits a work like this without incurring numerous (and happy) debts. I want to publish mine here. First off, I am grateful to my pioneering contributors for their wisdom, tenacity, and willingness to push beyond the borders of conventionality. Second, I applaud Allan Hale and Harry Elam for their many acts of kindness in answering a menagerieful of questions. I also want to thank the University of Southern Mississippi for repeatedly supporting and encouraging my research, especially Denise Von Herrmann, Dean of the College of Arts and Letters, and Michael Mays, Chair of the Department of English. I am also grateful to our English Department secretary Danielle Sypher-Haley for her continuing good cheer and assistance.

To my family—extended and blood kin—go my prayers and love: Margie and Al Parish; Deacon Ralph and Mary Torrelli; and my children—Kristin Julie, Eric, Theresa, and grandchildren Evan Philip and Megan Elise Kolin. To Lois and Norman Dobson go my gratitude for their prayerful support. Finally, I thank Diane Dobson for her love and faith—in me and in God!

Contents

Preface

Tennessee Williams deserves the honor of being recognized as one of the most prolific and influential playwrights America has ever produced. His energy was miraculous. Spanning five decades, his expansive canon shaped and defined what American theatre meant by how it was performed. No stranger to controversy, Williams mapped the uncharted territory of sexuality and the subconscious on the American stage. His characters, symbols, poetic dramaturgy and language, and plots have often been the models by which other playwrights were measured and/or appreciated. Every dramatist in the American theatre has been touched by his presence. Inevitably, whenever a new, poetically endowed playwright arrives on the scene, a reviewer hails him or her as Williams's heir.

Yet, surprisingly, there has not been a vigorous study of the breadth and depth of his influence. Scattered articles over the years have sporadically linked Williams to various playwrights, though few of these studies went beyond pointing out echoes and announcing shared sympathies, usually sexual ones. Closer to the mark, a special issue of the *South Atlantic Review* that I co-edited in 2005 was devoted to Williams's legacy but covered only six kindred playwrights.

The Influence of Tennessee Williams is the first book to consistently and exclusively investigate the powerful ways he entered the works of fifteen diverse yet representative American playwrights, both his contemporaries and those dramatists who have survived him by almost three decades. The fifteen essays and one original interview assembled here reassess Williams's importance while providing new contexts in which to read the works of these other dramatists. Some of the essays in this collection focus on writers who admired Williams, learned from his craft, and modeled or modified theirs along the lines of his. In this category stand William Inge, Tennessee's earliest protégé, Edward Albee, his ideological compatriot, Sam Shepard, his fellow mythographer of performativity, and Tony Kushner, whose plays dealt with many of the scandals that lurked in Williams's queerdom. Other essays turn to playwrights who gently (Neil Simon) or savagely (Christopher Durang) parodied him. Other essays look at playwrights not customarily associated with Williams but who nonetheless share emerging dramatic conventions with him, such as David Mamet. This volume also places special emphasis on African American playwrights — from Lorraine Hansberry to Adrienne Kennedy to August Wilson to Anna Deavere Smith to Suzan-Lori Parks — and their complex relationships to Williams.

Of course, these fifteen playwrights are not the only major ones Tennessee Williams influenced. But they do represent a valid cross-section of major female and male, white and black, straight and gay, traditional and experimental, prize-winning dramatists whose work, like Williams's, has left or is leaving a legacy of greatness to the American theatre. Obviously, many more playwrights could step forward — in particular, Lanford Wilson and David Henry Hwang. But, happily, Williams's influence on their plays has already been convincingly

1

researched by Milton Tarver (Wilson) and John Bak (Hwang) for the *South Atlantic Review* issue on Williams.

Appreciated from different critical perspectives (feminist studies, racial identity, queer theory), each of the playwrights in this volume further enlightens our understanding of the concept of influence. In fact, each essay here interrogates and develops the idea of influence slightly differently, thus reformulating the construct itself and its diverse applications.

Not limited to searching for allusions or finding ways in which Williams plots were borrowed, expanded, or truncated, the essays in *The Influence of Tennessee Williams* as a whole illustrate the varied, subtle, complex, and provocative ways Williams relates to these playwrights and they to him. Sometimes they reinvested his capital features in their plays, but many times, too, they challenged or even subverted and radicalized his dramaturgy. A few of the essays here (on Albee, Henley, and Smith) deconstruct the idea of a linear influence, showing how these playwrights may have anticipated, influenced, or even redirected Williams's own works. But however they responded to his work, he energized their canons in powerful, lasting ways.

P.C.K.
September 2008

Introduction:
The Panoptic Tennessee Williams

Philip C. Kolin

Dakin Williams, younger by eight years than Tennessee, was fond of predicting that in two or three hundred years his older brother might be more famous than Shakespeare. Fraternal hyperbole aside, Tennessee Williams is, unquestionably, the most influential playwright America has ever produced. From the 1940s onward he entered the American imagination as no earlier playwright had, and he has been a commanding presence ever since in the theatre as well as in film and in popular culture. Fellow dramatist and ideological compatriot Lillian Hellman explained why.

> With *The Glass Menagerie* of 1944 and *A Streetcar Named Desire* of 1947, he brought to the theatre the greatest talent of the post-war generation. There are many good writers who do not influence men who come after them ... influence is not the only measure of worth — but I think it safe to guess that Williams's influence on the theatre will be there a hundred years from now because the mirror he held in his hand announced a new time, almost a new people, and the mirror will remain clear and clean [qtd. in Van Antwerp and Johns, 255].

Looking into his own mirror, Williams wrote what he saw. A self-fashioning author, he became his plays. As Shakespeare did in the *Sonnets*, Williams unlocked his secrets (and hurts) in his plays for generations to come. And America couldn't know enough about Williams the man because of the plays and vice versa. He wanted and needed the fame. Williams lived in a constant swirl of premieres, interviews, parties, controversies, and peripatetic escapes, junkets into his subconscious. He was always the fugitive artist searching for acceptance but, ironically, even when it was securely his, as after *A Streetcar Named Desire* won every major award, he grew habitually self-critical, self-destructive. Throughout his long career, Williams could never exorcize the blue devils — debilitating bouts of despair and anxiety — that terrorized him. Admittedly, he was the target of some of the most vicious attacks ever recorded in the American theatre, and after *Night of the Iguana*, the critics continued to write his postmortem for the 20 years before he died in 1983.

But what critics demonized as Williams's flaws were really the fountainhead of his strengths. He drew sustenance from the inner world of his own excesses and madness — from the early, recently (re)discovered journeyman plays through his last outrageous, experimental works such as *Kirche, Kuche, Kinder* or *The Remarkable Rooming House of Mme. Le Monde*. According to fellow playwright Romulus Linney, Williams claimed that art lived in the unconscious (qtd. in Wilmeth 199). His art represented selfhood, desire, sexuality — his own and his characters' — more openly and boldly than had any playwright before. As C.W.E. Bigsby appropriately contends, the underlying metaphors for Williams's work and life were "the self as actor, society as a series of coercive fictions" ("Tennessee Williams: the Theatricalizations of Self" 64). His name, like his plays, became synonymous with raw desire, the untamed, the taboo, the Southern grotesque. He charted the uncharted, enticing audiences to experience, vicariously, something wild in the country. He lived by and yet suffered because of the cruel psychic paradoxes that generated and infused his works. As Robert Anderson painfully observed, Williams "wrote about what bugged him" (qtd. in Bryer 43) — his family, his sexuality, the condemning paternalistic South, deliberate cruelty, puritanical proscriptions, capitalist doxologies, and, always, the fear of going mad. At the same time, though, there was — suddenly and powerfully — God in Williams's works. A product of his "own divided personality" (Bigsby 68), his plays breathed flesh and spirit — existential yet indeterminate.

Despite the vagaries of critical opinion, Williams's canon towers above any other American dramatist's. His plays seem ubiquitous. Although no one can say with certainty just how many he wrote, we do know that he created more than 75 full length ones, not to mention the bulging archives of earlier drafts and later revisions now coming into print.[1] His plays broke records and traditions. *Glass Menagerie*, which ran on Broadway for 16 months, introduced the Plastic Theatre that became his venerated signature. *A Streetcar Named Desire* dazzled audiences for a full two years on Broadway (1947–1949), spawned two road companies, and was voted the number one American play of the twentieth-century by the Association of Drama Critics. *Streetcar* is an American icon and perhaps our finest literary export. Within two to three years after its opening, Williams's play traveled to over 30 national premieres around the globe (Kolin *Streetcar*). The world has been mesmerized by those star-crossed lovers, Blanche and Stanley, ever since. *Streetcar* has been made into a film, a teleplay, a ballet, an opera, and inspired a Thomas Hart Benton painting. It has been the subject of countless variations, imitations, and parodies.

Cat on a Hot Tin Roof was both a commercial success and an iconoclastic affront. When President Eisenhower was America's Big Daddy, Williams dared to bring homosexuality out of the closet and onto the Broadway stage premiere for nearly two years in *Cat*. Director Elia Kazan insisted on a different last act than what Williams wrote to highlight Big Daddy, and he complied but returned to *Cat* later to write still another third act. *Cat* won audiences over in the 1958 film version which paired the steamy Elizabeth Taylor with crutch-hopping Paul Newman, and made Williams a fortune — a half million dollars (*Selected Letters* 2: 586). It has since been televised, adapted, and acted by theatre companies with a host of ethnic, racial, and political interpretations. *Cat* has proven incalculably proleptic. According to C.W.E. Bigsby, the play's attack on mendacity has made it perfect as a Watergate commentary for cover 17 years. *Orpheus Descending*, perhaps Williams's most reworked script, was also turned into a controversial film (*The Fugitive Kind*) in 1960, starring Marlon Brando and Anna Magnani, whom Williams christened "the Tigress of the Tiber"; a teleplay of *Orpheus* came out in the late 1980s with Vanessa Redgrave; and an opera based on the play was composed by Bruce Saylor in 1994, with a libretto by J.D. McClatchy.

In the 1960s, his "Stoned Decade," and well into the 1970s, Williams showed the world that he could remake himself by writing avant-garde, highly complex plays. Though too often dismissed, or unfavorably compared with his earlier works, Williams's later canon is justifiably being recuperated today, unshackled from myopic, biographically-rooted criticism (Kolin *Unknown Country*). The cocaloony-sieged Gnädges Fräulein in the play of the same name does not, after all, have to be seen as Blanche DuBois metamorphosized into an aging, dockside baglady. Nor should *Something Cloudy, Something Clear* be reduced to the status of a second-string *Glass Menagerie* manqué. *Vieux Carré, Small Craft Warnings, Clothes for a Summer Hotel* and so many of his other late scripts should not point to a Williams in decline but rather celebrate a playwright in the ascendancy of his powers of experimentation. Worth recalling, too, is that in sheer quantity, Williams's later plays outnumber those of the 1940s and the 1950s. These later works may best be regarded as postmodern canvases on which Williams was painting the agony of his canon. Seeing them in this light, they can more profitably be linked to the earlier plays through their continued emphasis on transformation and transcendence.

Williams the playwright also exerted a tremendous influence on Hollywood. He crafted his dramas as if they were films and rightly deserves the honor of being America's first truly cinematic playwright. Father Gene Phillips reminds us that "Fifteen screen adaptations of Williams works were produced between 1950 and 1970" ("Film Adaptations" 63). Although he wrote few of the screenplays himself—*Baby Doll* (1956) being his most famous credit in this genre—Williams's reputation for many has been, ironically enough, based on the blockbuster film versions of his plays (Bray and Palmer). Millions of Americans who never went to the theatre to see his plays saw them nonetheless, albeit through a Hollywood-colored lens. Allean Hale has perceptively gauged how extensively film versions of Williams's plays influenced popular culture, and the overall American economy in the process. After *A Streetcar Named Desire*, she points out, sales of T-shirts surged. Previously, many American men had worn one-piece "union suits." "Marlon Brando appeared in a plain white t-shirt in *Streetcar* in 1951 turning it into a cult status as an outwear garment" (Sweeney). *Cat* illustrates another change a Williams's film wrought. In Act 1, Big Mama points to the bed in her son's room and says to Maggie, "When a marriage goes on the rocks, the rocks are there, right there!" This line, argues Hale, accounted for the sudden increase of sales of double beds over twin beds which had long been predominantly popular before the play was filmed.[2] Moreover, *Cat* became the inspiration for the long-running popular CBS drama "Dallas," according to its producer ("Television").

But Williams's reputation extends beyond plays and films. He triumphed in many other genres. Gore Vidal, a confidant to the "Glorious" Bird, as he affectionately baptized Williams, declared that the "stories are [his] true memoirs" (xx). Had Williams written only stories, he would still have merited a high place in American letters for his narrative techniques, provocative symbols, lusciously depraved characters, and outrageous plots and settings. He published more than 100 stories (and only the Almighty knows how many more unpublished ones will surface sooner or later); two novellas; and a highly provocative novel, *Moise and the World of Reason* (1975), that anticipates many of the techniques, characters, and inert malaise valorized in postmodern fiction. Freed from the prying eyes of censors, imperious producers, and box-office results, Williams revealed in his fiction, even more daringly than in his plays, what plagued him, what demons he battled in his unconscious. A talented poet as well, Williams produced an enviable body of work in this genre. His verse pulsates with the elegant contraries and nuanced conceits that align him with Hart Crane (about whom he wrote a play and from whose poetry came the epigraph to *Streetcar*), Wallace Stevens, Sylvia Plath, and maybe even Carl Phillips.

Added to all these genres are Williams's avowedly private-life writings—the *Notebooks*, the *Memoirs*, three volumes of letters, and a collection of nonfiction essays *Where I Live* (prefaces, reviews, memoirs, and observations on a life in the theatre), expanded and reissued in 2008 by New Directions, Williams's official publisher. In his introduction to the reissue of the *Memoirs*, John Waters celebrates Williams as a major influence on his own gay fantasias. In addition to his prose, plays, and poems, Williams painted canvases that looked at times like an amalgamation of Gaugin and Picasso. According to William Plumley, Williams' paints are "compelling not because of subtlety or technique," but because they give us a glimpse into the playwright "unguarded" (804). Williams also wrote ballads, and even penned libretti, e.g., for his one act play "Lord Byron's Love Letters." The panoptic Tennessee was a lyred Orpheus, providing a source for André Previn's music score the *Streetcar* opera and for Lee Hoiby who wrote the arias and rhapsodies for the opera of *Summer and Smoke*. Williams's creative energy was nothing less than miraculous.

Besides making bravura entrances in his own confessional works, crisscrossing genders in the process, Williams has come on stage in the American theatre through works scripted by a diverse range of playwrights, his contemporaries as well as those who survived him by several decades. The essays in *The Influence of Tennessee Williams: Essays on Fifteen American Playwrights* investigate the complex relationships between Williams's canon and the works of other major playwrights — male and female, white and black, heterosexual and gay, popular and radical. Their connection(s) to him reveal as much about Williams as they do about themselves and the directions American theatre has taken over the last seven decades. Entering the textual spaces of his dramas, these and many other playwrights define themselves and, in turn, help us to read and (re)define Williams.[3] Many dramatists welcomed and shared his characters, themes, and techniques in their works, extending, celebrating, and further empowering what Williams wrote about sexuality and the performativity of self. Others reshaped and recast him, borrowing but parodying his art, sometimes with the (un)kindness of strangers. Still other playwrights radicalized and racialized him, resisting and subverting his white male Southern gentility, his nostalgia, and his color-coded images, characters, settings, and resolutions. For over half of a century, Williams was, paradoxically, both the barometer and lightning rod for the American theatre and the playwrights whose work defined it.

Of the fifteen playwrights covered in this volume, Williams exerted perhaps his most demonstrable influence on the career and plays of William Inge, born only two years after him in 1913. Incontrovertibly, Inge's successes in the 1950s bear much in common in theme and sometimes dramaturgy with Williams's own work. In his essay on the two playwrights, Michael Greenwald points out how and why Williams was instrumental in getting Inge's first works produced in Dallas and in New York. As a drama critic in St. Louis, Inge first saw *The Glass Menagerie* as it was being readied for its New York premiere and was immediately captivated by Williams's haunting poetical style and his gallery of lonely hearts. Undoubtedly, Williams and Inge shared numerous connections through their representation of regional prejudices, portraits of frustrated women, sexual anxieties, and compelling portraits of loneliness and isolation. But if Williams was hailed as the voice of the Old South, Inge, according to Greenwald was honored as the playwright of the Midwest. Their relationship was, at first, a mixture of immense admiration for each other's plays, but, then, as Inge's four Broadway hits (*Come Back, Little Sheba*; *Bus Stop*; *Picnic*; *The Dark at the Top of the Stairs*) rivaled Williams's own successes, he cooled toward Inge, distancing himself from his admiring protégé. Incidentally, a pompous, sybaritic Inge is skewered in Edward Albee's one-act play *Fam/Yam*, which Williams would have greeted in the early 1960s as a well-deserved, wicked parody of his once devoted pupil. The underlying rivalry between these two leading dramatists raises thorny question about who exactly influenced whom, and how.

In the next essay in this volume, Susan Koprince looks at how another immensely popular playwright, Broadway's "King of Comedy" Neil Simon (born in 1927), has been influenced by Williams. Initially, admits Koprince, Williams's influence on Simon might appear to be as distant as graphic novels are from *War and Peace*. Yet Simon's victories, according to Koprince, can be traced to Williams's own success. She argues that Simon's plays actually rework Williams's as parodies, not as ridiculing imitations but as playful and respectful recastings of his dramas. Parody helped Simon to come to terms with the legacy of a theatrical giant while at the same time staking claim to Broadway as his territory for romantic comedies. Koprince reads Simon's classic portrait of incompatibility, *The Odd Couple* (1965), as an extended parody of *A Streetcar Named Desire*. The incorrigible slob Oscar Madison and his prissy, neurotic roommate, Felix Ungar, became parodic versions of the hypermasculine Stanley Kowalski and the delicately feminine Blanche DuBois — the "odd couple" of Williams's play. As Koprince argues, *Streetcar* reverberates throughout Simon's canon, particularly Blanche whom Koprince sees in various guises in *The Gingerbread Lady* (1970), *California Suite* (1976), *Brighton Beach Memoirs* (1983) and *Broadway Bound* (1986). Although Simon's characters owe much to Williams's Southern belles and lost souls, he treated Williams's themes such as sexual desire, loneliness, alcoholism, and homosexuality as subjects for humorous popular drama. In fact, Simon also translates Williams's memory play *The Glass Menagerie* into his own semiautobiographical *Brighton Beach Memoirs* and *Broadway Bound* and incorporates the image of the dysfunctional family from *Menagerie* in *Lost in Yonkers* (1991).

Examining the plays of Edward Albee (1928–), David A. Crespy discovers many of Williams's ghosts. Albee has consistently praised (and incorporated) Williams over five decades of achievements in the American theatre, evidenced by the plentiful tributes in numerous interviews, including a new one exclusively on Williams at the end of this volume. Comparing the creative nuances among Albee's and Williams's characters, language, and symbols, Crespy delineates their mutual influences, and argues that Williams's work consistently informs Albee's dramaturgical technique. Their mutual appreciation ranges from Albee's inserting lines from *Streetcar* in *Who's Afraid of Virginia Woolf* to Williams's honoring Albee as one of the leading playwrights of the century. After Williams, in fact, Albee may be the most important voice in post World War II American theatre. Paradoxically, as Crespy suggests, Albee's successful experimentation may have given Williams the impetus to create a new dramatic style and form. Using a performance-based ideology of "the reality of doing," Crespy illustrates how both playwrights pushed beyond the limits of language in their dramas. Moreover, Williams, like Albee, crafted characters who revel in a virtuosity of performativity — simultaneously artificial and yet deadly serious, utterly believable and real. Crespy also cogently identifies and confluences between Albee's and Williams's dynamic and controversial women and their surprisingly delicate men. Common to both playwrights, too, are their use of beast allegories, symbolic landscapes, and the underlying musical structures orchestrating their plays.

Although popularly deemed to occupy different bands of the playwriting spectrum, Tennessee Williams and A. R. Gurney (1930–) each discovered significant creative energy in the conflicts between fathers and sons, which is the subject and scope of Arvid F. Sponberg's following essay on these two playwrights. Guided by Paul Ricoeur's insights on the paradoxical roles the father figure has in relationship to sonship, Sponberg examines the crucial father/son dynamic in three Williams plays (*The Glass Menagerie*, *A Streetcar Named Desire*, and *Cat on a Hot Tin Roof*), and several works by Gurney (especially *The Cocktail Hour* and *Crazy Mary*). Sponberg argues that confronting and dramatizing these conflicts in their life as well as in their art forced Williams and Gurney to "crack the shell of literalness" in their creative methods. Gurney is one of the many playwrights surveyed in this volume who respected Williams's pain because it reminded them so much of their own.

Like several playwrights here, Lorraine Hansberry (1930–1965), whose *Raisin in the Sun* ran opposite Williams's *Sweet Bird of Youth* on Broadway in the late 1950s, could surely claim different gender, racial, and ideological allegiances. Yet she and Williams both deserve singular honors for writing perhaps two of the most influential plays of the post–1945 American theatre—*Streetcar* and *A Raisin in the Sun*. (Only Arthur Miller's *Death of a Salesman* can rank with them.) Scholarship, especially David Krasner's recent analysis in *American Drama 1945–2000*, has just begun to plumb the complex (inter)relationships between Hansberry and Williams. Nancy Cho's essay advances the case for understanding and appreciating their shared themes and techniques even further. First investigating the biographical and historical connections between them, Cho then juxtaposes *Raisin* and *The Sign in Sidney Brustein's Window* and Hansberry's two posthumous works—*Les Blancs* and *To Be Young, Gifted, and Black*—with *Menagerie*, *Streetcar*, and *Cat*. She believes that Hansberry, like Williams, created universal works rooted in a biting social critique that scrutinized the construction of categories of class, race, gender, and sexuality. While Cho admits that Hansberry's plays are far more explicitly political than Williams's, she nonetheless convincingly maintains that the two dramatists explored similar aesthetic and thematic territory, including interrogating the possibilities and limits of domestic realism, the fracturing of the American Dream, the politics of gender and sexuality, and the power of social and psychological violence. According to Cho, Hansberry's own anxieties and goals argue for a keen and receptive adaptation of Williams's racially sensitive works, a radically different way, of course, than how they influenced playwrights such as Neil Simon or A. R. Gurney.

In my essay on Adrienne Kennedy (born in 1931 when Williams was almost 21), I argue that while she was fascinated with Williams and his work, and repeatedly acknowledged her admiration in her autobiography *People Who Led to My Plays* as well as in her more recent life writings, such as "Passages, Paragraphs," she concluded that her strengths as a playwright lay elsewhere. Kennedy had to surrender Williams's characters and themes because they came from a world not her own. Yet even so, Williams's presence can be documented in the subterranean, nightmare world of her plays. She radicalized and racialized several of his works in a process that I liken to nuclear fission, or the splitting of an atom in two—in this case, splitting Williams's plays into fragments that she incorporated and transformed in her works.

There was much in Williams that attracted Kennedy's attention and helped her explore and develop her own nightmarish theatre—his quarrel with realism, the juxtaposition of the lyrical and the terrifying, recurrent character types such as hysterical artists, maidens, taboo sexual unions, and frightful beast allegories. Elements of *Glass Menagerie* and *Streetcar* disintegrate in such Kennedy plays as *Funnyhouse of a Negro* and *The Owl Answers*, providing unmistakable echoes of her rejection of Williams. The ending of *Owl*, for instance, evokes through Kennedy's surrealistic techniques the conclusion of *Glass Menagerie* with its candles, derelict father, and forlorn, mentally disoriented daughter. Absent, though, is Williams's sentimental longing for a sister he left behind. *Streetcar*, I believe had an even more profound effect on Kennedy. Blanche DuBois with her multiple selves and harrowing excursions into the subconscious implode in *Funnyhouse* as Sarah the Negro adopts in her madness, many of the traits and habits of Williams's southern belle. Vestigia of Williams's plays reside in but are surrealistically transformed in Kennedy's canon. They are the photographic negative of his canon.

John Guare (1938) has readily acknowledges the impact of Tennessee Williams whose work permeated the culture in Guare's formative years. For Thomas Mitchell, the two playwrights share a sly wit exposing the banality of the American middle-class and questioning the assumptions about the nuclear family exemplified in *Glass Menagerie* and Guare's *House of Blue Leaves*. Each crafted compellingly strong and sensual female characters as the hallmarks of their plays. Guare developed a cycle of plays around the hypnotic Lydie Breeze as Williams had created the iconic Blanche DuBois. Additionally, both examined the danger and destruction of the social outsider in plays like *Orpheus Descending* and *Six Degrees of Separa-*

tion. The major differences between the two, though, is in their tone and point-of-view. While Williams's plays tend to be tragic with a morose comic edge for Mitchell, Guare's are absurdly comic with a bitter undertone. Most significantly, both playwrights advocated a departure from naturalism, and preferred heightened theatricality as exemplified in John Guare's "War Against the Kitchen Sink," and Williams's pursuit of a "Plastic Theatre."

In the next essay, Annette J. Saddik turns to Williams's use of mythic images and the shifting boundaries of identity, key influences on Sam Shepard's plays from *Operation Sidewinder* (1970) and *The Mad Dog Blues* (1971) to later works such as *True West* (1980) and *Fool for Love* (1983). As earlier with Inge and Albee, Shepard's connection to Williams has been long standing and positive. Appropriately, Shepard's first play was a Tennessee Williams imitation written for a high school literary magazine in the 1950s, Williams's strongest Broadway decade. Biographically, too, Shepard consistently voices his appreciation of Williams in interviews that shed light on both their myth-laden canons. Myths, in fact, become the aperture through which Saddik reads Williams's influence on Shepard. She grapples with how both writers confront the postmodern question of essence versus appearance as they try to represent the slipperiness of "authentic" identity as it relates to the mythology of artistic fame. Paying special attention to *Camino Real* (1953), Saddik explains how Williams's early experiment in nonrealistic drama heavily influenced Shepard's first major play, *The Tooth of Crime* (1972). But as their canons evolved, Saddik maintains, Williams as well as Shepard realized that freedom was possible only through fluidity, instability, movement, as opposed to resting comfortably in stasis. Accordingly, their characters become fugitives surging forward, never resting, despite their desperate, romantic need to cling to an unattainable ideal. For Saddik, then, one of the most salient ways Shepard can be linked to Williams is through the inevitability of role-playing and the quest for freedom associated with constructing the self.

Sandra G. Shannon's essay surveys the common ground between August Wilson (1945–2005) and Williams as sons of the South. She juxtaposes these two playwrights and the interstices between Wilson's grand ten-play cycle and Tennessee Williams's trilogy of *Glass Menagerie, Streetcar,* and *Can on a Hot Tin Roof.* In the high profile world of theatre, both playwrights enjoyed a hugely successful working relationship with their directors who had a tremendous influence on their work. Lloyd Richards was to August Wilson what Elia Kazan was to Tennessee Williams. Shannon points out that both playwrights stretched the boundaries of realism to explore national, regional, and family identities. Like Williams, Wilson developed his plays around ancestral legacies that impact the past and help to define tragic modern characters coping with marginalization, be it racial or familial or both. As Williams had done throughout his career, Wilson exposed the corruption of power that altered psychic landscapes. Reading Wilson's *Jitney* in relation to *Cat on a Hot Tin Roof,* for example, Shannon shows how both plays interrogate one's inheritance or legacy. The tragic circumstances of Troy Maxson of *Fences* and Blanche DuBois in *Streetcar Named Desire* reveal characters who wage (separate) battles against history, a recurrent theme uniting Williams and Wilson.

On the surface, David Mamet's plays appear radically different in style and substance from Williams's. Yet, as Brenda Murphy usefully points out, Mamet greatly admired Williams, referring to his works as "the greatest dramatic poetry in the American language." Born the year that *Streetcar* premiered on Broadway, Mamet, like Williams, has achieved fame in several genres and media, with continuous credits in film. Exploring these two playwrights, Murphy contends that Williams's importance in Mamet's plays is more overt than critics have stintingly conceded. An early Mamet play, "The Blue Hour" (1979), for instance, imitates Williams's style and imagery closely for Murphy. But even more revealingly, she argues that Williams's relationship with the American theatre and with his audience served as a paradigm of the plight of the aging artist for Mamet. According to Murphy, Williams's representation of the artist *in extremis* in his plays after 1960 provided a substantial context for Mamet's contemporaneous treatment of the aging artist, a crucial type he developed at the very beginning of his own career. Examining the treatment of the artist in three of Williams's later plays, *The Gnädiges Fräulein* (1966), *In the Bar of a Tokyo Hotel* (1969), and *Clothes for a Summer Hotel* (1980), Murphy relates this key figure found in Williams to Mamet's early treatments of the same character type in two of his early, yet highly proleptic, plays: *Squirrels* (1974) and *A Life in the Theatre* (1977).

Unlike most of the dramatists in this collection, fellow Mississippian Beth Henley (1952–) can readily claim a cultural kinship with Williams. Exploring the parameters of this kinship, Verna A. Foster declares that Henley's early plays drew on Williams's best-known work for characters, themes, and symbolic geographies. Concentrating on *The Miss Firecracker Contest* and *The Debutante Ball*, Foster reveals how Henley reimagines Williams's tragicomic characters and themes from *The Glass Menagerie* and *A Streetcar Named Desire* for her own darkly comic purpose. As so many of the essays in *The Influence of Tennessee Williams: Essays on Fifteen American Playwrights* reveal in diverse ways, *Streetcar* has to be one of the most protean scripts in American theatre, resurfacing, reconfiguring, and renewing a plethora of later plays. According to Foster, Henley's plays, not unlike Simon's, feature "Southern belles" who are distorted/split versions of Blanche DuBois or dominating mothers derived from Amanda Wingfield. Most importantly, though, Williams's earlier plays are inscribed in exaggerated and more literal form in many of Henley's works. But, as Foster also provocatively argues, Henley's works share an even closer dramaturgical connection with Williams's later plays of the 1960s and 1970s, an affinity not studied as closely as it deserves to be. Even though Henley, like Williams, was influenced by a Southern Gothic tradition, by Chekhov, and by absurdist theatre, Foster contends that her plays should be read as more literal and grotesque enactments of other Williams's motifs, such as disablement, the desperate need for love as a remedy against despair, and the symbiosis of desire and death, all abundantly manifested in his later canon. These dramaturgical similarities between Williams's later plays, such as *The Mutilated* and *A Lovely Sunday for Creve Coeur,* and Henley's canon cast light on Williams's own experimental dramatic trajectory that led him, ironically enough, to where Henley (like Mamet) began in the 1970s.

Williams also had a strong pull on the earlier works of Christopher Durang who claims Williams as his favorite playwright. John M. Clum focuses on the echoes of Tennessee Williams's work that can be heard in Durang's two notorious parodies—*For Whom the Southern Belle Tolls* (1994) and *Desire, Desire, Desire* (1987). The former, produced frequently, is a queering of *The Glass Menagerie*. Also reflecting Durang's attachment to *Menagerie* is his autobiographical play, *The Marriage of Bette and Boo* (1985), which demonstrates how Williams's "memory play" also served as a model for Durang's more serious work. Like Williams's Tom Wingfield, Durang's Matt narrates and comments on the family memories depicted in the play. Yet, as Clum argues, both Williams and Durang have a complex, pessimistic interpretation of marriage. Williams's views can be seen most clearly in his one attempt at a commercial Broadway comedy, *Period of Adjustment* (1960). In this play, as in so much of Williams's work, we hear the cries of the playwright's own mother making her way into his central character. Just as Durang's, his mother Isabel is a model for his Bette. While Williams's comedy mixes realism and symbolism to offer a picture of marriage literally teetering on the edge of an abyss, it is only sex, loneliness, and economic necessity that ultimately hold his couples together. Still, Williams makes a convincing case for the survival of the marriages he presents. On the other hand, Durang's less linear, more absurdist play constantly questions the meaning of the marriage it depicts and, in doing so, questions marriage itself.

Tennessee Williams's influence on Tony Kushner (born in 1956) is vibrantly strong — consistent, grateful, yet disturbingly complex. As Kirk Woodward stresses in his study of the two, it is also centered in controversy, an element common to both writers. He claims that Williams's influence on Kushner may be approached in three ways: through the historical and social contexts in which Kushner's plays are written; through the theatrical assumptions and techniques Williams made available to Kushner; and through the resonances from specific Williams's plays in Kushner's canon. According to Woodward, Williams profoundly influenced Kushner both as a "Southern author" and as a gay writer. In fact, Williams's frankness about sexuality points toward Kushner's self-identification as an author of a "gay fantasia" for Woodward. Williams's bold experiments with theatrical form and content, particularly in *Camino Real*, lighted the way for Kushner's intricate, emotional, and often sprawling dramas. Woodward contends that clear echoes and subtle resonances from *Cat on a Hot Tin Roof* inside *Angels In America* are powerfully revealing, even emancipatory. Juxtaposing these scripts, he traces the voices, occasions, victims, and outcomes of the scandals on which each play is based. Scandals become the centerpiece of each playwright's theatre of fantasia, *O Tempora, O Mores!*

An important goal of this volume is to show how Williams's plays have been radicalized in the works of several African American playwrights from Hansberry and Kennedy to August Wilson and beyond. He also has played a particularly significant, but underappreciated, role in the works of two foundational African American women playwrights of the late 20th/early 21st century – Anna Deavere Smith and Suzan-Lori Parks. Exploring the works of performer and playwright Anna Deavere Smith (born in 1950) and Williams, Harvey Young claims that both are theatre personalities as well as theatre practitioners whose auteur status shrouds their later works. Revealingly, too, for Young, their plays should be read as travelogues which grant the spectator a privileged glimpse into their nomadic but social lives. Furthermore, their plays not only pursue taboo topics but center them onstage. Both playwrights, according to Young, challenge conventional theatrical realism by incorporating poststructuralist elements in their works. In tracing the connections between Smith and Williams, though, Young does not seek to privilege those moments when Smith behaves or sounds like the white canonical playwright. Instead, he proposes that we flip the equation and consider those moments when Williams behaves and sounds like Smith, asking, "What happens when we read Tennessee Williams through the same critical lens applied to Smith with the aim of locating those moments when the poststructural, the postmodern, and the socially disruptive appear within his plays?" The answers are epiphanic and illuminates yet another way the traditional notion of "influence" is itself redefined and renegotiated again an again in *Tennessee Williams's Influence on the American Theatre*.

The youngest playwright in this volume to be contextualized in terms of Williams's canon is Suzan-Lori Parks (born in 1964) who was the first African American woman to win the Pulitzer Prize (in 2002). And while it seems strange even to imagine that Suzan-Lori Parks, a contemporary, experimentalist black woman writer, would be indebted to an established white male playwright, Harry J. Elam, Jr., convincingly emphasizes that she does in fact repeatedly posit Williams as a source of inspiration and admiration. Elam demonstrates that Williams fueled Parks's wrenching sense of theatre, most cogently reflected in his language and dramatic reality. The shared pathway to the gut for both playwrights, according to Elam, was through the "gutter" depiction of sexual indiscretions and transgressions, an insight demanding comparison with Kirk Woodward's powerful idea of "scandal" linking Kushner to Williams.

The revelation and representation of sexual desire in Parks evidences the legacy of Williams. As Elam insists, sex and sexuality operate in Parks and Williams at the gut level for the disclosure of dirty little secrets. Exploring how Williams's radical inventiveness is evoked in Parks's representation of sexual desire, Elam claims she follows him in challenging sexual taboos and dealing forthrightly with carnality and passion. Yet, significantly, sex for each of these playwrights exists not simply as subject matter but as psychic and dramatic conduit, a lever providing deeper access into the cultural mores and motives of the worlds their characters inhabit.

Demonstrating Parks's affinity to Williams, Elam reads *In the Blood* (1999) through *Cat on a Hot Tin Roof*, comparing Hester's sexual body politics with Maggie's. Questions of gender roles as well as motherhood bond these two plays for Elam. In *Cat on a Hot Tin Roof*, family secrets, questions of sexual impropriety, and deviance lurk behind closed doors while other (hidden) truths are exposed and reverberate loudly. The dividing line between the normal and the prurient is tenuous. Moreover, the multiple confessions of sexual proclivities found throughout *In the Blood* compel audiences to contest the purported morality of the social order and to reconsider who is the victimizer and the victim, just as Williams challenged heterosexual normativity and the legitimacy of traditional family values in *Cat*. Forty-five years after *Cat* premiered on Broadway, Parks's play evidences Williams's legacy as it shows Hester's power and the unfettered possibilities of this homeless woman, cast as a sexual deviant and social outcast.

Concluding this volume is an original interview with Edward Albee conducted by David A. Crespy. In it Albee defines his relationship to and with Tennessee Williams, and explains the influence that flowed between them. Albee felt they were both deeply indebted to Chekhov for the creation of their characters who are real but complicated and refuse to be merely symbolic. Albee also professes a lyric sensibility that transports the words of human beings in desperate situations into a kind of music, just as Williams did earlier in plays like *Summer and Smoke* and *Streetcar*. The interview reveals, too, that both Albee and Williams experienced a "tragic sense of life" which reflects their mutual concern for a humanity that fails to live life fully aware. Sadly, Albee regrets that he was unable to connect further with Williams who, by the time Albee met him, was ravaged by years of alcoholism and substance abuse. In the end, though, Crespy's interview further validates the strong connection between these two playwrights who were targets of fierce criticism because of their sexual orientation but who defied the bigotry that tried to interfere with the creation of their art.

The works of the fifteen dramatists surveyed in *The Influence of Tennessee Williams* span seven decades. In all that time, Tennessee Williams, whether alive or posthumously proactive, has had a powerful voice in the artistic world of representation the politics of gender and race. *The Influence of Tennessee Williams: Essays on Fifteen Playwrights* records that voice in different genders, tones, dialects, and degrees of affinity and separation. To readers, I end with Williams's own motto: *En avant!*

NOTES

1. For the last decade or so, a new Williams's manuscript — usually for a one-act or an early version of an established play — crops up every few months. In 2005, New Directions published ten new one act plays, *Mister Paradise and Other Plays*, and Annette Saddik has recently edited *Tennessee Williams: The Traveling Companion and Other Plays* (New York: New Directions, 2008).

2. I am grateful to Allean Hale for these perceptive observations.

3. In 2005, I guest-edited a special issue of the *South Atlantic Review* that contained articles on Williams's influence on Hwang and Lanford Wilson.

Works Cited

Bigsby, C. W. E. "Tennessee Williams: The Theatricalizations of Self." *Modern American Drama: 1945–2000.* Cambridge: Cambridge UP, 2000.

Bray, Robert and Barton Palmer. *Hollywood's Tennessee: The Williams Films and Postwar America.* Austin: U of Texas P, 2009.

Bryer, Jackson. "An Interview with Robert Anderson." *Speaking on Stage: Interviews with Contemporary American Playwrights.* Eds. Philip C.. Kolin and Colby H. Kullman. Tuscaloosa: U of Alabama P, 1996.

"Cat on a Hot Tin Roof." Newsweek 17 Nov. 1980: 70.

Devlin, Albert J. and Nancy Tischler, eds. *Selected Letters of Tennessee Williams.* Vol. 2. *1945–1957.* New York: New Directions, 2004.

Kennedy, Adrienne. "Passages, Paragraphs, and Pages That Changed My Life." *Yale Theater* 36, no. 1 (2006): 6–19.

_____. *People Who Led to My Plays.* New York: TCG, 1987.

Kolin, Philip C., ed. *The Undiscovered Country: The Later Plays of Tennessee Williams.* New York: Peter Lang, 2003.

_____. *Williams: A Streetcar Named Desire.* Cambridge: Cambridge UP, 2000.

Krasner, David. *American Drama 1945–2000: An Introduction.* Malden, MA: Blockwell, 2006.

Phillips, Gene, S.J. "Film Adaptations." *Tennessee Williams Encyclopedia.* Ed. Philip C. Kolin. Westport, CT: Greenwood P, 2004.

Plumley, William. "Tennessee Williams's Graphic Art: 'Two on a Party.'" *Mississippi Quarterly* 48 (Fall 1995): 789–806.

Saddik, Annette, ed. *The Traveling Companion and Other Plays.* New York; New Directions, 2008.

Sweeney, Michele. www.ffwdmagco.uk/85 The T-shirt-html.

"Television." *Newsweek.* 17 Nov. 1980: 70.

Van, Antwerp and Margaret A. and Sally Johns, ed. *Tennessee Williams. Dictionary of Literary Biography.* Documentary Series 41. Detroit: Gale, 1984.

Vidal, Gore. Introduction. *Tennessee Williams: Collected Stories.* New York: New Directions, 1985.

Waters, John. Introduction. Tennessee Williams: *Memoirs.* New York: New Directions, 2007.

Williams, Tennessee. *Moise and the World of Reason.* New York, 1975.

_____. *Mister Paradise and Other One-Act Plays.* Ed. Nicholas Moschovakis and David Roessel. New York: New Directions, 2005.

_____. *Notebooks.* Ed. Margaret Bradham Thornton. New Haven: Yale UP, 2006.

Wilmeth, Don. "An [Interview] with Romulus Linney." *Speaking on Stage: Interviews with Contemporary American Playwrights.* Eds. Philip C. Kolin and Colby H. Kullman. Tuscaloosa: U of Alabama P, 1996. 193–208.

"[Our] Little Company of the Odd and Lonely": Tennessee Williams's "Personality" in the Plays of William Inge

Michael Greenwald

While history has anointed Tennessee Williams and Arthur Miller as the preeminent American playwrights of the 1950s (and obviously beyond), such was not always the case. The first seven years of that decade found William Motter Inge (1913–1970) the most popular and critically successful dramatist on Broadway. *Come Back, Little Sheba* (1950, 190 performances) earned Inge the title of "Most Promising New Playwright" (New York *Times*, July 23, 1950, II.1), while his second work, *Picnic* (1953, 477 performances), received the Pulitzer Prize. *Bus Stop* (1955, 478 performances) and *The Dark at the Top of the Stairs* (1957, 468 performances) gave Inge a then unprecedented four consecutive successes among critics and audiences, an extraordinary accomplishment for serious drama. To add to his luster, each of these plays became popular films that introduced Inge to an American public distant from Broadway.

While Miller followed *Death of a Salesman* (1949, and a Pulitzer) with *The Crucible* (1953) and *A View from the Bridge* (1955), and Williams received a second Pulitzer for *Cat on a Hot Tin Roof* (1955), neither dramatist quite matched the adulation enjoyed by Inge in the 1950s. In his 1962 study of post-war American drama, John Gassner, despite some misgivings about Inge's need for "a larger and original vision than psychotherapy affords" (173), proclaimed the Kansan to be "one of the most talented playwrights of our mid–century theatre, and those of us who have known him since he began his career in the mid–Forties [see below] would not hesitate to testify under oath that his probity as a writer is unquestionable" (168–9).

Ultimately, Inge proved to be more super nova than legitimate star as his career faded almost as quickly as it flared. Both Williams and Miller continued to write exceptional plays in the 1960s and beyond (e.g., Williams's 1961 *The Night of the Iguana*, Miller's 1968 *The Price*), while Inge's subsequent plays —*A Loss of Roses* (1959), *Natural Affection* (1963), *Where's Daddy?* (1966)— failed to realize the potential he exhibited earlier, although he did win a "Best Screenplay" Oscar for *Splendor in the Grass* in 1963. That same year John McCarten, writing for the *New Yorker*, abruptly dismissed Inge as "a junior varsity Tennessee Williams" (66). As his acclaim waned, Inge fell further into the severe depression and alcoholism that plagued much of his adult life, and in 1973 he committed suicide. Nonetheless, the Kansas-born Inge remains the dominant, if dark, dramatic voice of the American Midwest, a "world which lay behind the *Saturday Evening Post* covers" (Bigsby 153), just as Williams is the voice of the (Old) South.

Although Williams and Inge contested for the approbation of the public and theatre critics throughout the 50s (Williams received more critical lashes than Inge, partly because his newer works were eclipsed by the brilliance of *Streetcar*), theirs was mostly a friendly rivalry born of a long-standing relationship dating back to 1944 when Inge met Williams as the latter prepared *The Glass Menagerie* for a pre–New York production in Chicago. Thus it was fated that Williams exerted demonstrable influence on both Inge's career and his dramaturgy. None of the other playwrights in this collection has been affected so directly by Williams as they launched careers in the theatre. While each can claim some thematic or technical kinship to Williams in their play craft, Inge — who frequently shared drafts of his plays with Williams, and vice versa — most benefited from Williams's mentoring. And there may be instances when the relationship was reciprocal: on occasion, as shall be shown, Williams may have been inspired by Inge's work.

Curiously, Inge rarely admitted that Williams was a primary influence on his work. In a 1967 interview with Walter Wagner, Inge cited the Irish playwrights Synge and O'Casey as influences, adding that Chekhov "opened up the whole world for me when I first began writing as a student back in college" (122). (Williams also admits to Chekhovian influence: in his 1941 one act, "The Lady of Larkspur Lotion," a young writer — clearly Williams's alter-ego — identifies himself as Anton Chekhov.) Thornton Wilder and Williams received minor credit from Inge, who quickly adds, "I think my viewpoint — whatever viewpoints I have — are quite separate from these men" (122). In his forward to *Four Plays by William Inge*, the playwright further asserts that his plays "all represent something of me, some view of life that is peculiarly mine that no one else could offer in quite the same style and form" (vi).

His declarations notwithstanding, there is substantial evidence that Williams was integral to Inge's career. Externally, Williams was the principal promoter of Inge's earliest works, while internally an examination of his plays suggests that many of Williams's thematic concerns are present throughout Inge's scripts. Williams's external influence on Inge may be more important than the internal ones: Inge may not have had a playwriting career but for the former's encouragement and direct assistance (see Voss: "An Alignment...").

Williams's Contributions to Inge's Career

Inge's principal biographers, Baird Schuman (1965) and particularly Ralph Voss (1989), provide significant material about Inge's youth, for Inge, much like — or because of? — Williams, drew upon family experiences in the creation of his characters and their conflicts. The Williams-Inge saga began in the autumn of 1944. Dissatisfied with his teaching position at Missouri's Stephens College (despite mentoring from Maude Adams, the acclaimed early-twentieth century actress and head of Stephens's theatre department), Inge took a job in 1943 as the substitute (for a draftee) theatre critic for the St. Louis *Star-Times*, for which he wrote over 400 reviews and feature stories until 1946. Inge's near-nightly encounters with a variety of plays no doubt contributed to his subsequent skills as a playwright, much like Bernard Shaw and Tom Stoppard benefited from their pre-playwriting careers as critics.

In late 1944 Inge heard that a promising young playwright with St. Louis ties was returning to that city to visit his mother, Edwina. He requested an interview for a "local-boy-makes-good" story (Williams: *Memoirs* 89), and fortunately Tennessee Williams accepted Inge's offer, agreeing to visit the journalist at his residence. Williams and Inge took an immediate liking to each other, partly because Inge had a print of Williams's favorite Picasso painting hung in his modest home (consider the Picasso connection in *Picnic*: 90). The two shared their enthusiasm for the arts and attended the St. Louis Symphony and other cultural events together. Williams recalls that Inge "was embarrassingly 'impressed' by my burgeoning career as a playwright.... He made my homecoming an exceptional pleasure" (*Memoirs* 89). Their fondness for one another also prompted an apparent, though unproven, sexual relationship during the St. Louis years (Spoto 112), for both men were gay (although closeted in the '40s), a not insignificant point given that each playwright includes homoerotic material in his plays.

Inge journeyed to Chicago to see *The Glass Menagerie* on New Year's Eve 1944, an event that singly transformed Inge and his artistic career. He spoke enthusiastically about the play and of Laurette Taylor's superb rendering of Amanda Winfield, although, curiously, he did not write a review for the *Star-Times*. He judged that Williams's play was "so beautiful and deeply moving" that he "felt a little ashamed for having led an unproductive life" and thus determined that "being a successful playwright was what he most wanted in the world for himself" (Gould 268). Audrey Wood, Inge's literary agent (importantly, also Williams's), cites a passage from an unpublished journal that confirms that Williams's family drama provided the epiphany that prompted Inge to write *for*, rather than *about*, the theatre:

> I rode the train back to St. Louis and gave my experience in Chicago deep thought. Tennessee had shown me a dynamic example of the connection between art and life. I could see, from what he had told me about his youth and family life, how he had converted the raw material of his life into drama. I had been wanting to write plays myself, but I had never known where to look for material.... Now I knew where to look for a play — inside myself [Wood 222].

That spring Inge began work on a play "formed from pretty nostalgic memories of childhood, without being very autobiographical ... a belated attempt to come to terms with the past" (*Four Plays* ix). Borrowing a phrase from a Thomas Hood poem, Inge called his play *Farther Off from Heaven*. Like *The Glass Menagerie*—though more conventional and realistic in form and diction — it was a family drama based upon details extracted from Inge's youth in Independence, Kansas. The father, Andrew Campbell, is a harness salesman (cf. Inge's father, Luther Clayton Inge) who has more-or-less fallen in love with long distances (cf. *Menagerie*). The family has two children: a young boy fond of reciting Shakespeare, dressing as female movie stars, and collecting film memorabilia (cf. Inge as a pre-teen in Kansas: Voss's biography provides photos of Inge dressed as "a young girl," p. 20, and as "an old lady with a monocle," p. 18); an exceptionally shy teenage girl (much like Inge's sister, Helene) who anxiously anticipates the arrival of a "gentleman caller" (cf. Laura in *Menagerie*), himself an outsider because of his Jewish heritage. The play's central figure is a weary mother, Sarah (Inge's mother's middle name), who alternately smothers her children with love and stifles them with harsh demands (cf. Amanda Wingfield and Inge's mother, Maude Sarah Gibson, a descendant of the Booth family of actors; Edwin Booth is referenced in the play). These plot elements may sound familiar: a decade later Inge reworked *Farther Off from Heaven* where it appeared on Broadway as *The Dark at the Top of the Stairs*. (Inge's major plays were typically derived from earlier, usually shorter, works).

Inge shared his script with Williams, who received it warmly and forwarded it to Wood in New York. Although she admired its potential, Wood judged it as being not Broadway-ready (Voss 89). Though Inge despaired at her rejection, Williams persisted and sent the play to a Dallas friend, Margo Jones, who had served as the assistant director to actor Eddie Dowling, who also played Tom, in *The Glass Menagerie*. (Williams first met Jones, whom he called "the Texas Tornado" because of her extraordinary energy, in Pasadena, California, in

1942.) After several directing experiences on Broadway, Jones launched a new theatre project in Dallas: Theatre 47 (i.e., 1947; Jones updated the year with each new season), which evolved into one of America's leading regional houses, the Dallas Theatre Center. Jones so admired Inge's drama that she selected it to open Theatre 47's first season, which also included Williams's *Summer and Smoke*. That she chose Inge's play as the inaugural production over one by Williams — by then an established playwright whose masterpiece, *A Streetcar Named Desire*, opened in New York later in 1947 — suggests much about the quality of Inge's initial playwriting effort. Texas and New York critics alike admired *Farther Off from Heaven* and the other plays in Jones's first season (Voss 93; see also footnote 32).

Encouraged by his first success, albeit it farther off from Broadway than he preferred, Inge began work on a second play. He read a draft to Williams — "in his beautifully quiet and expressive voice" (*Memoirs* 89) — who was so "deeply moved by the play" that he sent it to Wood with the promise that he — now a kingmaker because of the phenominal success of *Streetcar*— would personally put up the seed money for *Come Back, Little Sheba* should she not accept it or secure financing for a New York production. Fortunately for Inge, Wood recognized the play's quality which she labeled "a sensitive and well-written drama about two very ordinary people ... [Tennessee] was absolutely right" (Wood 223). After a successful tryout in Westport, Connecticut, the play opened on February 15, 1950 to mostly enthusiastic reviews for Inge's writing and Shirley Booth's stellar performance as Lola. Williams himself lauded the play and its performances in a telegram in which he praised "the greatest ensemble playing [he could] remember ... since *Juno and the Paycock* in 1940." Williams further added that the play had "an unaffected truth and controlled passion that will give it nobility to our theater and warmth to many hearts in need for a long time to come" (Wood 9–10).

Sheba evidenced some of Williams's dramaturgical trademarks that will be explored throughout this essay: central characters who flee from their dilemmas into alcohol (Doc) or a fantasy bordering on madness (Lola); the lust of an adult for an attractive young person (cf. Blanche and the paperboy with Doc and Maria); a young hunk's muscular torso that arouses an older woman's sexual cravings (Blanche for Stanley, Lola for Turk). Whether Inge consciously mirrored Williams is uncertain, but the parallels certainly suggest that the fledgling dramatist had learned some lessons well from his mentor.

With *Sheba*'s success Inge emerged as his own man in the commercial theatre; he no longer needed Williams to open Broadway's doors for him. His next play, *Picnic,* and particularly the Pulitzer Prize it earned him, put Inge on equal footing with Williams. It also contributed to a fissure in the Inge-Williams friendship. Shortly after *Picnic* premiered in 1953, Williams's [*Ten Blocks on the*] *Camino Real*—written as a project for the Actors' Studio — opened to hostile reviews. Walter Kerr condemned it as "the worst play yet written by the best playwright of this generation." It closed after only 60 performances and is rarely performed today. (This scenario repeated itself in 1957 when Inge's *The Dark at the Top of the Stairs* upstaged Williams's *Orpheus Descending*.) While lunching at the Algonquin Hotel, Inge — whose intentions should be considered honorable — asked Williams if perhaps he felt "blocked as a writer" (Williams's to Audrey Wood, October 14, 1953; Devlin 503). Williams was offended by Inge's insinuation, in no small part because he still considered the Kansan an apprentice and his pupil. And because he was jealous of Inge's success?

A year after the Algonquin incident, Williams attacked Inge in a letter to Audrey Wood (March 6, 1954):

I was terribly disturbed by the one-acts he gave me to read.... I think he is going through what I went through after "*Streetcar*," post [Williams's deleted "trauma" here] shock. But he is overcompensating in the wrong way. To exhibit this work is extremely damaging. I think you must deal with him as candidly as you do me when I send you "crap." It's the only way to help a panicky writer [Devlin 519].

Williams was fully aware of his jealousy, as evidenced by a letter to Brooks Atkinson (March 25, 1955) in which he admitted his "invidious resentment" at Inge's success at a time of his own failure: "I was consumed with envy of his play's [i.e., *Bus Stop*] success.... Hideous competiveness which I never had in me before! But after '*Camino*' I was plunged into such depths I thought I would never rise from" (Devlin 569). Years later, when Inge suffered a similar fate — negative reviews, abrupt closings, declining popularity among audiences and critics — Williams, perhaps a bit too callously, said of his colleague: "Bill's primary problem was one of pathological egocentricity; he could not take a spell of failures after his run of smash hits: so eventually he was cared for by two male nurses" (*Memoirs* 225).

The line about "two male nurses" rings with irony. Both men suffered from bouts of depression and ill-health, in part the by-products of alcohol and substance abuse. Each "rescued" the other in time of need — or at least tried to do so. In 1967, Inge sent his personal psychiatrist to Williams's home near Los Angeles as Williams lay "drugged in [his] back bedroom," while two young men (one named Ryan, Williams's apparent lover at that time) had a violent fight in an outer room. The playwright arose to find "a strange and formidable man" (the psychiatrist) in his living room. Williams first called the police (which, Williams wrote, sent the psychiatrist "hot footing it" out if the house) and then Audrey Wood, who, like Inge, interceded to help the drugged playwright. Williams accused Inge of attempting to "put him away," although Williams soon thereafter checked himself into a treatment center because he was "headed for the bin" (*Memoirs* 215–16). Williams also aided Inge under similar circumstances, particularly in the last days of Inge's life: he pleaded unsuccessfully with Inge's sister, Helene, to have her alcoholic brother committed to a hospital "for an indefinite period of time" (Voss 270).

The playwrights, however, remained close friends despite their apparent animosities. In a recent addendum to his autobiography of Inge in *American Drama* (Winter 2006), Voss speculates that Williams may have borrowed the plot of *Sweet Bird of Youth* (1959) from Inge's most produced one-act play, "Bus Riley's Back in Town" (written in the mid–50s, published in 1962). Williams's secretary, John Connolly, showed him a copy he had received from Inge as the two writers continued to share drafts of plays with one another even after the Algonquin incident. It is therefore possible that the "Bus Riley" plot may have had a more-than-coincidental influence on *Sweet Bird of Youth*. (Ironically, a 1998 *New York Times* review of "Bus Riley" by Wilborn Hampton labeled the Inge one act "a sort of low-rent version" of Williams's play.) Inge added to the intrigue of this situation by including dialogue in *Natural Affection* that references *Sweet Bird of Youth*: a character asks, perhaps ominously, "I don't know where that Tennessee Williams finds the characters he writes about, do you?" (82). Although Voss doesn't draw a definitive conclusion to his speculation, his essay suggests an intriguing possibility about these feuding friends. Actor Barbara Baxley, likely the closest friend Inge had in New York, admits to the strain in the Williams-Inge professional relationship but emphasizes that "when push came to shove, those two were very good friends" (Voss 153). Williams, who outlived Inge by ten years, eulogized his dead friend in a New York *Times* essay, "To William Inge, An Homage:"

It is pleasant to believe that the work of an artist gives him a certain life after death, usually a thing for which he paid an enormous price. But surely Bill with [his] deep humanity would be happy to know ... how much of his heart remains with us cliffhangers ["Homage" 8].

Williams's "Personality" in the Plays of William Inge

Although Inge downplayed Williams's influence on his playwriting in the Wagner interview, there are discernable commonalities shared by the playwrights. Robert Brustein, in a controversial (and devastating for Inge) assessment of Inge's playwriting for *Harper's Magazine* (November 1958), noted that *The Dark at the Top of the Stairs* was "the first of Inge's works not to be largely dominated by Williams's personality" (Kernan 72). Brustein's commentary implies that *Come Back, Little Sheba, Picnic,* and *Bus Stop* each manifests Williams's "personality" or what Milton Tarver calls "emulative authority," that is, "the mesmerizing power of an individual with enough affective presence to occupy another person's consciousness ... such that the actual and imaginary characteristics that define the individual become both intentionally and unwittingly assimilated" (23). The point was made earlier that the largely autobiographical *Farther Off from Heaven,* the 1947 draft of *The Dark at the Top of the Stairs,* was obviously inspired by Inge's admiration for *The Glass Menagerie,* the first demonstrable instance of Williams's emulative authority on Inge.

Recall, also, that *Farther Off from Heaven* opened the Theatre 47 season in Dallas, which also featured Williams's *Summer and Smoke,* originally titled *A Chart of Anatomy* and revised later that year as *Eccentricities of a Nightingale.* In the altered version, the central character, a lonely woman named Alma, talks wistfully about her "little company of the faded and frightened and difficult and odd and lonely" (75), an apt profile of so many of Williams's central characters and, significantly, those of Inge. Although the latter's are in most cases not as "eccentric" as those of Williams, Inge's Midwesterners, like Williams's Southerners, attempt to escape from a stifling existence in isolated, unnamed towns in Kansas and Oklahoma. And like Williams's most memorable characters, Inge's loneliest, most vulnerable creations are women: for every Amanda and Laura Wingfield, Alma Winemiller, Blanche DuBois, and Hannah Jelkes, Inge offers a Lola Delaney (*Sheba*), the collected women of *Picnic, Bus Stop*'s Elma, Grace, and, to another extent, Cherie, and Cora and Reenie Flood in *The Dark at the Top of the Stairs.* Collectively these women embody Inge's dominant themes: "loneliness, frustration, loss, despair, and, perhaps above all, the human need for love" (Voss 183), attributes Voss elsewhere ascribes to the playwright himself ("Savior" 26). Little wonder that Williams and Inge are considered among the most eloquent spokes*men* for alienated women in the modern American theatre. If Harold Clurman's observation that "no one in American drama has written more intuitively of women than Williams" is valid (*Eight Plays* x), surely his protégé stands not far removed.

Consider the mothers contrived by each playwright in the mid–1940s (and further developed by Inge in 1957, as cited here), keeping in mind that Inge — in oft-stated admissions — was profoundly influenced by Williams's portrait of the Wingfield family. Though not as flamboyant as Amanda (then, who is in American realistic drama?), Cora Flood (*Heaven*'s Sarah Campbell), a staid Midwestern mother for whom flamboyance would be unthinkable, is overly protective of her children, Reenie (Irene in *Heaven*) and Sonny: "...maybe I've hurt you more by pampering. You. And Sonny, too," she admits to her daughter (*Stairs* 285). (Perhaps too protective of Sonny? Theirs is a decidedly Oedipal relationship, an issue which Inge explored more fully in the short-lived *Natural Affection*). Against the protestations of Rubin (Andrew in *Heaven*), her oft-absent, overbearing, and philandering husband, Cora defends her right to buy surreptitiously an expensive party dress for Reenie's date with Sammy Goldenbaum, her gentleman caller "all the way from California" (256). Realizing that her painfully shy daughter is "a plain girl with no conscious desire to be anything else" (235), Cora, like Amanda, envisions a life for her daughter beyond the confining walls of the family household "out here in this sandy soil" (293) of rural Oklahoma.

In reality, Cora, again like Amanda, seeks escape from the claustrophobia of her own situation, partly through fantasies about her daughter's future being brighter than the dreary existence the Flood women face on the arid Plains. Just as Williams uses decaying homes in the Old South (e.g., Belle Reve or Big Daddy's house on the Delta) and the seedy apartments in the Vieux Carré or St. Louis as metaphors for people trapped in a world that is passing them by, Inge uses the flat, unchanging horizons of Kansas and Oklahoma as "prisons" for his protagonists. *The Fugitive Kind* (1959), the retitled film version of Williams's *Orpheus Descending*, serves as an incisive label for Inge's women and some men, as well as those in Williams's canon, who seek an escape from psychological incarceration.

Williams himself identified "claustrophobia" as a primary concern in Inge's plays as well as in his personal life. In a testimonial to his deceased friend, Williams wrote that, based on his "long association" with Inge, he knew that his colleague "suffered from extreme claustrophobia" ("Homage" 1). Inge wrote in an uncompromisingly naturalistic style befitting the conservative, literal-minded disposition of his Midwestern roots. This accounts, in part, for the single-settings of his plays. Critics, notably Craig Clinton, remark that the fixed stage picture, coupled with relatively unobtrusive lighting/sounds effects (the theatrical kind of which are endemic to Williams's best work), heighten the "claustrophobic nightmare" of an Inge play (32). Even Inge's lone exterior in *Picnic* (originally conceived to feature six locales: Voss 128) calls for "two small houses that sit *close* beside each other in a small Kansas town..." (75, emphasis added). True, we occasionally hear the sound of train whistle in the distance, which only reinforces that Inge's women are taunted by a world beyond their suffocating, finite surroundings, which prompts Madge to declare wistfully, "Whenever I hear that train coming into town, I always get a feeling of ... (*Hugging her stomach*) ... right here" (79).

Of more importance than the claustrophobia induced by settings that mirror the small town and small-minded people who imprison Inge's heroines is the mental claustrophobia they experience. Inge, a homosexual in a repressively conservative environment in his native Kansas, certainly understood this phenomenon. Consider a speech from his 1960s one-act, "The Boy in the Basement," in which a mother (much like the citizens of Independence?) reacts to the news that her son is gay:

> Dear God, my own son! My own flesh and blood! Corrupting himself in low degeneracy. Going to some disgusting saloon, where men meet other men and join together in ... in some form of unnatural vice, in some form of lewd degeneracy [*Summer Brave et al.,* 177].

Philip C. Kolin credits Williams with revolutionizing "the American stage by not representing conflict as merely an external, outer force of opposition" and thereby advancing "an experimentation with self" (49) largely through the use of lengthy interior monologues/ soliloquies. Although Inge followed his mentor's lead in privileging the private soul, he only rarely used the extended monologue to illuminate anxieties of his principal characters (*Sheba*'s Lola is an exception): his taciturn Midwesterners don't think/speak like that, nor do they use the eloquent flights of language that mark Williams as American drama's foremost poetic realist. One cannot imagine an Inge character saying, as Blanche does, "Don't you just love these long rainy afternoons ... when an hour isn't an hour — but a little piece of eternity dropped in your hands — and who knows what to do with it?" (*Streetcar* 149) Rather, Inge's people speak in terse sentences, often punctuated by clichés learned (apparently) at Sunday church services. After Sammy's suicide (aggravated, in part, by Reenie's painful shyness at the country club dance where his Jewishness is unwelcomed), Cora reminds her daughter:

> There are all kinds of people in the world. And you have to live with them all. God never promised us any different. The bad people, you don't hate. You're only sorry they have to be [294].

Such seemingly trite dialogue is, as Jane Lange illustrates by using media advertisements from the 1950s, Inge's "conscious artistic device" to objectify in verbal terms the strict social conformity imposed by Midwestern conservatism that stifles his characters (62). Shuman also rebuts critics (Weales 41, Brustein 71) who deride Inge's commonplace dialogue: "Such criticism is unjust, for the people of whom Inge is writing do 90% of their thinking and speaking in clichés. Were he to present them in any other way, he could justly be accused of presenting unrealistic and unconvincing dialogue" (83). In a more recent study (2005), Jeff Johnson argues that "Inge's plays prove how lives held together by clichés [both linguistic and situational] *can* be dramatically rendered without the plays themselves being wrecked by the very clichés they purport to explode" (42). Williams himself said Inge had "a perfect ear for [his characters'] homey speech" (Homage, 8). One might, in fact, argue that Inge's precise use of "homey speech" constitutes a kind of poetry, much as David Mamet valorizes the clipped and vulgar speech of Chicago's mean streets. The same may be said of Williams's Southerners — e.g., Amanda, Blanche, Alma — and their "affectations" in speech (see *Eight Plays* 227–29).

Other of Inge's female protagonists are as trapped as Cora Flood. Inspired by memories of the troubled past of his maternal aunt (Shuman 23), Inge borrowed two characters from *Farther Off from Heaven*, Ed and Lola Delaney, to create *Come Back Little Sheba*. In the new play Lola, perhaps Inge's most compelling character, is ensnared in a failing marriage of some 20 years. A former high school beauty queen (14; cf. Madge Owens, Queen of Neewollah, in *Picnic*; is she the specter of Lola as a teen?), Lola, 18 and pregnant, was forced to marry the once-handsome, upwardly mobile Doc because of their one-night indiscretion as teens. Embittered that his plans for a medical career were aborted, Doc — much like Inge himself — turned to alcohol as an escape from his circumstances. (If Inge was a spokesman for trapped women, he was no less so for alcoholics; consider Dr. Lyman in *Bus Stop*, who, like Inge, is a drunken professor with unconventional sexual predilections). Lola seeks escapes routes, also: in rambling phone conversations with her mother; in a steamy radio soap opera titled "Taboo," which promises listeners that they can, for fifteen minutes, abandon those quintessential Inge concerns: "the dull cares that make up your day-to-day existence" (22); in her Blanche-like fantasies about, and flirtations with, other men (the athletic Turk and the postman); and especially in her dog, Sheba, a mental substitute for the baby that died in childbirth (7). Clearly Lola, again like Blanche (who was then new to Broadway audiences), frantically seeks to "recover her vanished years [which] waxes more pathetic than poetic" (Johnson 54). She fails — her dreams are as dead as her dog and "smeared with mud, with no one to stop and care for her" (69) — but attempts to carry on by "fixing [Doc's] eggs" for breakfast (69) in what appears to be a positive, traditionally domestic resolution. The ending can be read as ironic as that of *Streetcar*, in which Stanley attempts to soothe Stella's grief for her sister's forced removal to a mental institution (196–97). Just as audiences sense that the fracture in the Stanley-Stella marriage is permanent (he raped her sister even as Stella was in labor: 187), so, too, have we seen the ugly side of the Doc-Lola relationship. Doc has threatened his wife with a hatchet (56–7), exposing a predilection for violence that is not likely to dissipate with time, despite his apparent repentance (67) or a hearty breakfast. Elsewhere, Doc has shown a cruel side that unmistakably recalls Williams's men in *Streetcar*: disillusioned when he learns that the beautiful border, Marie, his "ideal" woman and perhaps a projection of the younger Lola, has been sleeping with the track star, Turk, Doc angrily "jerks the cloth off the [dining] table, sending dishes rattling to the floor" (56), a reenactment of Stanley's angry plate-tossing episode at Blanche's "dismal birthday supper" in scene 8 (168–9). Doc's line — "My mother didn't buy those dishes for whores [i.e., Marie] to eat off" — echoes Mitch's dismissal of Blanche: "You're not clean enough to bring in the house with my mother" (180). Even as Inge was scripting *Sheba*, *Streetcar* was the most popular — and sensational — play on Broadway; that Inge's first Broadway play should resonate with elements of Williams's phenomenal success is not surprising.

Instead of focusing on the loneliness of a single woman as he did in *Sheba*, Inge diffused his focus in *Picnic*, a reworking of *Front Porch*, which he had written in the late 40s, a sketch about middle-aged women in a small Kansas town in late summer. Inge had also begun a draft of a "The Man in Boots" (Voss 94), in which we meet the prototype of Hal Carter who brags that his "old man" left him a pair of boots and some macho advice: "There'll be times when the only thing you got to be proud of is the fact that you're a man. So wear your so people can hear you comin'..." (*Four Plays* 111). The two plays provided the foundation upon which Inge built his most successful and still produced play.

In *Picnic* Inge portrays three generations of women who are stirred emotionally and sexually when Hal, a young drifter and the antithesis of the "gentleman" caller, comes to town in time for the annual Labor Day picnic. Was Inge again influenced by an earlier play by Williams? In his introduction to *Orpheus Descending*, Williams describes an earlier work — *Battle of Angels*, which was produced in Boston in 1940 — as "the tale of a wild-spirited boy who wanders into a conventional community in the South and creates a commotion like a fox in a chicken coop" (*Eight Plays* 540). Had Inge read and/or discussed *Battle* with Williams, a not uncommon practice between the playwrights that has been documented here? On the other hand, might we ask if Williams, admittedly jealous of *Picnic*'s Broadway and film successes, decided to revise his early play to compete with Inge's popular tale about "a conventional community" in the Midwest? Williams does not say so in his preface to *Orpheus*, but once again the offstage Williams-Inge drama is as intriguing as those on their respective stages.

In *Picnic* we first see Mrs. Potts, a 60-ish woman shackled to her home to care for her octogenarian, mean-spirited mother (87), who has hired Hal to do some yard work. Next door lives a trio of Owens women: Flo, yet another struggling mother now without a husband (who, Stanley Kowalski–like, was philandering the night his daughter was born: 14); her teenage daughters, Madge (eighteen and "the pretty one," says her jealous little sister, 52) and Millie, 16, a bookish tomboy on the verge of womanhood. Mrs. Potts and her neighbors spend considerable time on the porch because, as the former laments in a trademark Inge-ism, "I hate for the neighbors to see me there all *alone*" (88, emphasis added). A fourth and equally alienated woman central to the play, Rosemary Sidney, is "an old maid school teacher" (85), a comically pathetic representative of the small town mindset that censors new works (e.g., Carson McCullers's *The Ballad of the Sad Café*, a popular novel among the gay community: 89) and classical statuary for its erotic potential (acting edition 55). Again, we are privy to the very landscape from which Inge longed to escape as a youth in (how ironic!) Independence.

Picnic represents Inge's attempt to write his most Chekhov-like full-length play, employing what Francis Fergusson calls "realistic ensemble pathos" (163). Rather than center his attention, and importantly the audience's emotional investment, on a single character (e.g., Lola) or family (e.g., the Campbell/Floods in *Heaven*/*Stairs*), Inge spreads his focus on several figures simultaneously, a technique he expanded in his subsequent effort, *Bus Stop*. Although *Picnic*'s primary story centers on the Hal-Madge relationship, itself a rather standard romance fable, it is through the eyes of the other women (Mrs. Potts, Flo, Millie, Rosemary and her two teacher-colleagues) that we better understand Madge's fantasies of escape "from the dime store" (79–80). As her mother, who knows well the frustration of the limitations of small town life, counsels her beautiful daughter: "...the years'll start going by so fast you'll lose count of them. First thing you'll know, you'll be forty, still selling candy at the dime store" (81). Again we hear echoes of Williams, especially Amanda's insistence that Laura attend secretarial school: "I know so well what becomes of unmarried women who aren't prepared to occupy a position. I've seen such pitiful cases in the South..." (*Glass* 28). Later, in the most pathetic speech in the play, the sexually repressed Rosemary, begs Howard, the local hardware store owner, to marry her after a night of dalliance, because "it's no good livin' like this ... meetin' a bunch of old maids for supper every night" (130).

And Madge does escape. With Hal — on that outbound train that has tempted her for years. At least that's what Broadway audiences saw in 1953. Actually, the script that Inge submitted for production had Madge remaining in the small Kansas town, even as Hal fled the police. Inge initially envisioned a more realistic denouement for his play: girl doesn't get boy. However, director Josh Logan, with whom Inge worked on the *Picnic* script for a year and a half (*Four Plays* x), convinced Inge to amend his original design by providing a more satisfying conclusion for Broadway (and certainly film) audiences accustomed to romantic endings in which boy-gets-girl. Logan was motivated, in part, by the poor reception the play received in its tryouts in St. Louis and Cleveland. A minor furor ensued when Harold Clurman — whom Inge labeled as "the only real intellectual I know in the theater" (*Four Plays* x) — wrote an essay for the *Nation* criticizing his fellow director, Logan, for turning Inge's vision into "a prurient popular magazine story" (Voss 136). Although Inge and Logan said little publicly about the altered ending, the playwright remained committed to his first draft of *Picnic*: years later (1962) he revised and re-titled it (*Summer Brave*) to restore "the attenuated rosary of disappointments" to which Logan had objected (Voss 129). *Summer Brave*, then, is more in the Williams's tradition of the bittersweet, truer-to-life ending in which, for instance, Laura can only "blow out [her] candles" (90) after the gentleman caller leaves. And Madge can only walk yet again to the five-and-dime to a chorus of catcalls from the local boys who themselves are not going anywhere (*Summer* 112–113). They — Alma, Lola, Cora, Madge, Rosemary and so many more — are prey to the ultimate enemy in a Chekhov, Williams, and Inge play: "life's destroyer, time" (*Eight Plays* 302).

Based on his early 1950's one-act "People in the Wind" (inspired by an incident the young Inge witnessed while traveling on a bus to Kansas City: Voss 73), *Bus Stop* is unique among Inge's four major plays: it is not a family-centered drama, and, upon first impression, it is his most conspicuously comedic work. Furthermore, it seems to bear the least resemblance to a Williams drama, despite Brustein's earlier comment about it (as were *Sheba* and *Picnic*) being infused with Williams's "personality." *Bus Stop* most resembles Inge's other works, and to some extent those of Williams, in its depiction of a diverse group of "fugitive kinds" fleeing circumstances in which each feels alienated.

Rather like the hotel-of-fools Williams devised for *The Night of the Iguana* (1961, six years after *Bus Stop*), in which a disparate and desperate collection of travelers converge on an isolated beach in Mexico, Inge's love/lust-sick characters find shelter from a paralyzing blizzard in a crossroads café, "a dingy establishment" in rural Kansas that serves "as an occasional rest stop for the bus lines in the area" (153). As he did in *Picnic*, Inge focuses on a group of individuals rather than a central protagonist. We meet four travelers and their bus driver (Carl): a Montana cowboy (Bo); his older, wiser sidekick (Virgil); a drunken philosopher and pedophile (Dr. Lyman, excised from the screenplay in the conservative 1950s); and a would-be torch singer from the Ozarks (Cherie, perhaps Marilyn Monroe's finest film role). The passengers eventually pair off with the diner's regulars: the sheriff and town's conscience (Will); a high school waitress (Elma) who, like Blanche DuBois, uses literature, especially Shakespeare, to escape her small town existence; and an older, "experienced" woman (Grace) who owns the joint. Like Williams, notable for his extensive use of symbols (both objects and names), Inge invests his characters with allegorical names to further the morality-play elements of this study of the "varying kinds of love, ranging from the innocent to the depraved" (*Four Plays* viii), a précis that might be applied to any number of Williams's plays. Virgil, so like his Roman namesake in his detached observations on human folly, and Will (as in Schopenhauer's "will" of the world) watch the sexual parings. Lyman — whose depraved life is indeed built on "mendacities," that favorite Williams term for lies — lusts after the youthful Elma (a near homonym of Alma, Williams's "soulful" heroine in *Summer and Smoke*). The worldly Grace and Carl rendezvous upstairs because, as she says, "makin' love is one thing, being lonesome is another" (155), a line echoed in Williams's *Orpheus Descending* two years later: "The act of lovemaking in almost unbearably painful ... I do bear it because to be not alone, even for a few moments, is worth the pain" (*Eight Plays* 592). Bo (i.e., "beau," one who is good looking and one who is betrothed) and Cherie are fore grounded in the ballad of this sad café, but unlike *Picnic*, in which the "stud" Hal charms the sexually awakened Madge, here it is Cherie — she of "the voluptuous pair of lips that are not her own," a product of watching too many movies (157) — who reins in the seemingly macho cowboy, who admits he's "kinda green" when it comes to women and love (210). "Seemingly" may also be applied to Cherie, the chanteuse: like Bo, she is more "front" than "fact," an imposter who presents herself as more worldly than she actually is. Were Bo to hold that notorious light bulb to her face, as Mitch does to Blanche (*Streetcar* 177), he would see, not the vamp she pretends to be, but, in Jeff Johnson's estimation, "a mother (who) tames him, and negotiates their future together on her terms" (*Subversion* 71). After the snowfall ceases, Bo and his would-be bride board the bus for Montana and an apparent happy ending.

But is it? Is there validity to Vincent Canby's observation (in a 1996 review of *Bus Stop*) that Inge — much like his mentor, Williams — was "too clear eyed to be an outright sentimentalist [who] longed for happy endings, but the ones he provided ... always left the door open for disaster"? Is Inge's biographer, Voss, correct in his belief that "Inge was not about happy resolutions" ("Williams and His Contemporaries" 113)? If so, we can only imagine the disillusionment facing Bo and Cherie in isolated Montana, her dreams of being an entertainer shelved, the shallowness of his awe for the beautiful "chantoosie" exposed during long, cruel Rocky Mountain winters. Might we actually expect the Bo/Cherie marriage to be any more felicitous than that of Stanley/Blanche or Maggie/Brick? Brick's sardonic curtain line in the original script for *Cat on a Hot Tin Roof* (the Broadway version was altered) likely rings as true for Bo's and Cheri's purportedly happy-ever-after ending (as well as that of Doc and Lola, Hal and Madge, Rubin and Cora): "Wouldn't it be funny if that were true?" (505).

Brustein's 1957 dismissal of Inge's four successive Broadway hits — which may have triggered Inge's mental and emotional collapse, and about which Williams remained silent because he felt a response would dignify Brustein's argument (Voss 183) — was predicated on his belief that the Kansan's cumulative work "is not really different from the Midwest of Rogers and Hammerstein, a land where the gift of milky happiness is obtained when some obstacle ('pore Jud' or resistance to love) is removed ... [Inge] is the first spokesman for a matriarchal America" (78–79). Brustein, then a young critic perhaps looking to make a name for himself by challenging the commercial theater's reigning dramatist, submits that Inge wrote "she-dramas" in which seemingly rugged men (Doc, Hal, Bo, Rubin) ultimately capitulate to their respective women's "power to comfort and provide his life with affirmative meaning" (73). In the context of the 1950s — when Über-Moms like June Cleaver, Harriet Nelson, and Donna Reed dominated sentimental family sit-coms on television — Bruistein's interpretation merits consideration, as Shuman attested in his 1965 biography: "Essentially Inge's women are bent on ... emasculating their men so they can dominate them and thereby bolster their own egos" (170).

"Not so" argues a subsequent generation of critics, notably Janet Juhnke who critiques Brustein's (in)famous critique by tracing the evolution of feminist discourse [Betty Friedan, Barbara Ehrenreich, Germaine Greer, Eve Merriam] from the 1950s into the 1980s. In particular, Juhnke says that, in her interrogation of Inge's plays and germinal feminist studies, Inge actually "anticipates not Friedan's *Feminine Mystique* [1963], but her more recent views expressed in *The Second Stage* [1981] about "shared responsibilities" among marriage partners. She concludes her analysis of those issues articulated by Brustein: "In exploring these human problems ... Inge should ultimately be seen not as a narrow provincial but as an intelligent articulator of some of the most significant dilemmas of modern times" (110). If Juhnke's argument has merit, then perhaps Inge's endings may indeed be more upbeat than those of most of Williams's plays, which are more sadly realistic than pessimistic, much like those of Chekhov, to whom both playwrights acknowledged an indebtedness. The degree to which Inge's plays end positively — or otherwise — depends on the choices made by the director and actors who breathe life into his words. His resolutions are ambiguous enough to tolerate a range of interpretive possibilities, perhaps even more so than those of Williams.

With *Streetcar*, Williams — and to be sure Marlon Brando on stage and especially in film — introduced an essentially new figure in American popular entertainment, perhaps best defined by Val Xavier, "the stud at hire," in *Orpheus Descending* (1957). Brando's ruggedly handsome, bare-armed, tight and/or torn t-shirt wearing Stanley Kowalski sired a 50s generation of hunky males who titillated young and older women alike: Brando in *The Wild One* (1954), James Dean in *Rebel Without a Cause* (1955), as well as Elvis, *et al.*) Whereas the "pin up girl" (e.g., Betty Grable) had been the object of the male gaze through the war years (and of course long before), women, who had proved their mettle on the home front during the war, could now more freely ogle muscular young men in the theatre, a more conservative medium than film, which had given women such well-sculpted Olympic stars as Johnny "Tarzan" Weissmuller and Buster Crabbe primacy throughout the 1930s. Following the Williams/Kowalski lead, Inge created what Jane W. Lange, in fact, refers to as a "subversive hunk." She argues that it was Inge, perhaps more so than Williams, who anticipated the youth cult's social revolution of the 1950s and especially the 1960s: "The perception of youth, particularly the virile young male, as a threat to conventional society is a historical reality that cannot be underestimated in appraising William Inge's *Picnic*" (58). Lange's argument is augmented by R. Barton Palmer who spoke on a panel at the 2006 Williams Scholars' Conference. Palmer notes that on the poster for the film version of *Picnic*, it is Hal's "bodice" that is torn, not Madge's: "...in many ways Inge schematizes this cultural change in much more interesting ways [than Williams] by actually presenting the [male] characters as objects of the gaze within the action of the play or ... in the films themselves" ("Williams and His Contemporaries" 114).

In truth, Inge brought the muscular young stud to Middle America in *Come Back, Little Sheba* via the javelin thrower Turk, Marie's male model and sometime lover, who obviously evokes comparisons with Stanley. His manly presence becomes the catalyst for Lola's erotic and none-too-subtle Freudian dream about Doc reverting to his former masculine appeal: "...you came out on the field [to replace Turk] just as big as you please ... you picked up the javelin ... you threw it, Daddy, clear, *clear* up in the sky and it never came down" (68). Again it is worth noting: *Streetcar* was Broadway's most titillating play as Inge began scripting *Come Back, Little Sheba* in the late 40s. Thirty seconds into *Picnic* Hal emerges through Mrs. Potts's back door wearing a T-shirt that is soon "wrapped around his neck," leaving him "bare-chested" (90). Soon he, as Turk did for Marie, poses for Millie-the-Sketch-Artist, much to the delight of Mrs. Potts and to the consternation of the town's prudes. Though Bo doesn't partially disrobe, as do Turk and Hal, he is nonetheless intended to be *Bus Stop*'s stud who is "...rumpedly picturesque [who] could pass for an outlaw ... tall and slim and good looking in an outdoors way ... [wearing] faded jeans that cling to his skin like shedding skin..."(169). (Notably, Val Xavier, among Williams's sexiest studs, is called "Snakeskin.") Although almost past his prime (an issue in *Stairs*), Rubin Flood, who impregnated Cora before marrying her, retains his masculine appeal: "a good looking man ... still robust, dressed in Western clothes — a big Stetson, boots, narrow trousers..." (226). Inge's he-men more than rival the Stanley Kowalskis, Alvaro Mangiacavallos (*The Rose Tattoo*), and Val Xaviers that walk tall across Williams's sultry landscapes.

But to what purpose? For the sexual energy they incite in the frustrated women in the out-of-the-way towns into which they drift? Surely they fulfill that dramatic purpose, as do the *machismos* rendered by Williams. But there other possibilities, as suggested by twenty-first century readings of Inge's plays.

The first has to do with Inge's closeted homosexuality. In his study of "suspected" artists in the 1950s, David Savran writes that Williams's "homosexuality is both ubiquitous and elusive, everywhere in his work and yet nearly impossible to pin down" (92). In a 2002 collection of essays devoted to, as its subtitle proclaims, *Queer Readings of American Theatre History*, Albert Wertheim asserts that "much the same may be said of Inge" (197). Wertheim further contends that "Inge knew that the presentation of an overtly homosexual character or theme and Broadway success was an oxymoron ... [therefore] a gay sensibility informs his major plays, is refracted in them, and most importantly permits him special insights ... derived from his personal experience of gay alterity to write movingly and knowledgeably of his characters" (198). Only later in his career did Inge deal openly with gay characters and themes, most notably in the previously cited one-act, "The Boy in the Basement," in which a mortician must sneak out of town to pursue his sexual desires, and in his none-too-subtle autobiographical novel, *My Son Is a Splendid Driver* (1971), written two years before his suicide.

Williams had opened the (closet) door for gay themes in *Streetcar*: Blanche talks about her short and tragic marriage to a young boy, Allen, who possessed "a softness and tenderness that wasn't like a man's, although he wasn't the least bit effeminate looking." Blanche discovers her boy-husband with an older man when she "came suddenly into room that [she] thought was empty—which wasn't empty but had two people in it" (158–9). Humiliated, Allen later shoots himself, much like Sammy, the fragile Jewish boy—"a darkly beautiful young man of seventeen ... [who] offers a limp hand when being introduced" (262–3)—in *Dark at the Top of the Stairs*. There are intimations that Brick, the former University of Mississippi football player and now failed stud in *Cat on a Hot Tin Roof*, may have lusted after his team mate and best friend, Scooter (*Eight Plays* 472). And we customarily accept that Tom in *The Glass Menagerie* is actually a self-portrait of the gay Thomas Lanier Williams.

As has been noted, Williams, like Inge, also paraded numerous handsome young men across his stages, perhaps — has Wertheim suggests in specific regard to Inge's beefcake boys — to "enable and even for his audiences to overcome its innate homophobia and find its humanity ... capable of embracing and understanding all of his characters, male and female, gay and straight" (215). Or as Williams advocated so simply in *Summer and Smoke* through Alma, who enjoys the company of "different" men and women: "I say that life is such a mysteriously complicated thing that no one should really presume to judge and condemn the behavior of anyone else!" (*Eight Plays* 226).

There are indeed instances throughout Inge's major plays that permit readings suggesting that Inge's "It Boys" represent a sub-textual homoeroticism through which the playwright challenges, even subverts, the Midwest's prevailing social norms — echoed in the taunts that the town boys hurl at Sonny in *Stairs* (231) — that had tormented him as a child in Independence. Are the apparently conventional middle class homes, so instantly recognizable to Inge's audiences, themselves subterfuges meant to dislodge conventional thinking by exposing the sexual realities behind their picket-fence façades? Current discourse raises questions concerning such possibilities. Is Doc's disillusionment with Marie's tryst with Tank actually jealousy, not for Marie's body, but for Turk's? Inge's stage direction notes that Turk's laughter is like that "of sated Bacchus (Dionysus)" — classical mythology's notoriously hermaphroditic god. Does Doc overreact to Tank's posing for Marie as she sketches him based on prudery — or a recognition that he, too, gazes too long(ingly) on Turk's muscular form? Doc is, Wertheim reminds us in his summary of the play, "a character drawn by a dramatist who brings his knowledge of gay lives, gay neuroses ... to bear, employing that knowledge to create a moving and tragic portrait" (206).

In both *Picnic* and *The Dark at the Top of the Stairs* we find prominent instances of homoerotic behavior that may seem merely playful to straight audiences but that would have been appreciated by gays. When Hal meets his former school pal Alan, they play a game of "motorboat" in which Alan is seen "clasping his legs around Hal's waist, hanging by one hand wrapped about Hal's neck" (90). Throughout the play Inge goes to some lengths to "feminize" Alan, who, says Madge, "is not like most boys" (80). (Irony: Alan was played by Paul Newman in the original Broadway production; that actor became Williams's leading "hunk" in the film versions of several of his later plays.) In act two Hal and Howard dance together (118) in a parody of the hetero-erotic dance between Hal and Madge at the conclusion of the act. Rosemary, the town's moralist and most pronounced homophobe, demands that Hal and Howard cease their dance. In *Stairs* we find an even more provocative example of what Wertheim labels Inge's "gay inflections" (206 and *passim*): Sammy allows the obviously effeminate Sonny to mount him like a horse while brandishing the young military school student's sword. The dialogue (267–68) is rife with Freudian double entendres that heighten the phallic nature of the sword and the homoerotic horseplay. Even *Bus Stop*, which seems confined to heterosexual love and lust, suggests gay possibilities. Virgil may well be attracted by Bo's virility and admits he's more comfortable in a bunkhouse with his buddies than with women (185), an inflection that a post–*Brokeback Mountain* audience might recognize more readily than those in the 1950s. Virgil seems particularly forlorn after Bo leaves with Cherie, especially in light of Grace's ominous line ("you're just left out in the cold" 219). Wertheim tries to make the case that Dr. Lyman is attracted to Elma because she is more like a boy actor in the Elizabethan theatre in her love of Shakespeare's sonnets, some of which were written to a man. Wertheim may be stretching to make his point by noting that "Elma" is an anagram for "male" (208 — it is also one for "lame"), but much of his essay makes a credible case that Inge, like Williams, "brilliantly inscrib[es] a gay text within the margins of a straight one" (208).

Or, perhaps more accurately, we might paraphrase Wertheim to say Inge "brilliantly inscribes a *human* text within the margins of a too-often inhumane world." In a 1969 interview, Inge reflected on his career and that of his old friend and mentor, Williams, about whom he said, "...there is always, in most of his plays, the suffering spirit that gives his plays their beauty and appeal" (Steen 116–17). At his best, much the same may be said of Inge, who, according to John S. Bak, "tugged at America's heartstrings [while] Williams touched the nation's nerve" ("Williams and His Contemporaries" 115). Although not as poetic or as dazzlingly theatrical as Williams, Inge nonetheless understood "the suffering spirit" wrought by small town, small minded people in the Midwest. Daniel Mann, who directed Inge's first

Broadway hit, *Sheba*, (as well as his first failure, *A Loss of Roses*), believes that "Bill, in the simplest way, gave us the greatest insight into the profundity of the human spirit in order to be able to overcome" (M. Wood 8).

Works Cited

Bigsby, C.W.E. *Modern American Drama, 1945–1990*. Cambridge University Press, 1992.

Brustein, Robert. "The Men-Taming Women of William Inge." In *Modern American Theatre: A Collection of Critical Essays*. Alvin B. Kernan, ed. Englewood Cliffs, N.J., Prentice-Hall, 1967. 70–79.

Canby, Vincent. "Inge's Bus Passengers, Stranded Overnight." *The New York Times*, February 23, 1996.

Devlin, Albert J. Ed. *Selected Letters of Tennessee Williams: 1945–1957*. New York: New Directions Books, 2004.

Fergusson, Francis. *The Idea of a Theatre: A Study of Ten Plays; The Art of Drama in Changing Perspective*. Garden City, N.Y., Doubleday, 1953 [(c)1949].

Gassner, John. "William Inge and the Subtragic Muse: *The Dark at the Top of the Stairs*." In *Theatre at the Crossroads: Plays and Playwrights of the Modern American Theatre*. New York: Holt, Rinehart and Winston, 1960. 167–73.

Inge, William. *Four Plays by William Inge: Come Back, Little Sheba; Picnic; Bus Stop; The Dark at the Top of the Stairs*. New York: Random House, 1958. [All quotations from these plays are from this anthology.]

_____. *Natural Affection*. New York: Random House, 1963.

_____. *Picnic*. New York: Dramatists Play Service, 1955. [Note: This acting edition contains speeches not found in *Four Plays by William Inge*.]

_____. *Summer Brave and Eleven Short Plays*. New York: Random House, 1962.

Johnson, Jeff. *William Inge and the Subversion of Gender*. Jefferson, NC and London: McFarland, 2005.

Juhnke, Janet. "Inge's Woman: Robert Brustein and the Feminine Mystique." *Kansas Quarterly* 18:4 (Fall 1986): 103–11.

Kolin, Philip C. "The Fission of Tennessee Williams's Plays into Adrienne Kennedy's." *South Atlantic Review*. 70: 4 (Fall 2005): 43–72.

McCarten, John. "Tour de Force." *The New Yorker* 9 (February 1963): 66–68 *(pasim)*.

"The Most Promising Playwright," *New York Times*, July 23, 1950. Sec. II, 1.

Savran, David. *Communists, Cowboys and Queers*. Minneapolis: University Press of Minnesota, 1992.

Shuman, R. Baird. *William Inge* (Revised Edition). Twayne's United States Authors Series. Warren French, ed. Boston: Twayne Publishers, 1965 (Rev. 1989).

Spoto, Donald. *The Kindness of Strangers*. Boston: Little Brown, 1985.

Steen, Mike. "William Inge [Interview]." *A Look at Tennessee Williams*. New York: Hawthorne Books, 1969. 96–123.

Voss, Ralph F. "An Alignment of the Stars: Tennessee Williams, William Inge, and Margo Jones's 'Theatre '47.'" *Tennessee Williams Annual Review* 9 (2007): 41–52.

_____. *A Life of William Inge: The Strains of Triumph*. Lawrence, KS: UP Kansas, 1989.

_____. "Tennessee Williams's *Sweet Bird of Youth* and William Inge's "Bus Riley's Back in Town: Coincidences from a Friendship." *American Drama* XX (Winter 2006): 33–39.

_____. "William Inge and the Savior/Specter of Celebrity." *Kansas Quarterly* 18:4 (Fall 1986): 25–43.

Wagner, Walter, ed. "William Inge" [Interview]. *The Playwrights Speak*. New York: Delacourt Press, 1967. 110–139.

Weales, Gerald. "The New Pineros" in *American Drama Since World War II*. New York: Harcourt Brace and World, 1962. Pp. 40–49.

Wertheim, Albert. "Dorothy's Friend in Kansas: The Gay Inflection of William Inge." In *Staging Desire: Queer Readings of American Theatre History*. Eds. Kim Marra and Robert A. Schanke. Ann Arbor: The University of Michigan Press, 2002. 194–220.

"Williams and His Contemporaries: William Inge" (Scholars' Conference Panel: Annette Sadick, Moderator). *Tennessee Williams Annual Review* 9 (2007): 109–130.

Williams, Tennessee. *Eccentricities of a Nightingale and Summer and Smoke: Two Plays by Tennessee Williams*. New York: New Directions Books, 1964.

_____. *Eight Plays*. New York: Nelson Doubleday, Inc. 1979. [All quotations from Williams's plays are from this collection, unless otherwise noted.]

_____. "Introduction" in William Inge, *The Dark at the Top of the Stairs*. New York: Random House, 1958. vi–vix.

_____. *Memoirs*. NY: Doubleday & Company, Inc. 1972.

_____. "To William Inge: An Homage." *New York Times* July 1, 1973, Sec. 2, 1–8.

Wood, Michael. "An Interview with Daniel Mann: The Director of Inge's First Success and His First Failure." *Kansas Quarterly* 18:4 (Fall 1986): 7–23.

Wood, Audrey. "Come Back, Sweet William." *Represented by Audrey Wood*. New York, 1981. 220–237.

Neil Simon's Parodies
of Tennessee Williams

Susan Koprince

Let no one parody a poet unless he loves him.
— *Sir Theodore Martin*

In a scene from Neil Simon's comedy *Laughter on the 23rd Floor* (1993), a group of 1950s television writers and their eccentric star, Max Prince, read aloud from a sketch in which they playfully make fun of the current film version of *Julius Caesar*, starring Marlon Brando:

KENNY. What dost thou seekest in the constellations, Caesar?
MAX. (Reads, doing Brando.) A clustuh a stahs in da heavens.
BRIAN. And by what name dost this cluster be called, oh, Caesar?
MAX. It is called Stelluh ... *Stelluh!* ... Stelluh for Stahlight! [4: 283].

Echoing an iconic moment in *A Streetcar Named Desire*, these lines probably represent the most overt parody of Tennessee Williams in Simon's canon. Yet during his long reign as Broadway's king of comedy, Simon actually created a number of subtler and more extended parodies of Williams's dramas. Indeed, it can be argued that Simon's typical response to the plays of Tennessee Williams comes in the form of parody. Such imitation does not seek to ridicule or to devalue but, as Linda Hutcheon has suggested, "to recontextualize, to synthesize, to rework conventions — in a respectful manner" (33). By incorporating Williams's texts into his own, Simon found that he could pay homage to an esteemed literary forebear and, at the same time, carve out his own creative territory. He could learn, as he once explained in an interview, "to write [...] drama and tell it as comedy" (*Studies* 157).

On the surface, Neil Simon would appear to have little in common with Tennessee Williams. Whereas Williams was a gay Southern playwright who came to prominence in the 1940s and 1950s, Simon is a heterosexual New York Jew who began his forty-year career on Broadway in the 1960s. Whereas Williams has been recognized for his poetic tragedies and his Southern Gothicism, Simon is known for his lighthearted comedies and his realistic portraits of middle-class urban life. Williams, of course, has been the subject of a vast — and ever expanding — body of scholarly research, whereas Simon, despite his perennial box-office appeal, has failed to garner the same amount of critical attention.

Yet there are some striking affinities between Williams and Simon. Both playwrights experienced unhappy childhoods, suffering from the fallout of their parents' stormy marriages and seeking escape through books and movies. Both faced turmoil in their own romantic rela-

31

tionships — Williams taking on a long series of casual sexual partners or companions, and Simon (after his first wife's death) going through multiple marriages and divorces. As dramatists, Williams and Simon explored similar themes: marital discord, family conflict, mental instability, sexual desire, and the longing for human connection. They shared a common reverence for Chekhov, with Simon even adapting a group of Chekhov's short stories for his play *The Good Doctor* (1973). And, most notably, both playwrights achieved enormous popular success, each terming his sudden rise to celebrity a "Cinderella story" (Simon interview in *Playwright's Art* 232), yet each becoming acquainted with what Williams called "The Catastrophe of Success" (135). Like Williams, Simon discovered that he was at the mercy of the critics and that "there was no safety or refuge in prominence" (Simon, *Rewrites* 32). And like Williams, he underwent psychoanalysis in order to cope with depression and anxiety.

Although the two writers never met, Simon identified Williams as an important mentor and role model: "When I was in my late teens and early twenties, I went to the theater a lot. There was always a Tennessee Williams play to see or a great English play. It was such an education" (Interview in *Playwrights at Work* 225). Simon admired Williams's discipline and his devotion to his craft: "I read that Tennessee Williams wrote practically every day of his adult life, whether at home, traveling, or vacationing. He had set up a regular schedule of hours which only illness might cause him to take a respite from" (*Rewrites* 329). Simon also respected Williams for having the courage to experiment with his art, applauding him for "[taking] such chances with plays like *Camino Real*" (Interview in *Studies* 174). Moreover, he was attracted to the humor that he found in Williams's work — even in plays that are traditionally labeled as tragedies. According to Simon, Williams taught him that humor need not come from gags and one-liners, but could arise naturally from the characters and their situations:

> The humor that I saw in *Streetcar Named Desire* came out of a new place for humor. It came out of the character of Stanley Kowalski saying, "I have this lawyer acquaintance of mine" and talking about the Napoleonic Code. It was the way he talked that got huge laughs, and I knew that this was not comedy; it was character comedy and that's what I aimed for later on" [Interview in *Studies* 157].

Simon clearly views Tennessee Williams as a masterful dramatist, listing him among "the illustrious crowd" that he wanted to emulate when he first contemplated a career in the theater. Extolling playwrights such as Williams, Miller, Odets, and Beckett, along with legends of comedy like Kaufman and Hart, Simon writes: "These were all giants, all members of the royal family of the theater" (*Rewrites* 32). How, he wondered, could he possibly join such a group and thereby "enter the gates of Playwrights Heaven"? (*Rewrites* 55). In a 1979 interview, Simon admitted that he initially believed he didn't have the talent to be a playwright: "After watching plays by writers like Tennessee Williams and Arthur Miller, I'd say to myself, 'That's big league, I can't do that'" (*Playboy* 68). Faced with this "anxiety of influence," as Harold Bloom has called it, Simon turned to parody as a means of confronting Tennessee Williams and coming to terms with his predecessor's legacy.

According to Linda Hutcheon, parody is a form of imitation that involves "revising, replaying, inverting, and 'transcontextualing' previous works of art" — i.e., giving them new and often ironic contexts (11). Although parody is a form of literary recycling, it should not be branded as "parasitic and derivative" (3). Parody does not merely copy a borrowed text; it transforms it — establishing an opposition or contrast between texts and thus creating "difference at the heart of similarity" (8). This difference, Hutcheon argues, typically comes in the form of ironic inversion. Deriving its name from the Greek "parodia" or "counter-song," parody (particularly in its contemporary forms) involves much more than mocking imitation. Its range of intent is broad — "from the reverential to the playful to the scornful" (26). Unlike many critics, Hutcheon also asserts that parody need not be inherently comic: "The pleasure of parody's irony comes not from humor in particular but from the degree of engagement of the reader in the intertextual 'bouncing'" (32) between the original source and its new, reconstituted version.

The Tennessee Williams play that Simon parodies most frequently is *A Streetcar Named Desire*—a work that he claimed he "could see over and over" (Interview in *Playwrights at Work* 225). According to Simon, *A Streetcar Named Desire* and *Death of a Salesman* made deeper impressions on him than any other American dramas, and he noted that if there were one play that he wished he could have written himself, "it would be *Streetcar*" (Interview in *Studies* 157). Discussing his comic view of the world—a view deeply influenced by the tradition of Jewish humor—Simon confessed, "I can't write a play as dark and bleak and wonderful as *A Streetcar Named Desire*" (*Playwrights at Work* 220). Through parody, however, Simon comes as close as possible to "writing" Williams's masterpiece, incorporating the earlier drama into his own work and refashioning it for his own comic purposes.

The Odd Couple (1965), Simon's classic study of two newly single—and wildly incompatible—men, might well be understood as an extended parody of *A Streetcar Named Desire*. Like *Streetcar* (a play that Williams initially titled "The Poker Night"), *The Odd Couple* spotlights the game of poker, presenting three card-playing scenes (one in each act) and ending, as *Streetcar* does, with a repetition of the poker game ritual. In both plays, the poker scenes serve to create a distinctly masculine environment, where men gather to eat, drink, and play cards with their friends—and where women are definitely not welcome. In *Streetcar*, Blanche DuBois tells her brother-in-law, Stanley Kowalski, "I understand there's to be a little card party to which we ladies are cordially *not* invited!" (276). Similarly, in *The Odd Couple*, the poker players meet for a "boys' night out" at Oscar Madison's apartment—a setting which, since the time of Oscar's divorce, has been "without the touch and care of a woman" (1: 217). The poker scenes also provide a common dramatic structure: both plays focus on the arrival of an intruder in the masculine world of the poker game and conclude with the departure or expulsion of that intruder. In *Streetcar*, of course, the intruder is the aging Southern belle Blanche DuBois, whose dainty appearance, complete with white suit, gloves, and hat, is said to be "incongruous to this setting" (245). In *The Odd Couple*, the intruder is Oscar's new roommate, the frustrated homemaker Felix Ungar, who is completely out of his element in the unkempt male enclave of Oscar's apartment.

Representing the manly half of Simon's odd couple, Oscar Madison has much in common with the hypermasculine Stanley Kowalski. In his stage directions, Williams stresses Stanley's "animal joy" in living: his powerful sexual appetite, "his heartiness with men, his appreciation of rough humor, his love of good drink and food and games" (264–265). In *The Odd Couple*, Simon likewise introduces Oscar as a man who "seems to enjoy life to the fullest. He enjoys his weekly poker game, his friends, his excessive drinking and his cigars" (1: 220). In Simon's screenplay for *The Odd Couple* (1968), Oscar even goes bowling—one of Stanley's favorite masculine pastimes. Like Stanley, Oscar has a strong sexual drive, insisting that he and Felix arrange a double date with their neighbors, the Pigeon sisters, because "unless I get to touch something soft in the next two weeks, I'm in big trouble" (1: 263). Like Stanley, Oscar is also straightforward, unpretentious, and down-to-earth. Indeed, Stanley's line, "Be comfortable is my motto" (266) would apply equally well to Oscar.

Despite these parallels, however, Oscar is really a parody of Stanley Kowalski—an over-the-hill, humorous version of Williams's famous character (Koprince 34). Forty-three years old and divorced, Oscar can no longer hope to be the male sex symbol or "gaudy seed-bearer" that Stanley represents. His attempts to romance the Pigeon sisters prove fruitless, and his only meaningful contact with a woman comes through nagging phone calls from his ex-wife — whose name, quite significantly, happens to be Blanche. In *Streetcar*, Stanley is described as sloppy — flinging watermelon rinds to the floor during the poker game or making his face and hands "disgustingly greasy" (371) when he eats his dinner. But in Oscar's case, this sloppiness becomes a signature trait. His apartment is said to be "a study in slovenliness" (1: 217) — the furniture in disarray and the living room littered with dirty dishes, garbage, old newspapers, and cast-off clothing. The poker players themselves complain about the mess, asking Oscar, "How can you live like this? Don't you have a maid?" (1: 222). Another trait that Simon parodies is Stanley Kowalski's propensity for violence — his image as "brute force incarnate" (Brustein 10). When an enraged Oscar throws a plate of linguini into the kitchen, covering the walls with Felix's dinner; or when he chases Felix around the furniture, forcing him to protect himself with a lamp, Oscar is clearly portrayed as more laughable than menacing. He is Stanley Kowalski brought into the realm of comedy.

Just as Oscar can be seen as a parodic image of Stanley, so can Felix be viewed as an ironic version of Stanley's adversary, Blanche DuBois. At the end of *The Odd Couple*, Oscar even refers to Felix as "Blanche" (1: 301) — conflating the image of his prissy roommate with that of his nagging ex-wife. Although Simon has reversed the gender, Felix in many ways resembles Williams's Southern belle heroine. Like Blanche DuBois, Felix has been cast out of his home and is forced to seek shelter with others. Like Blanche, he comes into conflict with an uncouth, untidy man whom he compares to "an animal" (1: 291). And like Blanche, Felix is ultimately expelled from this temporary haven, becoming dependent on "the kindness of strangers" (i.e., the Pigeon sisters). Emotionally unstable like Williams's heroine, Felix even sinks into a suicidal depression after the collapse of his twelve-year marriage and exhibits so many signs of neurosis that Oscar labels him "a hopeless mental case" (1: 261).

Exaggeration has been described as "the meat that parody feeds on" (Macdonald 560); and in creating his parody of Blanche, Simon particularly exaggerates her desire for neat, attractive surroundings. Scolding Stanley's friend Mitch in *Streetcar*, Blanche says, "Take your foot off the bed. It has a light cover on it. Of course you boys don't notice things like that. I've done so much with this place since I've been here. [...] "You saw it before I came. Well, look at it now! This room is almost — dainty! I want to keep it that way" (382). In *The Odd Couple*, Felix Ungar is pictured as compulsively neat — a man who, after moving in with Oscar, totally transforms his friend's apartment — cleaning and redecorating it until it resembles a scene "out of *House and Garden*" (1: 268). For the second poker game, Felix even washes the playing cards and reminds the men to use their cloth napkins and coasters. "Try to eat over the dish," he warns them. "I just vacuumed the rug" (1: 253). Just as Stanley Kowalski resents Blanche's efforts to cleanse and beautify his apartment (e.g., placing a paper lantern over a light bulb or spraying perfume as if she were "the Queen of the Nile" [398]), so does Oscar resent Felix's attempts to feminize his home, telling him: "I don't think that two single men living alone in a big eight-room apartment should have a cleaner house than my mother" (1: 259).

By parodying *A Streetcar Named Desire*, Simon not only creates an amusing study of sexual stereotypes — replaying (and recasting) the crude masculinity of Stanley Kowalski and the delicate femininity of Blanche DuBois — but he also calls attention to the "odd couple" in Williams's own play. Stanley and Stella are, to be sure, the married pair in the Kowalski home, but Stanley and Blanche are the "odd couple" — hopelessly mismatched from the beginning — just like the inveterately sloppy Oscar and the absurdly neat Felix. Whereas Blanche is well-bred, Stanley is "common as dirt" (377); whereas Blanche is fragile and dependent, Stanley is powerful and controlling; whereas Blanche represents the decadent culture of the Old South,

Stanley embodies a harsh new proletarian order. Given the extreme differences between the two characters (at least on the surface), it is no surprise that Williams's tragic "odd couple," like Simon's comic one, would find it impossible to live together and would move inexorably toward a violent confrontation. Indeed, when Stanley, dressed in the silk pajamas from his wedding night, picks up Blanche and carries her into the bedroom to rape her, the scene "takes on, according to Thomas P. Adler, 'the aura of a desecrated marriage'" (Londré 60).

Although *The Odd Couple* is the most extended parody of *Streetcar* in Simon's canon, there are echoes of Williams's masterpiece in other plays as well. *The Last of the Red Hot Lovers* (1969) reworks Williams's central theme of desire — presenting the protagonist, Barney Cashman, as another inversion of Stanley Kowalski. Convinced that the sexual revolution of the 1960s is passing him by, Barney seeks to prove his virility by engaging in an extramarital affair. He yearns to be seductive and powerful — a "red-hot lover" in the mold of Stanley.[1] During a scene that recalls Stanley's aggression toward Blanche, Barney makes crude advances toward one of his potential conquests, saying, "I'm a pro, baby. I know the ropes. [...] Now, are you going to take off that dress, or do I rip it off with my fingers? (1: 653–654). In reality, however, Barney is not a "red-hot lover" at all. The owner of a fish restaurant, he is forty-seven years old, married, and overweight, with the smell of fish clinging to his fingers. Far from a male sex symbol, he is simply an ordinary man who has become aware of his mortality and who is experiencing a mid-life crisis.

Barney can also be seen as an exaggerated version of Mitch — Blanche's suitor and Stanley's foil in *Streetcar*. (In some ways, in fact, Mitch represents Williams's own parody of Stanley.) Oafish and insecure on his date with Blanche in scene 6, Mitch is shown to be incapable of achieving his amorous goals — even "fumbling to embrace her" (389) in scene 9 when he confronts Blanche more forcibly. Similarly, in *Last of the Red Hot Lovers*, Barney Cashman is portrayed as an awkward, bumbling suitor whose sexual overtures fail with three different women. Like Mitch, Barney is unskilled in the language of seduction — speaking to prospective sexual partners about the menus in his fish restaurant, his excess weight, and his habit of reading the obituaries. Like Mitch, Barney is also overly attached to his mother, so much so that he foolishly selects her empty apartment as the setting for his adulterous trysts. According to Philip Kolin, Mitch belongs to a group of "unsuitable suitors" in Williams's dramas who "suffer from interrupted/incomplete sexuality" (132). Barney Cashman can surely be viewed as a descendant of "the Family of Mitch" (Kolin 132). Filled with desires that will never be satisfied — even during the sexual revolution — Barney is a hopeless dreamer, an "incompetent wooer" (Kolin 136), or, as Simon has called him, "an Everyman" (Interview in *Studies* 174).

Parodic versions of Blanche DuBois can likewise be found in a number of other works by Simon, most notably in one of his darkest dramas, *The Gingerbread Lady* (1970). Evy Meara, the play's forty-three-year-old protagonist, is a former nightclub singer whose addiction to alcohol has ruined both her career and her marriage, sending her life into a downward spiral. Out of loneliness, Evy has turned to casual sex, eventually engaging in an affair with an abusive musician and attempting suicide after her lover deserts her. Less than a month after returning home from a sanitarium, the heroine resumes drinking. As Michael Abbott writes, Evy "is acutely aware of the scathing truth about herself: she is an unstable, self-obsessed, nymphomaniac alcoholic" (131). In other words, she is an incarnation of Blanche DuBois. But unlike Blanche, Evy is also a comic figure — a wisecracker who jokes about her drinking problem and her promiscuity, masking her despair with a caustic wit. In contrast to Blanche, Evy does not play the role of the demure Victorian lady. She calls herself "a congenital filthy talker" (2: 171) and speaks openly about her alcoholism and her sexual escapades.

Neither self-deluded nor dishonest, Evy admits that she has "only one more chance at this human-being business ... and if I blow it this time, they'll probably bury me in some distill-ery in Kentucky" (2: 173).

By parodying Blanche DuBois in *The Gingerbread Lady*, Simon focused on more serious themes than he had in previous plays; e.g., alcoholism, domestic violence, and self-destruc-tion. Furthermore, he made his first real effort to combine tragedy with comedy. According to Simon, Lillian Hellman once warned, "Never mix comedy and drama in the same play; the audiences won't understand it" (Interview in *Studies* 166). But Simon's own life experi-ence told him otherwise. Tragic situations, he reasoned, could suddenly develop out of the most benign circumstances, and "if that can happen in life, why can't it happen in the the-atre?" (Interview in Konas 221). Although many critics faulted *The Gingerbread Lady* (espe-cially for its tacked-on, upbeat ending), Simon adhered to his plan "to deal in comic fashion with [contemporary subjects] which were not intrinsically comic" (Johnson 59). He did so, to a large degree, through the art of parody, creating in the person of Evy Meara "the most vivid and tormented" of his female characters (Abbott 130).

In the "Visitors from London" playlet from *California Suite* (1976), Simon presents a more nuanced parody of Blanche DuBois as he addresses the topic of homosexuality. A high com-edy in the style of Noël Coward, this short piece focuses on Diana and Sidney Nichols, a sophisticated British couple who have come to Los Angeles to attend the Academy Awards ceremony, where Diana is a contender for best actress. Like Blanche, Diana is portrayed as alcoholic, emotionally insecure, and promiscuous. Like Williams's character, she is also pic-tured as an accomplished performer — a role player who is happiest when immersed in a world of make-believe.[2] "Why am I always so much more comfortable as someone else?" she won-ders (2: 594). Excessively concerned about her appearance, Diana recognizes that her youth has slipped away from her. "I've aged, Sidney," she laments, after losing her bid for an Oscar. "I'm getting lines in my face ... I look like a brand new steel-belted radial tire" (2: 607). But the most important link between Blanche and Diana is that both women are depicted as hope-lessly in love with a gay/bisexual husband. In *Streetcar*, Blanche reveals that she adored her young husband, Allan Grey, who committed suicide after Blanche cruelly confronted him about his homosexuality. In "Visitors from London," Diana makes it clear that she is similarly devoted to Sidney, though she, too, is capable of homophobic outbursts. "Faggot!" she cries in a moment of anger. "If it's anything I hate, it's a bisexual homosexual" (2: 612).

The key difference in Simon's parody (aside from its use of witty repartee) is that Diana is still married to Sidney, who himself admits that he has only been "half a husband" to her (2: 600). Indeed, Diana and Sidney are shown to have become "a closet couple" (2: 610) — staying together for twelve years for the sake of appearances, fighting about Sidney's prefer-ence for men, yet managing somehow to value each other's company. At the end of "Visitors from London," as the couple go to bed together, Diana implores Sidney not to close his eyes and think of another lover: "Look at *me* tonight," she begs. "Let it be *me* tonight" (2: 614). By reminding audiences of Blanche DuBois's failed marriage, Simon not only underscores Diana's desperate need for intimacy, but he also foreshadows the tragic end of the Nichols' union.[3] In a sequel to their story in *London Suite* (1995), in fact, Simon reveals that Diana and Sidney are long divorced, that Diana still loves him, and that Sidney is dying of AIDS. According to Richard Grayson, Simon's empathy with his gay characters gradually increased over the decades, reflecting changing middle-class values in America and a new open-mind-edness in his audiences (137). Following a trail blazed by Tennessee Williams, Simon reveals a nascent understanding in "Visitors from London" of "the difficult self-imprisonment and deception of the closet" (Grayson 143).

Presenting one last parody of Blanche DuBois in his Brighton Beach trilogy, Simon even names his character "Blanche" and uses the technique of inversion to give her story a happy ending.[4] A secondary figure in *Brighton Beach Memoirs* (1983), Blanche Morton has come to live with her sister's family after the death of her own husband. Dependent and self-pitying, she recognizes that her presence in the household (along with that of her two daughters) produces stress for her brother-in-law, Jack Jerome, who now has more mouths to feed during the Depression. Seeking a way out through courtship, Blanche encounters an "unsuitable gentleman caller" in the form of an alcoholic neighbor, Mr. Murphy, and determines thereafter not to rely on others for support. But in the final installment of the trilogy, *Broadway Bound* (1986), the audience learns that Blanche is now married to the wealthiest man in the garment district. She lives on Park Avenue, has a Cadillac and a chauffeur, and "wears a mink coat and fur hat" (3: 715). In short, Simon's Blanche is living out the very dream that Williams's heroine once imagined for herself: rescue at the hands of a Cadillac-owning suitor like Shep Huntleigh.[5] By devising this fairytale ending, Simon separates himself from Williams's tragic story and demarcates his own territory as a writer of comedy. As Hutcheon explains, "while the act and form of parody are those of incorporation, its function is one of separation and contrast. Unlike imitation, quotation, or even allusion, parody requires that critical ironic distance" (34).

Although Simon was influenced most deeply by *A Streetcar Named Desire*, he was also inspired by *The Glass Menagerie*— a drama that he identified as one of the works that "made [Williams's] reputation" (Interview in *Studies* 174). Confronting his family history and Jewish heritage for the first time in *Brighton Beach Memoirs*, Simon presents a semi-autobiographical memory play in the style of *The Glass Menagerie*. Like Tom Wingfield, Simon's protagonist, Eugene Jerome, speaks directly to the audience, recalling his adolescence in New York in 1937 (the same time period as Williams's play) and detailing the financial anxieties and turbulent lives of his Jewish American family. Like Tom, Eugene serves as the play's narrator — introducing other characters, commenting on the action, and forming a confidential bond with the audience. Furthermore, like Williams's narrator, Eugene imbues his story with a sense of nostalgia — so much so that T. E. Kalem called *Brighton Beach Memoirs* "Neil Simon's love letter to his past" (348), and Clive Barnes referred to the playwright as "the poet of all our forgotten yesterdays" ("Memoirs").

Yet *Brighton Beach Memoirs* is really a lighthearted parody of *The Glass Menagerie*. Appropriating the technique of the memory play, Simon inverts Williams's approach, turning Eugene Jerome into a comic raisonneur. Eugene confesses, for example, that he hates his name: "How am I ever going to play for the Yankees with a name like Eugene Morris Jerome? You have to be a Joe ... or a Tony ... or Frankie ... If only I was born Italian ... All the best Yankees are Italian ... My mother makes spaghetti with ketchup, what chance do I have?" (3: 485). Reflecting a tradition of Jewish humor that is central to Simon's plays, Eugene presents himself as a beleaguered victim and self-deprecating jokester. He relates serious or tragic events in a comic manner, using humor as a defense mechanism. As Peter Hays observes, *Brighton Beach Memoirs* would appear on the surface to have the makings of a tragedy: it's the middle of the Depression; Eugene's brother has been fired at work; Jack Jerome has suffered a heart attack after losing one of his two jobs; and Hitler has moved into Austria, highlighting the looming threat of World War II. Yet these serious circumstances are filtered through the mind of Simon's wisecracking, teenage narrator, creating what Hays calls "an autobiographical chronicle of personal catastrophe, recounted comically" (66).[6]

Simon further parodies *The Glass Menagerie* in *Brighton Beach Memoirs* by inverting or recasting key elements of Williams's play. He transforms the overbearing Southern belle

Amanda Wingfield into a nagging Jewish mother, Kate Jerome, who worships cleanliness, treats Eugene like an errand boy, and "wields guilt like a scalpel" (Schiff 52). Moreover, Simon converts the absent Mr. Wingfield into the very palpable — and seemingly ideal — father, Jack Jerome, who is respected and beloved by everyone in the family. Indeed, as Glenda Frank suggests, *Brighton Beach Memoirs* might aptly be subtitled: "Father Knows Best" (114). Finally, Simon alters the ending of *The Glass Menagerie*, composing a comic finale in which members of the Jerome family not only reconcile with each other but also plan to open their doors to refugee relatives from Poland. Whereas Williams's drama closes with a sense of tragic separation (as Tom remembers deserting his sister, Laura), Simon's play, in the tradition of classical comedy, includes "as many people as possible in its final society" (Frye 165). Through this jocund parody of *The Glass Menagerie*, Simon thus offers a rose-colored vision of his own childhood as well as an idealization of the family itself. As the playwright explained, "It's like looking back on your family album and seeing it better than it was" (Interview in *Studies* 175).

In *Broadway Bound*, however, set twelve years later in 1949, Simon presents a more serious — and reverential — parody of *The Glass Menagerie*, constructing a vision of the Jerome family that is far less idealized. Like the faithless Mr. Wingfield, Jack Jerome eventually abandons his wife and family, revealing his true identity as a flawed, disappointed man. Like Tom Wingfield, the twenty-three-year-old Eugene soon follows "in [his] father's footsteps" (*Glass Menagerie* 237) — leaving home for good to pursue a career in show business and thus contributing to the breakup of the family unit. Most of all, like Amanda Wingfield, Kate Jerome suffers the pain and indignity of losing the only man she ever loved; and like Amanda, she finds solace in memories. During a touching scene that takes place right before Jack deserts her, Kate recalls trying to impress her future husband long ago when she danced at the Primrose Ballroom with the movie star George Raft. Reliving this magical evening by dancing with Eugene in the kitchen, Kate is momentarily transformed into the vibrant, attractive girl that she once was. "You're so graceful, Mom," says Eugene. "I never knew you were so graceful" (3: 788). As a parodist, Simon preserves, to be sure, the technique of the comic raisonneur and even offers a somewhat optimistic ending. (Eugene's professional future is bright, and he is seemingly free from the guilt that Tom Wingfield feels for abandoning his family.) Nevertheless, Simon's parody comes close at times to replicating the poignancy of *The Glass Menagerie*. Describing *Broadway Bound* as "a play of forgiveness" and "an attempt [...] to understand my family and my own origins," Simon admitted that this last chapter in the Brighton Beach trilogy could be interpreted as "a love letter to [my] mother" (Interview in *Studies* 168).

The influence of *The Glass Menagerie* can be felt as well in Simon's Pulitzer-Prize winning drama *Lost in Yonkers* (1991), which focuses on a dysfunctional Jewish American family in 1942. Bella Kurnitz, an emotionally arrested (and probably mildly retarded) woman in her mid-thirties, is especially reminiscent of the physically handicapped Laura Wingfield. Desperate for love, the tender-hearted Bella dreams of finding the right man, getting married, and having children of her own. But her disability prevents her from leading a normal life; and when she does meet a "gentleman caller" (a mentally handicapped theater usher named Johnny), he proves to be more helpless and dependent than she is. Like Laura, Bella seems doomed to a life of lonely spinsterhood, living out the remainder of her days with an authoritarian mother who stifles her development. In fact, Grandma Kurnitz — a nightmarish version of Amanda Wingfield — is shown to have damaged the lives of all of her adult offspring, turning them into "emotional cripples" (Winer). Striving to teach her children to be strong "like steel" (4: 108), Grandma has abused them physically and has withheld from them almost any sign of motherly affection. As a result, Bella's brother Eddie has become a broken man, afraid to challenge his mother's authority; another brother, Louie, has taken to the streets to become a gangster; and a third sibling, Gert, is afflicted with an unusual speech problem. As Eddie's teenage son Jay remarks to his brother, Arty, at the start of the play, "Did you ever notice there's something wrong with *everyone* on Pop's side of the family?" (4: 90).

Simon's portrait of this dysfunctional family becomes a parodic echo of *The Glass Menagerie*, however, largely because of the inclusion of these two boys, who offer a comic perspective on their ten-month ordeal living in the Kurnitz home. Jay pictures Bella as a lovable but daffy character, pointing to her tendency to get lost ("She missed the first year [of high school] because she couldn't find it"), and remarking that her mind is "you know — closed for repairs" (4: 90). The boys also find humor in Aunt Gert's speech impediment, imitating her tendency to say "the first half of a sentence breathing out and the second half sucking in" (4: 91). They are amused by the tough-talking gangster, Uncle Louie: "It's like having a James Cagney movie in your own house" (4: 122). (Indeed, Louie mirrors Tom Wingfield's outlandish image of himself as a "hired assassin" and member of the Hogan Gang [164].) Finally, Jay and Arty manage to uncover a comic side to Grandma Kurnitz herself, mimicking her German accent, joking about her Nazi-like demeanor, and describing her as "Frankenstein's Grandma" (4: 89). Although Jay and Arty don't narrate the play directly in the manner of Eugene Jerome, they serve nonetheless as a humorous Greek chorus, commenting on the scene and providing a comic twist to many of the problems that beset the Kurnitz household.

By imitating *The Glass Menagerie* (especially Williams's portraits of Laura and Amanda Wingfield), Simon was able to go deeper in *Lost in Yonkers* than he had gone in previous plays — exploring serious topics such as child abuse and mental disability — and setting such themes against the dark background of World War II and the Holocaust.[7] At the same time, Simon managed to treat these serious subjects in a comic fashion, even offering a slightly upbeat ending in order to highlight the resilience of his characters. As the boys are about to leave Grandma's apartment to reunite with their father, Jay says, "We made it, Arty. Ten months here and we're still alive. We got through Grandma and we're all right" (4: 153). Indeed, as Barnes notes, "the motto of the [Kurnitz] family is survival" ("Lost"). Grandma has survived anti–Semitism in Germany; Uncle Louis has survived the mob; and despite their scars, the Kurnitz children and grandchildren have survived living with Grandma. Although Simon's characters may be "lost" — and, in Bella's case, perhaps even doomed — they display the same capacity for endurance found in many of Williams's characters, especially Amanda Wingfield. "Life's not easy," Amanda tells her son, Tom. "It calls for — Spartan endurance!" (172). Unlike Grandma Kurnitz, Amanda also recognizes that such endurance is made easier when the family itself becomes a refuge rather than a battleground. "In these trying times we live in," she says, "all that we have to cling to is — each other" (171).

Written throughout his lengthy career on Broadway, Neil Simon's parodies of Tennessee Williams are ultimately more than amusing copies of his predecessor's work; they are a mode of stylistic confrontation — a way of coming to terms with "the rich and intimidating legacy of the past" (Bate 4). Through the craft of parody, Simon simultaneously pays tribute to Williams's drama and distances himself from it — incorporating the master's texts into his own, but imprinting them with his unique comic style. As Israel Davidson has observed, the age-old tradition of Jewish parody "did not spring from the desire to disparage, but rather from the wish to emulate" (xviii). The same can be said for Simon's modern-day parodies of Williams, which are surely not intended as mocking attacks. Instead, when Simon "plays against" dramas such as *A Streetcar Named Desire* and *The Glass Menagerie*, he does so in a spirit of "creative embrace and rivalry" (Brower 4) — acknowledging his debt to Williams while at the same time seeking "to clear imaginative space" for his own comic art (Bloom 5). Most of Simon's parodies are humorous reworkings of Williams's texts — designed to demonstrate that even the grimmest of subjects can be treated in a comic manner. However, in several of his best dramas (i.e., *Broadway Bound* and *Lost in Yonkers*), Simon at times shifts his tone from the playful to the reverential — revealing the raw anguish and loneliness of his characters, and occupying a kind of border territory between parody and pure imitation. During moments such as these, Simon signals not only his increased confidence as a playwright, but his ability to respond to the legacy of Tennessee Williams with a true "greeting of the spirit" (Bate 134).

NOTES

1. Simon's title echoes the tamale vendor's cry of "red-hot!" outside the Kowalski apartment in *Streetcar*. For further discussion of the "red-hot" image, see Kolin, "Red-Hot!"

2. As Felicia Hardison Londré notes, numerous critics have commented on Blanche's identity as an actress — her penchant for "playing roles detached from the reality of her situation, costuming herself from the trunk containing fake furs and costume jewelry, [and] designing the lighting effects that will show her to advantage" (55).

3. Diana may also remind audiences of Maggie Pollitt in *Cat on a Hot Tin Roof*, who pleads with her (latently homosexual) husband, Brick, to have sex with her.

4. Simon invites comparisons to Williams in *Brighton Beach Memoirs* by naming two of his characters "Blanche" and "Stanley." However, aside from his sexual experience and his brief interest in playing poker, Stanley Jerome (Eugene's brother) bears little resemblance to Stanley Kowalski. Furthermore, the play as a whole is more indebted to *The Glass Menagerie* than to *Streetcar*.

5. According to Blanche, the Texas oil millionaire Shep Huntleigh had "a Cadillac convertible; must have been a block long!" (316). At the end of the play, she imagines that Mr. Huntleigh will rescue her by taking her on a cruise of the Caribbean.

6. *Biloxi Blues* (1985), the second installment of Simon's Brighton Beach trilogy, also makes use of a comic raisonneur. But this play, which focuses on Eugene Jerome's basic training in the army rather than on his family life, has less in common with *The Glass Menagerie* than do the other two plays.

7. For a discussion of how the Holocaust "casts its shadow" over *Lost in Yonkers*, see Mandl.

WORKS CITED

Abbott, Michael. "Neil's Women." Konas 127–135.

Barnes, Clive. "Lost in Yonkers, Happily Ever After." *New York Post* 22 Feb. 1991. Rpt. in *New York Theatre Critics' Reviews* (1991): 377.

———. "'Memoirs' is Simon's Best Play." *New York Post* 28 Mar. 1983. Rpt. in *New York Theatre Critics' Reviews* (1983): 345.

Bate, W. Jackson. *The Burden of the Past and the English Poet.* 1970. Cambridge: Harvard UP, 1991.

Bloom, Harold. *The Anxiety of Influence.* London: Oxford UP, 1973.

Brower, Reuben. *Mirror on Mirror.* Cambridge: Harvard UP, 1974.

Brustein, Robert. "America's New Culture Hero: Feelings Without Words." *Tennessee Williams's A Streetcar Named Desire: Modern Critical Interpretations.* Ed. Harold Bloom. New York: Chelsea House, 1988. 7–16.

Davidson, Israel. *Parody in Jewish Literature.* New York: AMC Press, 1966.

Frank, Glenda. "Fun House Mirrors: The Neil Simon-Eugene O'Neill Dialogue." Konas 109–125.

Frye, Northrop. *An Anatomy of Criticism: Four Essays.* 1957. New York: Atheneum, 1970.

Grayson, Richard. "'The Fruit Brigade': Neil Simon's Gay Characters." Konas 137–147.

Hays, Peter L. "Neil Simon and the Funny Jewish Blues." Konas 59–68.

Hutcheon, Linda. *A Theory of Parody: The Teachings of Twentieth-Century Art Forms.* New York: Methuen, 1985.

Johnson, Robert K. *Neil Simon.* Boston: Twayne, 1983.

Kalem, T. E. "Speak, Memory: 'Brighton Beach Memoirs,' by Neil Simon." *Time* 11 Apr. 1983. Rpt. in *New York Theatre Critics' Reviews* (1983): 347–348.

Kolin, Philip C. "The Family of Mitch: (Un)suitable Suitors in Tennessee Williams." *Magical Muse: Millennial Essays on Tennessee Williams.* Ed. Ralph F. Voss. Tuscaloosa: U of Alabama P, 2002. 131–146.

_____. "'Red-Hot!' in *A Streetcar Named Desire*." *Notes on Contemporary Literature* 19.4 (1989): 6–8.

Konas, Gary, ed. *Neil Simon: A Casebook*. New York: Garland, 1997.

Koprince, Susan. *Understanding Neil Simon*. Columbia: U of South Carolina P, 2002.

Londré, Felicia Hardison. "A streetcar running fifty years." *The Cambridge Companion to Tennessee Williams*. Ed. Matthew C. Roudané. Cambridge: Cambridge UP, 1997. 45–66.

Macdonald, Dwight. "Some Notes on Parody." *Parodies: An Anthology from Chaucer to Beerbohm — and After*. Ed. Dwight Macdonald. New York: Random House, 1960. 557–568.

Mandl, Bette. "Beyond Laughter and Forgetting: Echoes of the Holocaust in Neil Simon's *Lost in Yonkers*." Konas 69–77.

Schiff, Ellen. "Funny, He Does Look Jewish." Konas 47–58.

Simon, Neil. *Brighton Beach Memoirs*. *The Collected Plays of Neil Simon*. Vol. 3. New York: Random House, 1991. 479–593.

_____. *Broadway Bound*. *The Collected Plays of Neil Simon*. Vol. 3. New York: Random House, 1991. 693–803.

_____. *California Suite*. *The Collected Plays of Neil Simon*. Vol. 2. New York: Plume, 1986. 547–632.

_____. *The Gingerbread Lady*. *The Collected Plays of Neil Simon*. Vol. 2. New York: Plume, 1986. 147–227.

_____. "An Interview with Neil Simon." By Jackson R. Bryer. Konas 217–232.

_____. "An Interview with Neil Simon." By Jackson R. Bryer. *Studies in American Drama 1945-Present* 6 (1991): 152–176.

_____. Interview. *The Playwright's Art: Conversations with Contemporary American Dramatists*. Ed. Jackson R. Bryer. New Brunswick: Rutgers UP, 1995. 221–240.

_____. Interview. *Playwrights at Work*. Ed. George Plimpton. New York: Modern Library, 2000. 193–230.

_____. *Last of the Red Hot Lovers*. *The Collected Plays of Neil Simon*. Vol. 1. New York: Plume, 1986. 583–657.

_____. *Laughter on the 23rd Floor*. *The Collected Plays of Neil Simon*. Vol. 4. New York: Touchstone, 1998. 231–298.

_____. *Lost in Yonkers*. *The Collected Plays of Neil Simon*. Vol. 4. New York: Touchstone, 1998. 87–156.

_____. *The Odd Couple*. *The Collected Plays of Neil Simon*. Vol. 1. New York: Plume, 1986. 215–301.

_____. "Playboy Interview: Neil Simon." By Lawrence Linderman. *Playboy* 26 (Feb. 1979): 58ff.

_____. *Rewrites: A Memoir*. New York: Simon and Schuster, 1996.

Williams, Tennessee. "The Catastrophe of Success." *The Theatre of Tennessee Williams*. Vol. 1. New York: New Directions, 1971. 135–141.

_____. *The Glass Menagerie*. *The Theatre of Tennessee Williams*. Vol. 1. New York: New Directions, 1971. 123–237.

_____. *A Streetcar Named Desire*. *The Theatre of Tennessee Williams*. Vol. 1. New York: New Directions, 1971. 239–419.

Winer, Linda. "Simon Gets Darkly Comic." *New York Newsday* 22 Feb. 1991. Rpt. in *New York Theatre Critics' Reviews* (1991): 380.

Zimmerman, Paul D. "Neil Simon: Up From Success." *Newsweek* 2 Feb. 1970: 52–56.

"Inconspicuous Osmosis and the Plasticity of Doing": The Influence of Tennessee Williams on the Plays of Edward Albee

David A. Crespy

Tennessee Williams's influence on Edward Albee is fluid—it may very well have flowed in both directions, moving one way, then the other, at different points in these two writers' careers. As Helen Thompson notes, Albee prefers to think of this influence as "a process of 'osmosis'; an inconspicuous element that is only recognized when the damage has already been done and is irreversible" (110). And what Albee may have drawn upon in Williams's work, and what Williams may have drawn from Albee's work, is far more subtle, and yet far more profound, than the shared direct quotation in other writers. At the heart of the influence that flowed back and forth between Tennessee Williams and Edward Albee was deep sense of the "reality of doing," realized through an extraordinary plasticity of technique—the "plasticity" being Williams own notion of theatricality, non-linearity, and magic set forth in his production note to *The Glass Menagerie*.

Of course, at times, Albee did purposefully quote Williams's work, perhaps even to amuse the older playwright. Albee actually quotes Williams's *Streetcar Named Desire* quite openly in *Who's Afraid of Virginia Woolf?* This occurs in George's snap dragon moment and his line "flores para los muertos?" which is an ironic play on the flower woman in *Streetcar* (Amacher, 103). Similarly, in his later plays Williams attempted the experimentation that fascinated him in Albee and other Absurdist writers—drawing heavily upon the neo-vaudevillian style of Albee's *American Dream* and the character of the Young Man (Ben Zvi, 183). The differences between Albee and Williams are enormous, of course. Williams's southern, grotesque, fantastic lyricism contrasts with the austere Yankee minimalism of Albee's lean, angular modernism. And as much as Williams seemed to focus upon lower middle-class lives of quiet desperation, Albee has almost exclusively explored the wealthy worlds of decadent emptiness. These are exceedingly different playwrights who really don't seem to have much in common in terms of style, content, and sensibility, at least at first glance.

However, Williams was an early advocate for Albee's work and Albee found in Williams a playwright with whom he finally felt some kind of connection. Both struggled personally with their fame, wrestling with alcohol abuse, though Thompson challenges Mel Gussow's premise that Albee was the playwright Williams *would* have been, if he hadn't succumbed to his substance abuse. They were different writers entirely. Yet, Albee was deeply disturbed by and regretted Williams's personal excesses, primarily because it put a screen between them, limiting their personal connection. Biographically, they were connected as well, socializing at least on a fairly casual level — Albee invited Williams to dinner and cocktail parties in Greenwich Village; Williams infrequently visited Albee at him home in Montauk, swimming in his pool, and indicated some appreciation (or perhaps awe) of Albee's dogs, which Williams thought were "as big as ponies" (St. Just, 190).

Because of his own relentless and successful experimentation, Albee gave Williams the impetus to continue to experiment himself, especially in the later period of Williams's career, and to write the plays Williams had always wanted to write, confounding the critics, without the interference of directors and producers who had always sought more commercial plays from him. When asked by Studs Terkel about his being inspired by the younger generation of playwrights, including Albee and Pinter, Williams said that he liked "their attitude toward the commercialism of the theatre" and that they say, "take a flying jump at the moon" (Terkel, 79). Ironically, of course, because of this relentless spirit of adventurism both Albee and Williams suffered equally at the hands of the critics, often for the same reasons — including attacks on their sexual orientation, their portrayal of women and heterosexual relationships, accusations of self-indulgence, and charges that both had exhausted the limits of their talents and were dallying with recycled material. And yet, both still pressed on with their work — Albee disregarded these same critics, and battled the same irrelevant, homophobic, and disturbing reactions to their work that never seem to change, year after year.

There are elements of character, structure, language and symbol that occur in Albee's plays which have earlier precedent in Williams's work. Albee has admitted that he may have done so to amuse Williams — and both writers were close enough, and shared similar career triumphs and set-backs, personally, to share artistic homage. Norma Jenckes argues that Albee and Williams are linked by a "resurgent American Puritan optimism," and "have sought to expand the experimental possibilities for dramatic art in America." But perhaps, more importantly, she observes "both created space in their work for the marginalized, the dispossessed, and the silenced" (Jenckes, 7). In addition, there is the innate power of both writers' command over a deeply naturalistic and yet, in complete contradiction, highly artificial language, built on an almost operatic sense of the power of their "arias," the most crucial dramaturgy linking them, combined with a deep, complex understanding of character. However, I will argue, in addition, that a deeper underlying of dramaturgical techniques unite their writing which demonstrate a "reality of doing." Based upon a broader appreciation of Williams's and Albee's plays, I believe there is a fundamental subtextual structure of non-realistic, non-linear plasticity in real action that establishes a powerful commonality of character, thought, and spectacle in Williams's and Albee's plays.

I interviewed Edward Albee at his home in Montauk, New York, to ask him point blank about what drew him to Williams's plays and what links their work together. The contents of that interview are included at the end of this chapter. In our early conversations, before the interview, Albee highly recommended that I read Walter Davis' study *Get The Guests*. Davis' book uses psychoanalysis to "get" at our own real connection as critics with these writers's work — in other words, according to Davis, we are the eponymous Guests in his hermeneutic study of O'Neill, Miller, Williams, and Albee. The book is an analysis of the "wounds" that Albee's and Williams's plays have made upon their audiences, readers, and critics. For Davis, *A Streetcar Named Desire* and *Who's Afraid of Virginia Woolf?* are mousetraps with no escape for the audience, "[*A Streetcar Named Desire*] opens up desire not to offer us Lawrentian possibility but to show us all the ways in which desire is death" (91). The project of both plays is to break into the crypt which imprisons our souls to get at our basic wounds, "Our task is no less than to reverse ourselves from the 'ground' up" in order to undo the "psychological structures" which have been wrought by our "failure to face" the wounds which have shaped us (254). Davis comes very close in his analysis of both plays to what I would argue is the essence of linkage between these two writers, the "real doing" of unmasking the audience and revealing what lies below — the scarred remains of an American psyche which cannot bear its own face.

For Albee, Williams's work was "Chekhovian." Williams wrote *real* characters, as opposed to those that Albee considered to be "Ibsonian," that is, characters who are symbols or devices to promote a useful social message (a technique Albee felt was closer to Arthur Miller's style). In this case, realism converges on naturalism and Albee prefers the latter. Of course, Albee unquestionably admires the "absurd," insisting the absurdist minimalism of Beckett explains his own plays, like *Tiny Alice*. In response to Steve Capra on the inaccessibility of some absurdist drama, Albee's emphasizes, "If *Waiting for Godot* had been set in a living room, nobody would have had any trouble with it" (179). Albee's character-driven, yet deeply symbolic, Chekhovian naturalism, reflects the Russian's representation of a character's desires without a strong interest or focus in language per se as a stylistic element. But yet, language is at the heart of both Williams's and Albee's stylized plays — which despite their artifice have the uncanny knack of seeming terribly real.

The coinciding element that brings Chekhov, Albee, and Williams together can be called the "reality of doing," a force that moves deeply beneath characterization, language, image, and plot in their plays. "The reality of doing," a Stanislavsky-based acting term, is tied very closely with the teachings of Sanford Meisner, and deals with the very real, concrete, and most importantly, *specific* underlying actions that these characters *really do* in order to get what they want (Soloviova, 136–155). These are the "doings" that characters make subconsciously, making them profoundly "actable" in Albee and Williams. In combination with the plasticity of language, both Albee's and Williams's plays offer that "mystic naturalism" underscoring a deep and shared influence between them and that Chekhov had on them, which both Albee and Williams acknowledge. Because their characters are committed to often subterranean, but very real, tasks, the extraordinary language that Albee and Williams use takes flight and moves beyond poetry and lyricism to something much more important — and powerful — the language of drama. As Sanford Meisner, the great American acting teacher, was fond of saying, "an ounce of behavior is worth a pound of words" and in the case of Williams and Albee, both these writers managed to do something which has been quite elusive in American drama — write lyrical (in the case of Williams) or musical (in the case of Albee) language and have it be *real*. "Quite a trick," Albee noted in his interview with me.

One of the more controversial elements that link these two writers tied to their ability to coincide naturalistic, deep "doings" with extraordinary characterization, is their depiction of women. While both playwrights have written the most complex, fascinating, and extravagant women in American drama, their characters are not, as many critics and theatre artists have assumed, "men in drag." This critical reaction to the female characters has challenged their work. Rather than seeing such readings as legitimate queer readings which as Stacy Wolf has brilliantly done in a study of the American musical, empowering sexual identity, critics have censored Albee's and Williams's plays, using their orientation as a critical sledge hammer. Jo Coubert, for example, wrote to the editor of the *New York Times* shortly after Albee's *Who's Afraid of Virginia Woolf?* premiered: "And there, it suddenly struck me, is the key to the play: it is not about men and women; it is about male homosexuals." According to Coubert, Albee has extrapolated the "vicious, waspish, gratuitous destructiveness of people living in special circumstances" and projected it on heterosexual couples (Coubert, 23). Coubert expresses what has been an oft-repeated response to the women in Albee's and Williams's plays, and also which questions whether a gay playwright is even able to write a heterosexual relationship out of a lack of conjugal knowledge. This opinion has then been followed over the course of many years by similar disturbing notions about both Williams and Albee by distinguished critics, including writers as Stanley Kauffman, Philip Roth, Walter Nadler, William Goldman, and others, including, recently, David Mamet.[1]

Fintan O'Toole, in his review of Albee's recently published collection of plays, entitled "These Illusions are Real" notes that these criticisms have long since been proven false by the testament of the performers and performances themselves (2006). In the article, "Tom and His Feminine Mystique," actresses Estelle Parsons, Zoe Caldwell, Eve Marie Saint, and Rosemary Harris touch upon their personal experiences of working with Tennessee Williams himself and what seemed to be at the heart of his ability to write great roles for women. Estelle Parsons sums up it up this way: "Everything he wrote was larger than life, and so much, so much more poetic than the real people the characters were based on" (quoted in Osgood, 91). And of course what makes the women of Williams and Albee so real are the powerful, specific underlying actions that grow out of the writers' profound understanding of the "reality of doing" running underneath the external realities of their female characters.

Marion Seldes, when interviewed about her role as the "Woman" in Albee's *The Play About the Baby* claimed "Every second on the stage, there always has to be something you want, and for her, it's the need to help, to assist. She's almost desperate to do that" (quoted in Marks, 2001). Seldes' was coached by Albee himself in that production, who told her that there was no "too far" in the playing of that character. Seldes's comments echo Rosemary Harris's discussion of her work performing the "lengthy, syntactically complex speech" given to Agnes in opening moments of *Delicate Balance*, "'It was like clutching a tidal wave,' she said, 'and you caught it at the crest, knowing that eventually you would land on the shore because Edward takes you there — if you trust him'" (quoted in Watt). Language itself provides a score for the real actable doings running underneath it and the humanity bursts through this same arched language in a "hyper-punctuation" that is "a grammatical defense against insanity" (Watt). Agnes's aria is built on a complex powerful web of real actions, as she makes sense of, wrestles with, and finally tames the terror of her own mind slipping away from her.

Tennessee Williams, for all his humorous protestations to the opposite (see his essay "Tennessee, Never Talk to an Actress") was similarly supportive of his actresses and they were deeply attached to him.[2] Frank Rich, in his review of Vanessa Redgrave in *Orpheus Descending* notes that Redgrave fills "out each moment, however tiny, with the dramatic (if sometimes funny) conflict of emotions" and "subtly reveals the countervailing forces tugging within" (Rich). Redgrave explores the rich emotional life of Williams's Lady Torrance as she inhabits this character, and it is this network of actions within the maelstrom of imagery and lyricism of his language that provided a strong, clear, and specific spine of doings that moves Williams's language from poetic lyricism into a volatile dramatic magma of behavior.

Both Williams and Albee often noted that they are perfectly capable of writing "real women." When interviewed by Rex Reed, Williams noted, "If I am writing a female character, goddamnit, I'm gonna write a female character, I'm not gonna write a drag queen!" (Reed, 146). Albee's response, when questioned by *New York Times* theatre critic, David Richards, reiterates that of Tennessee Williams, but then touches upon an even more pernicious, hurtful, and twisted response to the plays — the actual suggestion that his plays should be performed in drag. He also notes that both he and Williams have been attacked on this issue, and calls Stanley Kauffmann's article, "disgusting" and considers the idea that "gays were writing about gays, but disguising them as straights, and writing about men, but disguising them as women," as "preposterous." Albee notes that he has had to shut down productions of *Who's Afraid of Virginia Woolf?* with all-male casts "for the same reason I don't allow all-female casts of *The Zoo Story*. They're incorrect." But he also notes that "the sniping has never gone away" (Richards, 1991).

Deconstructionist directors, even gay directors, such as William Ball, whose controversial production of *Tiny Alice* had Albee racing backstage to protest, have purposefully "misinterpreted" Albee's and Williams's work as their own artistic *cri de coeur*— ostensibly "outing" a playwright's hidden sexual orientation. But these purposeful "misinterpretations" that cross-dress Albee's and Williams's women are equally insulting and censorious to writers who happen to be gay and would like to write any kind of character they would like to write — regardless of their gender and sexual orientation. Albee touches upon this, taking it to its "imbecilic extreme" by noting that writers who are censored from writing anyone who differs from her/himself in anyway is finally only allowed to write about himself.[3] The dangerous curves of brutal desire that Albee's and Williams' women that Ben Brantley calls "Albee's Tigers" have been etched out of the blood of their constant oppression. Brantley notes that "whether life givers or death angels" Albee's women are "blazing sources of energy that both nurture and scorch" and make even Albee's most "impenetrable" plays interesting.

Interestingly, their striking out has come from the peculiar inactivity, the quietness, the passive aggression, of the men in both writers' plays. Brantley notes that the men who hover around these tigresses "merely stammer, hedge and wilt, latter-day Hamlets choking on contemplation." What is striking about both Albee's and Williams's men is their inability or refusal to act. As John Clum points out, it is Albee's sensitivity to the "strong women who are failed by the men they married" that actually drives the power of these plays (Clum, 59). With the exception of Stanley Kowalski in *Streetcar Named Desire*, and the very elegant, controlling Man in *The Play About the Baby*, these men are utterly frustrating in their passiveness, and yet they prove to be the perfect catalyst for the women in their plays to react against. The same can be said of the spousal relationships between Maggie and Brick in *Cat on a Hot Tin Roof*, George and Martha in *Who's Afraid of Virginia Woolf*, and Agnes and Tobias in *Delicate Balance*, in both plays the women plead for the men to somehow take charge of their lives, and finally are driven to extraordinary measures themselves to deal with the passive aggressiveness of their husbands. And it is clear, in both of these plays that the real doing running underneath the waves of language hinge on decisions that the men must make.

Williams was an influence on Albee long before Williams knew him — and this influence was tied directly to the ostensibly gay character who is dead before the play begins — a link between these two playwrights. Albee recalled that his first encounter with Williams's work began in "the late 1940s," although he couldn't remember any specific production. However, as Mel Gussow observes, it was when Albee saw Williams *Suddenly Last Summer*, that some kind of a deep connection was made with Williams's work, when he and William Flanagan saw *Suddenly Last Summer* together, and according to Flanagan, the play "had a profound hypnotic effect on both of us." Whether it was the performance by Anne Meacham, and Williams' powerful technique of Catherine's intense aria, or the grotesque, gothic horror show of Sebastian's final end, it's clear that for Albee, seeing Williams was, according to his contemporary, playwright Robert Heide, "like a light bulb going off, or as a release for his own pain" (Gussow, *Singular Journey*, 89). Looking back at the plays themselves, the haunted surreal quality of the violently grotesque and ultimately tragic relationship between a mother and her son can be seen in many of Albee's plays, including *the American Dream, Who's Afraid* of *Virginia Woolf, Delicate Balance*, and *Three Tall Women*, even *Tiny Alice*. Albee's ability to wed the unreal, the extravagant, and the highly stylized theatricality is similar to what Williams did in *Suddenly Last Summer* with a concrete, real doing that makes the play so powerful. This is the craft that underlies the real doings of these characters and it is this influence that has inconspicuously "osmosed" between these two writers.

Taking a closer look at two arias created by each of these authors, one can see specific linkage of doings between *Suddenly Last Summer*, which Albee saw, predating his earliest work, and Albee's own *The Goat, or Who is Sylvia?* which was produced recently in 2005. The scenes take place near the end of both plays, and in each case, the characters are fighting for their lives — and this powerful driving action unleashes an explosion of language from both. In each case the situation is extreme, surreal, and there is an uncanny quality to the situation, as if the plays have moved beyond traditional psychological realism, and channel deeper, more ancient, dramatic sacrificial rituals.

At the end of *Suddenly*, Catherine is fighting for her life, and at the heart of her aria, her poignant retelling of a Sebastian's death — is a story so horrific that Violet Venable would like to "cut this hideous story out of her brain!" Here is a level of real stakes that forces the character to use language that has an almost talismanic effect on the audience, casting a spell through the ritual of keening. Catherine recounts the tale of Sebastian's being cannibalized by homeless naked children, stating that they, like a "flock of featherless little black sparrows ... had torn bits of him away and stuffed them into those gobbling fierce little empty black mouths of theirs." And by the end of the speech, Sebastian is described as being almost a sacrificial offering himself looking like "big white-paper-wrapped bunch of red roses had been *torn, thrown, crushed!* — against that blazing white wall" (Williams, 147). Catherine's ritualistic evocation of the death and dismemberment of Sebastian Venable not only presents the off-stage violence in a way that echoes the work of Sophocles and Euripides, but also channels a deeper sense of tragedy, a tragic loss of a great poet, a great artist who might have been the voice of a new generation.

This similar act of mourning, of sacrifice, of ritualized speech may also be seen in the character of Stevie in the Albee's *The Goat, or Who is Sylvia?*, who finally, after listening to her husband's attempt, in the traditional meek, broken mutterings of Albee's broken men, to somehow justify his coupling with the beast, finally explodes: "You have brought me down, you goat-fucker; you love of my life! You have brought me down to *nothing*.... You have brought me down, and, Christ!, I'll bring you down with me![4] Stevie is fighting for her marriage, fighting for what is left of her dignity as Martin's wife, and finally, fighting for her life. The speech is filled with half-thoughts, remembrances, corrections, realizations, asides, as she makes sense of what has been said to her, and claws her way back from the abyss that Martin has made of their relationship.

What becomes clear, just by considering the quality of the language of both Catherine in *Suddenly Last Summer* and Stevie in *The Goat*, is that at the heart of these fundamental dramaturgical parallels is the structure of subtextual "doings" in the throb and flow of actions running underneath the dialogue. The minds of the two characters are similarly racing, checking and rechecking their language, their facts, jogging their memories, trying to get it right in their minds, and at the same time trying — desperately trying — to make a connection with their listener. In Williams's case, the aria is colored by remembered images, descriptions that drip with emotion and are painted with strokes of desire. Catherine attempts to evoke the memory of the carnage she has seen in order to make the deepest impression she can on the doctor. Freed from the constraints of her fear of her Aunt Violet, her language is liberated and yet simultaneously taken prisoner by her cousin Sebastian's poetry. It is as if she is channeling him, allowing him to describe his own death. The images she invokes, the children as black birds, their mouths like the bills of fierce raptors hacking away at Sebastian's body, are in service to a larger ritual, an almost dithyrambic hero story that is more akin to an offering before an angered god than a beautiful young woman pouring her heart out to an equally young, attractive doctor. And of course, the physical reality, the physical attraction between Catherine and the young doctor, is deeply woven into the play — is that also Sebastian's influence reaching beyond the grave?

In the case of Albee's *Goat*, Stevie's lament is built on a musical structure of theme and variations and a rhythm that pulses with the ebb and flow of the character's reasoning process, because in her case, she's making a decision right then on what she is going to do — she's pulling it together even as she wrestles with the very notion of what it is she's having to deal with. There is a distinct lack of imagery — outside of the imagined bed that Stevie and Martin shared together — and at the same time, a ritual pounding pushes through the aria. This seems to grow out of the same sacramental keening that Catherine brings to bear on Sebastian's story in *Suddenly*. The repeated deep dull roar of pain, "You have brought me down..." pounds in the ear three times until it devolves into a dark rumbling threat, "You have brought me down, and, Christ!, I'll bring you down with me!" which summons a kind of dithyrambic incantation of Greek tragedy with just a hint of Christian sacrifice thrown in for good measure — linking pagan and Christian traditions, which is not surprising for Albee — who has often cited his own fascination with the historical Jesus.

These ritualized acts of revelation point to other connective tissue of influence between Williams's and Albee's writing — and these are their shared central philosophical concerns, which directly tie into their mutual exploration and unmasking of the "mendacity" (using William's term) or "false illusions" that seem inherent in the myth of the American Dream. And both of these writers are reacting, in essence, at least from Albee's point of view, to Eugene O'Neill's notion of "pipe dreams" as articulated by Hickey in O'Neill's *The Iceman Cometh*. Albee observes in an interview with Richard Farr observing that there isn't any problems with having false illusions, as long as you don't kid yourself "that they're not false" and he notes that "it is the playwright's job to show you that they are" (Farr). Once again, Albee's stated responsibility for the playwright ties in very closely with Davis's project of exploring the "mousetrap" action of both writer's plays, moving characters, and thereby, the audience, inexorably toward a powerful self-revelation of the wounds within themselves. This is also echoed in Thompson's notion of the ephemeral dreams that flow between Blanche's southern past in *A Streetcar Named Desire* and the imaginary son of George and Martha in *Who's Afraid of Virginia Woolf*, and how, in each case, these dreams are stripped of illusion by "spoiled occasions" (Thomson, 112–113). And interestingly, it is at these moments that the characters are stripped of their ability to manipulate language.

In the case of both plays there is a birthday party — Blanche's party is spoiled by the gift of a one-way greyhound ticket to Laurel, Mississippi, and Martha's birthday party for her son is spoiled by George's announcement that their son had been killed in a car accident. In each case, interestingly enough, the moment that ties these two scenes together is a failure of language — Blanche tries to smile, then laugh and she hastily exits into the bathroom where we hear her coughing and gagging. Martha's response, in a play that has been essentially verbal warfare, is Martha's eruption — "YOU CAN'T DO THIS!" and "YOU CAN'T DECIDE THESE THINGS!" — followed by Martha drifting off into strangely inarticulate ramblings that end the play. Language fails because in both plays, language has been the mask, the means of keeping up the illusions, and in the end, it too must be destroyed. As Albee notes himself, these are the moments that the playwright is holding a mirror to the audience and saying "here's what you look like. Change." In Albee's opinion, it is the job of art to be useful, not unlike the African art that he cherishes in his own home; otherwise, "it's a waste of time" (Academy of Art Interview).

However, for both Williams and Albee, the process of getting to an useful art, the real doing of challenging an audience to release their hold on their own personal myths, is a brutal one — and there is an inherent cruelty to both writers, a quality of merciless and unflinching sadism inflicted on and by the characters in both Albee's and Williams' plays. In his own remarks on Tennessee Williams's brutal honesty, Albee observed that "A good play is an act of aggression against the status quo of people's smugness. At his best, Tennessee was not content with leaving people when they left a play of his the way they were when the came in to see a play of his" (Brockway). This can be seen, of course, in the major works like *Who's Afraid of Virginia Woolf?* and *A Streetcar Named Desire*, but it is manifested with a subtle level of horror in the small jewels of both playwrights work — their short plays, and in particular, their short plays which veer away from naturalism.

For both writers, experimental, non-linear, "magic" playwriting technique was intrinsic to their art, and both expounded upon it, in Williams case, he explores his notions of a "plastic theatre," and he goes to some length to discuss his attachment to this non-realistic technique as early as his first major commercial success, *The Glass Menagerie*, in the 1940s. Albee writes about non-linear technique with an ironic point of view in, "Which Theatre is the Absurd One," first published in the *New York Times* in 1962 — where he points out that the avant-garde theatre is not only fun, "it is free-swinging, bold, iconoclastic and often wildly, wildly funny." And finally what he recommends to understand it is a "child-like innocence" to approach it on its own terms. However for both writers, there is more than a hint of Artaud's cruelty to their work, and it is here that influence between the two writers swings wildly back and forth.

One of the fascinating aspects to the linkage of these writers' work is the flow of influence between them, and for the most part, it was Williams who was doing a good deal of the influencing, but after 1960, Albee's star was in ascension, and Williams was his relentless supporter, attending opening night after opening night, and in countless interviews, commending Albee's work. So it is not surprising that as Albee's biggest fan, Williams began to emulate Albee's experimentation, and this can be seen directly in Williams's *Slapstick Tragedy* which incorporated two one-acts, *The Mutilated*, and *The Gnädiges Fräulein*, both of which used techniques which, though Williams claimed otherwise, could not have come anywhere but from his own assimilation of a generation of writers, including Albee, who had experimented with the absurdist techniques of Beckett, Genet, Ionesco, and Pinter. In particular, it is fascinating to compare the figure of the Young Man at Grandma's death in Albee's *The Sandbox* with the final moments of Williams's *The Mutilated* and the entrance of the seductive Jack-in-Black and the virile, insatiable Indian Joe in *The Gnädiges Fräulein*. In Albee's play the Young Man is well aware that he is merely playing a role, that of the Angel of Death, a kind of movie role that he is not sure he's entirely expert at, and confesses as much to Grandma, even as he acknowledges his true identity. And at that moment of revelation, Grandma is gently, if somewhat awkwardly, killed by the Angel of Death with a kiss, to the elegiac strokes of the cello. The cruelty here is perhaps less one of brutality than of a kind of sudden shock of recognition, a moment of horror, as Grandma realizes that what has felt perhaps like a lucid dream has become the nightmare of her own undoing. The Young Man, a beautiful, muscled creature of masculine sexuality, clearly identified as a Hollywood actor, and a vain one at that, is emblematic of the kind of sexual passion that is identified with commercial film and pop culture, and of course, as John Clum would perhaps label as the antithesis of the "sacrificial stud," an icon of gay virility, and yet, simultaneously as the deathly personification of the American Dream (Clum).

The figure of Jack-in-Black in *The Mutilated* appears as a representation of Trinket's breast cancer, her pain personified — yet he also, oddly enough, has the sexual bravado of an El Gallo, the all-knowing, all-seeing commedia puppet master of Jones's and Schmidt's *The Fantasticks*. Like the *Sandbox* and *The American Dream*, Celeste and Trinket, the fading prostitutes in the play, are essentially clown-like commedia figures, who simultaneously exist as allegorical, expressionist impressions of characters, and yet all-too-real, fully realized human beings. Despite their freakish and seemingly senile, attempts at winning over the attentions of sailors, Celeste and Trinket still seek an all too real buffer against loneliness and the brutal, cruel reality of the street — the kindness of ... old friends. In the final moments of the play, which is essentially a fractured Christmas carol, the action is sung after the appearance of "Our Lady," who is perhaps Mary, but not the Mary we think — rather she is the Mary who is the saint of prostitutes, the one who brings both Celeste and Trinket into a trance and heals them. With her cry, "The pain in my breast is gone!" Trinket is allowed a final miracle, tied perhaps to her final forgiveness of Celeste, and more importantly to a grant by Jack-in-Black, perhaps the ultimate "john," despite the tolling of the death nell, of further life.

What links these two scenes and ties them deeply to the real doing in these essentially absurdist, non-linear, and finally abstract comedies, is the use of a paralyzing attraction to the beautiful young man who simultaneously symbolizes death and a small tsunami of male libido. If the Young Man and Jack-in-Black are both the Angel of Death, and we keep in mind that *Sandbox* was written in 1961, and *The Mutilated* was written by the end of 1964, then it is clear that here is a moment of influence which may have flowed from Albee to Williams, a freedom of image and metaphor that is being handed back and forth between the two. Arguably this same young man could said to have originated as Stanley in *Streetcar* or Val in *Orpheus Descending*, but the use of this figure simultaneously as both a figure of death and a overwhelming scent of male sensuality is clearly flowing from Albee's own lean imagery of the Young Man of the *American Dream* and *Sandbox* transformed by Williams into a much more theatrical, comical, and perhaps more romantic, image of Jack-in-Black in *The Mutilated*.

And in a sense, this same figure appears again, in *Gnädiges Fräulein*. Another correlation of this handsome, young Angel of Death figure is that of Indian Joe — who is clearly tied very closely to the blonde, blue-eyed, Hollywood boy toy that Albee plays with in the Young Man of *Sandbox*. Only here, Williams takes the image to a new level of expressionist irony, playing with the ironic notion of the "Hollywood" version of a Native American. Once again, at the heart of these images, is the real, deep-running desire for this lovely, handsome young male Adonis that plays underneath, for Granny and Mommy in *American Dream* and *Sandbox*, and for Celeste and Trinkett in *The Mutilated*, and Polly and the Gnädiges Fräulein in *Gnädiges Fräulein*. In fact, at the heart of the tale of *Gnädiges Fräulein* is a broken heart — the broken heart of the fish-catching *Gnädiges Fräulein*, half-woman, half-bird, for her Viennese lover ... personified by the ever-hungry, ever-masculine Indian Joe. Her frantic bid for fish is tied to a deep wound that has been left forever opened by her "Viennese dandy."

Continuing for a moment in the short plays of Albee and Williams, we see the influence of cruelty and perhaps the grotesque shared between them in a different way with the intense, powerful longing found in the monstrous hatreds and deep passions of the Nurse in Albee's *The Death of Bessie Smith*, and, oddly enough, in the pathetic weakness and victimization of the very frail, though enormous Flora in Williams's *27 Wagons Full of Cotton*. A deeply ambiguous blend of sexuality, sensuality, and violence is inherent to both. Here the influence clearly flows from Williams — the rapid, violent wooing and rape of the massive Flora by the vicious, vengeful yet tiny Vicarro culminates in a rapid-fire exchange of banter between them as Vicarro closes in for his final vengeance against Jake who has burned down his gins (Williams, 324). The terse interchange of questions, demands, orders, and pleas is physically contrasted with Vicarro's tiny, tense presence, and the contradictory enormous flab of Flora, who is genuinely terrified of Vicarro. And yet, here is that same pulse of sexuality, of a blend of sadistic, unwelcome seduction tied to a longing, a hunger for satiation which ends ultimately in inevitable sexual violence. Contrast this scene from *27 Wagons Full of Cotton* with the exchange between the Intern and the Nurse in *The Death of Bessie Smith*, just after the young intern has, half-facetiously proposed to the Nurse. Here the Nurse promises to "fix" the intern, promising, "Honey, your neck is in the *noose* ... and I have a whip ... and I'll set the horse from under you ... when it pleases me" (Albee, 69). Once again the threat of the whip is here, coming from the Nurse, who clearly, despite the contradictory signals we're getting in this scene, is the one who is in charge. The scene between the Intern and the Nurse is filled with a kind of wild, laughing sexuality that signifies for the intense physical relationship between them — the sexual horseplay that takes place each night between them in the Intern's car, as it is parked in front of the Nurse's father's home. And the intensely violent threat that the Nurse hisses at the Intern is a kind of romantic foreplay — because she fully intends for the Intern to continue this strange violent courtship — a sado-masochistic relationship that also has a whip stinging beneath the language. It is a scene that rings like a bell with the Nurse's wild, throaty, lustful laughter serving as a contrapuntal note beneath the threats of violence, and sickeningly laced, finally, with the tragedy of Bessie Smith's pathetic death hovering over all that happens in the play.

Perhaps one of the most fascinating parallels both in terms of cruelty and the power of a kind of cleansing sadism is directly tied to the fates of two characters in Albee's and Williams's plays — the character of Julian in *Tiny Alice* and that of Shannon in *Night of the Iguana*, and here the flow of influence or at least mutual fascination, is tied to the ultimate cruelty of crucifixion — for both Julian in *Tiny Alice* and Shannon in *Night of the Iguana* are subjected to a ritualized act of contrition. Julian is mortally wounded by the Lawyer in an "accident" and left to the mysteries of Alice; Shannon is bound in his hammock by Maxine and his confessor is Hannah. Both Albee and Williams professed a kind of attachment to Christianity, Williams was converted to Catholicism by his brother Dakin, and Albee has, on several occasions, confirmed his own attachment to Christianity, albeit a high secular one, tied directly to Jesus himself. In the case of Julian, his sacrifice, his outpouring lead to a level of acceptance of his "priesthood" which is his marriage to Alice in the model, Alice the monstrous being, who is his ultimate confessor. And simultaneously he is abandoned by the imposter Alice, who goes on, for an eternity, with the Lawyer and the Butler, to continue their hellish deeds.

For Shannon, the cruelty abruptly ends with a bolt for freedom, he looses his own ropes and makes his way to the liquor that imprisons him and his "need to believe in something or in someone — almost anyone — almost anything ... something." Unlike Julian, who is tested, sacrificed, and finally furiously accepting of his fate, Shannon makes his connection with his "Alice" who is Hannah, and then tragically gives it up for the "imposter Alice," in this case, Maxine. The characters of Julian and Shannon are both mock "priests" and both have fallen, and in both plays the dramatic structure of cruelty is built on the real doing of two men who seek a connection with their god — their god who is a woman longing for them, longing for their connection, and yet ultimately completely separate from them. When Julian finally dies, he is cut loose from the ties that have held him and Shannon, once he has sliced through the rope holding the iguana, has played "God tonight like kids play house with old broken crates and boxes."

Finally, in what might be the most fascinating linkage of influence flowing between the two writers, are Albee's and Williams's wonderful control of the metaphor and physical realities of animals in their plays. From Albee's own wonderful animal tales, including the magnificent aria that is the "dog story" in *The Zoo Story*, to Tobias's sadly evocative tale of his relationship with his cat in *Delicate Balance*, to the submerged, subversive threat of the lizard-like creatures at the end of *Seascape* to the frightening, earth-shaking revelations in *The Goat, Or Who is Silvia?*, Albee's evocative mix of metaphorical animal imagery to the actual presence of non-human characters, both onstage and off, provides enormous clues to Albee's own sensibilities regarding man's relationship with nature, and man's own intolerance for creatures who do not live in a world with false illusions — because they are incapable of illusions. Albee's animals contrast neatly with those conjured by Williams, who deals with them in a far more metaphorical manner, although animals certainly do appear in Williams's plays — Maggie, the cat, in *Cat on a Hot Tin Roof*, Blanche's appearance as a moth in *Streetcar*, Stanley's appearance as a "richly feathered male bird among hens," Shannon's association with the iguana in *Night of the Iguana*, the strangely omniscient parrot in *A Perfect Analysis Given by a Parrot*, and Alma Winemiller's singing in *The Eccentricities of A Nightingale*. In each of these cases, the human beings take on the qualities of the animals, and at the same time, the images of the animals offer clues to the real doings of the characters. A great actor playing in either Williams's or Albee's plays would ignore the resonance these animal behaviors offer at their peril.

What is particularly striking when one compares Williams' use of the very real cocaloony birds in *Gnädiges Fräulein* with equally "present" lizards in *Seascape*, are the similarity of the threat that each of these beasts seem to make in both plays. The Cocaloony bird is a grotesque, frightening beast that pecks out the eyes of its human competition, the Gnädiges Fräulein — while the Lizards that appear in *Seascape* are no where nearly as grotesque, although for that reason they are all the more frightening — since they are so real. The Cocaloony bird, not unlike the Bird Girl in *The Mutilated*, is a fairly cartoonish creature, and the violence they pursue, while bloody, seems to be by no means as threatening as the violence suggested by Leslie and Sarah, the two lizards in *Seascape*. And this is because Leslie and Sarah are so "real." They are given names, they talk, they are reasonable, and yet, they remain very threatening. While in contrast the simple "AWK!" of the Cocaloony bird which suddenly appears in Polly's and Molly's midst in *The Gnädiges Fräulein*, Leslie and Sarah seem to be evolving — while in contrast, the Gnädiges Fräulein seems to be devolving. Since Williams produced his strange combination of one-acts, *The Mutilated* and *The Gnädiges Fräulein* in 1966, nearly 10 years before *Seascape*, it may very well be that Albee borrowed the idea of actor-sized non-humans from Williams, but it is much more likely that both writers brought the non-humans on the stage to get at that deep contradiction in the human nature — that is both fascinated by nature, and yet, at the same time wants to control it, so that the collision between human beings and animals isn't a disastrous one. What is lurking in these creatures is not just an evocative image or an emotional metaphor, but a suggestion for a much deeper sense of the desire that flows beneath — the real doing that is at the heart of both Albee's and Williams work.

Like Chekhov, both Albee and Williams share a common interest in the natural world — and it is not surprising that animal imagery figures so strongly in both playwrights' plays — for here is the basis of what links these writers so closely together — their understanding of the basic metaphor of characterization. Here, in the non-human world of strange creatures, both writer were able to plumb the depths of the human psyche, and in the mousetraps that their plays ultimately resemble, the animals portrayed there are symbols of the kind of behaviors and real doings that drive dramatic action, and at the same time, allow these writers to wright behavior on the wing of metaphor, and take advantage of language to its fullest dramaturgical advantage. If the question of influence must begin and end there, then what finally links these two writers is a deep sense and connection with the ritual action of drama — that of *catharsis*, the purgation of, not pity and fear, but rather the false dreams, mendacity, and illusion that plague the modern imagination, and weaken its core strength, the "real doings" and desires of fragile, believable human beings caught in surreal, frightening landscapes that resemble, and then at times, don't bear any resemblance to, the dream of America, a dream that has at its core, an unwavering quality of illusion.

NOTES

1. See Stanley Kauffmann, "On the Acceptability of the Homosexual," *The New York Times*, January 23, 1966.; Philip Roth, "The Play That Dare Not Speak Its Name," *The New York Review of Books*, February 25, 1965.; William Goldman, *The Season: A Candid Look at Broadway* (Harcourt, Brace, 1969), pp. 234–240; David Mamet , *Bambi Vs. Godzilla: On the Nature, Purpose, and Practice of the Movie Business*, New York: Pantheon, 2007, 107.

2. Williams, Tennessee, "'Tennessee, Never Talk to an Actress'" *New York Times*

3. Edward Albee in *Tennessee Williams: Orpheus of the American Stage*, dir. Merrill Brockway, 97 min. 1994, videocassette.

4. Edward Albee, *The Goat, or, Who Is Sylvia?* Woodstock: The Overlook Press, 2003.

WORKS CITED

Academy of Art Interview, "Edward Albee: Who's Afraid of Virginia Woolf" 2 June 2005. Http://www.achievement.org/autodoc/page/alb1int-1, Accessed 8/31/07.

Albee, Edward "The Death of Bessie Smith," in *The Collected Plays of Edward Albee: Volume 1, 1958–65*, Woodstock: *Overlook Duckworth*, 2004.

Albee, Edward. Personal Interview. 25 July. 2007.

Albee, Edward. *The Goat, or, Who Is Sylvia?* Woodstock: Overlook, 2003.

Amacher, Richard E., *Edward Albee*. New York: Twayne, 1969.

Ben Zvi, Linda. "Playing the Cloud Circuit: Albee's Vaudeville Show." *The Cambridge Companion to Edward Albee*. Ed. Stephen Bottoms. Cambridge, England: Cambridge University Press, 2005. 178–197.

Brantley, Ben. "Albee's Tigers, Albee's Women." *New York Times*, 12 April 1996. 2: 7.

Brockway, Merrill. *Orpheus of the American Stage*. Videocassette. International Cultural Programming Inc. 1994.

Capra, Steve. "Interview with Edward Albee." *Stretching My Mind*. Ed. Edward Albee. New York: Carroll & Graf, 2005. 175–188.

Clum, John M. "The Sacrificial Stud and the Fugitive Female in Suddenly Last Summer, Orpheus Descending, and Sweet Bird of Youth." Ed. Matthew C. Roudané. *The Cambridge Companion to Tennessee Williams*. Cambridge: Cambridge UP, 1997. 128–146.

Clum, John M. "'Withered Age and Stale Custom': Marriage, Diminution, and Sex in *Tiny Alice, A Delicate Balance*, and *Finding the Sun*." *The Cambridge Companion to Edward Albee*. Ed. Stephen Bottoms. Cambridge, England: Cambridge University Press, 2005. 59–74.

Davis, Walter. *Get the Guests: Psychoanalysis, Modern American Drama, and the Audience*. Madison: U of Wisconsin P, 1994.

Farr, Richard. "Edward Albee." *Progressive* 60, no. 8 (1996).

Gussow, Mel. "Tennessee Williams on Art and Sex." *New York Times*, 3 November 1975. 49.

Gussow, Mel. *Edward Albee: A Singular Journey*. New York: Simon & Schuster, 1999.

Jenckes, Norma. "Structures of Feeling in Tennessee Williams's *The Night of the Iguana* and Edward Albee's *A Delicate Balance*." *South Atlantic Review* 70.4 (2005), 4–22.

Kolin, Philip, ed. "Edward Albee." *The Tennessee Williams Encyclopedia*. Westport, Conn. Greenwood, 2004.

Marks, Peter. "The Stage Is Her World, Albee Her Province." *New York Times*. 15 April. 2001. 2:5.

O'Toole, Fintan "These Illusions are Real." *New York Review of Books*. 51.14 (2004). 44–46.

Osgood, Charles & Randy Gener. "Tom and His Feminist Mystique." *American Theatre*, Sept. 2004. 34+.

Reed, Rex. "Tennessee Williams Turns Sixty." Conversations with Tennessee Williams. Ed. Albert J. Devlin. Jackson: University Press of Mississippi, 1986. 184–207.

Rich, Frank. "Vanessa Redgrave in 'Orpheus': Matching Artistic Sensibilities." *New York Times*. 25 Sept. 1989. 2:5.

Soloviova, Vera, et al. "The Reality of Doing." *The Tulane Drama Review* 9.1 (1964): 136–55.

St. Just, Marie. *Five O'Clock Angel: Letters of Tennessee Williams to Maria St. Just 1948–1982*. New York: Knopf, 1990.

Terkel, Studs. "Studs Terkel Talks with Tennessee Williams." *Conversations with Tennessee Williams*. Ed. Albert J. Devlin. Jackson: University Press of Mississippi, 1986. 78–96.

Thompson, Helen. "Who's Afraid of A Streetcar Named Desire? The Influence of Tennessee Williams on Edward Albee." *Publications of the Mississippi Philological Association* (1990): 110–116.

Williams, Tennessee. *"27 Wagons Full of Cotton." Plays 1937–1955*. New York: New Directions Publishing Corporation, 2000.

_____. *"Night of the Iguana." Plays 1957–1980*. New York: New Directions Publishing Corporation, 2000.

_____. *"Suddenly Last Summer." Plays 1957–1980*. New York: New Directions Publishing Corporation, 2000.

Wolf, Matt. "Rosemary Harris Has a New Specialty: Albee's Women." *New York Times*. 30 June, 2002. C5.

"Cracking the Shell of Literalness": The Itinerary of Paternal Consciousness in Williams's Tragedy with Notes on Its Influence on Gurney's Comedy

Arvid F. Sponberg

Williams' Tragedy

STANLEY. In the state of Louisiana there is such a thing as the Napoleonic Code, according to which whatever belongs to the wife belongs to the husband and vice versa.... You see under the Napoleonic Code — a man has to take an interest in his wife's affairs — especially now that she's gonna have a baby.

BLANCHE. Stella? Stella's going to have a baby? I didn't know she was going to have a baby [*Streetcar* 29].

In the passages leading to and surrounding these lines, Stanley, first with Stella and then with Blanche, lays the foundations for taking up his duties as a father. In the years since Kazan's production of *A Streetcar Named Desire* launched Brando's career as a star, critical and popular response to the play has focused so relentlessly on Stanley's crude sexuality that other dimensions of the Kowalski-DuBois family dynamics have received comparatively little attention. Yet, as these passages make clear, Williams himself saw rich dramatic possibilities in what many other playwrights might have passed over as dry, unpromising material. Williams, for example, risks melodramatic triteness by concocting a fight between Stanley and Blanche over the fate of Belle Reve. Wills, inheritances, decrepit estates — these are rags and bones in the dramatist's workshop.

In performance, Stanley's invoking the Napoleonic Code always becomes a convenient dramaturgical pretext to launch his conquest of Blanche. It's easy to judge it as a ploy because Blanche does ("My but you have an impressive judicial air"), a tactic justifying the ransacking of Blanche's clothes and papers that foreshadows the sexual assault to come. Taking their cue from Blanche, directors, actors, and audiences do not take Stanley's exposition of the Code seriously. It's a serious mistake.

I argue, on the contrary, that Williams's assigning a *paternal motive* to Stanley opens a view into both Williams' most profound aims as a playwright and to his similarities and differences to other playwrights who explore a vital, fruitful source of conflict in American drama: transient sons vs. absent fathers.

55

The list of playwrights is long; one branch runs all the way back to Robert Montgomery Bird (1806–1854) whose play *The Gladiator* (1831) treats Spartacus as a man forced by Roman oppressors into combat as the price for saving his wife and family. (Bird's play launched Edwin Forrest's [1806–1872] career in a manner that may be compared to the way *Streetcar* launched Brando's.) Enduringly popular in the part, Forrest played Spartacus until the end of his life and the play itself entertained audiences until the end of the century. The story, of course, retains its appeal and was picked up successfully as recently as 2000 in the Ridley Scott Film, *Gladiator*, earning Russell Crowe an Oscar in the title role.

Am I arguing that we should view Stanley Kowalski as a gladiator? Not in the Roman sense, directly, but as Lyle Leverich's biography makes clear, Williams knew that his own family tree included notable fighters (Leverich viii–ix). Williams's own combativeness, especially toward those he saw as threatening people unable to protect themselves, became a colorful part of both his public and private personality.

Stanley, after all, is a modern gladiator. He served in World War II. As a first gesture on stage he slams a chunk of red meat on the table. Audiences may regard this as an emblem of Neanderthal-ic brutality — Kowalski as a twin of O'Neill's Hairy Ape — and so it may be. But more supple-minded viewers may also see the meat as the burden Kowalski carries from the war — a burden imposed on him by society both to protect it from its enemies — which he has done — and to safeguard the integrity of its traditional values — which, as he informs Blanche, he is determined to do.

The portrait of Stanley can also be seen as the second panel of a dramatic triptych that included *The Glass Menagerie* and *Cat on a Hot Tin Roof*. An interpretive key to the triptych is provided by Paul Ricoeur's thinking in his essay "Fatherhood: From Phantasm to Symbol" (Ricoeur, 468–97).

Ricoeur's working hypothesis has three parts: (1) "Father figures" are dynamic and protean, not static and fixed. The father figure is a concept capable of migrating through diverse semantic environments. For example, in some contexts we may see the father figure as a "phantasm" and a "castrater who must be killed"; in others as a symbolic sacrificial offering who "dies of compassion." (2) With the growth of our imaginations, it is possible to "resituate" father figures within the spectrum of possible human relationships. When we are young, we limit the meaning of "father" to our literal parent. As we mature, people outside the family "crack the shell of literalness" and free the father figure for a variety of emotional, spiritual, and intellectual duties. (3) From the point of view of philosophical (and I would add artistic) development, the father figure must be killed so that it can be resurrected and repeated at "higher" levels. The return after its death is, for Ricoeur, "the central problem" if the father figure is to become a useable symbol. The fact of the father figure's "susceptib[ility]" to various "actualizations" creates the possibility and need for interpretation. These interpretations are, one way or another, governed by the memories of the initial father figure. For Ricoeur, then, fatherhood becomes a "*process* rather than a *structure*" (Ricoeur 468–9; emphasis Ricoeur's).

Of course, Ricoeur is not pursuing the interpretation of a particular playwright's work — as I am. He's on the trail of a broader principle of fatherhood as it applies to all philosophical — and especially theological — interpretation. So I'll need to proceed warily to avoid a charge of *anmasslichauslegung*. On the other hand, if Ricoeur has stumbled into truth, then we ought to not to be surprised if a genius such as Williams taps into the same truth while working in drama, a powerfully evocative form with a history rooted in myth.

Williams's connections to myth have been stimulatingly explored by Judith J. Thompson. In discussing *Streetcar*, Thompson points to parallels between the play and Euripides *The*

Bacchae. Under these terms, Thompson sees Stanley as Dionysus to Blanche's Pentheus. Noting Dionysus' alternating lion-like and fawn-like phases, Thompson states that so, too, Stanley is depicted as "a powder keg" one moment — hurling cards onto a poker table, plates onto the floor, the radio out the window, or Stella across the room — and "good as a lamb" in the next. Finally, as the sociable leader of the pack who spends his time with the boys playing poker, bowling, and drinking beer, Stanley represents the Dionysian spirit of "unthinking physical enjoyment, of the instinctive group-personality, of anti-intellectual energy" (Thompson 38–9).

This tantalizing mythic view of Stanley, however, unhelpfully aggrandizes Stanley's function in the play by narrowing our vision of the power of his character. Of course, myth-icizing can result in just this sort of paradox and artists and critics invoking mythical analogies risk falling into this "trap," if it is a trap. After all, we want an artist of Williams' authority and passion to draw deeply on the imaginative powers bequeathed us by ancient stories. We want Williams to stand on the same level as Euripides. We confer honor on our age and ourselves by doing so.

Nevertheless, modesty might better become us than overreaching ambition. In grasping for the star of eternal grandeur we may carelessly stumble into the bog of impossible performance — and it's to Stanley's perform-ability that I wish to pull focus. To be blunt, under the axioms of twentieth century acting in the United States, there's no use casting an actor as Stanley and then asking him to "play Dionysus." Nobody living knows who Dionysus really is. Everyone, on the other hand, has parents of some kind and most actors can say who their fathers were even if they can't say they knew them well. Williams surely knew his.

Stanley's power in the play derives from sources much closer to home both for Williams and for us. The actor playing Stanley may, instead of invoking Dionysus (at least right away), see how the situation *in his own apartment* looks to Stanley. From this perspective, the passages negotiating the Napoleonic code, quoted at the beginning, give the actor a helpful clue. Stanley is a man who cares about protecting his money and his property and whose home *has been invaded.* As a father-to-be, he calls down the authority not of an old Greek God but of the law of the state of Louisiana. By his own lights, in other words, he behaves rationally and with restraint.

True, Blanche, the invader, is his wife's sister. Well-brought-up middle class audiences might reasonably expect Stanley to show Blanche a more gracious, hospitable countenance than he does. Let's remember, though, that Williams wrote this play immediately after World War II when housing shortages were epidemic, especially for ex-service men. The Kowalskis feel fortunate to have a place at all to call their own. When asked by Blanche, full of memories of the elegance of Belle Reve, "Why didn't you let me know ... that you had to live in such conditions?" Stella replies, "Aren't you being a little intense about it? It's not that bad at all. New Orleans isn't like other cities" (*Streetcar* 11). Because Williams has made her alert to the perilous contingency of her own predicament, Blanche hears the warning twisting under the skin of Stella's last sentence and does not press the point.

By saying that New Orleans is not like other cities Stella signals to Blanche and to the audience that nothing in the play will be like anything they've seen before — definitely not her relationship with Stanley. While placing us in the most intensely real predicament, Williams — aided, let us ever remember, by Kazan's staging — simultaneously "cracks the shell of literalness."

With 60 years of perspective, we can see even more clearly the significance of Williams's breakthrough in *Streetcar.* American producers and audiences have always been wedded to realism in some mode or another and American playwrights have always strained against it in one fashion or another. No one, for example, bloodied his fists against the cell walls of realism longer than Eugene O'Neill. The ragged trail of his dramatic productions — success, failure, success, failure — through the 1920s and 30s can be accounted for in good part by his quest for some way to invest the paltry patrimony, in his view, of American theater with the grandeur of Greek tragedy. O'Neill essentially scaled up his plots, casts, rhetoric, and scenery. The economics of commercial theater between the wars encouraged this strategy. Ironically, the one play that continues to be produced often in the professional theater — *Long Day's Journey Into Night*— brings plot, characters, language and scene down to life-size. Had O'Neill lived longer and been healthy, he might have won the title that has fallen to Williams — the *poet* of American theater.

The playwright Jeffrey Sweet has written insightfully about the crucial nature of theater's metaphorical power. He reminds us that theatrical rooms have one less wall than they ought and that time and light (unless your lamps have gels) behave in bizarre ways. And where is that music coming from? "All this is palpably unrealistic, yet, when it's all working the way creators hope, the audience *believes*. Toss something too realistic into the middle of this, the metaphor evaporates" (Sweet 122; emphasis Sweet's).

Williams not only understood theatre's metaphorical power more completely than any of his American predecessors, but, more importantly for the sustained future of his dramatic vision, he also learned to help his audience experience the poetry he felt. One of the keys to his learning seems to be an evolving grasp of the feelings all Americans have about their fathers. More specifically, as I am arguing, he fulfilled an arc connecting *Glass Menagerie* to *Streetcar* to *Cat on a Hot Tin Roof*. He realized that actors could "play" and audiences could "read" father-son conflicts with intense, rising pleasure.

In *Menagerie*, Williams devised a fable that works *because* of the absence of Tom and Laura's father. In Riceour's scheme, as summarized above, Father Wingfield is "problematic, incomplete, and in suspense" (468). I'm not suggesting that *Menagerie* is a less-excellent play than it is because it lacks a father character. It's pointless to criticize a writer for not writing a different play. I'm only pointing out that, when viewed as the first part of a triptych with *Streetcar* and *Cat*, the absence of a father character is particularly striking. And I'm arguing that from that absence follow two artistic choices that have shaped the performance history of the play since its premier.

The more obvious choice is the decision to make *Menagerie* a "memory" play. Habitually regarded as the most attractive feature of the play, this "framing device" actually challenges the actors to struggle against a stasis that is alien to the essence of dramatic construction.

The second choice that less apparently follows from the absence of Father Wingfield is the creation of Jim, the "Gentleman Caller." After thousands of performances, this choice seems so inevitable to us that its almost impossible to imagine that Williams could have achieved nearly equivalent — or even greater — dramatic power with any other choice. And, indeed, it may have seemed inevitable to Williams as he composed the play; I have not been able to consult his recently published notebooks and so I don't know if they shed light on this choice. Nevertheless, a short trip into Williams' biography hints at possibilities.

Lyle Leverich, always interested in the relationship among "Tennessee," Tom, and C. C. Williams, sees psychological significance in the absence of a father character in *Glass Menagerie*. After noting that Williams formed a friendship with D. H. Lawrence based in part on their "failed relationship with their fathers." Leverich continues: "Tennessee began to exonerate his father early on in his plays and stories, whereas Tom in his personal life found this an impossibility." Leverich adds that Tom's desire for "affection and respect" for his father amounted to hero worship. The contrast between Tom's attitude and Amanda's "bitter and rueful" memories accounts for most of the play's dramatic tension. Leverich argues that Williams nurtured similar admiration for his own phantasmal father. Williams's "drunkenness, poker playing, candor, and sensual desires" attest to his emulating drives (Leverich 322–3; emphasis Leverich's).

But Leverich doesn't speculate about the effect of this absence on the artistic choices Williams had to make in writing *Glass Menagerie* nor on the audience's reception of the play. History, of course, as Churchill famously reported, does not disclose its alternatives and speculation about hypotheticals rarely advances our knowledge, however entertaining a pastime it may be. And yet Leverich's perception of an exoneration of the father, as part of Williams's rite of passage as both person and artist, opens a fresh perspective on two key sources of *Glass Menagerie's* power.

One source of the play's power is Tom's monologues. I count seven of them: Beginning of the play, opening and closing of scene three, just after the opening of scene four, just after the opening of scene five, opening of scene six, and closing of the play. These monologues have many functions in the play, as we expect of writers of Williams's artistry. I suggest that their most important purpose is to keep the absent Father Wingfield alive in the mind of the audience. Two examples of how Williams stages these monologues must suffice.

Among the play's many famous lines, those in the opening monologue most directly present Father Wingfield to us and have become emblematic not only of *Glass Menagerie* but of the entire Williams oeuvre exactly because they announce and amplify Tom's prophetic power within the world of the play. Referring to the "larger-than-life-size" photo of "our father" above the fireplace, Tom says, "This is our father who left us a long time ago. He was a telephone man who fell in love with long distances; he gave up his job with the telephone company and skipped the light fantastic out of town" (*Menagerie* 993).

The dramatic tension that explodes sarcastically, comically, and painfully in scene three sparks the conflict that we first witness here between Tom's physical captivity in his mother's apartment and his psychological capacity for freedom and creativity beyond its walls. This capacity is represented by Tom's absent/present father and Tom's language. Tom's power to speak — to us, about Laura, Amanda, and Jim — substitutes dramatically for the person who should be actually and not just photographically present. In this sense, Williams' artistry comes within the meaning of Ricoeur's understanding of the aspect of father he categorizes as a "phantasm." The role of the father phantasm in emergence of self-consciousness — which I take to be the true and deepest subject of *Glass Menagerie*— Ricoeur adumbrates as follows, quoting Hegel's *The Phenomenology of Mind*: "...self-consciousness is thus only assured of itself through sublating this other, which is presented to self-consciousness as an independent life; self-consciousness is *Desire*. Convinced of the nothingness of this other, it definitely affirms this nothingness to be for itself the truth of this other, negates the independent object and thereby acquires the certainty of its own self...."

And then Ricoeur adds a notable insight — that self-consciousness arises when fathers and sons experience a "movement of recognition" and that this movement — like that of master and slave — is "reciprocal" in a sense also expressed by Hegel. The action of one is the act of one as well as another. The roles need to be equal to be reciprocal (474–5).

Reader's wanting more of the context for his coupling of father-son and master-slave will have to go Ricoeur's essay. But the point of connection, for our purposes, between Williams' dramaturgy and Ricouer's philosophy lies in the terms "doubling of consciousness" and "master-slave." Let me be clear: it's not my argument that Williams's work merely illustrates Ricouer's analysis. Rather, I'm arguing that Ricoeur's analysis opens a way to see more clearly one source of the power of Williams's art to enthrall us. Each of us must, one way or another, both embrace our parents spiritually while we separate ourselves from them psychologically and physically. *The Glass Menagerie* arises from this struggle in Tennessee Williams's life. Tom's monologue opening the play proposes the "double consciousness" of Tom's relationship with his father. Tom's departure at the end of the play is the reciprocal action of his father's departure. Tom, too, falls in love in with long distances. This reciprocal action also partly constitutes the exoneration that Leverich proposes in his biography.[1]

The idea of exoneration opens a perspective on a second source of *The Glass Menagerie*'s poetic power: the figure of Jim O'Connor, the gentleman caller — "a nice, ordinary, young man," as Williams lists him. In his opening monolog Tom describes Jim as "the most realistic character in the play, being an emissary from a world of reality that we were somehow set apart from." Tom then confesses "a poet's weakness for symbols" and labels Jim as the emblem of "the long delayed but always expected something that we live for" (*Menagerie* 993).

In the relation of this play to Ricoeur's scheme of "mutation" of the father figure from phantasm to symbol, I attach significance to Tom's description of Jim immediately preceding his description of the Father. The description of Jim also follows that of the descriptions of Amanda, the mother, and Laura, the sister. In a different and, perhaps, more "natural" order of introduction we would expect the description of the father to follow that of the daughter — closing the family circle, so to speak, before introducing an "outsider." One might even expect the description of the father to occur first in the monolog, an honor due to the "head" of the family, absent or not. Instead, Williams places Tom's description of Jim between the descriptions of his mother and sister and the description of his father. Another way to emphasize the significance is to say that Jim takes the father's place and, in doing so, "crack[s] the shell of literalness of the father figure and liberate[s] the symbols of fatherhood and sonship" (Ricoeur 468).

The complex dynamism of this moment in *Glass Menagerie* is easy to overlook and I hasten to admit that no actor can "play" the symbolism of this moment any more than we can ask the actor playing Stanley in *Streetcar* to enact Dionysus. And yet I do not hesitate to label this moment as the seed of every subsequent act and thought in the play.

Williams gives Jim a double nature — realistic character and symbol. Williams cracks the shell of American theatrical literalness by having Tom announce directly to the audience: "Jim is a symbol." Is this evidence of the influence of Brecht? Of Wilder? (I'll say more about self-reflexivity in the following section on Gurney). Then Williams pairs the all-too-present Jim with the all-too-absent father who is present to our senses *only* as an image, a phantasm. In watching a performance, we must quickly pick up our cue to see that in talking about Jim and his father together, Tom is really talking about himself— the only character in the play missing from his opening monologue. Tom is also a phantasm.

As part of the play's climax, Williams compounds these ironies by making Jim's "fatherly" advice to Laura have a far greater effect on Tom. Tom really needs no urging to "think of yourself as *superior* in some way" or to see that he lives in "a world full of common people!" and his frustration with life at home and at the shoe warehouse has taught him that, indeed, "everybody excels in some one thing. Some in many!" (*Menagerie* 1013). We already know that Tom believes that he can excel as a writer. These platitudes of American success-mongering, as common today as they have ever been, have also torn at Tom's soul when his mother accuses him of selfishness and "jeopardizing your job." This accusation triggers Tom's explosion.

> Look! I'd rather somebody picked up a crowbar and battered out my brains — than go back mornings! ... And you say self—*self's* all I ever think of. Why, listen, if self is what I thought of, Mother, I'd be where he is — GONE! *(Pointing to father's picture)* As far as the system of transportation reaches! [*Menagerie* 998; emphasis Williams's].

In order to fulfill his promise to "give you truth in the pleasant guise of illusion" (*Menagerie* 993) Tom confounds himself, his father, and Jim. This experiment in father/son figuration provides a potent psychological correlative to the devices of theatrical design — theme music, legends and images projected on screens, dim lighting, the emphasis on softness and delicateness in costumes and furniture, the glass animals themselves — so often remarked as the outward signs of Williams' breaking the "rules" of American stage literalism.

It would comply with a certain logic, therefore, to say that in *Cat on a Hot Tin Roof* the appearance of a literal, fully-realized father on stage, and in the heart of the plot, marks Williams's return to the conventions of stage realism. And when we consider the prominence of literal fathers in a long line of American plays[2] we see how easy it would be to take this approach. But a closer look at the father/son dynamic in *Cat* indicates, I think, no lessening by Williams of his drive to give audiences truth in the guise of illusion. Here, again, we can turn to Ricoeur for guidance about what happens between Brick and Big Daddy:

> To complete the constitution of this paradigm of fatherhood according to the spirit, we still have to say how *death* — the death of the son and eventually the death of the father — is inserted into this genesis of meaning.... The true kinship bond ... is that which is established on the level of ... the concrete ethical life; now this bond raises fatherhood above the contingency of individuals ... the death of the father is thus blended into the representation of the bond of fatherhood which dominates the sequence of the generations ... there is, therefore, somewhere a death of the father which is no longer a murder and which belongs to the conversion of the phantasm into symbol [Ricoeur 491–2].

In the second act of *Cat*, Williams shows Big Daddy's confrontation with death making it the occasion for Brick to face the truth about his denial of both his love for Skipper and his guilt that his denial caused Skipper to kill himself. Big Daddy and Brick describe themselves as living in a morally disordered world. They establish a bond based on this recognition of "mendacity," which becomes the code word signifying their bond.

Big Daddy says, "What do you know about this mendacity thing? Hell! I could write a book on it! Don't you know that ... think of all the lies I got to put up with! — Pretenses! Ain't that mendacity? Having to pretend stuff you don't think or feel or have any idea of?" Big Daddy "then declares his disgust with his family and his community except" for Brick: "*You* I *do* like for some reason, did always have some kind of real feeling for — affection — respect — yes, always.... You, and being a success as a planter is all I ever had any devotion to in my whole life! — and that's the truth... (*Cat* 80–1).

This declaration breaks Brick's silence which we, along with Maggie, have endured for half the play. The appropriateness of Brick's name is striking, with its connotations of cold, stony inertness while yet being man-made and carrying associations with fire. Maggie notes the latter early in the first act. "When something is festering in your memory or your imagination, laws of silence won't work, it's just like shutting a door and locking it on a house on fire in hope of forgetting that the house is burning" (*Cat* 25).

But Brick breaks open only under the pressure applied by Big Daddy. Prior to and during this extended scene, there is a great deal of physical movement and much struggling for possession of Brick's crutch, Big Daddy taking it and Brick trying to get it back. The psychological battle so strongly visualized resembles that between Stanley and Blanche over the contents of her trunk, and especially her letters.[3] Williams follows Brick's reference to "fairies" with a stage direction that indicates Williams's desire to link Brick and Big Daddy in revolt against moral disorder masked by "the Normal." Big Daddy is not satisfied with an explanation that he senses leaves out crucial information. He digs further, unable to discern that penetrating Brick's deepest secret will also reveal the mortal secret that his family has withheld from him: "We have tracked down the lie with which you're disgusted and which you are drinking to kill your disgust with, Brick. You have been passing the buck. This disgust with mendacity is disgust with yourself. *You!*— dug the grave of your friend and kicked him in it!— before you'd face the truth with him." Brick reciprocates: "Who can face the truth? Can you? ... *How about these birthday congratulations, these many, many happy returns of the day, when ev'rybody but you knows there won't be any!*" (*Cat*, 92).

The power of *Glass Menagerie* derives in part from the *absence* of the father and Williams' dramaturgical — and, perhaps, autobiographical — need to substitute a three-faceted *phantasm* of the father. The power of *Streetcar* derives in part from Stanley's becoming a father and his struggle — and failure — to integrate that role with his past as a warrior/dominator/protector and his present as a lover/husband. The power of *Cat* derives in part from the shattering *presence* of the father — the only person capable of forcing Brick to face the truth. But the painful price of confronting truth *without illusions*[4] is knowledge of your own mortality. To live is to lie; to see truth is to die.

Again, we may turn to Ricoeur's triple-faceted analysis for an assessment of Williams's sojourn in fatherhood in these three plays. In *The Glass Menagerie* we see "the retreat of physical generation in favor of a word of designation." In *A Streetcar Named Desire* we see "the replacement of a doubly destructive identification by the mutual recognition of father and son"[5]; finally, the access to a symbol of fatherhood detached from the person of the father. In *Cat on a Hot Tin Roof*, we see "this last trait which is the most exacting for thought, for it introduces not only contingency but death into the building-up of the symbol" (Ricoeur 497).

Gurney's Comedy

At first glance, any relationship between Gurney and Williams appears nonexistent. Such a view, however, would indicate lack of knowledge or thoughtful reflection on Gurney's art and a curious pigeon-holing of Williams as a playwright. People justly admire Williams as the tragic poet of the vulnerable and wounded. This view was poignantly expressed by the great director Jose Quintero who recalled his reaction to seeing the original production of *The Glass Menagerie*. Seeing it, he said, confirmed his decision to make theatre his career. After seeing the performance, he remembered, "'I walked all night long. I knew then something had made me feel whole. Here was someone who could feel my pain, my loneliness, and put it into such beautiful words.'" He remembered this as the first time in his life that he stopped feeling alone" (Leverich 574). However, the light brightly shining through Laura's fragile glass animals, or dimly illuminating Blanche together with the strains of "Varsouviana" and Maggie's odes to the "charm of the defeated" often seem to blind these admirers to Williams' comic spirit.

Though skepticism about Williams's influence on Gurney could plausibly be predicated on differences in their social backgrounds, another brief trip into biography suggests powerful affinities between the playwrights. Both Gurney and Williams are middle children with an older sister and younger brother and both were reared, more or less, in the Episcopal Church. Gurney comes from an upper-middle-class family of successful business people in declining Buffalo. He was a good student at all the excellent private schools and universities in New England that he attended. His close, stable family provided an extended network of relations whose lavished attention on him. His parents had a long and stable marriage. His father had also grown up in Buffalo and remained a strong, daily presence in the lives of Gurney and his older sister and younger brother. Gurney spoke of him in an interview:

I think my father had the best sense of humor of anyone on both sides of the family. He had a great sense of humor, a particularly public sense of humor. He was a great public speaker. He could get up and make a toast at a small family gathering and have people in stitches. Or he could speak to a really large group — I'm not talking about two thousand — but a big banquet of two hundred — and he would be equally professional. And if anybody heckled him, and, of course, everybody liked to because that was another ritual, he would deal with the heckler in a brilliant way. I really admired the man. He could think on his feet quicker than anyone I've ever met. So he became kind of a master of ceremonies, toastmaster, for a large number of functions in Buffalo and sat on a great many boards simply because he was the one who could give the best speech. My father would always [use literary allusions]. And he was very clever — he [would say], "As we all know ..." and then he'd give this obscure quote and he'd make the audience feel good. He'd assume they knew even though, of course, they didn't. And I follow, maybe, in that tradition [Sponberg 6].

Williams's roots in the lower-middle class of the Midwest and south — though not without with some connections to commercial and political influence — were continually disturbed by his father's long absences and the resulting need of his mother to move he children to and from her parents' home. Consequently, Williams' education featured attendance at a variety of big city and small town public schools.

Other personal factors seem to distance the two artists. Gurney has been married for over fifty years and is a father of four children and a grandfather. Williams was gay, aggressively promiscuous and left no children. Williams became a brilliant star in the firmament of the American theater. Gurney's brightness, however, possesses a different quality because the American theatre had changed by the time Gurney's first plays earned national attention. Coming out of Yale in 1958, after a tour in the Navy, a stint of high school teaching, and the birth of his children, Gurney found no opportunities for Broadway productions. Consequently, the rising non-profit theater, with its smaller theaters, modest resources, and its media-free productions, became the seedbed of his developing art.

However, the comparative study of their plays renders all this biography trivial. In a number of ways, Gurney and Williams, separated by only 19 years, worked the same side of the comic street in their plays. The "keys" to their comedy are:

• the "battle" between men and women;
• the dilemmas posed for youth by age, usually represented by a "Senex," or father figure;
• an extravagant formal imagination that delights in upsetting audience expectations, frequently characterized by self-reflexive commenting on the conventions of drama;
• verbal virtuosity that channels the energy flowing from rhythms of ordinary American speech into passionate, precise, speakable lines actors love to perform.

In discussing early influences on his writing, Gurney reached out to Williams for a revealing example:

I liked to read a lot. I liked to read novels when I was little. But whenever I had a school assignment for a composition — and in those days we were always assigned compositions — I remember a number of times I'd say, "Can I write a play instead?" I always seemed to like the dialogue form. I remember as a little kid I used to hate what I called "I books," books that were told in the first person. I always felt as a kid that that was such a limited perspective. I liked the third-person narrative where you had an outsider. Now that's not necessarily dramatic. You can have a third-person narrative without going into drama, but the reverse is certainly true; it's very hard to write a play from an individual perspective. Tennessee Williams tries in *The Glass Menagerie,* but in the end that's not what it's about. The most significant scene in *The Glass Menagerie* takes place when the narrator isn't there. In any case, something about my sense of perspective made me veer toward drama, too [Sponberg 7].

Notice here the emphasis on fulfilling the assignment in a different way, on listening to dialogue, on not wanting to take the "I" position. Ruling out stories that put "I" in the limelight leaves stories in which a group or an ensemble holds center stage. Many voices, rather than one voice, interest Gurney. As he matured, Gurney found additional ways to multiply voices. He mixed classical and contemporary characters in many of his early one acts (*The Comeback, The David Show, The Golden Fleece*) so that the past comments on the present. He uses this technique again in *Overtime*, mixing modern and Renaissance sensibilities by extending into our time the lives of the characters from *The Merchant of Venice*. He mixed present and absent characters, underscoring the experience of separation and loss (*Children, What I Did Last Summer, The Cocktail Hour, The Old Boy*, and *Love Letters*). He wrote plays in which actors play more than one character, deploying the resources of acting to the greater delight of both actor and audience (*Scenes from American Life, The Dining Room*). He wrote a play (*The Wayside Motor Inn*) in which multiple scenes play simultaneously. And in what remains his most the most striking experiment even if it is not regarded as his best work (*Sweet Sue*) he wrote a play in which different actors play the same characters, so that the audience experiences alternating interpretations of actions and feelings within a single performance. Most recently, he pushed theatrical boundaries beyond merely human perspectives and created a dog, the title role in *Sylvia*.

Gurney shares a dramatic aim that Williams expressed most effectively in the following stage direction from *Cat on a Hot Tin Roof* just as Brick begins to tell Big Daddy about Skipper:

> ...The bird that I hope to catch in the net of this play is not the solution of one man's psychological problem. I'm trying to catch the true quality of experience in a group of people, that cloudy, flickering, evanescent—fiercely charged!—interplay of live human beings in the thundercloud of a common crisis. Some mystery should be left in the revelation of character in a play; just as a great deal of mystery is always left in the revelation of character in life, even in one's own character to himself. This does not absolve the playwright of the duty to observe and probe as clearly and deeply as he *legitimately* can; but it should steer him away from the "pat" conclusions, facile definitions which make a play just a play, not a snare for the truth of human experience [*Cat* 85].

Debra Mooney, a favorite actress of both Williams and Gurney, played Blanche in a production that Williams admired and she also played Sally in Gurney's *The Perfect Party*. She compared the two, taking note of how their senses of humor spring from an affirmation of life.

> MOONEY: I've been so lucky. I've known and worked with David Storey and Neil Simon and Jules Pfeiffer and Tennessee Williams and Arthur Miller and Lanford Wilson and Pete Gurney. As I said I wanted to work with live authors. I think the wonderful thing about all of them, particularly Tennessee, who was my first, so that then I see the others sort of through those eyes, have this wonderful affirmation of life, and in the end are looking at the positive. The first time that I met [Tennessee] after the play, after *Streetcar* that night, he walked up to me at this party and said, "Of course, she doesn't stay there." And I said, "Of course not, she marries the doctor, right?" He laughed and said. "And then she invites Stella over for tea, and says, 'but don't bring that brute of a husband.'" [laughs] I mean he always had a sense of humor and a positive outlook on everything.
> Q: And you see that Gurney shares those qualities as well?
> MOONEY: Yes, because at the end of [*The Perfect Party*], you think how is he going to get out of it. And he gets out of it in a wonderful, positive affirmation of life in this marriage. You know that they have a wonderful marriage [Sponberg 60].

Two of Gurney's most recent plays pay direct homage to Williams. *Post Mortem*, a satire on American values set at a university in the future, makes Gurney the research subject of an eager undergraduate in love with his literature professor. The play opens with the professor, a frustrated actor, rehearsing one of Blanche's speeches. When her impressed student suggests that she perform the speech in class, she rebukes him:

> Tennessee Williams? A homosexual playwright? Who wrote about rape, castration, and murder? You want me to perform him out *loud*? Here? In a border state? At a faith-based university, supported by public funds? ... We are allowed to read silently, and refer to occasionally, certain writers like Tennessee Williams, but we're asking for trouble to go much beyond that [*Post Mortem* 2].

In *Crazy Mary*, Gurney's latest play, the homage is somewhat more diffuse. The title character's disappointments in love aggravated her bi-polar disorder, leaving her confined to a private psychiatric institution for more than thirty years, completely forgotten by her few remaining relatives. The situation may be imagined as the sort of thing that happened to Blanche Du Bois after the end of *Streetcar*. The burden of the play involves Mary's being "recalled to life" first by the attention and then by the affection of her college-age relation, Skip. (His mother sometimes addressed him as Skipper.)

About a half hour into the play, Skip, alone, comes to the institution to visit Mary. The aides, Jerome and Pearl, must decide:

> PEARL: Should we have Mary waiting for him, or him waiting for Mary?
> JEROME: How about the latter? He's an admirer, making a call. And she's the lady of the house coming downstairs to see who it is [*Crazy Mary* 38].

Gurney makes this oblique reference to *The Glass Menagerie* more explicit five minutes later.

> JEROME: Mary thinks you're a gentleman caller.
> SKIP: What is this? Tennessee Williams?
> JEROME: Without the Southern accent [*Crazy Mary* 42].

The allusive habit which Gurney says he inherited from his father clearly provides an artistic path between his own work and Williams'. It's not surprising that thoughts of Williams flicker at the edge of Gurney's thoughts. At the time Gurney entered the theatre, Williams shone most brightly on the American scene. Gurney has been measured repeatedly against the Williams standard. In the most widely read newspaper article about him, the New York Times reporter Alex Witchel reported that Gurney believes that he has created "a body of work, somewhat interconnected" about urban Easterners suffering a decline as American power moves west. When Witchel asked him how his own works might be taught, Gurney emphasized that his point of view was "primarily comic" and that he saw "a reconciliation possible at the plays end between the individual and the world. And that's not terribly American. If you look at the European tradition — Molière, Coward, Congreve — the world is always put back together by the end. In American comedies, there's anarchism at the end — Huck Finn says goodbye and shoves off for the territories, Holden Caulfield ends up in the madhouse. So, I see what I do as going against the grain of the American embracing of private freedom" (Witchel).

The note of reconciliation returns to the problem of fatherhood. As much as Gurney admired his father, his choice of an academic career and playwriting alienated them from each other. Witchel reported that the lack of his father's approval "drives" Gurney to create works about "fathers and sons in adversarial relationships." In Witchel's view, it is possible to speculate that "an irrational hope" of gaining his father's approval has blocked Gurney from "writing a character capable of an all-out tantrum," spurning his father's world as it has rejected him (Witchel).

In four plays, *Children, The Middle Ages, What I Did Last Summer* and *The Cocktail Hour,* we see another itinerary of paternal consciousness moving from phantasm to symbol. In *Children*, the father has died, leaving his wife to cope with the resistance of their children to her wish to marry an old family friend. Gurney revisits this basic situation again in *What I Did Last Summer*. In this memory play about a fatherless family, the main character, 14-year-old Charlie, directly addresses the audience, as does Tom in *The Glass Menagerie*. Charlie is the object of a struggle between his mother, who embodies the values of upper-middle-class respectability, and Anna, a bohemian artist, who appeals to Charlie's innate desire to rebel. In *The Middle Ages*, a domineering father and rebellious son battle with each other over the values of a fading age, represented by the family's membership in a prestigious club, and the desires of youth. In this play, the father appears on stage in a strong role, but the encounters with the son are brief and conflictual.

In *The Cocktail Hour*, as in *Cat on a Hot Tin Roof*, Gurney brings father and son together for three acts of truth telling. There is reconciliation at the end but plenty of turmoil along the way. One particularly painful moment embroils John, the son, Nina, his sister, and his parents, Bradley and Ann. All are disturbed that John, a professor, has written a play that is more or less about them. He has also, against the wishes of his parents, arranged for his brother, Jigger, to take a job in a distant city.

> BRADLEY. You kind of like playing God around here, don't you?
> ANN. Yes, John, I really think you should stop managing other people's lives.
> BRADLEY. Yes. Do that in your plays if you have to, not in real life.
> JOHN. Oh, yeah? Well, I'm glad we're talking about real life now, Pop. Because that's something we could use a little more *of*, around here. Hey, know what? The cocktail hour is over, Pop. It's dead. It's gone. I think Jigger sensed it thirty years ago, and now Nina knows it too, and they're both *trying* to put something back into the world after all these years of free ride...
> BRADLEY. ...your mother and I, and your grandparents on both sides, and Aunt Jane and Uncle Roger and Cousin Esther, and your forbears who came to this country in the seventeenth *century* have all spent their lives trying to establish something called civilization in this wilderness, and as long as I am alive, I will not allow foul-mouthed and resentful people to tear it all down. *(He storms off and upstairs. Long pause.)*
> ANN. Well. You were right about one thing, John: the cocktail hour is definitely over [*Cocktail Hour* 58–9].

Astute readers may see here the conflation of elements that Williams separates in *The Glass Menagerie* and *Cat on a Hot Tin Roof*. John's threatened exit resembles Tom Wingfield's, not excluding business with a raincoat. Bradley's social background differs sharply from Big Daddy's, but they share fierce pride in what they think their lives stand for. They defiantly resist what they see to be mendacious depredations on their heritage from any quarter, from outside or inside the family.

In the "court" of American theater, we can see Williams and Gurney as twin jesters, mockers of morals, prickers of pretension and pomposity, critics of social and artistic convention. To see this similarity we need to see beyond differences in subject matter, setting, and situation. They use these to hold our attention while their plays perform their real work — angling, inverting, and reversing audiences' expectations. If, in this way, like John, and Tom, Williams and Gurney wish to be God-like creators, at least in the theater, they can be so only by participating in a "teleology of hope" to which Ricoeur refers at the end of "Fatherhood: From Phantasm to Symbol" (496). This is the hope implicit in Tom's poignant farewell to Laura, "I tried to leave you behind me, but I am more faithful than I intended to be" (*Menagerie* 1017).

NOTES

1. Between the opening and the closing of the play, the photograph of Father Wingfield occupies our consciousness. No experienced playgoer, I think, can fail to see the allusion to that other famous paternal image that stands at the head of modern drama: the portrait of General Gabler in Ibsen's *Hedda Gabler*. The struggles of Hedda and Tom with their fathers' influences indicate the persistence of this powerful theme down the decades and suggest a couple of waypoints for an interesting journey in dramatic criticism. Other "must-see sites" to visit on the same journey would include: *The Father, Major Barbara, Inheritors, Long Day's Journey Into Night, Death of a Salesman, A Raisin in the Sun, Painting Churches, The Piano Lesson, W;t(Wit)*, and *Anna in the Tropics*.

2. Martin Van Der Hof in *You Can't Take It With You*, Willy Loman in *Death of A Salesman*, James Tyrone in *Long Day's Journey Into Night*, and Troy Maxson in *Fences* come to mind first.

3. See Jeffrey Sweet, "Lesson Two: Negotiation Over Objects," in *Solving Your Script: Tools and Techniques for the Playwright* (Portsmouth, NH: Heinemann), 21–32, for practical wisdom on this widely used method.

4. Williams's theme in *Cat* resembles O'Neill's in *The Iceman Cometh* with Williams's play being both artistically more accomplished and theatrically more successful. With this contrast in mind, one reads with added interest Leverich's account of Williams's meeting of Jordan Massee, Sr, a model for Big Daddy, during a 1941 visit to St. Simon's Island, Georgia. There, Leverich writes, "Tom was exposed to still another southern way of life ... this was the kind of southern grandeur that Tom had never seen before, and a mansion he would have noticed. The Casa Genotta (so named for Gene and Carlotta), had once been the home of the Eugene O'Neills..." (418).

5. A little tricky, this one, since Ricoeur means a father and son mutually recognizing each other — as happens in *Cat*. However, I have argued that it is Stanley's struggle to recognize *himself* as a man about to become father to a son that drives, in part, his struggle with Blanche.

WORKS CITED

Gurney, A. R. *The Cocktail Hour*, New York: Dramatists Play Service, 1989.

_____. *Crazy Mary*. New York: Broadway Play Publishing, 2007. References here, however, are to the play in manuscript.

_____. *Post Mortem*. New York: Broadway Play Publishing, 2006.

Leverich, Lyle. *Tom: The Unknown Tennessee Williams*. New York: Crown Publishers, 1995.

Ricoeur, Paul. "Fatherhood: From Phantasm to Symbol." *The Conflict of Interpretations: Essays in Hermeneutics*. Evanston, IL: Northwestern UP, 1974.

Sponberg, Arvid F., "A. R. Gurney: An Introduction." *A. R. Gurney: A Casebook*, New York: Routledge, 2004.

Sweet, Jeffrey. *The Dramatists Toolkit: The Craft of the Working Playwright*. Portsmouth, NH: Heinemann, 1993.

Thompson, Judith. *Tennessee Williams' Plays: Memory, Myth, and Symbol*. New York: Peter Lang. Revised edition, 2002.

Williams, Tennessee. *Cat on a Hot Tin Roof*. New York: Signet, 1985.

_____. *The Glass Menagerie. Masters of Modern Drama*. Ed. Haskell M. Block and Robert G. Shedd. New York: Random House, 1962.

_____. *A Streetcar Named Desire*. Dramatists Play Service. 1947.

Witchel, Alex, "Laughter, Tears, and the Perfect Martini," *New York Times Magazine*, November 12, 1989. <http://query.nytimes.com/gst/fullpage.html?res=950DEED9163-F931A25752C1A96F948260&scp=3&sq=Alex+Witchel+Gurney&st=nyt>

"That gentleman with the painfully sympathetic eyes...": Re-reading Lorraine Hansberry Through Tennessee Williams

Nancy Cho

When contemporary playwright Lynn Nottage premiered *Crumbs From the Table of Joy* in 1995, Clive Barnes observed: "Imagine a pairing — artistically of course — between Tennessee Williams and Lorraine Hansberry, a memory play about a black family, a glass menagerie in the sun."[1] Barnes' review indirectly poses a seldom-asked question. What is the relationship between the work of Williams and Hansberry? In what ways might their legacies in American theater be intertwined? This essay examines Hansberry's brief but significant career in light of the work of Tennessee Williams, who dominated American theater in the mid-twentieth century. While obvious contrasts exist between the two writers, Barnes' review also implies a more dialectical tension. Certainly neither artist's canon can be worked neatly into a one-dimensional view, and their works share many affinities that have yet to be adequately examined.

Despite important contributions of Hansberry and Williams to mid-twentieth century American culture, scholars have been surprisingly silent on the subject of comparing them. In recent years, however, scholarly dialogue on both writers has opened up dramatically, enabling new comparative insights. The most significant research on Hansberry has explored the implications of her radical politics, while Williams' work has been re-framed by queer studies as well as questions of racial identity. [2] Most central for my purposes are recent attempts to re-write the theatrical history of the Cold War era; in book length studies, both David Krasner and Bruce McConachie devote significant attention to Williams and Hansberry. The emerging picture of both playwrights situates them at the unstable junction of mainstream culture and political resistance. In short, Williams' plays no longer register as merely "closeted" or evasive of explicitly political issues, while Hansberry is far from being the assimilationist or tidy realist that previous criticism had asserted. In my re-reading of Hansberry via Williams, I explore the nuances of their politics and esthetics by examining direct connections between particular works and contexts of production. Investigating biographical and textual links, I place Hansberry's complex negotiation of mainstream culture directly alongside that of Williams. Both writers achieve commercial appeal while at the same time unsettling deeply ingrained assumptions about the constitution of American identity. We might thus remember Hansberry not only as "young, gifted, and black," but also as a very public artist in dialogue with her peers and the larger sphere of Cold War America.

Hansberry and Williams were direct contemporaries, which makes the dearth of comparative analyses all the more curious. Indeed, Hansberry's debut in American theater, the landmark Broadway premiere of *A Raisin in the Sun* in 1959, almost exactly coincided with the premiere of Williams' *Sweet Bird of Youth*. Producer Philip Rose, remembered for his venturesome role in bringing Hansberry's work to Broadway, recalls in his memoir how rave reviews for Williams' play hovered above *Raisin*'s opening night. Evidently Rose and Hansberry worried "that the critics had used up all of their superlatives for the week, or even for the year. We wondered: even if they liked *A Raisin in the Sun*, what could they have left to say?" (11). *Raisin* would go on to win the coveted New York Drama Critics' Circle award for that year, defeating plays by Williams and Eugene O'Neill. One Hansberry biographer notes that Williams also had Hansberry in mind, sending her a telegram after the opening of *Raisin* dazzled the critics (Cheney 26). Although Hansberry's letters, speeches, and interviews only infrequently mention Williams, his work certainly informed her education in the theater. Rose recollects how readily she could "read and critique Shakespeare, Chekhov, O'Casey, Tennessee Williams, Arthur Miller, and many other classic and contemporary poets and playwrights" (46). While Sean O'Casey and *Death of a Salesman* appear frequently in the scholarly literature on Hansberry, her specific historical relationship to Williams has gone almost unnoticed.

Williams' enormous reputation and somewhat controversial status surrounded Hansberry as she was developing *A Raisin in the Sun* for the stage. Indeed, *Raisin* emerged at an interesting point in Williams' career: well after his resounding success with *The Glass Menagerie*, *A Streetcar Named Desire*, and *Cat on a Hot Tin Roof*, and just on the heels of his more surprising success with the controversial subject matter of *Suddenly Last Summer*. In 1959, in a closing address delivered to the First Conference of Negro Writers, Hansberry quoted both Williams and Sean O'Casey in order to highlight challenges facing the modern African American artist. In their 1981 reprinting of Hansberry's landmark speech, the editors of the journal *Black Scholar* present this address as Hansberry's "credo" and note its prominent timing just two weeks before the Broadway opening of *A Raisin in the Sun* (2). As a window into both playwrights' work, this address is quite revealing. Its appreciation of Williams' sense of social responsibility seems oddly prescient now and very much in keeping with current recognition of Williams as a politically engaged dramatist.

Hansberry's speech, "The Negro Writer and His Roots: Toward a New Romanticism," opens with quotes from O'Casey and Williams and calls for the African American writer's "participation in the intellectual affairs of men, everywhere" (3). Already conscious of her role as a public intellectual, Hansberry first cites O'Casey to portray the artist as a "warrior against despair and lover of humankind" (2). She then uses Williams to evoke a more controversial image of the artist. She quotes the following remarks from Williams she had recently read in the newspapers: "'Life is cannibalistic.... Someone is always eating at someone else for position, gain, triumph, greed, whatever. The human individual is a cannibal in the worst way'" (2). Anticipating her audience's aversion to such a condemnation of human nature, Hansberry rushes to Williams' defense, offering a paean to his artistry:

> That gentleman with the painfully sympathetic eyes and the sweetest of smiles, who is the gifted playwright Tennessee Williams, has presented to American culture a great body of work which significantly embodies the particular death agonies of a dying and panic-stricken social order. With horror and fear he has presented anguished indictments of that which too many others would actually celebrate. The poet Tennessee Williams is a mourner of beauty and decency, not their enemy [2].

I quote at length to underscore the particularities of Hansberry's reading of Williams; his willingness to "indict" American society for its failures informs his status as one of the "modern world's most important writers" (2). Entering into a dialogue with Williams, Hansberry encourages her listeners not to shrink back from his sense of despair, but to respond with "study and concern and involvement—and argument of equal stature" (3).

Hansberry's characterization of Williams in this 1959 speech seems a reminder to her audience of the figure who wrote "The Catastrophe of Success" roughly a decade earlier. This essay, written after *The Glass Menagerie* had catapulted Williams to fame, discusses how class privilege exposes the failings of democracy. Williams defines "the good" not as riches or status but as "the obsessive interest in human affairs, plus a certain amount of compassion and moral conviction" that must be translated into art ("Catastrophe" 17). Such words, in their tenor and point of view, would not have been surprising as an epigraph for Hansberry's 1959 address, as she stood poised on the threshold of her own sudden celebrity.

Yet Hansberry, whose work has always been relegated to the realm of socially conscious theater, reveals in her letters, speeches, and interviews a prickly resistance to being stereotyped as a "message" writer. In one letter, published in the posthumously created work *To Be Young, Gifted, and Black*, Hansberry cites Williams in an attempt to complicate facile definitions of a socially conscious theater. As she insists with some urgency in this letter, "...there are *no* plays which are not social and no plays that do not have a thesis.... The fact of the matter is that Arthur Miller and Lillian Hellman and Henrik Ibsen are no more social playwrights than Tennessee Williams and Bill Inge..." (119). Resisting reductive formulations of art's relation to politics that would place Ibsen on one side of the equation and Shakespeare on the other, Hansberry again intimates that Williams' work compels her precisely because of its artful negotiation of the sociopolitical realm.

Hansberry's term "social playwright" might indeed prove more useful than "political" in describing the work that she and Williams produced, for their enormously popular plays are anything but doctrinaire. Notwithstanding the populist influences upon Williams in the 1930s and Hansberry's socialist journalism of the 1940s, one must keep in view their appeal to a middlebrow audience. While Williams probed the dark corners of humanity's "cannibalistic" nature and Hansberry used art to interrogate issues such as class exploitation and colonialism, both writers also enjoyed an astonishing degree of commercial success. In response to Williams' stated abhorrence of the pressure to produce blockbuster after blockbuster, critic Walter Kerr in 1959 maintained that "the blockbuster was born in him" (347). One important marker of this commercialism is the fact that so many of Williams' mid-century stage hits were made into Hollywood films —*A Streetcar Named Desire*, *Cat on a Hot Tin Roof*, *Suddenly Last Summer*, and *Sweet Bird of Youth*. Hansberry, for her part, produced one extraordinary blockbuster in her lifetime as well as a second play—*The Sign in Sidney Brustein's Window* (1964)—that ran on Broadway for 101 performances. *A Raisin in the Sun* also, of course, found an expanded audience as a major Hollywood film (1961) starring Sidney Poitier. Even posthumously, Hansberry's words have proven to reach the masses. The musical adaptation *Raisin* (1973) was a Tony award-winning Broadway hit, while *To Be Young, Gifted, and Black* (1969), created and culled from Hansberry's writings by her former husband, Robert Nemiroff, enjoyed a long run Off Broadway. In short, any assessment of Hansberry and Williams as "political" writers must also engage their significant commercial appeal. The challenge here is to see that commercial success need not cancel out left-leaning politics, but rather may inflect these politics in complex ways.

A Raisin in the Sun, Hansberry's best-known work, puts into stark relief the complicated status of the protest play as Broadway blockbuster. Entirely canonical as well as popular, this play thoroughly dominates the scholarly conversation on Hansberry, despite being an elusive text to assess. Like Williams' most famous dramas — *The Glass Menagerie, A Streetcar Named Desire*, and *Cat on the Hot Tin Roof—A Raisin in the Sun* has generated conflicting interpretations for generations of scholars and critics. Jacqueline O'Connor has argued that even Williams' signature works have, over the years, "been by turn ignored, scorned, morally condemned, or seriously misunderstood" (255). Current assessment of both Williams and Hansberry allows us to approach their popular domestic dramas as complex political texts, ones that sharply indict the American Dream even as they have come to serve as touchstones for understanding mid-century American culture.

Although a tradition of social protest theater and American family drama dates back to the 1930s and '40s, it is the decade of the 1950s that is key for understanding Hansberry's emergence into the theater and Williams' dominance of that world. In his recent survey of twentieth century American drama, David Krasner uses *The Glass Menagerie* and *A Raisin in the Sun* to frame an understanding of American drama at the mid-century mark. Stressing thematic parallels between Williams and Hansberry, Krasner draws connections between *Raisin*'s concern with social justice and Williams' challenges to "materialism, McCarthyism, and homophobia" (44). Bruce McConachie, is his monograph on the Cold War era and its "theater of containment," also sees links between Williams and Hansberry. He argues that of all the mid-century playwrights, they were the most successful in using conservative forms to "contest" the hierarchies of race, gender, and sexuality that defined "containment liberalism" (54). Such parallels between Hansberry and her white male contemporaries, it should be noted, have not always produced favorable or careful assessments of *A Raisin in the Sun*. One scholar, for instance, abruptly deems the play "old fashioned," "safe," and an example of "Arthur Miller in blackface" (Ashley 151). The point, of course, is not to see Hansberry as "second rate" Miller or Williams, but rather to see her work as actively in conversation with the same social milieu of those writers — the world of Eisenhower America and its ideology of economic prosperity and self-fulfillment.

If *Raisin* is sometimes seen as "safe" or "old-fashioned" in its style, I want to stress that the formal expression of Hansberry's political vision is a complicated issue that deserves careful scrutiny. The question of "kitchen sink" realism is not simply a matter of Hansberry using a conventional form to express "radical" ideas. Once again, a comparison with Williams might prove illuminating, given his own complicated stance towards realism. Williams viewed realism as a flexible medium and he relied on it, to some degree, in many of his mid-century works. In his famous "Production Notes" for *The Glass Menagerie*, Williams does not advocate an escape from reality, but rather calls for "a more penetrating and vivid expression of things as they are" (7). Hence Williams disparages not realism *per se*, but rather the "straight realistic play with its genuine Frigidaire and authentic ice-cubes, its characters who speak exactly as its audience speaks..." (7). At first glance, such "Frigidaire" realism seems accurately to describe the text and stagecraft of Hansberry's signature work, a play in which tired furnishings and "worn places in the carpet" set the scene for the Younger family's story (Hansberry *Raisin* 23).

Yet the very realism of *A Raisin in the Sun* — its naturalistic expression of "things as they are" — is arguably what makes the play just as groundbreaking as *The Glass Menagerie*. Notwithstanding earlier examples of serious black drama, such as Theodore Ward's *Big White Fog* (1938) and Alice Childress's *Trouble in Mind* (1955), *A Raisin in the Sun* marks the moment when black family life is finally *seen*— literally made visible to the wider American public. Glenda Gill's research reveals that black actors of the 1940s and '50s, in the absence of an established black theater repertoire, resisted "rigid segregation" in the Jim Crow south by performing classics such as *The Glass Menagerie* in non-professional venues (596). Yet it was Hansberry's 1959 work, with its intentional and strategic use of realism, which signaled the entry of African American family life onto the American stage. It is noteworthy, then, that at least one of the original Broadway reviewers responded precisely to this illusion of "life as the dramatist has lived it," while at the same time faulting Williams in *Sweet Bird* for losing his contact with "the tangible, diurnal world that formerly nourished his talent" (Tynan 100). In light of historian Judith Smith's recent work on popular culture in post–World War II America, we might even see Hansberry's strategic realism as a radical intervention. Arguing that Hansberry "reracializes" the 1950s American family, Smith suggests that *A Raisin in the Sun* "proudly asserted African American families as *American* families integral to the social fabric of American life, their inclusion requisite to fulfilling the promise of post-war democracy" (281).

If realism is one side of the equation that relates *A Raisin in the Sun* to Williams' canon, then lyricism is the other. Such lyricism works not to dilute social protest, but rather to fuse political resistance with the nuanced representation of everyday life. While Williams' "poetic realism" is almost a cliché in thinking about his work, the lyrical qualities of Hansberry's work are sometimes neglected. In light of this tendency, Robert Nemiroff takes care to remind us of moments of "poetic compression" in *Raisin*; for example, he cites the opening scene of Act II in which Walter Lee transitions from drunken ramblings to the poetic summoning of an African warrior spirit (Nemiroff "The 101" 167). Beyond moments when the play explicitly leaves the ground of naturalism, Hansberry deftly exploits the poetic potential of naturalistic elements. One memorable visual metaphor concerns the small plant that Mama nurses over the course of the play; the image of the plant dominates the end of Act I, Scene 1, and lingers at the play's conclusion, when Mama comes back into the apartment to get her plant before closing the door behind her. In *A Raisin in the Sun*, Hansberry fuses a political vision of social transformation with an entirely tender and expressive treatment of domesticity. The play explores and enacts metaphors for understanding African American family life — dreams deferred, planting one's garden — just as *A Streetcar Named Desire* and *Cat on a Hot Tin Roof* push the use of metaphor to interrogate American norms and values.

To capture the popular imagination, however, is also to experience what Williams called a "catastrophe." Plagued by the pressure "to deliver another *Streetcar*," Williams in the 1960s produced a variety of experimental, largely ill-received plays that represent his attempt to break free of commercial formulas (Hale 147). One might see Hansberry as similarly trapped by success. An important essay by the actor Ossie Davis, quoted by Robert Nemiroff, insists that Hansberry "deserved all" the success she got and more, but "in her success she was cheated, both as a writer and a Negro" (Nemiroff "Notes" xix). Davis argues that the extraordinary force with which the mainstream public saw the Younger family as "just like any other American family" worked to obscure the play's critique of race and class inequality and allow the audience to avoid critical reflection (xix). The marketplace, then, might usefully be seen as the conduit both enabling *and* stifling the non-conformist visions of Hansberry and Williams.

The shifting critical reception of *A Raisin in the Sun* demonstrates the importance of this tension between mass appeal and counter-establishment views. In a startling reassessment of the play, Amiri Baraka published his radically transformed views after seeing a 1986 revival. He praises Hansberry for accurately representing the struggles of the U.S. black majority and admits to his prior blindness in viewing the play as "conservative" in form and "middle class" in its decision to have the Youngers move into a white neighborhood (19). In another example of the play's vexed history of reception, Robert Nemiroff notes how 1959 audiences rejoiced in the "happy ending" despite the fact that the play leaves the Youngers on "the brink of what will surely be, in their new home, at best a nightmare of uncertainty" ("Notes" xx). While not wanting to deny the play's sharp political edge, I also want not to deny its more conservative qualities. On one level, the ending *is* undeniably resolved and uplifting — the Youngers' quest for self-determination meshes perfectly with deep-seated American values about staking a claim for your rights and risking a new start. At the same time, of course, the play is implicitly devastating in its exposé of institutional racism and class exploitation. It is this "both/and" quality to Hansberry's work, its conventional gestures coupled with explosive critique, that again makes parallels to Williams so compelling.

Williams' most canonical works abound with instances of this conflicting politics of representation. The ending of *Streetcar*, for example, seems to provide perfect closure — Stanley is victorious over Blanche and about to start over with Stella, baby in tow — while Williams also confronts the audience with the brutality of Stanley's actions. It is indicative of this delicate tension, however, that the original Broadway production actually tipped the audience's sympathy towards Stanley (McConachie 94–98). The case of *Cat on a Hot Tin Roof*, both in terms of its production and reception, proves especially illuminating with respect to *Raisin*. This play arguably does with sexuality what Hansberry does with race; both playwrights mediate their social protest within frameworks acceptable to mainstream audiences. Bruce McConachie posits that *Cat* both opens up questions about homosexuality and "defuses" them at the same time (54). Assessing elements of set design, changes to the text, and differences in vision between Williams and director Elia Kazan, McConachie demonstrates how Williams' "hope that *Cat* might promote a more fluid understanding of human sexuality" gave way to the terms of a "liberal melodrama" (116) in which spectators could feel titillated by unanswered questions concerning Brick's sexual orientation.

Just as the texts and productions of William's plays reflect the pressures of the marketplace, *A Raisin the Sun* has proven susceptible to the same forces. The 1986 Off Broadway revival restored certain scenes that the original production had cut, and research into the complicated production history of *A Raisin in the Sun* contains copious reminders that the "writing" of a play or film script extends far beyond the role of the author. Margaret Wilkerson, in an essay that resituates Hansberry's place within African American theater history, reveals how Hansberry's left-wing politics have been muffled and elided over the course of *Raisin*'s stage and screen life. Although the play might have been seen as conservative from the perspective of a nascent black nationalism, it was also potentially subversive within the context of white establishment norms. Wilkerson explains how Hansberry's attempts to add scenes for the 1961 screenplay — specifically to enlarge Walter Lee's role and develop his political consciousness — met with censorship from the film's producers as the new scenes "ended up on the cutting room floor" (Wilkerson 44).[3]

Debates over whether *A Raisin in the Sun* is mainstream or radical, assimilationist or revolutionary, force us to confront the undeniable complexity of Hansberry's career as a whole. Such debates mirror the struggle to define Williams' career in stable terms. Philip Kolin asks us to consider the enormous "fluidity" of Williams' canon, a body of work that is "indeterminate" and "paradoxical" ("Guest Editor's Intro" 1). Likewise, Steven Carter's biography of Hansberry underscores the "consciously paradoxical nature of Hansberry's world view and art" (14). He views her as "a fighter for her race" but also an internationalist; a conceiver of a black community theater in Harlem but also a "creator of black drama who frequently adopted and adapted techniques and material from the work of non-black writers" (14). Without suggesting that Hansberry directly felt influenced by Williams, I do want to stress that their shared complexity helps to illuminate our understanding of both writers as well as the conflicted American society they addressed.

The paradoxes of Hansberry are fully on display in her second work, *The Sign in Sidney*

Brustein's Window (1964). As the last play over which Hansberry had authority, *Sidney* is vital for understanding the range of her writing after *Raisin* and the trajectory of her artistic vision and political development. Yet *Sidney* is a play that alienated critics at its premiere and that scholars have by and large avoided. Its reputation probably has been tainted by the fact that a campaign was launched to keep it running during Hansberry's hospitalization with cancer. Yet other factors help explain the play's low profile in discussions of Hansberry's legacy: it centers on white characters and marginalizes issues of race; it openly rejects conventions of "well made" drama; and it tackles a huge range of topics ranging from Greenwich Village intellectuals, feminism, gay identity, prostitution, drugs, psychoanalysis, and the ethics of art. It is, in short, a "baggy monster" of a play. In a striking parallel, much has been made of the difficulty, strangeness, and diversity of Williams' output during the 1960s, the sense that this was a radically different Williams from the one who wrote *Streetcar*. *The Sign in Sidney Brustein's Window* makes abundantly clear that Hansberry, like Williams, was deeply engaged in artistic experimentation and similarly aware regarding her reception in the marketplace of commercial theater. Drawing upon recent work that provides new leverage on Williams' later plays, I offer a reading of *Sidney* that makes sense of its dissonance without passing judgment on its "success" or "failure."

Sidney, perhaps even more than *A Raisin in the Sun*, invites comparisons with Williams. In its fitful juggling of domestic drama, tragic-comedy, and social commentary, *Sidney* confronts the spectator with a number of familiar Williams elements. These include brutal verbal sparring between Sidney and his wife, Iris; characters with neuroses; references to cannibalism to describe society's inhumanity; and the use of music — a "white blues out of the Southland" (*Sidney* 218) — to disrupt the frame of realism. The play's penultimate scene, involving the suicide of a mistreated call girl, explicitly alludes to both Williams and Edward Albee. Described in the stage directions as an "absurdist orgy" and a "disintegration of reality to parallel the disintegration in Sidney's world" (328), this scene features drunken and violent psychological conflict. As Gloria, Iris's sister, contemplates overdosing with a bottle of pills, the stage directions strongly allude to Blanche in Scene Ten of *Streetcar*: "For a long moment her eyes dart frantically and she whimpers, trapped, seeking refuge" (*Sidney* 333). While faulting Hansberry for cribbing from Albee in this play, one Broadway critic inadvertently helps us see what Hansberry might have been doing with Williams and the dramatic idiom of the early '60s. The critic proclaims: "There is a sort of inverted miracle in the way Miss Hansberry manages to distort so many things — taste, intelligence, craft — and be simultaneously perverse as dramatist, social commentator, political oracle and moral visionary" ("Borrowed Bitchery" 101). Though the review unequivocally sees *Sidney* as a failure, its sense of the play's "distortions" is precisely an opening into re-reading its potential. This is a work that self-consciously quotes, scrambles, and parodies the American dramatic tradition (which Williams helped to define), much as Williams himself was doing during this period.

Throughout the 1960s, Williams was experimenting with form and subject matter in plays like *A Period of Adjustment* (1960), *The Milk Train Doesn't Stop Here Anymore* (1963), and *Slapstick Tragedy* (1966), all plays that confounded the critics. Even as early as 1953, with *Camino Real*, Williams had been pushing the boundaries of commercially viable drama. Annette Saddick argues that this "distinctly experimental" play was a "work ahead of its time in struggling with questions of personal freedom, authenticity, and role-playing in the midst of public surveillance during the height of the McCarthy era" (Saddick 80). With its huge cast, plethora of literary allusions, and emphasis on role-playing, *Camino Real* evokes the same sort of metatheatrical dizziness as *The Sign in Sidney Brustein's Window*. *A Period of Adjustment* might also prove illuminating here. Billed as a "serious comedy," this aptly named play departs from the "morbid" intensity for which Williams was known. Amusingly, it features a house with a crack running through it, almost as if to comment ironically and nostalgically upon the genre of domestic realism. As the 1960s dawned, both Williams and Hansberry were embarked upon parallel "periods of adjustment"; in the wake of commercial success, they were acutely conscious of their own fame and actively seeking new artistic forms.

Allean Hale's analysis of Williams' *In the Bar of a Tokyo Hotel* provides a model for how one might probe the difficulties of *Sidney*. After citing the almost unbelievably negative reviews that this play received upon its premiere Off Broadway in 1969, Hale argues that the play makes sense if we consider that "the medium is the message"; in short, she asks that we "consider this as a play written in code" (149). Hale goes on to decipher how *In the Bar of a Tokyo Hotel* responds to the conventions of Japanese Noh drama. Her reminder to consider "the medium as the message" proves illuminating when examining the intense self-consciousness of Hansberry in *The Sign in Sidney Brustein's Window*. Not only does the protagonist agonize over the sign to be placed in his front window, the play itself seems to be holding up a "sign." Although many critics have struggled with the play's sprawling range of subjects and "talky" script, I would like to suggest that the work opens up if we see it as a self-conscious exploration of the writer's relationship to the marketplace and an interrogation of the writer's ability to reach the public.

Certainly there is abundant textual evidence for reading *Sidney* as a meta-commentary on the process of producing and contesting art. Nearly all the characters in the play, as they drift in and out of the Brusteins' Greenwich Village apartment, prove to be artist figures of one sort or another. As the play opens, Sidney has just taken over a Greenwich Village weekly and is trying to discern how his newspaper will present itself to the world. Indeed, much of the play's first act animates debate between Sidney, Iris, and their friends about the design of the paper's masthead. Throughout the play, characters like Iris (an actress), Alton Scales (an activist), and David Ragin (a playwright) all comment self-consciously about the roles they play and the audiences who judge them. In a long monologue about the horrors of the audition process, Iris refers to "those blank director-producer-writer faces just staring at you like a piece of unfinished wood, waiting for you to show them something that will get them excited" (251). Not just Iris but all these characters see themselves holding up "signs" to the world, while on a literal level, Sidney wonders whether to support reform politics by posting a banner in his front window.

A Sign in Sidney Brustein's Window is almost obsessively concerned with names and labels, even as it also challenges the boundaries of social categories. While it is possible to see the play, like many of its original critics did, as a compendium of stereotypes, we might approach it now through the rhetoric of performativity or "passing." Hansberry takes great care to identify her characters — David is gay, Iris is Greek/Irish/Cherokee, Sidney is Jewish, Alton is black — while she also unhinges these identities from any stable ontological meaning. Alton, for instance, is explicitly identified as a light-skinned African American. When Iris mocks him for making a "cause" out of race, Alton rejoins: "I *am* a black boy. I didn't make up the game. And as long as a lot of people think there is something wrong with the fact that I *am* a Negro, I am going to make a point out of being one" (246). As one of the few moments in the play where racial issues are foregrounded, this scene deserves particular attention. Alton's reference to race as a "game" implicitly evokes complexities surrounding Hansberry's racial position in 1964. What did it mean for the author of Broadway's longest running play by a black American to produce a work like *The Sign in Sidney Brustein's Window*? To what degree did Hansberry feel defined, empowered, or constrained by racial categories? With its interrogation of identity politics across a vast spectrum, *Sidney* can be seen as performing or "encoding" Hansberry's *multiple* subject positions — as a middle-class African American, a lesbian, an activist, and a celebrity playwright. Unlike Johnnella Butler, who attempts to recuperate the play's merits by enfolding it within a "black esthetic," I read *Sidney* as a deeply self-questioning piece that explodes any singular configuration of identity or dramatic idiom (265).

Hansberry's posthumous works are no more uniform than *Sidney* in their topics and esthetic choices, yet I will not linger on these here. Any scholarly examination of these plays, including *Les Blancs* (1970) and *To Be Young, Gifted, and Black* (1969), must grapple with the role that Robert Nemiroff, Hansberry's literary executor, has played in their development and creation. While *To Be Young, Gifted, and Black* presents Hansberry's words, the piece also represents choices made by Nemiroff in the arrangement and editing of her writings. Still, a work like *Les Blancs*, which Nemiroff completed, provides an opportunity to consider briefly the political trajectory of Hansberry's work in comparison to that of Williams. Wilkerson and Carter have discussed how *Les Blancs* represents a logical extension of *Raisin* in its exploration of colonialism in Africa. In the earlier play, Hansberry evokes Africa through cultural references and the character of Asagai, while *Les Blancs* is set entirely in Africa and is directly concerned with the traumas of imperialism. *Les Blancs* is Hansberry's most explicit critique of colonialism and seems to be garnering new attention through a range of contemporary revivals. While Williams' political commentary was never so explicit, scholars have uncovered his support for civil rights and the variety of ways his theater explored and contested stereotypical images of African American culture. [4] Here I wish not to blur important distinctions between the specific political engagements of Hansberry and Williams, but rather to highlight the shape-shifting nature of their political involvement through art.

Throughout this brief comparative investigation of Williams and Hansberry, I have stressed their status as "social playwrights" — both deeply in tune with mid-century America and sharply critical of its values. If the term "social playwright" is vague, it is also usefully capacious, for there are few playwrights who are at once so iconic and so misunderstood. Both authors function in popular discourse as convenient placeholders — Williams for his forays into the so-called "Southern Gothic" and Hansberry for her pioneering dramatization of black family life — yet there are no stable frames to account for the diversity and heterogeneity of their careers. Hansberry's overnight fame, her career as a left-wing journalist, her death at the age of 34, and the complications of her posthumously published plays — all make the very question of her "canon" especially fraught. Yet the political, social, and formal complexity of her work, along with its historical contingency, deserves ongoing scholarly investigation, just as the full range of Williams' plays is prompting re-assessment of his career and its historical significance.

In the new millennium, it is perhaps becoming easier to see how both Williams and Hansberry boldly put social categories in flux, in motion. Their work contests boundaries of class, race, gender, sexuality, and nation, and they stage not the uniformity but the contradictions embedded in mid-century American culture. In an essay reviewing the renewed scholarly interest in American theater during the post–World War II period, Alan Ackerman reminds us of "the variety and vitality of the drama and theater of a liberal culture characterized by an always fluid set of relations between liberty and coercion, the democratic and the undemocratic" (765). Absolutely this calls for an active re-imagining and re-reading of such landmark playwrights as Hansberry and Williams, to hear the ways in which they unsettled the very society that embraced their work.

NOTES

1. See the Barnes quote at: http://www.2st.com/seasonArchives.php?menuItem=16.

2. Margaret Wilkerson discusses major shifts in the critical reception of Hansberry's work, arguing that *A Raisin in the Sun* and *Les Blancs* "affirm a political stance more radical than previously recognized" (40). Mary Helen Washington examines the left wing journalistic writing and socialist politics of Hansberry, "whose activities in the 1950s earned her a three binder FBI file" (194). For examples of recent scholarship examining constructions of race and sexuality in Williams' canon, see essays by Kolin, Bak, and Powers in the Special Issue of *South Atlantic Review* edited by Philip C. Kolin.

3. Communications scholar Lisbeth Lipari, doing extensive archival research on the film's production, reveals that over one-third of Hansberry's original screenplay was cut by the time the film was released. Lipari reads the film production process as an example of Hollywood's "cultural construction of whiteness" (81).

4. Moschovakis explores racial issues in Williams by looking at his use of blues music. Rather than see the plays as reinforcing stereotypes, he shows how Williams used blues music to question or disrupt racial binaries. See also Kolin's essay on the film *Baby Doll* (written by Williams, directed by Elia Kazan). Kolin reads the film as a radical work in how it protests racial oppression.

WORKS CITED

Ackerman, Alan. "Liberalism, Democracy, and the Twentieth-Century American Drama." *American Literary History* 17 (2005): 765–780.

Ashley, Leonard R. N. "Lorraine Hansberry and the Great Black Way." *Modern American Drama: The Female Canon.* Ed. June Schlueter. Rutherford: Fairleigh Dickinson UP, 1990. 151–160.

Baraka, Amiri. "A Critical Reevaluation: *A Raisin in the Sun*'s Enduring Passion." *A Raisin in the Sun and The Sign in Sidney Brustein's Window.* Ed. Robert Nemiroff. New York: Vintage Books, 1995. 9–20.

Butler, Johnnella E. "*The Sign in Sidney Brustein's Window*: Toward a Transformative Aesthetic." *Transforming the Curriculum: Ethnic Studies and Women's Studies.* Ed. Johnnella E. Butler and John C. Walter. Albany: State University of New York Press, 1991. 257–270.

Carter, Steven R. *Hansberry's Drama: Commitment and Complexity.* Urbana: U of Illinois P, 1991.

Cheney, Anne. *Lorraine Hansberry.* Boston: Twayne Publishers, 1984.

Gill, Glenda E. "The Transforming Power of Performing the Classics in Chocolate, 1949–1954." "Forum on Black Theatre." *Theatre Journal* 57 (2005): 591–596.

Hale, Allean. "*In the Bar of a Tokyo Hotel*: Breaking the Code." *Magical Muse: Millennial Essays on Tennessee Williams.* Ed. Ralph E. Voss. Tuscaloosa: U of Alabama P, 2002. 147–162.

Hansberry, Lorraine. *A Raisin in the Sun and The Sign in Sidney Brustein's Window.* New York: Vintage Books, 1995.

_____. "The Negro Writer and His Roots: Toward a New Romanticism." *The Black Scholar* 12 (March/April 1981). 2–12.

_____. *To Be Young, Gifted, and Black: Lorraine Hansberry in Her Own Words.* Adapted Robert Nemiroff. Englewood Cliffs, NJ: Prentice-Hall, 1969.

Kerr, Walter. "Sweet Bird of Youth." *New York Herald Tribune.* March 11, 1959. In *New York Theatre Critics' Reviews, 1959.* 347.

Kolin, Philip C. Ed. "Civil Rights and the Black Presence in *Baby Doll*." *Literature and Film Quarterly* 24 (1996): 2–11.

_____, ed. "Tennessee Williams in/and the Canons of American Drama." Special Issue of *South Atlantic Review* 70 (2005).

_____. "Guest Editor's Introduction." *South Atlantic Review* 70 (2005): 1–3.

Krasner, David. *American Drama 1945–2000: An Introduction.* Malden, MA: Blackwell Publishing, 2006.

Lipari, Lisbeth. "'Fearful of the Written Word': White Fear, Black Writing, and Lorraine Hansberry's 'A Raisin in the Sun' Screenplay." *Quarterly Journal of Speech* 90 (2004): 81–102.

McConachie, Bruce. *American Theater in the Culture of the Cold War: Producing and Contesting Containment, 1947–1962.* Iowa City: U of Iowa P, 2003.

Moschovakis, Nick. "Tennessee Williams's American Blues: From the Early Manuscripts through *Menagerie*." *The Tennessee Williams Annual Review* 7 (2005): 14–36.

Nemiroff, Robert. "Notes on This New Edition." *A Raisin in the Sun and The Sign in Sidney Brustein's Window.* Ed. Robert Nemiroff. New York: Vintage Books, 1995. xv–xxiv.

_____. "The 101 'Final' Performances of Sidney Brustein." *A Raisin in the Sun and The Sign in Sidney Brustein's Window*. Ed. Robert Nemiroff. New York: Vintage Books, 1995. 159–203.

O'Connor, Jacqueline. "The Strangest Kind of Romance: Tennessee Williams and His Broadway Critics." *The Cambridge Companion to Tennessee Williams*. Ed. Matthew C. Roudané. Cambridge: Cambridge UP, 1997. 255–264.

Rose, Philip. *You Can't Do That on Broadway!: A Raisin in the Sun and Other Theatrical Improbabilities*. New York: Limelight Editions, 2001.

Saddick, Annette J. "'You Just Forge Ahead': Image, Authenticity, and Freedom in the Plays of Tennessee Williams and Sam Shepard." *South Atlantic Review* 70 (2005): 73–93.

Smith, Judith E. *Visions of Belonging: Family Stories, Popular Culture, and Postwar Democracy, 1940–1960*. New York: Columbia UP, 2004.

Tynan, Kenneth. "Broadway." *New Yorker* 21 Mar 1959: 100–102.

Washington, Mary Helen. "Alice Childress, Lorraine Hansberry, and Claudia Jones: Black Women Write the Popular Front." *Left of the Color Line: Race, Radicalism, and Twentieth-Century Literature of the United States*. Eds. Bill V. Mullen and James Smethurst. Chapel Hill: U of North Carolina P, 2003. 183–204.

Wilkerson, Margaret. "Political Radicalism and Artistic Innovation in the Works of Lorraine Hansberry." *African American Performance and Theater History: A Critical Reader*. Eds. Harry J. Elam, Jr. and David Krasner. New York: Oxford UP, 2001. 40–55.

Williams, Tennessee. *A Streetcar Named Desire*. New York: New Directions, 1980.

_____. *The Glass Menagerie*. New York: New Directions, 1970.

_____. "The Catastrophe of Success." *The Glass Menagerie*. New York: New Directions, 1970. 11–17.

Author Unknown. "Borrowed Bitchery." *Newsweek* 26 Oct 1964: 101.

The Fission of
Tennessee Williams's Plays
into Adrienne Kennedy's

Philip C. Kolin

The theatre of Adrienne Kennedy seems far removed, dramatically and ideologically, from Tennessee Williams's plays, a point about which critics appear to agree judging by their silence regarding the existence of any relationships between their respective canons. Although Marc Robinson includes individual chapters on Williams and on Kennedy in his *The Other American Drama*, suggesting an affinity between the two playwrights, in point of fact he injects only one slight mention of Williams in his discussion of Kennedy. Moreover, the few scattered references to Williams in *Intersecting Boundaries: The Theatre of Adrienne Kennedy*, a major gathering of essays on Kennedy's life and theatre, are confined to reasserting that he was not her model and that she developed a distinctive style radically different from his (Bryant-Jackson 47; Wilkerson 71).

Beyond question, Adrienne Kennedy's plays fall into entirely different categories from Williams's. His luminous plots, romantic characters, evocative imagery, and naturalistic sets ruled Broadway from *The Glass Menagerie* in 1945 to *The Night of the Iguana* in 1961. With numerous long runs on Broadway and more than fifteen film adaptations of his works from 1950 to 1970 (Phillips 63), Williams was the most popular, and respected, playwright in American theatre history. Kennedy's plays, however, emerged from a different milieu — the highly experimental Off Broadway theatre of the 1960s. Because her works are disturbingly surrealistic, even phantasmagoric, they have not been staged as widely as they deserve to be. Radically departing from traditional notions of plot and character, Kennedy's plays often contain grotesque-looking characters split into multiple, warring selves, with no consistent or easily identifiable sense of a single individual. Time and place become on her stage a distorted world of shifting psychic landscapes where shrieks, bloodied heads, and funnyhouse mirrors symbolize her characters' schizophrenia. The influences on each playwright are also as dissimilar as their canons. Williams's plays have been honored as examples of the Southern Gothic, a site from which his theatre evolved but from which he recoiled as well. Still, he has been acclaimed for mythologizing the American South, especially New Orleans, in iconic plays that earned him the tide of "Orpheus of the American Stage" (*Tennessee Williams: Orpheus*). Kennedy's primary influences, on the other hand, are rooted in an African American nightmare marked by the prejudice of violence to the inner selves of her black and mulatta characters. Her theatre is painfully occupied with the tortured racial identities of these women who want to be white, or just to be accepted by the white world. Pointing out that her dramatic vision was shaped only after a 1960 trip to Ghana, Kennedy confessed: "I discovered a strength in being a black person and a connection to West Africa" (Betsko and Koenig 248).

Despite the gulf between these two writers, Williams was, inescapably, the dominant voice that any aspiring playwright had to listen to in the 1950's and 1960's, the decades when Kennedy struggled to become a writer and when she eventually won Off Broadway success. Either consciously or subconsciously, a young playwright like Kennedy would have formed a relationship with Williams. Indeed, she herself frequency affirms that he was both her catalyst and provocateur. Kennedy's acknowledgements of admiration for and indebtedness to Williams are prolific, even lionizing at times. They run throughout her interviews and in her scrapbook autobiography, *People Who Led to My Plays* (1987), where the subtitle of a chapter on "Marriage and Motherhood, 1953–1960" situates Williams in a pantheon of writers whom Kennedy revered — "Dreaming of Being a Writer, More of Williams, Lorca, Chekhov." Along with Williams, Kennedy enshrined Elia Kazan and Marlon Brando as the triumvirate of the American theatre, even including cameo-size photos of the three — director, actor, and playwright — on the top of one page in *People* where she asked herself: "Would I ever be part of an artistic brotherhood like this. Ever" (95). Kennedy further confessed that Williams was "The writer whose career and plays I coveted" (*People* 94). "Coveting" conveys praise for and indebtedness to Williams, to be sure, but may also suggest her desire to equal him perhaps.

One Williams play in particular was central to Kennedy's decision to become a playwright. "I was not interested in drama until I saw Tennessee Williams's *Glass Menagerie* ... [which] came to Cleveland when I was sixteen years old. They did it in the round. I had never experienced anything like that" (Binder 102). Throughout her college years at Ohio State University (1949–1953), Kennedy's fascination with Williams continued, especially with *Streetcar*, which was then "at the height of its fame" (*People* 78). Even after college, she studied his plays: "While I was pregnant I read as much of Williams as possible" (78). As she started her career as a writer, Kennedy again claimed Williams as her guide. In the 1950's, the years before her *Funnyhouse of a Negro* debuted in 1964, she revealed, "I had worked a long time before I did [*Funnyhouse*] ... I was very much in awe of Tennessee Williams at the time and so I imitated him" ("Growth of Images" 47). During this decade, she attended many writing workshops at Columbia University producing a novel and drafting several three-act plays, including *Pale Blue Flowers*, which reflect Williams's influence. But none of these works ever saw production, leaving Kennedy discouraged and wondering about her vocation.

Of course, a stream of other sources fed her talent, and Kennedy has not been reluctant to name them in *People* — everyone from Frankenstein and the Wolf Man to Beethoven and James Baldwin. She acknowledged that Lorca, who clearly had influenced Williams heavily, also played a major role in her desire to write a new type of drama. "After I read and saw *Blood Wedding*, I changed my ideas about what a play was. Ibsen, Chekhov, O'Neill and even Williams fell away. Never again would I try to set a play in a 'living room,' never again would I be afraid to have my characters talk in a non-realistic way, and I would abandon the realistic set for a greater dream setting. It was a turning point" (*People* 108). Surely, too, the trip to West Africa radically changed the direction and reception of her work, correlating with Lorca's profound impact on her. Retrospectively, she concluded, "It took me ten years to stop imitating [Williams], to stop using his form and to stop stealing his themes, which were not mine" (*People* 94).

Yet looking back at the 1950's, Kennedy elsewhere admitted, "It had been a long time since I thought of Williams, but now [1961] as I stood staring at volumes of *Streetcar*, *The Glass Menagerie*, and *The Rose Tattoo*, I realized how much I still admired what he did" ("Secret

Paragraphs" 235). She also recalls that when she attended Edward Albee's Playwrights' Unit at the Circle-in-the-Square Theatre in 1963, she "was waiting in the lobby to go to the last class, [and] Albee asked me would I be going to Actor's Studio every Tuesday." She continued, "Knowing that Tennessee Williams was the playwright I most admired, he said 'Tennessee Williams sometimes goes to Actor's Studio.' And turned and walked away" ("Sketches" 6). Though Kennedy does not record whether she met Williams at the Actor's Studio, she knew his works intimately. Contrary to her admission that it took ten years to stop imitating him, I believe she never really escaped from remembering Williams's plays as she developed her own dramatic form and characters. In *People*, for instance, she specifically refers to a Williams essay that strongly spoke to her sense of stage design. Honoring Williams as a master of painterly sets, she praised "His comments on the nature of writing and drama in the press and in *Theatre Arts* magazine, especially an essay on how he utilized the colors of greater painters in his work, and as well, actual scenes. He spoke of how he used a setting in Cezanne for inspiration in a scene in *Streetcar*" (105). Kennedy unquestionably continued to esteem Williams's techniques long after the 1950's.

I'm not arguing here for Williams as a unilateral, or even overriding, source for Kennedy's plays but, rather, prefer to see him more as a context for them, though the many explicit invocations of Williams in her non-fictional writings might support such an intentionalist argument. Doubtless, Williams wrote much to intrigue Kennedy through characters and dramatic techniques that surely interacted with her creative vision, as she attests. Responding to Williams at various levels, she certainly particularized her own racial heritage on stage. In negotiating his scripts, she found doomed heroines, eroticized plots, failed love affairs, interiorizing poetic monologues, and the ineluctable struggles of the human heart against a cruel, patriarchal world, all elements that could possibly be morphed into the psychic histories of her tragic black and mulatta characters. But, above everything else, she may have been drawn to Williams because of his mad maidens who were often "deranged artists" (O'Connor), a character type radicalized through her many black female voices. Kennedy's early plays — with their psychotically episodic plots, splintered characters with conflicting selves, and arias of lyrical hysteria — often incorporate the dramaturgy, if not the nostalgic effects, that Williams championed in his new "Plastic Theatre" of 1944 ("Production Notes"). Especially important, his works provided excursions into self which would also be at the core of Kennedy's theatre. Kennedy discovered in Williams's representations of self, and the distortion of time and space brilliantly realized in Jo Mielziner's scrims of gauze, a theatre that possibly prompted her to seek and to find alternative ways of rendering self and desire.

Claiming *The Glass Menagerie* as the catalyst for her career, Kennedy valotized a Williams's work most famous for breaking the rules of a realistic/naturalistic theatre. Though she judged the dialogue and setting of *Menagerie* as "realistic," the staging techniques were certainly not, an especially relevant fact for a study of Kennedy's work in relationship to Williams's. He provocatively challenged the way character, time, and space were represented. Destabilizing realistic presentations of character, Williams drew attention to the revelation of a character's self, and the many other selves inside her or him. Tom Wingfield in *The Glass Menagerie*, for example, is narrator, character, stage manager, and Williams's double, all embodied in one actor. Living in several worlds simultaneously, Tom escapes inside himself through his poems, his dreams, his travels, and especially through cinema, as Kennedy's Clara does even more compulsively in *A Movie Star Has to Star in Black and White* (1976). Thanks to Tom's (sub)consciousness, audiences moved from present to past and back, inside and outside, as Williams's experimental stage challenged the boundaries of realism ("Production Notes" 131).

To accommodate such revelations of self Williams created a new stage language from magic lantern slides, nostalgic music, and imaginative lighting combining "religious" clarity with the "dusky" atmosphere of an El Greco painting. Most memorably, he created multivalent symbols such as the glass unicorn or the fire escape in *The Glass Menagerie* (or the Chinese paper lantern and the blind Mexican flower seller in *A Streetcar Named Desire*) to reflect self. Articulating how this "poetic imagination" imparted its magic, Williams claimed that such dramatic techniques "can represent or suggest in essence, only through transformation, through changing into other forms than those which were merely present in appearance" (131). At work in *The Glass Menagerie*, then, this principle of "poetic imagination" resulted in an "episodic," "fragmentary" narrative, offering audiences a highly intensified "emotional appeal" (132). These performance ideologies of Williams's new theatre would have been nothing less than ground zero for an experimental dramatist like Kennedy in the early 1960's. With its emphasis on the "transformative" and "fragmentary," Williams's intensely poetic theatre almost certainly would have appealed to Kennedy's desire to tap into her own inner world of selves traumatized by race and gender. Though she resisted Williams's cultural and sexual codes, she interrogated, further reified, and transformed the dramatic techniques upon which they were based.

In light of *The Glass Menagerie*'s importance to Kennedy's desire to be a playwright, then, it may be possible to trace certain characters, sets, and images as they transform themselves from Williams, the central white, male Broadway playwright, to Kennedy, the quintessentially marginalized black female Off Broadway writer. Her experimental, revolutionary encounters with Williams's canon reflect the powerful boundary-crossing ways that gender, race, color, venue, and generation can confront, and disrupt, a script. Unlike the traditional literary influences that Harold Bloom and others have posited between established authors and their anxious disciples, a shockingly different kind of relationship exists between Williams's theatre and Kennedy's. This relationship might be compared to the violent collision and explosions accompanying nuclear fission, where one atom (or canon) is split in two, leading, in this case, to the complex transmutation of Williams's tropes into Kennedy's. As she forced Williams's script open for violent (re)creation, she rebelled against the very impositions of theatrical illusion and psychological realism associated with his white Broadway theatre. Engendering and empowering a black female voice, Kennedy resisted Williams's theatre, fragmenting and possibly recasting his characters into the tortured, surrealistic selves in her racialized scripts. As a result of this fission-like process, it might be possible to create a new map of intertextuality where the text of each playwright is visualized as an exploding scriptscape. In this essay, I use the term *fission* to explain these violent textual encounters between Kennedy's plays and Williams's. Relevant to this fission analogy, Williams's Gypsy in *Camino Real* (1953) asks: "Do you feel yourself to be spiritually unprepared for the age of exploded atoms?" (Block Three, 458). The emerging playwright Adrienne Kennedy was clearly prepared for the new age of "exploding atoms," and the radical transformation and disruption of the Williams canon they brought.

I must stress, though, that even while a gulf of racial and cultural differences separates Kennedy and Williams, a degree of interracial sympathy exists between her work and his in terms of the dramatization of self. Williams revolutionized the American stage by not representing conflict as merely an external, outer force of opposition. Arthur Miller aptly observed, "With *Streetcar* and other ... tonalities like those in *The Glass Menagerie*, the individual and his inner life moved to the center" ("Introduction" xiii). As Williams attempted to do, Kennedy broke out from the inside of this center. She took Williams's experimentation with self farther than any other American playwright has done (Robinson). Doing so, fragments of Williams seem to be converted into bursts of hysteria animating Kennedy's heroines. As she claimed, "I admire Tennessee Williams and Garcia Lorca — and I struggled for a long time to write plays — as typified by *Funnyhouse*— in which the person is in conflict with the inner forces, with the conflicting sides to their personality, which I found to be my own particular, greatest conflict ... it was an attempt to articulate ... your inner conflicts" ("Growth of Images" 47). By exploring the fission metaphor in *Camino*, we might profitably investigate how the most celebrated parts of Williams's theatre could be split, erupting into the most violent parts of Kennedy's canon, all revolving around "conflict(s) with the inner forces." Regardless of racial and gender differences, Kennedy and Williams would doubtless agree with poet Susan Wheeler that "Maybe it's our internalness/We're stuck on" ("Debtor").

Appropriately enough, both playwrights established their careers by writing self performance pieces, a theatre of self. Williams became a character in his own drama of self just as Kennedy would do. His plays of the 1940's and 1950's find him grappling with a self that was peripatetic, elusive, and transformative. In Tom Wingfield, he represented his own fears, guilt, dreams. Speaking of *Streetcar*, Williams confessed, "1 can identify with Blanche ... we are both hysterics" (Jennings 72) and, like Blanche, he fell deeply into self, exploring his closeted psyche. Kennedy's recognition of conflict in her plays began with interrogation of self as well. The credo of her theatre is "The characters are myself " (qtd. in Brown 86). Through one of her many fictionalized selves, Suzanne Sand in her novel *Deadly Triplets* (1990), Kennedy appropriately revealed that "the mystery and intrigue of unresolved identity ... seem to permeate my work" (76). Because of her frequent self disclosures, Kennedy has been honored for writing "the most personal plays of any playwright in the U.S.A." (Cummings 7), an attribution that could unarguably be applied to Williams in the 1940's-1960's, and, even more acrimoniously, in the 1970's with the publication of his *Memoirs*. But while Williams theatricalized his sexual dilemmas, and created a cast of androgynous characters in the process, Kennedy confronted the ghosts — white as well as black, female as well as male — haunting her traumatic racial history in *Funnyhouse*, *The Owl Answers*, *A Movie Star Has to Star in Black and White*, and other plays.

Williams's indeterminacy and Kennedy's unresolved identities, then, suggest powerful ways to chart the impact of his plays on hers, most significantly and radically, Kennedy transformed Williams's lyrical, expressionistic techniques of revealing self into surrealistic nightmares. In her theatre of (out)rage, Kennedy may have found in Williams's monologues potential for dramatizing the tormented selves and terrorizing cries of her talented, young black women. The dramaturgy behind Tom Wingfield's long monologues and Blanche's "hysterical outburst[s]" (260) detonate in the mad arias of Negro Sarah or Clara Passmore. Williams seems to erupt into hysteria in Kennedy. But quite possibly she simultaneously absorbed yet nullified his nostalgic temporality as she multiplied and racialized the voices of his hysterical women to create her own cast of alienated black women artists. Kennedy takes us on the other side of Blanche's shattered mirror, as it was represented at the end of Scene 11 in Elia Kazan's film of *Streetcar*, to show how her selves might look from a black perspective. For Kennedy that mirror revealed distortion, fragmentation, and deformity. Not surprisingly, Williams referred to his "public self" as an "artifice of mirrors and catastrophe" ("The Catastrophe of Success" 138). Unquestionably, mirrors are the dominant symbol in Kennedy's *Funnyhouse* where Sarah confronts the distorted reflections of her nightmarish selves, shattering her desire to be white into mad fragments.

Judging from her comments on seeing Williams's plays in the 1940's and 1950's, Kennedy was no doubt sensitive to the inner voices of his heroines besieged by numerous and contradictory selves. Amanda, Laura, Blanche, Alma Winemiller, and Serafina, for instance, articulate and battle conflicted selves. Amanda plays the Southern Belle, but she also unleashes the crueler voice of an angry, abandoned wife. At other times, she speaks to the Gentleman Caller as if she, and not her emotionally disabled daughter Laura, was the belle being courted while after the Gentleman Caller leaves she cries the heartbreak of the rejected woman. Living on the precipice of (dis)illusion, Amanda proclaims, with all her pretensions, her insatiable desire for acceptance by an empowered but disdainful white social group — the DAR — that ultimately rejects her. Even more prominently in *Streetcar*, Blanche DuBois is a tissue of selves — aristocratic, sexual, sacrificial. In her schizophrenic nightmares, she hears voices from a terrifying past, orchestrated in sleazy jazz ensembles and insanely elegant varsouvianas. In the 1951 film, Blanche's voices reverberate wildly in her head as they are magnified through an echo chamber. Serafina Delle Rose in *The Rose Tattoo* symbolically surrounds herself with falling manikins visualizing her dead and dying selves — as lover, bride, wife, historian of the heart, and her daughter's manic protector-interrogator. Further testifying to Williams's attempt to voice a character's various selves, Dr. John Buchanan in *Summer and Smoke* provocatively diagnoses Alma Winemiller as having "a Doppelganger," or another person [living] inside of me" (241). Lamenting the burden of her selves, Kennedy confessed, "Autobiography interests me, apparently because that is what I do best. I write about my family. In many ways I would like to break out of that, but I don't know how..." ("Growth" 42). Ironically enough, both playwrights were under the inescapable literary spell of their mothers. Edwina Dakin Williams's voice, prudery, and aristocratic pretense infuse Amanda Wingfield, Alma Winemiller, and Blanche DuBois. Correspondingly, Kennedy traces much of her work to her mother's companionship, reading, dreams, and desires (Parks 44). Williams's play, then, appears to have provided a nucleus around and through which Kennedy could explode her family's racial and cultural traumas, compellingly different from Williams's, of course, but eerily linked to them nonetheless.

As Kennedy reflected further on how she might represent family, *The Glass Menagerie* once more came to the forefront of her thinking In a 1985 interview, she admitted:

> Again, it was all centered on the obsession I had with *The Glass Menagerie*.
> I had come from a family that was very social, very prominent, but inside our house we had these seemingly endless conflicts, these arguments. And I really wanted to get them down. I couldn't understand that as young person. How could we be a certain way on the outside and another inside our house? And that really was the big motivation [qtd. in Binder 102].

In responding to *The Glass Menagerie*, she racialized this dialectic between outside and inside by dramatizing the warring disparity between a white façade that simultaneously conceals but betrays and the interior world of a black woman's hysteria fueled by racial injustice. *The Owl Answers* and *A Beast Story*, for example, traumatically record how well Kennedy, in her discomforting obsession with the conflicts foregrounded in *The Glass Menagerie*, got family "down." *In The Owl Answers*, Clara is denounced outside by her white father as well as inside by the black minister and his wife who earlier had adopted her. Caught in a world neither white nor black, she is metamorphosized into a harrowing owl whose yellow color suggests the tragedy of miscegenation (E. Barnesley Brown). Through Kennedy's multivalent symbolism, Clara becomes completely displaced from self and family. Rejection by the outside white world coalesces with the abjection she suffers inside. In the far less terrorized space inhabited by the white Southern gentleman Thomas Lanier Williams, Laura is preserved behind transparent glass where inside at last reflects outside. The broken unicorn symbolizes the translucent psychic rupture for Williams's white family — for Laura, Tom, and Amanda. Laura's brother and mother still love her, perhaps even more because of her rejection by the Gentleman Caller. Kennedy's heroines Sarah and Clara with their guilt are on the other side of the racial divide are existentially estranged, both inside and outside, from those who should love them — their family

Nowhere are Kennedy's textual encounters with Williams more telling than in a comparison of the last scene of *The Glass Menagerie* with the ending of *The Owl Answers*. The same religious icon — the candles — occurs at these climatic moments in both plays but is filtered through very different racial and sexual identities. As *The Glass Menagerie* ends, Tom asks Laura to "blow out your candles," suggesting a kindly, elegiac separation between brother and sister. As if demonizing memories of *The Glass Menagerie*, Kennedy transforms one of Williams's most well-known symbols into a horrifying tableau where a daughter is not simply disappointed by an illusory romance, or saddened by the guilt of a fugitive brother, but is assaulted by her own white father. If Williams's model for *The Glass Menagerie* was Chekhov, Kennedy's for *The Owl Answers* could easily have been Foucault, for *Owl* cities out from unrelenting sexual abuse and racial punishment. In the harrowing territory of her nightmare world, Clara Passmore in *The Owl Answers* is accosted by a Negro Man whom she entices to her apartment where a "*burning High Altar*" is foregrounded. As he "tries to force her down," Clara's dead father, "*the Richest White Man in Town, has been holding the candles,* [but] *now smiles.*" On Kennedy's phantasmagoric set, She Who is the Owl "*withdraws the butcher knife, still with blood and feathers on it*" and struggles with her father. As she falls "*at the side of the altar burning,*" "*her head* [is] *bowed, both hands conceal her face, feathers fly, green lights are strong....*" Metamorphosized into an owl, neither white nor black, Clara "*speaks*" like the tainted bird as her white "*Father rises and slowly blows out candles on bed*" (42).

Blowing out the candles is quintessential Williams while the same action, surrealistically translated, becomes painfully Kennedy-esque in *The Owl Answers*. As the extinguished candles in *The Glass Menagerie* quietly call Laura off stage, the burned-out candles on the bed in *The Owl Answers* signal the struggle and violation of a young black woman. Williams's lament over loss, softly conveyed through Laura's candles and Tom's gentle expression of sorrow, is transformed in Kennedy's scriptscape into an indictment of racist ideology justifying physical torture on a sexually punitive altar/bed. The burning altar and bed with its candles symbolize white religious piety and privilege that condemn children of mixed blood like Clara. Her psychic/sexual death is encoded as an (un)holy ritual, reminiscent of *The Glass Menagerie* that fragments into shrieks of horror in *The Owl Answers*. As Kennedy confessed in *People*, she was obsessed with *The Glass Menagerie* for ten years. Based upon the ending of *The Owl Answers*, Williams's climatic tableau in *The Glass Menagerie* still haunted her. *The Owl Answers* thus offers one of the most revealing and provocative encounters (fissions) between the plays of a white, Southern male who loved and mourned his sister throughout his life and an Off Broadway African American woman playwright who dramatized atavistic nightmares of blood-haunted daughters and white and black rapist fathers.

Streetcar Named Desire also seems to explode into early Kennedy plays such as *Funnyhouse*, *The Owl Answers*, and *A Beast Story*. In fact, *Streetcar* overflows with an abundance of dramatic elements found in Kennedy's early scripts — madness, hallucinations, cinematic flashbacks, poetic flights of rapture/rupture, nightmares, and violated bodies. But even more importantly, *Streetcar* most clearly embodies Williams's vision of the madwoman, a character at the core of Kennedy's early plays. As Jacqueline O'Connor argues, "For in no other play does Williams dramatize a woman's mental decline and fall so completely" (35). In recording her thoughts on first seeing Williams's play, Kennedy could have very well been responding to Blanche's harrowing "mental decline": "In *Streetcar* there is within the world, violence, danger" (*People* 89). The *Streetcar* world of hysteria — Blanche's dreams dissolving into nightmares — appears to be (re)cast "within" in Kennedy's theatre. Shards of *Streetcar* burst into racial violence and schizophrenic punishments in *Funnyhouse* and *Owl*. Blanche's self-dramatizing tendencies, her multiple, mad selves, violently interact with Kennedy's nightmarish black and mulatto figures. Blanche lives in a fantasy world of bad dreams just as Sarah in *Funnyhouse* and Clara in *The Owl Answers* do. Nightmares are central, of course, to many of Williams's and Kennedy's plays. Kennedy would unequivocally corroborate King Del Ray's dark credo in Williams's *Red Devil Battery Sign* (1977): "I believe in bad dreams."

Blanche's dreams, like those of Kennedy's heroines, render her a victim of her own fantasies, all of them linked to whiteness. In fact, one of the most readily intriguing explosions of Williams into Kennedy's canon is the way whiteness privileges but destroys desire. At the start of her career, Clive Barnes insightfully pointed to Kennedy's use of color symbolism as one of her most significant contributions: "Of all our black writers, Kennedy is most concerned with white, with white relationships, with white blood. She thinks black, but remembers white. It gives her work an eddying ambiguity." *Streetcar* is infused with the colored-coded cultural and psychic identities that in Kennedy turned into horrifying racial categories. The tortured selves within her works might be said to reprise Blanche's white hysteria through black voices that challenge the accepted boundaries/polarities imposed by the theatrical illusions of Williams's theatre. In exposing the ambiguities and contradictions "within" Williams's white world, Kennedy racially disrupts his Southern reflections of feminine gentility. Provocatively, whiteness in *Streetcar,* as in *Funnyhouse* and *The Owl Answers*, translates into self-destructive discourse. Desiring to be white, or valorizing things that are white, turns into a fatal attraction for Blanche, just as it does for Sarah and Clara Passmore. Though critics like Rachel van Duyvenbode have associated Blanche with the aristocratic heroines of plantation romances, she is systematically punished for encoding and enacting her cultural whiteness in *Streetcar*. Even her name (endangered white woods, echoing Chekhov's *Cherry Orchard*) is eponymous with a quintessential whiteness that condemns her just as it eludes and destroys Kennedy's heroines.

In terms of reading color codes in Kennedy against the backdrop of racial ambiguities in Williams's plays, it is significant that Blanche is victimized by a corrupt white patriarchy. As O'Connor again asserts, "Blanche's defeat is in part due to her powerlessness" in the patriarchy (46). She is evicted from Belle Reve because of her white male ancestors' "epic fornications" (284), and in New Orleans she is raped by the new father Stanley whose lie emboldens patriarchal truth at the conclusion of the *Streetcar* script, if not in the censored 1951 film version (Leff; Schleuter). The powerful white world strips Blanche of her life. She is fired from her teaching job by a principal named Graves and is expelled from Laurel to New Orleans, the city of night and shadows (Richardson). Along the way, she "slipped outside to answer" the calls of young soldiers who "the paddy-wagon would gather ... like daisies" (389), another symbolic white sign by which she is castigated by society. She is declared "Out-of-Bounds" (361) by the local army base, another bastion of white patriarchy where Stanley belongs as a highly decorated "Master Sergeant in the Engineers' Corps" (258). In New Orleans, Blanche becomes her own stranger seeking kindness as she alternates between being a paragon for the white world and a desperate outcast from it. She is the Lady of the Camellias wearing a white dress but she is also The East as the dark temptress of the Tarantula Arms.

Numerous instances of these color polarities envelop Blanche's psychic and cultural identities (artist, Southern belle, fallen woman) throughout *Streetcar*. Ironically, she is condemned to journey through two color-coded psychic spaces, one light, the other dark. Her encounter with Mitch in Scene Nine typifies the ambiguities of Williams's white/dark symbolism to represent Blanche's trauma. Deceived by her illusions all summer, an angry Mitch returns to Stanley's house to get a "look at [her] good and plain" (384). He contemptuously snaps at her, "It's dark in here" (384), and insists, "Let's turn light on here." Blanche frighteningly replies, "Light? Which light? What for?" (384). She knows that she is lost because of the delusions she has created for herself and for Mitch, all predicated on the white virtues of innocence, respectability, and genteel coyness she has performed. Yet this white world is in part a sham, an invention of the mind, symbolized in Blanche's song in Scene Seven, "Say, it's only a paper moon... But it wouldn't be make-believe If you believed in me" (360). The white imagery embedded in "paper" and "moon" calls attention to the ephemeral, the insubstantial, and the façade of selves Blanche wears. The flower seller Rosita in *Camino Real* appropriately links such indeterminacy (the moon, illusions) with Blanche's white flowers, "Camellias, camellias! ... whatever a lady finds suitable to the moon" (Block Seven, 489). Yet, in the end, Blanche is not destined for romantic, moonlit cruises. Forced into the harsh light of Mitch's proletarian realism, her other self emerges, a woman older, less attractive, nearly vanquished, the mad artist-self.

Refracting these interracial eruptions/fissions in Williams's canon, Kennedy's work exfoliates into a host of transformative white/dark registers as well. In confronting his plays, Kennedy brilliantly excavates the contradictions and ambiguities of the rhetoric of whiteness that undermine her own white-seeking black heroines. The white/dark subtext of *Streetcar* appears to splinter everywhere in *Funnyhouse* and *The Owl Answers* as Blanche's plight is grotesquely and racially magnified. In striving to represent themselves as white in a white world, Sarah and Clara Passmore seem to be shadowed by Blanche's delusions of an aristocratic white society with its otiose elegance, yet condemned to live in a ghastly/ghostly world of white suffocation. Blanche has been linked to Robert Graves's white goddess, a female deity "whose embrace is death" (qtd. in Kelly 128). Similarly, in *Funnyhouse* everything white is wedded to death. Victoria and the Duchess "wear a [white] mask" or are "*highly powdered*," giving them "*a hard expressionless quality and a stillness as in the face of death*" (12). Sarah's mother is "*dressed in a white gown.. .as in a trance.*" She stands before a curtain which is "*a ghastly white ... material that brings to mind the interior of a cheap casket*" (12). Given Blanche's symbolic associations with death, she may well be the type of companion, or confidante, that Kennedy's Negro Sarah longs for: "My white friends, like myself, will be ... intellectual and anxious for death" (14). When Kennedy's tormented black women are forced into discovery by the white world they want to join, they retreat into madness and hallucinate in color. But these black and mulatta characters do not intone the romantic cries of the heart in Williams; instead, they live in a blaring holocaust. Theirs is the danger "within" the *Streetcar* world that a black woman playwright like Kennedy had the courage to represent on her stage.

Like Blanche, too, who valorizes the arts and compulsively quotes from the canons of white male authors (Poe, Hawthorne, Whitman, Proust), Sarah immerses herself in white literary respectability. Her claustrophobic room in a "brownstone in the West Nineties in New York" (13), a truer synecdoche of her selves, is filled with old books, paintings of ruins from fallen white civilizations, and a "gigantic white plaster statue of Queen Victoria" that she fetishes into a Caucasian deity. Sarah spills herself in the service of copying the style and heritage of white authors: "I spend my vile days preoccupied with the placement and geometric position of words on paper. I write poetry filling white page after white page with imitations of Sitwell" (19), an English poet who, ironically enough, wrote a biography of Queen Victoria, the monarch synonymous with nineteenth-century white colonial power. Similarly attracted to but defeated by the white literary establishment, Clara in *The Owl Answers* travels to England to seek Chaucer, Shakespeare, and Eliot, "all my beloved English" (40), the progenitors of her adopted literary whiteness. But the culture of whiteness that Blanche espouses (teaching "bobby-soxers and drugstore Romeos" [302]) has expelled as it curses and condemns Sarah and Clara. Sadly, not even white books are a source of comfort for Sarah the librarian while Clara Passmore is fiercely denounced by the quintessential white male author, Shakespeare. There is no way for either of them to acquire a white literary identity, just as there is, paradoxically, no way for Blanche to survive because of hers.

Other fragments of Blanche's tragedy might be identified through the sexual exploitation of Kennedy's heroines, rejected and raped by their white fathers. In *Funnyhouse*, Sarah confesses: "My mother looked like a white woman, hair as straight as any white woman's," hoping she can inherit her mother's light skin. Clara in *The Owl Answers* is locked out of St. Paul's Chapel, her white ancestral home in England, and castigated by three white father figures — William the Conqueror, William Shakespeare, and William Mattheson, the latter her white biological father who sexually deflowers his daughter in "the garden" as well as in the "outhouse" (41). A similar sexual tragedy unfolds in Kennedy's *Lesson in Dead Language* (1968), where seven black girls in bloodied organdy Holy Communion dresses are punished for entering menarche by the cruel White Dog symbolizing the Greco-Roman world denouncing their procreative powers. Sarah's claim to maternal whiteness or Clara's because of a white father do not redeem these mulatta characters any more than Blanche's white ancestors protected her in Laurel or New Orleans. In fact, for all her whiteness, and because of it, Blanche descends into the shadows, as Kennedy's heroines do, except their psychic hells are darker, deeper — a clanging subway tunnel for Clara and a mind-ravaging *Funnyhouse* for Sarah. Of all the explosions of Williams's canon into Kennedy's scripts, Blanche's role playing, reflecting her multiple selves, may be the most resounding. Her excursions into sundry hallucinatory roles portend a shocking relevance for *Funnyhouse* and *The Owl Answers*. Blanche assumes the role of a queen and even the Virgin Mary, identities that Kennedy's heroines Sarah and Clara internalize in their theatre of self torture. "Boxed out of [her] mind" (381), Blanche, the sham queen, places "the rhinestone tiara on her head before the mirror of the dressing-table and murmur excitedly "to a group of spectral admirers" (391). She has proudly "decked herself out in somewhat soiled and crumpled white satin evening gown and a pair of scuffed silver slippers with brilliants in their heel" (391). Seeing a queenly Blanche, Stanley condemns her "lies and conceit and tricks!" (398). Like Mitch, he forces Blanche to confront her own illusions: "And look at yourself! Take a look at yourself in that worn-out Mardi Gras outfit, rented for fifty cents from some rag-picker! And with that crazy crown on! What queen do you think you are!" Stanley then compares her to the "Queen of the Nile" (398), a fallen Cleopatra (Kolin, "Cleopatra" 25).

Clearly, Blanche's disguised selves do not hide from the truth of her desperation, nor does Williams intend them to. In the performance of her self-deceptions, Blanche is at her most vulnerable. Easily wounded, she believes in the lie and yet must wear the truth. For Stanley everything about "dame Blanche" at this point is rotten, cheap, make-believe. His truth tragically belies her illusion in Scene Ten (Schlueter). But Blanche believes in the disguise of a queen, even though her aristocratic pretensions are covered in rags. In one of the most demanding roles in the American theatre, Williams asks the actor playing Blanche to voice multiple selves simultaneously — the respected and genteel lady whom she desires to be and the fallen woman she does not want to see in the mirror, and all the refraction in-between. The contrast between how Blanche envisions herself and how she is envisioned is caught by Stanley's scorning male gaze, providing a context for the rejections which most often are found at the center of Kennedy's plays. Later, in Scene Eleven, Blanche imagines herself as pure and blessed as the Virgin Mary, dressed in "Della Robbia blue. The blue of the robe in the old Madonna pictures" (409). Though she is taken to the madhouse, Blanche leaves the stage with her regal image in place as Mitch sobs and the gallant doctor in black at first courts and then escorts her off stage.

But where Williams's theatre capitalized on the synchronicity between the real and fictive Blanches, Kennedy forces her audiences to see her characters/selves as inescapably black women wearing white masks, their claim to a white identity and privilege harrowingly undercut by their self-indicting appearances. As if fragmenting pieces of the *Streetcar* scriptscape, *Funnyhouse* grotesquely suggests Blanche's tattered trappings and mad theatrics in the descriptions of the queenly robes and royal appointments of Kennedy's protagonists. Apropos of Blanche's royal and Marian selves, two of Sarah's selves aspire to regal representation as Queen Victoria and the Duchess of Hapsburg, and one of Clara's selves in *Owl* hailed as "the Virgin Mary." As we saw, the *mis en scene* for Victoria and the Duchess in *Funnyhouse* is a "white satin curtain of a cheap material and ghostly white, a material that brings to mind the interior of a cheap casket, parts of it are frayed and look as [if it] has been gnawed by [a] rat?" (12). Sarah's Queen Victoria and Duchess selves "*are dressed in royal gowns of white, similar to the white curtains; the material cheap satin. Their headpieces are white and have a net that falls over their face?*" (12). Although Sarah might believe she is a royal personage like Blanche, her tawdry costumes and settings in *Funnyhouse* ultimately disintegrate illusion, making it unable to sustain desire. This make-believe world of Sarah and her many selves is grotesque; their negritude is never absolved. The many-selved Blanche wearing "*crumpled white satin*" from a rag-picker collides with Kennedy's "queens" surrounded by "*white satin curtains of a cheap material*" which, like the extinguished candles at the end of *Menagerie* and *Owl* amounts to a textual explosion, a fission of Williams into Kennedy's canon. But while Williams recuperates Blanche through her deceptive roles, Kennedy's heroines are jarringly discontinuous with theirs. Wearing white masks that reveal their negritude rather than concealing it, her characters have black faces and "frizzy" hair that pushes through the façade of their whiteness.

Comparing the ways *Streetcar* and *Funnyhouse* end, as we saw with *The Glass Menagerie* and *The Owl Answers*, reveals how racial differences between the two playwrights privilege or deconstruct tragic dignity. It appears that Kennedy interrogates the subtext of *Streetcar* to publicize her outrage at how white art attempts to ennoble on stage. At the end of *Streetcar*, audiences commiserate with the tragic white woman from Belle Reve, despite Blanche's mad, frenzied illusions in Scene Ten and the conflicted color codes associated with her. In fact, Blanche's illusions actually contribute to her and the audience's desire for a tragically powerful fictionality. Yet Blanche's whiteness does not extend the dignity of psychic or cultural tragedy to Kennedy's heroines. There is no white place or white identity for Sarah or Clara. Role playing in *Funnyhouse* and *The Owl Answers*, however, only mocks any desire on the characters' part for a dignified escape/departure through illusion. The "net" that falls over Sarah's selves is the trap for their delusions, without any promise of Blanche's tragic departure in Scene Eleven. Kennedy's women never receive justification for grace that critics have bestowed on Blanche for her belletristic fervor. For Kennedy, unlike Williams, redemption in and through illusion is always and only a nightmarish impossibility. Unlike Blanche's noble departure, Sarah's suspended corpse onstage invites derision by the white world. She receives a contemptuous eulogy from Raymond, her Jewish boyfriend, who jibes: "She was a funny little liar" (25). Sarah is further mocked for her illusions by the "*laughing* landlady" as funnyhouse sounds and sights overwhelm in their absurd repression of desire. Raymond further undercuts and racializes Sarah's desire to be white: Her father "is a nigger who eats his meals on a white glass table" (26). Such is the devastating effect of Kennedy's resistance to the pretense of white tragedy in her racial and cultural fission of *Streetcar*.

Williams's representation of Blanche's rape by Stanley may further suggest a racialized fission of *Streetcar*, exploding fragments into *Funnyhouse*, *The Owl Answers*, and *A Beast Story*. As several critics maintain, the subtext for Stanley's character is rooted in stereotypical African

American traits of primitive brutality and sexuality (Crandell; van Duyvenbode). Crandell, for example, claims that in linking Stanley with "imagery traditionally associated with black characters," Williams symbolized "the prospect of miscegenation," and thus "obscures and confuses the boundaries between ethnic and racial groups at the same rime debunking the notion that 'race,' 'ethnicity,' and identity are unified, stable, and immutable features of the Self" (338). Correspondingly, several productions of the play by white and African American theatre companies alike have foregrounded Stanley's "blackness" (Kolin, *Williams: Streetcar*). In such a racialized context, Blanche's warning to Stella in Scene Four casts Stanley as a predatory outsider, the intruder from the jungle, separating him from the white world from which she believes Stella is dangerously estranged:

> He acts like an animal, has an animal's habits. Eats like one, moves like one, talks like one! There's even something — sub-human — something not quite to the stage of humanity yet! Yes, something — ape-like about him, like one of those pictures I've seen in — anthropological studies ... Stanley Kowalski — survivor of the Stone Age! Bearing the raw meat home from the kill in the jungle! [323].

In Blanche's Eurocentric dream world, Stanley represents "brutal desire," the dark other, smashing genteel women and other icons of white culture. Her images of him evokes the black male body stereotypically associated with rape. Insightfully, Arthur Miller characterized Brando's Stanley as a "sexual terrorist" ("Introduction" xii).

Stanley's sexuality, with its "animal force" (319) and violent entanglements in desire-ridden New Orleans, explodes into surrealistic representation(s) of predatory men in *Funnyhouse*. Negro Sarah describes her father in Stanley-like signifiers. He "is the darkest of us all, my mother the fairest ... I am in between ... he is a black man" (22). "He is arriving again for the night. He comes through the jungle to find me. He never tires of his journey" (12). A few lines later, the Duchess confesses that her mother, the white woman, died because "The wild black beast put his hands on her" (12). Speaking for Sarah's mother as well, the Man exclaims, "Black man, black man, my mother says, I never should have let a black man put his hands on me" (18). Sarah's Queen Victoria self situates the father in the same treacherous and primitive environment in which Blanche fixes Stanley. The black father and brutish Stanley share the traits of a looming predator — rapist, beast, dark, and wild. The fate of Sarah's white mother, the event which precipitated Sarah's tragedy, seems to excavate the *Streetcar* scriptscape absurdly. Both are driven to an asylum after the horror of being raped by a man characterized in Kennedy as "the darkest of them all" (12). In Kennedy's encounter with *Streetcar*, she reifies the metaphoric re-characterization of Stanley as a jungle predator but without any trace of his charisma or love for Stella. Again, colliding with Williams's play, Kennedy strips away any possibility for romantic attachments for her black heroines who are undone by their desire to be seen and preserved as white.

Yet the white Blanche and white-desiring Sarah are both caught in a trap because of this predatory beast. Stage directions from *Streetcar* alongside those in Kennedy suggest the splitting apart of *Streetcar* into *Funnyhouse* in creating an atavistic jungle of the mind. In Scene Ten of *Streetcar*, Blanche desperately tries, but fails, to reach her white, aristocratic redeemer, Shep Huntleigh. Blanche's tragedy is choreographed with inescapable racial overtones:

> *[She sets the phone down and crosses warily into the kitchen. The night is filled with inhuman voices like cries in a jungle.]*
> *[The shadows are lurid reflections and move sinuously as flames along the wall spaces.]*
> *[Through the back wall of the rooms, which have become transparent, can be seen the sidewalk. A prostitute has rolled a drunkard. He pursues her along the walk, overtakes her and there is a struggle. A policeman's whistle breaks it up. The figures disappear.]*

[Some moments later the Negro Woman appears around the corner with a sequined bag which the prostitute had dropped on the walk. She is rooting excitedly through it.]
[Blanche presses her knuckles to her lips and returns slowly to the phone. She speaks in a hoarse whisper.] [399].

Jungle cries, shadows, transparent walls, the Negro woman taking the harlot's bag — all expressionistically reflect Blanche's psychic torture. To break down the barriers, walls, and other conventions of a naturalistic theatre, Williams mapped the terrain of Blanche's nightmare in psychic language echoing O'Neill's *Emperor Jones*, one of the first American plays to cast an African American in a central role. Ironically enough, though, Blanche's nightmare is projected through the most threatening sights and sounds Williams could score from a city where ostensibly there is a *"warm and easy intermingling of races in the old part of town"* (243).

When Sarah expresses her fears of being raped by her black beast father, Kennedy also projects the action in jungle signifiers, possibly evoking the acoustics and sights of *A Streetcar.*

In the jungle, RED SUN, FLYING THINGS, wild black grass. The effect of the jungle is that it, unlike the other scenes, is over the entire stage.... By lighting the desired effect would be — suddenly the jungle has overgrown the chambers and all the other places with a violence and a dark brightness, a grim yellowness (23–24).

Though director Michael Kahn chose not to stage the "jungle" set in his production of *Funnyhouse*, it is, nonetheless, a central trope in Kennedy as it was in Williams — the bestial overtaking the vulnerable, the encroachment of the wild unconsciousness, the fear inherent in a schizophrenic-like nightmare, Blanche's and Sarah's both. (Incidentally, Williams's greatest fear was being sent to an asylum as his sister Rose was.) But Kennedy's dramaturgy uses Williams's signifiers to focus exclusively on the racial/apocalyptic traumas of *Funnyhouse.*

Other segments of Williams's expressionistic theatre seem to be racially intensified and reconfigured in *Funnyhouse.* Many places in *Funnyhouse* use Williamsesque directions reminiscent of Scenes Nine and Ten of *Streetcar*— blackouts, walls dropping down, etc. Kennedy's stage directions repeatedly notate "blackout" to represent her characters' nightmarish experiences to an audience frighteningly responding to and vicariously fleeing from them. Erin Hurley has ingeniously argued that the blackouts in *Funnyhouse* signal the transformation from non-being to immanence. Kennedy was well aware of the potential of the blackout cinematics in *Streetcar* to signal eminent sexual danger and psychic disintegration. Seeing the *Streetcar* film in 1951, she recalled: "I thought how I had first seen Brando ... the group of us from the dorm at Ohio State. We heard the movie had a rape scene. None of us quite knew where the rape scene was. It was when the light went out, someone finally decided" (Kolin, "Playwrights' Forum" 187). Foregrounding what she may have seen/not seen in Williams, Kennedy frequently blackened her theatre to announce the ominous arrival of the dark rapist from the jungle, the unrelenting terror that haunted Blanche as well as Sarah. But while Williams incorporated such experimental staging at key moments in Blanche's psychic disintegration, he comfortably returned audiences to a predominantly naturalistic space where Stanley, Stella, Eunice, and the poker players never leave their sordid New Orleans environment. *Funnyhouse*, on the other hand, relentlessly invades subconscious states to frighten and alienate.

Given the tremendous impact *Streetcar* had on Kennedy, as she herself attests, it is not surprising that the most influential actor associated with the play, Marlon Brando, would also have shaped her response to Williams's canon. She has attached multiple, and complex, meanings to Brando's performance that segue into her own dramatic strategies in *People* and in a "Playwrights' Forum" in *Streetcar.* As actor and artist, Brando lodged on several levels for

Kennedy. On the most public, conscious level, he symbolized the revolutionary, punitive function of art that Kennedy's own work validates. Honoring him as the ultimate "rebel," she admitted that "the myth of Brando fascinated me. You live in a 'walk-up,' you wear T-shirts, you disdain social events, you criticize society — this picture of the creative person was possibly the most powerful picture I had since I was twelve and saw *A Song to Remember*." Until she watched Brando's performance in *Streetcar*, Kennedy confessed that "rebellion was an abstraction to me" (*People* 78). Equating his creativity with rebellion — "disdain for social events" — Kennedy herself opened a way for Brando's iconoclasm to explode in her work. Her early plays like *Funnyhouse, The Owl Answers*, and *Lesson in Dead Language* rebel against an oppressive white society torturing creative young black women. Moreover, Kennedy's later works feature black male rebels in the spirit, if not costume and swagger, of Brando: Malcolm X in *Sun* (1967), a Vietnam veteran turned sniper in *An Evening with Dead Essex* (1973), and her own son, Adam, protesting racial profiling in *Sleep Deprivation Chamber* (1996). Racializing Brando's mythos as the rebel, each of these Kennedy's heroes protests a hateful white society.

But Kennedy's responses to Brando go deeper, shedding light on her thinking about role playing and its effects on her characters and audiences alike. She revealed that when she looked "at a photograph of an absolutely beautiful young man sitting by a window" in Daniel Blum's *Famous People in the Theatre*, at first she did not recognize Brando "as the man in the rape scene or [as] Emiliano Zapata [from *Viva Zapata*]. Then I realized this beautiful young man sitting by the window was both. And now it was indelible that he was Brando. It had never occurred to me that an actor or movie star would be unrecognizable from his characters. I had always recognized Paul Muni under his disguises" (Kolin, "*Streetcar* Playwrights' Forum" 187). Her shock at not being able to see the actor (Brando, reality) behind the character (the imaginary, the disguise) charts Kennedy's journey from conventional realism to surrealism. Indeterminacy, suggested in her remarks on Brando and his roles in *A Streetcar* or *Viva Zapata* became a defining feature of her characters who would hide within a series of identities, unable to distinguish a black self from their white mask. Her heroines try to escape behind the façade of character itself, a dramatic strategy whose genesis may possibly be associated with Kennedy's not recognizing Brando from his roles as Stanley or Zapata. Welding role to self would prove fatally deceptive in Kennedy's canon, early and late.

Even more provocatively, issues of Brando's identity and image surface directly in one of Kennedy's fictive selves, Clara in *A Movie Star Has to Star in Black and White*. A young, creative black woman, Clara turns her life over to a series of movie stars, Brando among them, to express her traumas and hopes. Mirroring events and sets from three movies, including *Viva Zapata! Clara* becomes a Jean Peters look-alike who talks to a Brando look-alike about her injured brother, her parents, and her failing marriage. Desperate for literary fame and Hollywood attention, both out of reach for a young black woman in the 1940's and 1950's, Clara transfers the ordinary details of her life into the voices of these glamorous, white movie stars. To Brando/Zapata, Peters (Clara) says, "I'm writing my play. It's about a girl who turns into an owl" (72), referring self-reflexively to Kennedy's own *The Owl Answers*. Still playing Clara, Peters "kisses Brando tenderly" (70), and the two of them make up a bed covered with black sheets. Kennedy's not recognizing Brando in and through his roles may explain why and how Clara in *A Movie Star* could blur fantasy and the real world from which she wanted to escape. In Clara's psychic cinema there is no difference between Jean Peters and herself or Brando and the black husband whom she hoped to romanticize into a Hollywood lover through Brando's rescue. Yet in reality, Zapata's or Stanley's Hollywood darkness starkly contrast with the white Brando. Brando's Stanley expresses the folly of role playing that robs Clara of her life: "Some men are took in by this Hollywood glamour stuff and some men are not" (*Streetcar* 279). Kennedy's self-interrogation of Brando's performative genius in *Viva Zapata* or *Streetcar* may well have anticipated, therefore, how she would frame her plays about identity, representation, and race. In seeing the complexity of Brando's real and fictional selves, Kennedy may have seen her own.

Having said all this, it would be grossly misleading and unfair to conclude that Kennedy simply blueprinted Williams's dramaturgy, his characters, and his actors. As I have argued, a much more complex process is at work between this experimental African American woman playwright and the most influential white Broadway dramatist of the 1940's and 1950's. Given her response to Williams in her nonfictional work as well as in her plays, Kennedy was fascinated by the expressionistic representations of self, family, and society in Williams. But, as she developed her unique voice, she renegotiated Williams's scripts and colliding with them, radically resisted and disrupted his characters and symbols. Through a fission-like process she split his canon apart, exploding the psychic traumas and contradictions submerged and/or surfacing in his Broadway hits. Through her textual encounters with Williams's hysterical women artists, Kennedy may have become further empowered to explore the soul-piercing nightmares of her black and hysterical women in a color-coded America. As she recalled Williams's earlier ways of dramatizing the inner conflicts of self, Kennedy entered her own undiscovered country, a world that grew more painful, treacherous, and absurd in the racial and psychic spaces her characters were condemned to inhabit in the 1960s and beyond.

AUTHOR'S NOTES

This article is reprinted with permission from the *South Atlantic Review* 70 (Fall 2005). I am grateful to Una Chaudhuri for reading an earlier draft of this essay and for her insightful responses.

WORKS CITED

Barnes, Clive. "*A Rat's Mass* Weaves Drama of Poetry Fabric." *New York Times*, 1 Nov. 1964: 24.

Betsko, Kathleen and Rachel Koenig, eds. "Adrienne Kennedy." *Interviews with Contemporary American Women Playwrights*. New York: Beech Tree, 1987. 246–58.

Binder, Wolfgang. "A MELUS Interview: Adrienne Kennedy." MELUS: *The Journal of the Society for the Study of the Multi-Ethnic Literature of the United States* 12 (Fall 1985): 99–108.

Bloom, Harold. *The Anxiety of Influence*. New York: Oxford UP, 1997.

Brown, E. Barnesley. "Passed Over: The Tragic Mulatta and the (Dis)integration of Identity in Adrienne Kennedy's Plays." *African American Review* 35 (Summer 2001): 281–96.

Brown, Lorraine, "For the Characters are Myself': Adrienne Kennedy's *Funnyhouse of a Negro*." *Negro American Literature Forum* 9 (Sept 1975): 86–88.

Bryant-Jackson, Paul K. "Kennedy's Travelers in the American and African Continuum." *Intersecting Boundaries: The Theatre of Adrienne Kennedy*. Eds. Paul K. Bryant-Jackson and Lois More Overbeck. Minneapolis: University Press of Minnesota, 1992. 45–57.

Crandell, George C. "Misrepresentation and Miscegenation: Reading the Racialized Discourse of Tennessee Williams's *A Streetcar Named Desire*." *Modern Drama* 40 (1997): 337–46.

Cummings, Scott T. "Theatre: Invisible Career: Adrienne Kennedy." *Boston Phoenix* 31 Mar.–6 Apr. 2000: 7.

Foucault, Michel. *Discipline and Punish*. Trans. Alan Sheridan. New York: Pantheon, 1977.

Hurley, Erin. "Blackout: Utopian Technologies in Adrienne Kennedy's *Funnyhouse of a Negro*." *Modern Drama* 47 (Summer 2004): 200–218.

Jennings, C. Robert. "Interview With Tennessee Williams." *Playboy* Apr. 1973: 69–84.

Kelly, Lionel. "The White Goddess, Ethnicity, and the Politics of Desire." *Confronting Tennessee Williams A Streetcar Named Desire: Essays in Critical Pluralism*. Ed. Philip C. Kolin. Westport: Greenwood, 1993. 121–32.

Kennedy, Adrienne. *The Adrienne Kennedy Reader*. Ed. Werner Sollors. Minneapolis: University of Minnesota Press, 2001.

_____. *Deadly Triplets*. Minneapolis: U of Minnesota P, 1991.

_____. "A Growth of Images." *Drama Review* 21 (Dec. 1977): 41–48.

_____. *People Who Led to My Plays*. New York: Knopf 1987.

_____. "Secret Paragraphs About My Brother." *The Adrienne Kennedy Reader*. Ed. Werner Sollors. Minneapolis: U of Minnesota P, 2001. 234–38.

_____. "Sketches: People I Have Met in The Theatre." *Ishmael Reed & Al Young's Quilts* [Berkeley, CA] 5 (1986): 1–34.

Kolin, Philip C. "Cleopatra of the Nile and Blanche DuBois of the French Quarter: *Anthony and Cleopatra* and *A Streetcar Named Desire*." *Shakespeare Bulletin* 11 (Winter 1993): 25–27.

_____. "*A Streetcar Named Desire*: A Playwrights' Forum." *Michigan Quarterly Review* 29 (Spring 1990): 173–203.

_____. "Williams in Ebony: Black and Multi-Cultural Productions of Williams *A Streetcar Named Desire*." *Black American Literature Forum* 25 (Spring 1991): 147–81.

_____. *Williams: A Streetcar Named Desire*. Plays in Production. Cambridge: Cambridge University Press, 2000.

Leff, Leonard. "And Transfer to Commentaries: The Streetcars Named Desire." *Film Quarterly* 55.3 (Spring 2002): 29–37.

Miller, Arthur. "Introduction." *A Streetcar Named Desire*, New York: New Directions, 2004.

O'Connor, Jacqueline. *Dramatizing Dementia: Madness in the Play of Tennessee Williams*. Bowling Green, OH: Bowling Green University Popular Press, 1997.

Parks, Suzan-Lori. "Adrienne Kennedy," *Bomb*. 5 (Winter 1996): 44–45.

Phillips, Gene, S.J. "Film Adaptations." *The Tennessee Williams Encyclopedia*. Ed. Philip C. Kolin. Westport: Greenwood, 2004.

Richardson, Thomas J. "The City of Day and the City of Night: New Orleans and the Exotic Unreality of Tennessee Williams." *Tennessee Williams: A Tribute*. Ed. Jac Tharpe. Jackson: University Press of Mississippi, 1977.

Robinson, Marc. *The Other American Drama*. Cambridge: Cambridge University Press, 1994.

Schlueter, June. "'We've had this date with each other from the beginning': Reading Toward Closure in *A Streetcar Named Desire*." *Confronting Tennessee Williams's* A Streetcar Named Desire: *Essays in Critical Pluralism*. Ed. Philip C. Kolin. Westport: Greenwood, 1993. 71–82.

Sichert, Margit. "The Staging of Excessive Emotions: Adrienne Kennedy's *Funnyhouse of a Negro*." *The Yearbook of Research in English and American Literature* 16 (2000): 229–51.

Tennessee Williams: Orpheus of the American Stage. American Masters. Alexandria, VA: PBS, 1994.

van Duyvenbode, Rachel. "Darkness Made Visible: Miscegenation, Masquerade, and the Signified Racial Other in Tennessee Williams's *Baby Doll* and *A Streetcar Named Desire*." *Journal of American Studies* 35 (2001): 203–215.

Wheeler, Susan. "The Debtor in the Convex Mirror." *Ledger*. Iowa City: University of Iowa Press, 2005.

Wilkerson, Margaret. "Diverse Angles of Vision: Two Black Women Playwrights." *Intersecting Boundaries: The Theatre of Adrienne Kennedy*. Minneapolis: University of Minnesota Press, 1994.

Williams, Tennessee. *Camino Real. Theatre of Tennessee Williams*. 2. New York: New Directions, 1971.

_____. "The Catastrophe of Success." *Glass Menagerie. The Theatre of Tennessee Williams*. 1. New York: New Directions, 1977.

_____. *Glass Menagerie. The Theatre of Tennessee Williams*. 1. New York: New Directions, 1971.

_____. "Production Notes." *Glass Menagerie*. New York, New Directions, 1971.

_____. *Memoirs*. New York: 1975.

_____. *A Streetcar Named Desire*. 1. New York: New Directions, 1971.

_____. *Summer and Smoke. The Theatre of Tennessee Williams*. 2. New York: New Directions, 1971.

Warriors Against the Kitchen Sink: Tennessee Williams and John Guare

Thomas Mitchell

John Guare declared war against the kitchen sink in the preface to his collected plays published in 1996. This manifesto articulated an approach to making plays that went beyond ordinary naturalism, into a world of fantastic possibilities. He called for a theatre that created more than surface reality, and more than "a real room with real water running into the kitchen sink" (ix). In the preface to *The Glass Menagerie*, Tennessee Williams similarly declared war against "the straight realistic play with its genuine Frigidaire and authentic ice cubes..." (xix). In Williams's view, as in Guare's, it is not enough to represent surface-level reality. Recall Blanche DuBois's preference, "I don't want realism. I want magic!" (*Streetcar*, 145). Neither playwright was satisfied with the theatre's ability to replicate the life-like qualities of a setting, the narrative presentation of action, or naturalistic behavior of characters. Williams and Guare both created extreme characters with large appetites and heavy emotional baggage. They used intentionally contrived plot elements to provoke major revelations and reversals. They both employed direct address and other heightened theatrical moments. Guare's "Kitchen Sink" essay describes his frustration with plays that fell short of the extra-realistic ideal, referencing the works of William Inge and John Osborne. In terms of acting, Guare rejected Lee Strasberg's method actors in favor of stage clowns like Judy Holliday, Zero Mostel, and Bert Lahr (Guare, *Volume 1*, x).

In his restlessness with naturalism and his fascination with theatrical possibilities, Guare exhibits the influence of Tennessee Williams, whose characters and situations regularly transcended the ordinary. Williams's characters are sometimes described as "southern gothics" who are extreme in their appetites, peculiar in their personal histories, and bold in their declarations. In a 1981 *Paris Review* interview, commenting on this southern gothic humor, Williams says "I make some serious, even tragic observations about society, but I make them through the medium of comedy" (179). Williams also ardently pursued the kind of theatre that broke the rules of structure and strayed from expected paths in style and tone. Even in his earliest plays like *Candles to the Sun* and *Not About Nightingales*, he rejected standard play structure for an episodic, film-like approach. In *Stairs to the Roof*, he embraced fantasy and science fiction. He called for the penultimate scene in *Fugitive Kind* to "veer sharply upward in its progression from the realistic to the lyrical plane" (124). He used blackout techniques, projected scene titles, and selective use of realistic details. He championed the "plastic theatre which must take the place of the exhausted theatre of realistic conventions..." (*Glass Menagerie*, xix). His "plastic theatre" included dance, music, pantomime, as well as innovative

95

stagecraft, and aimed to create a poetic truth. The productions of his major works *The Glass Menagerie, A Streetcar Named Desire, Cat on a Hot Tin Roof,* and *Night of the Iguana* were notable for using highly expressive scenic design, lighting, and musical scores, and they consistently used the extremely lyrical language of a dramatic poet. *Camino Real* in 1953 challenged audiences in form, content, and style. His late plays combined absurd situations, grotesque actions, and serious themes to create black comedies. By challenging traditional structure, using lyricism, fantasy, black comedy and gothic characters Williams was a model for the younger playwright, John Guare.

Born in 1938, John Guare, a native New Yorker, had access to Broadway, and didn't have to settle for movies, touring productions, and amateur theatres to see the latest and greatest plays as Williams had done in his St. Louis youth. Guare's family tree included vaudeville performers and talent scouts, and since his father was a clerk on Wall Street, the family's circumstances allowed John to attend the theatre regularly. As the only child of older parents, he didn't have to compete with siblings, but was the singular object of attention for his father, mother, and their circle of friends. He was educated in Catholic institutions, from elementary school through his bachelor's degree at Georgetown. Except for a brief period in upstate New York, Guare grew up in the urban environs of New York and later, Washington, DC. He came from a household that supported his writing as exemplified by the summer of 1949 when he and a pal wrote and produced plays in the family garage. The eleven-year-olds enticed photographers for *Life* magazine to cover their story by telling them that they were giving their profits to orphans. Guare's supportive parents rewarded his industry with a portable typewriter that he used for years (Cattaneo 75–76). This family anecdote contrasts with Williams's childhood stories of being called "Miss Nancy" by his father and being kicked by other students at school. While Guare's childhood story reveals the comic antics of two boys with ambition, Williams's childhood stories relate a tortured life in St. Louis with only vague hope of escape. These two perspectives exemplify the contrasting tones found in the works of the two writers: Guare's comic irony and Williams's tragic resignation.

Williams grew up part of the post World War I generation in which America had lost its innocence and the world community faced the horror that nations could combine to destroy half the planet. A child of the post World War II boom, Guare grew up in the post-nuclear cold-war age after the atom bomb had proven that man could not only destroy the world, but could do it easily. Williams entered college just as the Great Depression plunged the nation into chaos, and though his family lived in relative comfort, he was surrounded by others who struggled for economic justice. In those same years, international conflicts were roiling in Europe and Asia, and another world war was on the horizon. Guare's 1960s were as highly politicized as the 1930s had been for Williams. As a graduate student Guare faced the impending threat of the war in Viet Nam, and he was drafted after graduation. His career reflects his generation's bleakly absurd awareness that nuclear annihilation was imminent. Out of this absurdist perspective he observed that people of his generation who work in the theatre started out either because they saw *Annie Get Your Gun* or because they read Antonin Artaud (Cattaneo 72). It's not surprising that Guare's works balance in the place between these two. His plays employ a bit of "The Theatre of Cruelty" while celebrating that "There's No Business Like Show Business."

Also, Tennessee Williams and John Guare both had prolific careers. Although *The House of Blue Leaves* was John Guare's first major success in 1971, he had been amassing a significant number of short plays in Off Broadway venues. *The Loveliest Afternoon of the Year, A Day for Surprises,* and *Something I'll Tell You Tuesday* were presented in New York's Café Cino in 1966 and 1967, where Williams also had short plays produced. *Muzeeka* and *Cop-Out* were presented at the Eugene O'Neill Theatre Conference in 1967 and 1968. In 1969, *Cop-Out* and *Home Fires* played briefly on Broadway. Both writers' early plays had a political edge and were produced in small venues for audiences of true believers. Young Tennessee Williams was the beneficiary of several writing contests that provided him with financial support, education, and connections. Similarly, John Guare's career was bolstered by prizes and institutional opportunities. He won second prize in the 1960 Donn B. Murphy playwriting contest at Georgetown, and his plays were presented there. He studied in John Gassner's MFA Playwriting Program at Yale (Curry 7). Williams also studied with Gassner, but at the New School for Social Research in 1940. Guare's plays were supported by the Albee-Barr-Wilder Playwrights Unit and he was invited to take part in the first National Playwright's Conference at the Eugene O'Neill Theatre Center. Williams had his early work supported by a Rockefeller Grant, by the Group Theatre, and the Theatre Guild who produced *Battle of Angels*. In the 21st century climate of institutional cut-backs and precarious support of arts organizations, it is worth noting that both of these playwrights emerged from their roles as young firebrands into full-fledged professional playwrights with important institutional support. Like Tennessee Williams twenty-five years earlier, because of the awards and institutional backing, Guare was signed as a client by agent Audrey Wood. This super-agent for 20th century playwrights guided both playwrights in the development of their careers.

The House of Blue Leaves had a long Off Broadway run and won the New York Drama Critics Circle Award as had *The Glass Menagerie* in 1944. Guare followed the success of *The House of Blue Leaves* with an award-winning musical adaptation of Shakespeare's *Two Gentlemen of Verona*. Similarly, after his success with *The Glass Menagerie*, Williams hoped to make his fantasy, *Stairs to the Roof*, into a musical. Though it didn't materialize in that form, the play has some of the qualities of musical theatre: large spectacular "chorus" scenes, romantic "duets," and lyrical solo speeches. Williams's interest in a popular success with a musical theatre production parallels Guare's success with *Two Gentlemen of Verona* and later with his libretto for *The Sweet Smell of Success*. The desire for success in this quintessential American idiom emphasizes the show business savvy that both playwrights possessed, and though Williams never authored a Broadway musical, he went on to author major Broadway "hits." Though not as widely successful as Williams, Guare followed his early career success with four more major full-length plays, *Marco Polo Sings a Solo*, *Rich and Famous*, *Landscape of the Body*, and *Bosoms and Neglect* from 1973 to 1979. Each of these was filled with extreme characters, absurdist theatrical devices, and wonderfully contrived situations that challenged kitchen-sink realism. In 1982, Guare produced *Lydie Breeze* and *Gardenia*, the first parts of a multiple play cycle. Eventually, three plays about a charismatic 19th century native of Nantucket, Lydie Breeze, were written and re-worked during the 1980's. *Six Degrees of Separation* was produced in 1990 at Lincoln Center and won the New York Drama Critics Circle Award, the Obie, and was turned into a successful film in 1993. Williams's output was similar, turning out his major works during a twenty-year period. Both playwrights continued to experiment with form and content throughout their mature careers. Though Williams had begun writing in the late 1930s, for a period in the mid–1960s until his death in 1983, Williams and Guare were peers and competitors, sometimes producing for the same theatres or vying for the same audiences.

The two playwrights shared a sly wit aimed at exposing the banality of the American middle-class and questioning assumptions about the nuclear family. They each crafted compelling female characters that combined strength and sensuality. Each playwright examined the role of the social outsider, and the ways in which outsiders are crushed by powers that be. In each playwright, we can imagine a gleeful cackle in response to life's ironic absurdities. The major differences between the two is in their tone and point-of-view. The plays of Williams tend to be tragic with a morose comic edge. Guare's plays tend to be absurdly comic with a bitter, serious undertone. Williams's characters are often desperate to escape from torturous aspects of life, while Guare's characters desperately pursue unrealistic dreams or try to unravel confounding mysteries. Whereas Williams often captures the tragic irony of a situation, Guare revels in twisted comic ironies. Interestingly, Guare admired the title of Williams's production that played Off Broadway — *Slapstick Tragedy* (Guare, *Volume 1*, x). He recognized in the title a description of many of his own plays. Guare's interviews often cite stories from his early years that reveal a tone of self-deprecating comic irony. For example, he relates a desperate childhood audition for his Uncle Bill Grady, an MGM casting director, who was searching for an unknown child actor to play the role of Huckleberry Finn. Determined that he would be perfect for the role, the young John Guare packed his bags even before he auditioned. A frenzied performance left the uncle dumbstruck and he quickly hit the road, leaving Guare's mother in tears. The hopeful Huck Finn–wannabe gave up his dreams of stardom at eight years old (Cattaneo 75). The tone of this anecdote is not of tragic defeat, but of the absurd awkwardness experienced by the professional casting director facing his nephew's self-assured audition. The same story is slightly reworked into a major scene in *The House of Blue Leaves*. In an interview for the *Lincoln Center Theatre Bulletin*, Guare also describes the circumstances that led him to write that play. After serving in the Air Force, Guare traveled in Europe and the Middle East in order to find the inspiration to write. When he got to Rome in 1965, what did he see but a picture of his own neighborhood, Queens Boulevard, New York. The Pope had come to New York! In a comic discovery, he realized, "He's there and I'm here!" His recognition of the absurd irony of being in the wrong place at the wrong time and missing a life-changing event of global importance reflects Guare's general comic appreciation of life.

With the similarities and differences between these two playwrights in mind, there are parallels that reveal the influence of the older writer's works on the younger. Both playwrights had success with domestic stories that transmuted major elements of their own life experience. *The Glass Menagerie* and *The House of Blue Leaves* both draw significantly from their authors' life experiences, and both offer a wry commentary on the American nuclear family. Considering *The House of Blue Leaves* in the shadow of *The Glass Menagerie* illuminates Guare's play and anchors it in its historical place. In his play *Lydie Breeze*, and the several plays that make up the *Lydie Breeze* cycle, Guare created a character comparable to Blanche DuBois in *A Streetcar Named Desire*. The *Lydie Breeze* plays evidence Williams's influence on Guare in the latter's creation of this sexual, wise, and vulnerable woman. Finally, Guare's later play, *Six Degrees of Separation*, is a mature examination of contemporary New York life disrupted by a charismatic outsider. This outsider character was a hallmark of many of Tennessee Williams's plays such as *Orpheus Descending*. *Six Degrees* thus owes a debt to *Orpheus*, and both plays depict a view of the artist/outsider in a society that is both threatened and threatening.

The Glass Menagerie made Williams's career just as *The House of Blue Leaves* made Guare's. They both tell domestic stories that derive in large measure from the author's personal lives and family experience. Judging by the setting and the plot elements, Guare seems to have been directly influenced by *The Glass Menagerie*. It is easy to imagine that Guare's play was written as a meditation on the masterwork Tennessee Williams created a generation before. It is hard to ignore the fact that the shabby apartment of *House of Blue Leaves* bears a resemblance to the Wingfield apartment of *The Glass Menagerie*. The set description from *Blue Leaves* calls for a living room in a rundown Queens apartment filled with pictures of movie stars and jungle animals. A big bay window is upstage with security bars protecting the inhabitants inside from outside predators, or preventing the inhabitants from an easy escape into the freedom without. Outside the barred window is a fire escape. There is a piano with lots and lots of sheet music and beer bottles. Artie Shaughnessy's uniform shirt and pants are draped over a chair, and Artie is asleep on the couch, zipped into a sleeping bag (*Three Exposures* 16). While *Blue Leaves* features movie stars and jungle animals, *The Glass Menagerie* has "scores of transparent glass animals" and a portrait of the absent father, "ineluctably smiling" (4). The theatrical Wingfield apartment faces an alley and is entered by a fire escape, and though Williams calls for the dark tenement walls and fire-escapes to fade away as lights come up on the interior, they seem omni-present. Guare's fire escape is also always present outside the bay window with its metalwork construction copied in the criss-cross folding gate that bars the window. *The House of Blue Leaves* has the keyboard of a piano and pages of sheet music, while in *Menagerie*, it is a typewriter keyboard and shorthand diagram. The sofa in the St. Louis home becomes Tom's bed, just as in the apartment in Queens, Artie Shaughnessy sleeps on the sofa.

Both plays critique the idealized American dream home. The Williams St. Louis household is not that of the heart-warming *Meet Me in St. Louis,* the 1944 MGM musical that bustles with family holidays and neighborly romance. The Wingfield house is headed by a single mother who is both nagging witch and suffering saint abandoned by a husband who was good for little more than his charming smile. She is possessed by the American dream of an ideal husband for her daughter — the gentleman caller, an "emissary from a world of reality that we were somehow set apart from" (5). When he finally arrives, he bursts the illusion of a sentimentalized happy ending by announcing his engagement to another girl. The Shaughnessy household in *Blue Leaves* is headed by father and husband, Artie Shaughnessy, a zookeeper and shlocky songwriter. For all practical purposes, Artie is a single parent, looking after his wife, Bananas, who emotionally fragile and over-medicated, wanders randomly in and out of the household. Artie's girlfriend, Bunny, is as sexually expressive as Amanda Wingfield is repressed, but Artie has not been able to bring himself to divorce Bananas and make a final commitment to Bunny. On top of his marital dilemma, Artie's son, Ronnie, a cipher in army fatigues, has been called up for service in Viet Nam, but has gone AWOL.

Instead of a gentleman caller, the Shaughnessy household awaits two guests who hold keys for their future happiness. According to Artie, his friend Billy Einhorn is Hollywood's leading director and will use Artie's songs in the movies. In Artie's dreams it will only be a matter of time before he receives an Oscar as a cinematic songsmith. Artie and Bunny have as much invested in the Billy's visit as Amanda Wingfield invested in the visit of Jim O'Connor, Laura's Gentleman Caller. In the exaggerated and contrived nature of Guare's anti–kitchen sink theatre there is a second gentleman caller who happens to be visiting New York at the same time as Billy Einhorn. The second gentleman caller in *House of Blue Leaves* is no less than the Pope himself! Bunny, encouraging Billy, dreams that when the Pope passes by, she'll call out:

> "Your Holiness, marry us — the hell with peace to the world — bring peace to us." And he won't hear me because bands will be playing and the whole city yelling, but he'll see me because I been eyed by the best of them, and he'll nod and I'll grab your hand and say, "Marry us, Pope," and he'll wave his holy hand and all the emeralds and rubies on his fingers will send Yes beams [*Three Exposures* 21].

Artie and Bunny's dream of marriage in *The House of Blue Leaves* is similar to Amanda's dream in *The Glass Menagerie.* By 1971 family roles had changed, and marriage in Guare's play is for dad and his girlfriend. The nuclear family dream exploded with the atomic bomb. Artie and Bunny dream of a life of sensual pleasure and financial success, not the virtuous

American dream of domestic harmony, picket fences, and 2.4 children. Parenting is seen as a burden in both plays. Amanda suffers the torment of supervising the fragile Laura. Artie prays that Ronnie won't be sent to Viet Nam or get arrested for being AWOL. Reflecting an age of assassins, Guare takes a dark view of Ronnie's emotional fragility. Whereas Laura's fragile psyche dooms her to a lifetime imprisoned with her glass menagerie, Guare recognizes that the isolated loner may just as easily try to blow up the pope. Ronnie, is just such a loner. So while both playwrights deal with similar parental worries, Guare adjusts them to fit his "slapstick tragedy" view of life in a violent age.

Guare borrows Williams's stylistic choice for direct address to the audience. As in *The Glass Menagerie*, despite the play's "kitchen sink" realism, the playwright uses the meta-theatrical device of characters speaking directly to the audience. The audience becomes complicit with the character. In *The Glass Menagerie*, Tom describes his memory, and the audience sees the world not objectively, but by candlelight. In *The House of Blue Leaves*, Artie Shaughnessy is the host, but soon this role shifts. Bananas and Ronnie and Bunny and the Little Nun all speak directly to the audience. The truth becomes splintered. Guare consciously uses the device of direct address to take the audience into a world in which truth is subjective and morality is conditional. If one character is right, can the other be right? How can she be right when she doesn't even know what he's up to? The audience is arbiter of truth in a world of entertainment, where each character "performs." The ending of the play offers the darkest twist in this twisted world when Artie strangles the hapless Bananas in a spotlight singing "with bells on, Ringing out how I feel" (*Three Exposures* 87).

Beyond its homage to *The Glass Menagerie* in form and themes, the slapstick climactic scene of *House of Blue Leaves* also calls to mind a scene from *A Streetcar Named Desire*. M.P.s and nuns and starlets converge on the Shaughnessy apartment while men in white coats announce that they've come to pick up "Mrs. Arthur M. Shaughnessy." The scene with white-coated orderlies offering "the kindness of strangers" resembles the removal of Blanche in *Streetcar*. In Guare's play, however, they narrowly avoid taking Bunny instead of Bananas, and at the last moment Ronnie's bomb explodes, forever changing everyone's destiny.

The influence of *Streetcar* is not only evident in this climactic scene of *The House of Blue Leaves*, but it is also apparent in Guare's multi-play cycle *Lydie Breeze*. Just as Tennessee Williams struggled for more than a decade, converting *Battle of Angels* into *Orpheus Descending*, or shaping *Glass Menagerie* from short stories like *Portrait of a Girl in Glass*, or developing *Streetcar* out of "Blanche's Chair in the Moon" (Rader 152) for about 18 years, John Guare worked and re-worked a multi-play series based on a charismatic female character named Lydie Breeze. She is the center of a love triangle, the inspiration of a utopian community on Nantucket, and the mother of a haunted daughter who carries the same name. Identifying the difference between *Lydie Breeze* and Guare's earlier plays, Christopher Bigsby describes it as "a tone poem in which individual lives render up their meaning." He appreciates the relative stillness of *Lydie Breeze* in contrast with the zany action of *Blue Leaves* (20). This major work in Guare's formidable canon exhibits the influence of Tennessee Williams's masterpiece, *A Streetcar Named Desire*.

Williams's influence on Guare can be aptly explained in a story from the playwright's youth. Guare describes how his family moved to upstate New York and he became a writer. He had read a story in *Life* magazine about Josh Logan's play, *The Wisteria Trees* that was a re-setting of *The Cherry Orchard* into the American South. He also saw the dramatic Southern heroines performed by Kim Stanley and Geraldine Page on the black & white television showcases of the day. Together these impressions led him to Chekhov, where he discovered *Three Sisters*. This sparked the idea that he would imitate Josh Logan's creative interpretation.

He would re-interpret *Three Sisters*, give the sisters southern accents and a longing to return to New Orleans. "Every time the girls cried out for Moscow, I substituted New Orleans. Yes! That was theater! 'Get me to New Orleans!'" (Guare, *Volume 1*, vi). No theatre-goer from the period could have escaped the power of Tennessee Williams's southern dramas, and Guare was no exception. If Guare was going to create a New Orleans *Three Sisters*, he couldn't avoid comparisons to Blanche and Stella in *Streetcar*. At the time he was making this first dramatic attempt, Williams's compelling characters in *Glass Menagerie*, *Summer and Smoke*, and *Streetcar Named Desire* (along with Scarlett O'Hara) had established the faded southern belle as an identifiable character type on the American stage and screen. Young John Guare abandoned his adaptation of the Chekhov play, but his fascination with the passionate, sensual, complex woman re-emerged in *Lydie Breeze*. He re-located his female character out of the Deep South to Nantucket Island, but she possesses the same qualities that drew him to the roles he had seen performed by Kim Stanley and Geraldine Page.

The genesis of *Lydie Breeze* was in Guare's family history, just as *Streetcar* was sparked in part by an incident in Williams's early life. "Poker Night," an early form of *Streetcar*, grew out of his youthful experience when father, Cornelius, came home from late night card games. In one notorious anecdote, Cornelius had part of his ear bitten off by a rival poker player. Guare's own story comes from around 1950. His father, Eddie Guare, had bought into a "clubhouse" on the south shore of Long Island for veterans from the Great War who used it for their own "poker nights." Young John Guare had a privileged spot observing the antics of the adults around him. His father's good friend, Danny, was boisterous and charismatic, but one fateful day Danny grabbed young John and accused him of stealing his bottle of ginger ale out of the ice box. The adult grabbed the bottle away, cutting the boy's lip. John ran to his father, who was playing horseshoes on the beach, and Guare's father dropped the horseshoes and confronted his friend. "Your kid's a liar," Danny accused. Eddie punched the other man so hard that blood spurted out of his nose and mouth. A potentially fatal fight ensued. Both men lived, though they never spoke again. Life had changed and this event became a central plot element in *Lydie Breeze* (*Lydie Breeze 2001*, 8).

A Streetcar Named Desire, was produced on Broadway in 1947 and the unforgettable film with Marlon Brando and Vivien Leigh came out in 1951. It was in those same formative years John Guare became a writer, adapting Chekhov to New Orleans. In those years he saw his father's fistfight and the wreck of the utopian Long Island clubhouse. Out of this convergence of events, Guare created the *Lydie Breeze* saga that comments on the American moment in the same way that Williams's *Streetcar* commented on the American moment at the end of World War II. As early as 1939, Williams imagined a saga on American themes, something like Guare's. He wrote to Audrey Wood about a play he was conceiving, to be called "The Aristocrats," that would complement *Spring Storm*, and *Battle of Angels*. He also had in mind a projected novel, *The Americans*, using the same central character named Irene. According to Albert Devlin's notes, "The gifted young woman artist" intended for "The Aristocrats" first appears as Irene in a story entitled "Memory of an Aristocrat." She is one of "the aristocracy of passionate souls" who may fail in their art but retain their integrity" (Devlin and Tischler 220). Her story of mental illness echoes his sister Rose's experience, and foreshadows Blanche DuBois from *Streetcar*.

Clearly, the most obvious parallel between *Streetcar* and *Lydie Breeze* is the hypnotic, central female character. Blanche and Lydie are both mesmerizing women who, though not perfect or strong, demand attention. Both characters come from "important" families. Lydie's father was a ship's captain and his home an important place on the Nantucket shore. Blanche is the inheritor of Belle Reve, a quintessential southern plantation gone to ruin. Both women are psychologically volatile; they respond to impulses without much social filter or control. Most importantly, both characters are depicted as sexual predators. Whereas Blanche puts up a front of sexual propriety, she is clearly sensually hungry. Lydie puts up no pretense, but is open in her sexuality. Both characters are bathers, luxuriating in the sensual pleasure of their bodies in water. Lydie swims out to sea, and Blanche indulgently bathes in Stanley's bathroom. The predatory Lydie was christened "The Cannibal Princess" upon her birth at the earth's equator. Likewise, Blanche, confessing to her suitor Mitch, refers to herself as a spider at "The Tarantula Arms," a hotel where she brought her victims. Both plays deal with the results of what happens when a mesmerizing, predatory woman enters the male world of "poker night" and tries to change reality to "magic" or "utopia." It is interesting that Guare describes how a charismatic actress, Elizabeth Marvel, brought *Lydie Breeze* to the stage in 2000, after playing the role of Blanche DuBois at the New York Theatre Workshop the previous season. Her performance as Williams's heroine convinced Guare that she would be the ideal Lydie Breeze (*Lydie Breeze 2001*, 12).

Thematically, *Streetcar Named Desire* examines the twentieth-century South and how it had fallen from its once assumed glory. Instead of a lily-white monoculture in which all was well on the plantation, the 20th century dragged the South into a complex time where races and cultures mixed, where the pretenses of sexual propriety gave way to an awareness of animal instinct, and where illusions were stripped away and replaced by vulgar reality. Those who tried to hold on to the old ways were sacrificed. Blanche who desperately tries to hold onto the illusion of gentility is removed from the household and the crude, masculine, multi-ethnic card game resumes with the curtain line: "This game is seven card stud" (179). *Lydie Breeze* also looks back at a time in American culture: the idealistic years after the Civil War, and by inference the idealism of the 1960s. It examines the times when instincts for battle, greed and empire were set aside to rebuild a place built on equality, education, and love. The Nantucket utopia falls apart and decays very much like Belle Reve. Too many human shortcomings mark its demise: male rivalry, lust for money, infidelity, and deceit. At the end of Guare's play, however, there is a ray of hope. Joshua Hickman, the Civil War veteran, who served a jail term for the impulsive murder of his friend and rival, Dan Grady, sits with his daughter, Lydie, and teaches her to read from the idealistic poetry of Walt Whitman on the verge of a new century. Whereas *Streetcar* reflects the playwright's generation and mourns the loss of idealism and the triumph of brutality, *Lydie Breeze* reflects the later playwright's generation and celebrates the idealistic impulses that once enlivened it. Guare holds out hope that this idealism may be revived in future generations.

Very different from the manic comedy of *The House of Blue Leaves* or the elegiac and historical *Lydie Breeze* plays, *Six Degrees of Separation* reveals the artistically astute, socially liberal world that John Guare actually inhabited in the end of the 20th Century. His most popular and commercially successful play and popular film, *Six Degrees* is a sophisticated, witty piece set in contemporary Manhattan. This mature work doesn't display the same urgent emotional need expressed in *The House of Blue Leaves* or *Lydie Breeze*. As a mature play, the impact of Williams is more intellectual than the other plays in which the DNA of Williams seems to be threaded throughout. *Six Degrees of Separation* deals with a charismatic outsider who insinuates himself into the comfortable lives of the white ruling class. The outsider, Paul, is an artist of deception, and the play considers how his artistry is crushed when it begins to threaten the status quo. Tennessee Williams's plays often deal with outsider characters, but never as well as in *Orpheus Descending*. In that play, Val Xavier, the artist-outsider threatens the established, white ruling class with his very presence. In Williams's play, as in *Six Degrees of Separation*, the disruption provided by the outsider leads to his destruction.

Six Degrees of Separation is a fine example of Guare's war against the kitchen sink. The world of the play is that of upscale Manhattan: art galleries, restaurants, good colleges, and dinner parties. A two-sided painting by Kandinsky hangs over the set, rotating to reveal its alternate identities. The play is structured episodically, with brief scenes shifting immediately into subsequent scenes. The actors change costume pieces *a vista*, sometimes handed a jacket or bathrobe by other characters that observe from seats adjacent to the stage. The pretense of the kitchen sink is ripped away, and the audience acknowledges this as a contemporary morality play performed on a neutral stage. No more kitchen sink! Art dealer Flan Kittredge and his wife Ouisa are confronted by a young, black man, Paul, who shows up at the apartment, apologizing for seeking sanctuary there after a mugging. He is, he claims, among their son's circle of friends at Harvard. And he claims to be the son of Sidney Poitier. Paul is charismatic, engages easily in witty conversation, dresses well, cooks, and makes them laugh. His presence offers comfort and excitement. Ouisa, in particular, grows close to Paul. After welcoming him into their home, adopting him as a surrogate son, and even clothing him in their son's clothes, Paul betrays their trust, and he is thrown back out on the street. Ouisa makes one final unsuccessful attempt to redeem Paul, but in the end it seems that he has taken his own life.

Val Xavier of *Orpheus Descending* is a soulful musician who finds himself descended into the hell of a southern dry goods store. Like Ouisa Kittredge in *Six Degrees*, Lady Torrance in *Orpheus Descending*, is attracted to the outsider, Val. Like Paul in *Six Degrees*, Val possesses a surprising level of wisdom and charisma for his circumstances. He comes from New Orleans where he was entertainer and stud, though like Paul, he has a sexually ambiguous poetic sensitivity. Likewise, his snakeskin jacket and fondness for the blues, create a racial ambiguity. Though he is white, he is very "black" in his taste and behavior. Like Paul, Val communicates both worldliness and vulnerability. In some ways akin to Blanche DuBois and Lydie Breeze, Val and Paul are both innocents in new surroundings, but also predators looking for their next conquest. In *Orpheus Descending* as in *Six Degrees of Separation*, the threat of the outsider cannot be tolerated. Though each of these itinerant studs seduce the lady of the house, they can't stay. There can be no happy ending. Paul disappears, but likely dies a violent death. Val dies with Lady, murdered by her jealous husband.

As intellectual and cool in tone as *Six Degrees of Separation* is, Tennessee Williams's *Orpheus Descending* is emotionally hot. In its earlier form as *Battle of Angels* it was the author's first professional dramatic statement. It followed the politically bold early works: *Candles to the Sun*, *Fugitive Kind*, and *Not About Nightingales*, and the sexually bold student work, *Spring Storm*. The difference in tone and emotional "heat" is an excellent indication of the fundamental difference between young Tennessee Williams and mature John Guare. Out of his personal desperation and florid southern influences, Tennessee Williams poured emotionality into his characters. Out of his relative sense of comfort and ironic sense of humor, John Guare shaped plays with the objective eye of a removed observer. Guare recounts an anecdote from his freshman year in college at Georgetown. *Orpheus Descending* had just opened in Washington, and he went to the first performance. When a latecomer fell down the balcony stairs during the first act, Guare yelled out, "It's Orpheus descending!" and everybody laughed. His mocking comment places him on the outside of Williams's emotionally desperate world. "Oh, if only I could be European or Southern" he reflects, "and not be cursed with the nothingness of my surroundings!" (Cattaneo 80). He seems to acknowledge that his circumstances had shaped him into a much cooler and emotionally reserved writer than Williams.

Guare's *House of Blue Leaves, Lydie Breeze, and Six Degrees of Separation* nonetheless reflect the influence of *The Glass Menagerie, A Streetcar Named Desire*, and *Orpheus Descending*. Williams's plays, especially through the period from 1945 to 1960, left a huge impression on the American theatre. Commercial successes and the fuel for controversy, Williams's plays could not be ignored so it is not surprising that Guare's plays, written in the wake of Williams's masterworks, show their influence. He acknowledges the influence of Williams in interviews and essays on his career. Ironically, as Guare began his Off Broadway career with peculiar, absurdist one-act plays at the Café Cino, Williams was trying to assert his relevance with peculiar, absurdist plays at the same venue (*Slapstick Tragedy: The Mutilated* and *The Gnädiges Fräulein*). Williams's two short plays were extremely bizarre. Linda Dorff referred to them as "outrageous" and "bawdy, over-the-top farces that ... parody the state of contemporary theatre." Dorff observed that the outrageous qualities of the plays "are too often interpreted as uncontrolled, autobiographical excesses on Williams's part," but she viewed these outrageous works as expressing a justified, violent critique of the theatre that Williams considered corrupt (13). Guare cites Williams's absurd (or outrageous) plays as exemplars of his alternative to the kitchen sink. "He showed one way to that part of our brain or our souls," Guare says, "the part of theater that's vaudeville" (Guare Volume 1, x). Williams's final production, *A House Not Meant to Stand* combined elements of his own autobiographical memory play, *The Glass Menagerie*, with a new sense of "slapstick tragedy." *House Not Meant to Stand*, in fact, might have existed down the block from Guare's *House of Blue Leaves*. Both plays possessed tragic truths and absurd, broad comic surprises.

In an interview in the *Paris Review*, John Guare was asked about the playwright's purpose. He answered, "I think it's to break the domination of naturalism and get the theater back to being a place of poetry, a place where language can reign" (Cattaneo 102). In 1943, Williams described the "new" theatre he imagined that would dispense with "the myriad little nervous business of realistic drama." He went on to call for an emotionally passionate and lyrically articulate theatre very similar to that which Guare promoted. "The War Against the Kitchen Sink" essay concludes with an observation that the way in which contemporary playwrights deal with the naturalistic form will tell the story of twentieth and twenty-first century theatre. Whether playwrights continue to create kitchen sink realism that placates audiences with comfortably recognizable surface reality, or instead dismantles the kitchen sink to take audiences into a realm of the imagination and psyche will be the measure of what the theatre is becoming. Like Williams, Guare wonders how playwrights might restore theatre to its true nature as "a place of poetry, song, joy, a place of darkness where the bright truth is told" and he asserts that the "war against the kitchen sink is ultimately the history of our theatre" (Guare v. 1, xii). As Linda Dorff observed, the current generation is "longing for something that is based not just on materialism, not just on a kitchen-sink sort of realism ––they're looking for something spiritual, for some sort of poetry to lift them up and out into a new vision, a new imagination of the future" (25). Williams, in her estimation, tried to fill that desire. Guare seems to have been inspired by the passion of his predecessor and his plays show the influence of his predecessor's work — in subject matter, theme, style, and character there are elements of Tennessee Williams. By considering these two playwrights as comrade warriors, we can appreciate their contributions more completely.

AUTHOR'S NOTE

I am indebted to Allean Hale and Philip Kolin for their insights, opinions, and resources.

WORKS CITED

Bigsby, Christopher. *Contemporary American Playwrights*. Cambridge: Cambridge University Press, 1999.
Cattaneo, Anne. "John Guare: The Art of Theatre IX," *Paris Review*, 125 (Winter 1992): 69–103.

Curry, Jane Kathleen. *John Guare: A Research and Production Sourcebook.* Westport, CT: Greenwood, 2002.

Devlin, Albert J. and Tischler, Nancy M. eds. *The Selected Letters of Tennessee Williams. Vol. 1, 1920–1945.* New York: New Directions, 2000.

Dorff, Linda. "Theatricalist Cartoons: Tennessee Williams's Late, 'Outrageous Plays,'" *Tennessee Williams Annual Review* 2 (1999): 13–33.

Guare, John. *John Guare, Volume One: The War Against the Kitchen Sink.* Lyme, NH: Smith and Kraus, 1996.

_____. *Gardenia.* New York: Dramatist Play Service, 1982.

_____. *Lydie Breeze.* New York: Dramatist Play Service, 1982.

_____. *Lydie Breeze.* Woodstock and New York: Overlook Press, 2001.

_____. *Three Exposures: Plays by John Guare.* San Diego: Harcourt Brace Jovanovich, 1982 (*The House of Blue Leaves, Landscape of the Body, Bosoms and Neglect*).

_____. *Women & Water.* New York: Dramatist Play Services, 1990.

Martin, Robert A., *Critical Essays on Tennessee Williams.* New York: G.K. Hall, 1997.

Plunka, Gene A. *The Black Comedy of John Guare.* Newark: U of Delaware P, 2002.

Rader, Dotson. "Tennessee Williams: The Art of Theatre V," *Paris Review* 81 (Fall 1981): 145–185.

Rizzo, Frank. "Raising Tennessee," *American Theatre* (October 1998) 20–25.

Sarran, David. *In Their Own Words: Contemporary American Playwrights.* New York: Theatre Communications Group, 1998. 84–99.

Scott, Thomas. "A Conversation with John Guare," 31 May 2001. *Lincoln Center Theater*, 26 May 2006: <http://www.lct.org/index.cfm>

Williams, Tennessee. *The Glass Menagerie.* New York: New Directions, 1999.

_____. *Notebooks.* Margaret Bradham Thornton, ed. New Haven: Yale U P, 2006.

_____. *Orpheus Descending with Battle of Angels.* New York: New Directions, 1958.

_____. *A Streetcar Named Desire.* New York: New Directions, 1980.

Image, Myth, and Movement in the Plays of Sam Shepard and Tennessee Williams

Annette J. Saddik

"We all have in our conscious and unconscious minds
a great vocabulary of images, and I think all human
communication is based on these images as are our dreams."
—*Tennessee Williams,* The New York Times, *1953*

"Myth speaks to everything at once, especially the emotions."
— *Sam Shepard,* The Drama Review, *1977*

"The man I made up is me."
— *Crow,* The Tooth of Crime

In a 1974 interview for *Theatre Quarterly,* Sam Shepard vaguely recalled one of the earliest plays he ever wrote — a "very bad" Tennessee Williams imitation "about some girl who got raped in a barn and her father getting mad at her or something..." (Marranca 190). In his biography of Shepard, Don Shewey reveals that indeed Shepard's first play, *The Mildew,* was a Williams-style melodrama for his high school literary magazine, "a Tennessee Williams imitation about a girl who is raped and then taunted by her stepfather" (Shewey 23). Born in 1943, Shepard would have been leaving high school just as Williams's most critically successful plays were behind him and his career was beginning its post–1961 decline into what he would later call his "stoned age." As an emerging writer and actor, Shepard would have been familiar with many of Williams's major works of the 1940s and '50s: *The Glass Menagerie* (1944), *A Streetcar Named Desire* (1947), *Summer and Smoke* (1948), *Camino Real* (1953), *Cat on a Hot Tin Roof* (1955), *Orpheus Descending* (1957), *Suddenly Last Summer* (1958), and *Sweet Bird of Youth* (1959). He seems to have had the physical and emotional violence of *Streetcar, Orpheus Descending, Suddenly Last Summer,* and *Sweet Bird of Youth* in mind (with the rape, dismemberment, castration, and murder saturating these plays) when he composed his first drama in imitation of "America's Greatest Living Playwright." Throughout Shepard's career, Williams's melodramatic images continued to filter through his writing, as the hysterical excesses of Williams's plays were transformed into the textual eruptions that characterize Shepard's works.

Williams's influence on Shepard in terms of theme, language, use of music, technique, and style has been articulated by several critics. Christopher Bigsby, for example, has suggested a direct comparison between the work of Williams and Shepard, pointing out that both writers admired Chekhov, both were concerned with what Arthur Miller called "a politics of the soul" ("Born Injured" 9), and that Shepard's characters, "like Tennessee Williams's, are drifters, seekers after a truth in which they can no longer believe. On occasion they reach out a hand, hoping to find some momentary consolation, only to find that passion carries its own virus of violence and despair" (*Modern American* 165). He locates "something of Tennessee Williams in Sam Shepard," as each writes characters who "inhabit a broken world" and "cling to one another with the same desperation, damage each other with the same inevitability." Both, he argues, "are romantics observing the collapse of form and beauty. They acknowledge the power of love, but, in a world so inhospitable to selflessness, see it distorted..." (*Modern American* 192). In the Introduction to *Sam Shepard: Seven Plays*, Richard Gilman writes that Shepard's characters "move in our minds like signals from a particular human and geographical environment, one that vibrates simultaneously with sadness and violence, eccentricity, loneliness and self-assertion, bravado and the pathos of rootless existence" (xx). This description could easily be applied to Williams' ouvre, especially when one considers the pivotal figure of the "fugitive kind" and the futile search for stability stemming from the "pathos of rootless existence." Both writers give voice to and romanticize America's outsiders, outcasts living on the fringes of conventional society who are ultimately seen as all the more noble for their fugitive status and frustrated desire. In Williams's case, the drifter moves through the seamy underbelly of rooming houses and secret passions, while in Shepard's plays it is the cowboy out on the Western desert, or his contemporary counterpart, the rock star, who is at the center of this mythology.

Williams's plays can be read as profoundly mythic, both directly and indirectly. In *Orpheus Descending*, for example, he deals overtly with the Eurydice/Orpheus myth, while a play such as *The Glass Menagerie* is more subtle in its mythic applications. *Menagerie* transcends the boundaries of time and eschews the notion of a fixed reality by locating the action in Tom Wingfield's consciousness and shifting in and out of memory, where the "present" is represented by Tom's narration as a merchant marine who has escaped the confines of the Wingfield home and is removed from the past. While the play's highly experimental structure centers the action around Tom, his mother Amanda serves as a larger-than-life archetype that generates the action. The tension between Tom, who yearns for freedom, and Amanda, who is determined to keep him domestically fixed so that she and his sister Laura — who are completely dependent on him financially — will be able to survive, struggles with timeless questions of what it means to be family and the balance between obligation versus freedom, questions which Shepard often deals with as well in plays such as *Buried Child* (1978), *True West* (1980), and *Fool For Love* (1983), for example. In all three of these plays, memory and identity are called into question, and the "natural" connections that are supposed to accompany family ties are precarious, as human relationships prove unstable. In *Buried Child*, Dodge doesn't recognize his own grandson who has returned to the family home, asking him "Who are you to expect anything? Who are you supposed to be?" (89). In *True West*, "Mom" returns home to find her two sons in heated conflict and the house trashed, claiming that she doesn't " recognize it at all" (59). And in *Fool for Love*, the "Old Man," who is a non-realistic character that "exists only in the minds of [his children] May and Eddie" (20), represents memory, history, and connection, as he occupies a place on the side of the stage, observing and commenting on the action. Yet he is similarly dissociated from his past and his kin, claiming that neither May nor Eddie "look a bit familiar" to him, and that he can't doesn't recognize himself in either one of them. He "can't even remember the original circumstances" of their births, and insists they "could be anybody's" children (40). Family ties are presented as a myth with no real origin and no substantial value.

In 1977 Shepard asserted that exploring a sense of myth, which "speaks to everything at once, especially the emotions," is essential for his writing process (Marranca 217). He went on to clarify that "By myth I mean a sense of mystery and not necessarily a traditional formula. A character for me is a composite of different mysteries. He's an unknown quantity" (Marranca 217). Williams's work similarly relies on this sense of mystery rather than the revelation of a fixed truth, since "Every moment of human existence is alive with uncertainty" (Dey 73). Defending charges of "evasiveness" in *Cat on a Hot Tin Roof* from critics, Williams explained that he wants audiences to leave the play "feeling that they have met with a vividly allusive, as well as disturbingly elusive, fragment of human experience, one that not only points at truth but at the mysteries of it, much as they will leave this world when they leave it, still wondering somewhat about what happened to them, and for what reason or purpose" (Dey 73–4).

While the thematic concerns of both Shepard and Williams merge at several points, Stephen J. Bottoms suggests that similarities between them are actually more stylistic than thematic. He compares their use of sound and light, which "blur[s] the line between realism and subjective expressionism" (208), and proposes that they both share a "distinctly unorthodox, experimental streak" (268). Specifically, he feels that Shepard

> shares with Tennessee Williams a defiant obsession with what the latter once called "the incontinent blaze of live theatre, a theatre meant for seeing and for feeling," and both have drawn on the inspiration of musical improvisation in the attempt to realize this. Williams's foreword to *Camino Real* (1953) predated Shepard's own jazz experiments by a decade, but his description of feeling "a new sensation of release, as if I could 'ride out' like a tenor sax taking the breaks in a Dixieland combo or a piano in a bop session" could come from any Shepard interview [268].

Williams continues to describe this kind of freedom, a "sensation of release," in the foreword to *Camino Real,* writing that his desire was to give audiences a sense of

> something wild and unrestricted that ran like water in the mountains, or clouds changing shape in a gale, or the continually dissolving and transforming images of a dream. This sort of freedom is not chaos nor anarchy. On the contrary, it is the result of painstaking design, and in this work I have given more conscious attention to form and construction than in any work before. Freedom is not achieved simply by working freely [vii].

This was a "freedom" that Williams had sought as early as *The Glass Menagerie* in his description of a "plastic theatre," or in the one-act play "The Purification," written in 1945 and published in 1953, which he describes as "A play in verse to be performed with a musical accompaniment on the guitar" (6:40). Williams was working on both "The Purification" and *Camino Real* during the mid–1940s, and he had completed a one-act version, "Ten Blocks on the Camino Real" in 1946, publishing it in *American Blues* in 1948.[1] Bonnie Marranca sees this connection between jazz improvisation and a sense of controlled freedom in Shepard's work as well, claiming that for Shepard the "appeal of jazz is more than structural. As an approach to composition it embodies an attitude that is at the heart of Shepard's work: spontaneity of expression. Not chance, but improvisation" (20–1).

The use of music in the theater interested both Williams and Shepard throughout their careers, and they often call upon music or painting — genres that generate images beyond the delineations of rational language — to accentuate or describe the central structure of their plays. In 1961 Williams told Studs Terkel that he had "written a few Blues lyrics ... which have been set to music by Paul Bowles" and collected under the title *Blue Mountain Ballads* (Devlin

93), and several of his plays contain songs he had written. *Orpheus Descending*, for example, contains a blues lyric, "Heavenly Grass," that yearns for the comfort of spiritual origins while wandering here on each. Music specifically underpins the action in *The Glass Menagerie*, and in his note on the music in the play, Williams indicates that a "single recurring tune" is "used to give emotional emphasis to suitable passages" (1:133). Visual imagery also figures strongly in his conception, as he suggests that the lighting should bear "a certain correspondence to light in religious paintings, such as El Greco's" (1:134). In a later work, *A Lovely Sunday for Creve Coeur* (1979), a play that, like *The Glass Menagerie*, takes us back to St. Louis in the middle or late 1930s and resembles both *Menagerie* and *A Streetcar Named Desire* in theme and tone, he describes the mise-en-scène of surrounding apartment buildings as "vistas that suggest the paintings of Ben Shahn: the dried-blood horror of lover middle-class American urban neighborhoods" (8:119). In a 1972 interview, Williams indicated that his inspiration comes from images rather than language or ideas, and that he focuses on a "vision" instead of characters or a clear story line when he begins to work on a play, letting the story then emerge "like an apparition out of the mists" (Devlin 215). Referring to *Streetcar*, he explained: "I *see* somebody, you know? Like I saw Blanche sitting in a chair with the moonlight coming through a window onto her. My first idea for the title was 'Blanche's Chair in the Moon'" (Devlin 215). Story line and language are subordinated to image in Williams's imagination, serving it rather than the other way around: "I don't work for the beginning to the end of a play. Usually, I have a vision of the most dramatic scene, the central scene, and then I work around it for the approach and the denouement" (Devlin 215).

Williams' post–1961 work focused even less directly on elaborate language and character psychology, and more on the physical and visual aspects of theater, which was in keeping with the new dramatic styles in the theater that emerged during the 1960s: not only the work done by Beckett, Pinter, and Albee, for example, but also avant-garde theater troupes such as The Living Theatre, The Open Theatre, and the Performance Group — troupes that heavily influenced Shepard — which all did away with domestic realism, the style that had dominated the American theater in the 1940s and 50s, and experimented with the theater conventions from all over the world. In 1959 Williams himself went to Japan to visit Yukio Mishima, and was introduced to Kabuki theater, which very much influenced his later work. *The Day on Which a Man Dies* (which is actually dedicated to Mishima; the first version was written in 1960, and a later one was published as *In the Bar of a Tokyo Hotel* (1969),[2] *The Milk Train Doesn't Stop Here Anymore* (1963), and *I Can't Imagine Tomorrow* (1966) all exhibit the influences of Japanese Kabuki and Noh plays. These plays were more anti-realistic in their treatment of language, character, and action. Like Japanese Noh plays and the avant-garde European playwrights of the time, meaning is found not through language, but in the pauses and silences, in what is not said. The focus is less on character and conventional plot development, and more on tone, mood, and theme.

Shepard too eschewed the dramatic conventions of realism for a more visceral theatrical experience, focusing on the visual and aural aspects of theater and exploring the relationship between language and music. In 1974 he said that he wrote spontaneously, starting from "a picture." Speaking of his early work, he explained that he "would have like a picture, and just start from there. A picture of a guy in a bathtub, or of two guys on stage with a sign blinking — you know, things like that" (Marranca 191). He then went on to insist that music in the theater "adds a whole different kind of perspective, it immediately brings the audience to terms with an emotional reality" (Marranca 201). Shepard wrote songs for several of his plays; the influence of jazz, rock 'n' roll, and country western music is present both in the rhythms of Shepard's dialogue and in his direct use of live bands and music in his productions. *Angel City*

(1976), *Suicide in B Flat* (1976), and *Savage/Love* (1979), for example, use live jazz instrumentation, often with bluesy undertones. Shepard prefaces *Angel City* with his "Note on the Music," explaining that the "dominant theme for the saxophone is the kind of lyrical loneliness of Lester young's playing, occasionally exploding into Charlie Parker and Ornette Coleman," and giving the musician freedom to "explore his own sound within that general jazz structure" so that he may find places in the script "to heighten or color the action" (61). Like Williams, he finds inspiration in a less literal Japanese theater, as he notes that "It might be useful for the musicians to listen to some of the recordings of Japanese theater to hear how the actor's voice is used in conjunction with the instruments" (61). He follows this with a "Note to the Actors," suggesting that the actor should "consider himself a fractured whole with bits and pieces of character flying off the central theme. In other words, more in terms of collage construction or jazz improvisation" (61–2). Shepard's *The Tooth of Crime* (1972) is influenced more by rock 'n' roll than Jazz, and Shepard wrote the music for the play himself, instructing that the opening song should have a sound that resembles "Heroin" by the Velvet Underground (203). In a 1971 program note he asserted his connection with music in what has since become a well-known statement: "First off let me tell you that I don't want to be a playwright. I want to be a rock and roll star" (Bottoms 66), and clearly many of his plays are presented with the style and energy of a rock concert.

In 1972, Richard Schechner and The Performance Group mounted the New York production of *The Tooth of Crime*. While working on the play, Schechner explained to Shepard that The Performance Group strives for "a musical treatment of words" that is similar to opera (Marranca 162). In a letter to Shepard, he wrote that he wanted "to look at the play nakedly, approach its language not as dialect but as a way into the heart of the play" (163). While Shepard had no objection to Schechner's exploration of the play to "uncover what is to be uncovered" in rehearsals (163), he was very particular about how the music would be used. In his reply to Schechner, Shepard insisted that, similar to Williams's emphasis on the function of music as a sort of emotional punctuation in *Menagerie*, "All the music is written down and fits each section of the play according to the emotional line that's going down" (165) and that there is "No other way for it to work" (164). Ultimately, however, Shepard decided to "be adventurous" and trust The Performance Group's process, letting Schechner "go ahead with *Tooth*" (167).

It is at the intersection of theme and style, however, that one of the most salient connections between these playwrights is apparent, one which articulates a central contradiction of their characters. Bigsby observes that the two writers "have found in performance a symbol of lives which are the enactment of stories with their roots in the distant past of ritual and myth as well as in a present in which role and being have become confused" (*Modern American* 193). This "confusion" of role and being, performance and authenticity, is at the center of both Shepard's and Williams's characters' search for a stable identity, a fixed reality that both eludes and threatens to trap them as they perform the instabilit(ies) of postmodern identity in the late twentieth century. Bigsby addresses this dilemma in terms of a sense of inconsistency and instability in the work of the two playwrights:

> There is no consistency [in Shepard's plays]. Moods, dress, identity can switch in a second; characters are fractured, divided, doubled until the same play can contain, as independent beings, what are in effect facets of a single self.... But if this fluidity contains a threat of anarchy the opposite is equally menacing. As a writer, Shepard has spoken of his desire "To not be fixed." This is what keeps his characters on the move. Again like Tennessee Williams's figures they fear stasis, over-definition, even the trap of language [*Modern American* 166].

In several of their experimental plays, characterized by truncated and fragmented dialogue, highly symbolic language, and characters lifted from the mythic discourses of Hollywood film, rock 'n' roll, or literature, both Shepard and Williams are concerned with the postmodern question of essence versus appearance and the slipperiness of "authentic" identity as it relates to image, particularly the image associated with artistic fame. *Yet while their characters crave the stability of a fixed core identity and a return to origins, the inevitable contradiction is that they ultimately realize that freedom is possible only through fluidity, instability, movement. They must, therefore, remain fugitives and surge forward, never resting, despite their desperate, romantic need to cling to an unattainable ideal, a core of Truth. Stasis signifies death or confinement (a kind of death), and freedom lies in flexibility and individual agency, the ability to mold image(s) of the self and remain in process.*

Despite the critical establishment's tendency to see Williams as a "poetic realist" or southern Gothicist, he always saw himself as a radical playwright, experimenting with form and content in his quest to represent the inconsistencies and contradictions of the human situation, and Shepard's status as an experimental artist — "the unofficial star of the alternative theatre scene" (Roudané, *Sam Shepard* 3) — is indisputable. Both playwrights were interested in exploring the experimental dramatic forms that emerged in Europe after World War II and took root in the off- and off-off-Broadway American theater scene during the 1960s and '70s.[3] Shepard was, of course, associated with such downtown experimental theaters as Café Cino, La MaMa E.T.C., and Theatre Genesis, where he got his start in 1964 with *Cowboys* and *The Rock Garden*. During Williams's later period, specifically after *Garden District* (a double-bill of *Suddenly Last Summer* and "Something Unspoken") was staged at the York Playhouse in 1958, Williams too was very much interested in Off Broadway. His one-acts were among the plays that were produced at Café Cino during its early days, and Ellen Stewart, founder of La MaMa E.T.C., produced a dramatic adaptation of Williams's short story "One Arm" (Smith 164). While he essentially saw himself as a Broadway playwright, Williams began to expand his horizons as productions of his plays in the 1960s, '70s, and '80s were increasingly staged Off and Off Off Broadway at venues such as the Eastside Playhouse, Truck and Warehouse Theatre, Hudson Guild Theater, and the Jean Cocteau Repertory Theatre, and in 1975 he told Charles Ruas that his "great happiness in the theatre" was now Off Broadway and Off Off Broadway (Devlin 291).

The Off and Off Off Broadway theater scene of the 1960s and '70s was interested in exploring the period's concern with personal freedom and authenticity apart from political oppression, with locating an individual essence or reality outside social conformity or roles. Williams's interest in the slippery and ephemeral distinctions of identity was at his height during the 1960s and '70s with experimental plays such as *The Gnädiges Fräulein* (1966), *In the Bar of a Tokyo Hotel*, and his several versions of *Out Cry/The Two-Character Play* (1967, 1973, 1976),[4] especially in terms of the image of the artist and the breakdown of distinctions between the individual and his work that could lead to madness. His late plays often address the issue of psychic fragmentation and the collapse of stable identity. The setting of *The Two-Character Play*, for example, suggests the "disordered images of a mind approaching collapse" (5:308) and presents a brother and sister, performers who "have the same thought at the same time" (5:366) and are not sure of the boundaries that separate themselves from each other or from the play they perform. *In the Bar of a Tokyo Hotel* uses truncated dialogue to echo the emotional, existential breakdown of Mark, an artist who no longer sees any separation between himself and his work (7:21). The Fräulein in *The Gnädiges Fräulein* was once a great performer who now offers only grotesque re-enactments of her past glory, documented as a fixed image in the graveyard of her scrapbook. She is fragmented both psychically and physically, as she is prone to "Temporary amnesia resulting from shock" (7:247) and her body is progressively ripped apart by the cocaloony birds throughout the play, "streaked and dabbled with blood," with "Patches of her fuzzy light orange hair ... torn away" (7:260). She does, however, survive and go on; the play's last image is of the Fräulein bravely starting "a wild, blind dash for the fish-docks" (7:262), going off to meet the cocaloonies that will, more than likely, tear her apart once again as she fights them for the fish that allows her to earn her keep.

Similarly, many of Shepard's works of the 1960s and '70s such as *La Turista* (1967), *Action* (1975), *Angel City*, and *Buried Child*, followed by *True West* and later, *Simpatico* (1994) also deal with the fragile boundaries of identity and the impossibility of locating an authentic self outside of the roles, masks, images, and performances that mark human action. In *Action*, Shooter acknowledges this lack of authenticity, claiming that all human action is a performance: "You act yourself out" (178). At the same time, however, this protean lack of stability brings liberation. Megan Williams reads Shepard's *True West* as an illustration of theories of postmodern identity, and contends that Austin and Lee allegorize "two ways modern man attempts to solve his feelings of placelessness and alienation." While Austin initially clings to a lingering nostalgia for a stable sense of identity, relationships, and history, Lee "registers a potentially positive sense of freedom which accompanies man when he loses his nostalgia for history and realizes that identity and the past are only myths to be performed and manipulated." Lee, she argues, "challenges the precept behind postmodern theory which assumes that contemporary man's loss of subjectivity and history must necessarily be a negative experience" (58). Since Lee "possesses the almost miraculous ability to appear, disappear, and change identities" in contrast to Austin, who "is 'stuck' in his search for a world where identity and history are fixed" (69), Austin "wishes to ... relinquish himself to the positive freedom and anonymity of Lee's present" (60). Even though Lee craves "somethin' authentic. Somethin' to keep me in touch" (56), freedom is ultimately only possible through the fluidity of performance. Shepard's earlier play *La Turista* is similarly replete with discourses of shape-shifting, instability, transformation, and escape, although this fluidity is represented more physically: "He disappears and becomes the wall. He reappears on the opposite wall. He clings to the floor and slithers along.... He becomes a mouse and changes into a cobra and then back on the floor" (293). At the end of the play, Kent escapes being trapped by Salem and Sonny who "make a lunge" for him. He "runs straight toward the upstage wall of the set and leaps right through it, leaving a cut-out silhouette image of his body in the wall" (298). All that is left of him is a representation, an image. As Doc says, "Just keep yourself movin', son. It's the only way out" (287).

Both Williams and Shepard escape from a kind of "confinement" thematically as well as stylistically in their plays through their treatment of archetype and myth, and in their use of cultural figures who are brought together, transcending time and historical circumstance, in order to express unconscious, emotional truths beyond these limitations. Confinement was Williams's self-proclaimed worst fear, characterized by his well-known dread of institutionalization, a fate that befell his sister Rose. He traveled extensively and internationally, always on the move and refusing to set down roots. Shepard's need for open spaces, the sense of freedom he finds in the American West, as well as his desire to escape metaphysical confinement also comes through clearly in his writing and his interviews:

> [Y]ou have this personality, and somehow feel locked into it, jailed by all of your cultural influences and your psychological ones from your family, and all that. And somehow I feel that that isn't the whole of it, you know, that there's another possibility. [...] You can't escape, that's the whole thing, you can't. [...] But there is always that impulse towards another kind of world, something that doesn't necessarily confine you in that way [Marranca 208].

In both *Operation Sidewinder* (1970) and *The Mad Dog Blues* (1971), the confines of physical and historical boundaries are transcended, as characters are lifted from American mythology and brought together in a new context to perform their own fluid identities. Bonnie Marranca writes that the Shepard character

> knows he is a performer, and takes the opportunity whenever he wants to, to leave, mentally and in another time frame, the play and verbalize or act out his emotional responses to events around him. There is no such thing as illusion vs. reality, only shifting realities [25–6].

In *Operation Sidewinder*, characters are essentially named either for their functions (Mechanic, Young Man, Captain, General) or they take on archetypal, mythic identities (Mickey Free, Dukie, Spider Lady). They are searching for origins, for certainty, since "everything [...] goes down in doubt" (232). The Spider Lady recalls the myth of the "two great clans of man," the Snake Clan, which was given "a giant spirit snake to communicate with the Gods and keep peace in the hearts of the people" and the Lizard Clan, which grew jealous, resulting in a tug-of-war between the two clans. The giant serpent was then split into two parts, and "the people lost all knowledge of their origin," wandering "endlessly with no purpose" (265). The characters imagine a recoverable past that was secure and stable, one with "order," that they can return to. Captain Bovine declares that "Over the past few years there's been a breakdown of law and order and a complete disrespect for the things we've held sacred since our ancestors founded this country. [...] It's time for a change!" (269–70).

This nostalgia for the past, however, is perverted through the play's central image — a computerized sidewinder snake that was invented by the government "in an effort to produce a tracing computer which would help solve the questions of whether or not unidentified flying objects actually existed" (252), but "Operation Sidewinder" has gone disastrously wrong. The snake "has chosen to go off on its own accord. It has chose to be free and exist on its own" (251), and now the military is trying to track down the escaped computer. The computerized snake symbolizes a clash of cultures in the tension between a death-centered, static technology versus an ongoing spiritual awe of nature, represented through Native American myth and ritual. A respect for mystery has disappeared from modern military culture, replaced by society's attempts to control and dominate the natural world, a world of flux and possibility. Yet while the play begins with the sidewinder snake as an image of strangulation, death, and stasis, it ends with the promise of rebirth. The final image is of the Hopi snake dance, incorporating the sidewinder as it "lights up" simultaneously with the sky (287).

The Mad Dog Blues is an even stronger example of a play that relies on central mythic figures who inhabit our cultural imagination, as these figures appear as characters — Marlene Dietrich, Mae West, Captain Kidd, Waco, Paul Bunyan, Jesse James — that all interact in the same time and space and support the two central ones, Kosmo and Yahoodi. In this highly allegorical play all the "places the characters move through are imagined and mimed," they "speak directly to the audience" (291), and songs intermittently interrupt the action. The play's theme centers around a search for buried treasure, and the sense of futile searching is presented symbolically from the beginning in Kosmo's search for meaning and stability, as he self-consciously defines himself to the audience as someone groping "in the dark without a game" and moving "from spot to spot across the planet hoping to find a home" (291) — unstable and constantly in motion. Kosmo has "lost touch with [his] roots" and wants to get back to them (297), to find stability and a home. Yet Kosmo and Waco seem to find freedom in the promise of shifting identities — being "able to go anywhere and do anything and be anyone we want to" (304). When Waco asks if he could be "Jimmie Rodgers," Kosmo replies "Sure, why not?" but Kosmo himself is not sure who he wants to be. The only thing he knows for certain is that, at the very least, he will be "A different me" (304). The boundaries between authentic and performative identity are blurred, and when Ghost Girl tells Captain Kidd that she was warned about "imposters," claiming that he is "as phony as they come," Kidd indignantly protests: "I'm real! I'm the real Captain Kidd!" (318). Waco knows that he himself lacks a sense of stability, as he is "Just a driftin' fool" (320), and "One place is just as good as another" for him (327). His sense of spiritual and physical dislocation is disorienting, however, and he ultimately feels like "Just a ghost. Stuck somewheres between livin' and dyin'" (328). The play ends with Mae West suggesting that the characters "all go back home together [....] Back where we belong!" (340), as all gather and sing the final song, "Home" (340–1). But the ending is ironic and abrupt, and the tension between freedom and stability is not finally resolved.

While several of Williams's and Shepard's plays deal with this question of identity and freedom, I will focus more specifically on two works, *Camino Real*, which was Williams's first full-length experiment that departed from his more realistic plays, and *The Tooth of Crime*, which is often considered Shepard's first major play, and was a logical follow-up to *Operation Sidewinder* and *The Mad Dog Blues*. All three Shepard plays deal with image, movement, and shifting identities, and *Operation Sidewinder* especially addresses the need to escape the prison of social scrutiny. Williams maintained that the distinctly experimental *Camino Real*, a work that was ahead of its time in struggling with questions of personal freedom, authenticity, and role-playing in the midst of public surveillance during the height of the McCarthy era, was "one of his five best plays" (Devlin 298), despite its initial unsuccessful run. Just as in *Operation Sidewinder* and *The Mad Dog Blues*, the characters in *Camino Real* are lifted from the discourses of myth and literature — Jacques Cassanova, Baron De Carlus, Lord Byron, Marguerite Gautier, Don Quixote — romantic pioneers of personal freedom in the face of social oppression. They have all been brought together outside of time or place on the Camino Real, a totalitarian state of limbo that both imprisons and protects them from the "Terra Incognita," and their situation is a far cry from the elusive time "when the street was royal" (145). The main character, Kilroy, especially exists outside of time or place, a "Traveler" of "unknown" origins (111) who ultimately refuses to be a "patsy." Like *Operation Sidewinder*, *Camino Real* is a myth about regeneration, and both plays ran at the Repertory Theater of Lincoln Center in 1970: a revival of *Camino Real* ran from January 8 to February 21, followed by *Operation Sidewinder*, which was first produced on March 12.[5] *The Tooth of Crime*, a drama of confrontation presented through discourses of Hollywood Westerns and rock 'n' roll, centers around the characters Hoss, who is "stuck in [his] image" but refuses to be trapped as "a slave" (225), and Crow, whose "image is [his] survival kit" (249). Both *Camino Real* and *The Tooth of Crime* present a triumph of individual agency, but not through locating a stable Truth or an authentic core of identity. Rather, hope is to be found in the acknowledgment of the inevitability of role-playing and the freedom associated with the ability to construct the self, to remain a work-in-progress. Liberation lies in directing our own performances.

In "Reflections on a Revival of a Controversial Fantasy," an essay that first appeared in the *New York Times* on May 15, 1960 before the Off Broadway revival of *Camino Real* directed by Jose Quintero, Williams presented what he called a "TV commercial" for the play, emphasizing the ubiquitous commodifications of postmodern culture, asking "Has your public smile come to resemble the grimace of a lion-tamer in a cage with a suddenly untamed lion.... And do you have to continue your performance betraying no sign of anxiety in your heart? Then here is the right place for you, the Camino Real..." (Day and Woods 111). *Camino Real* is Williams's statement of his "own philosophy ... that romanticism is absolutely essential" (Devlin 142), as he insists on the need for tenderness and sincerity, associated with a triumph of the human spirit. Yet hope in this play ultimately rests in movement and process, the possibility that "the violets in the mountains can break the rocks if you believe in them and allow them to grow" (*Camino* 97).

In his 1947 essay "On a Streetcar Named Success," Williams laments how success traps the artist in image. He called his "public self" an "artifice of mirrors" (Devlin 19), a "fiction created with mirrors," and insists that "the only somebody worth being is the solitary and unseen you that existed from your first breath and is the sum of your actions and so is constantly in a state of becoming under your own volition" (Devlin 21). This "somebody worth being," the "solitary and unseen you that existed from your first breath," implies an original, authentic self that is separate from public image. But for Williams this self is still defined by "the sum of your actions" and is in flux, "constantly in a state of becoming." The self is in process, unstable, but we have the freedom to shape it according to our "own volition." Williams sees the world too as "an unfinished poem" (Devlin 92), and "Humanity is just a work in progress" (*Camino* 113). Hope therefore lies not in a return to origins or Truth, an unattainable stable center, but in the mysterious process of living, uncertainty, moving forward into the "Terra Incognita," where all we can do is *Make voyages!—Attempt them!—* there's nothing else..." (*Camino* 78). Williams's banner, of course, was the ultimate call to going on: "En Avant!" or, as Quixote says in *Camino Real*, "Forward!" (5).

Almost all the characters in the play, excepting, of course, the oppressive representatives of the State, are "fugitives" on the Camino Real, but Kilroy, the main character who wanders onto the scene, is the ultimate fugitive. The identification of Kilroy as the fictitious American soldier, created by troops who left the inscription "Kilroy was here" around the world during World War II, is related in the play to the more general use of the term to describe an extensive traveler, someone who wanders around the world, and indeed the characters on the Camino Real are all wanderers, displaced from their original literary texts. They exist in a limbo which is "a port of entry and departure, there are no permanent guests" (*Camino* 96), steeped in slogans that signify their spiritual dislocation:

> Gypsy's Loudspeaker: Do you feel yourself to be spiritually unprepared for the age of exploding atoms? Do you distrust the newspapers? Are you suspicious of governments? Have you arrived at a point on the Camino Real where the walls converge not in the distance but right in front of your nose? Does further progress appear impossible to you? Are you afraid of anything at all? Afraid of your heartbeat? Or the eyes of strangers! Afraid of breathing? Afraid of not breathing? Do you wish that things could be straight and simple again as they were in your childhood? Would you like to go back to Kindy Garten? [28].

The hysterical tone and paradox of existence that marks this passage ("Afraid of breathing? Afraid of not breathing?") echoes the existential dilemma of Beckett's characters, who can't go on yet still go on and simultaneously crave silence and speech. It expresses a desire to return to origins, to "childhood," in search of an essence or purity—the "unseen you that existed from your first breath"—that is characterized by an infantile breakdown of language ("Kindy Garten"). Historical progress is presented as not only "impossible" in this play, but undesirable. The gypsy's speech suggests that it is in looking backwards, not forwards, that real or essential identity—something "straight and simple"—is to be found, and with it, the peace and stability that Kilroy craves in the age of "exploding atoms."

In the timelessness of the Camino Real, however, there is no going back, and no origin to which to return. This is clear from the beginning of the play, as Quixote and Sancho arrive on the scene:

> SANCHO [urgently]: Let's go back to La Mancha!
> QUIXOTE: Forward!
> SANCHO: The time has come for retreat!
> QUIXOTE: The time for retreat never comes! [5].

For the moment, they cannot go forward, but they cannot go back either. The future is unknown, it is the Terra Incognita, and the past or history is unattainable and irrelevant, as the Baron asserts that "Used to be is past tense, meaning useless" (37). His desire to "Make a departure" from his "present self" to himself as he "used to be" (73) is answered by Gutman, "a lordly fat man wearing a linen suit and a pith helmet" (3) who presides over the Camino Real: "*That's* the *furthest* departure a man can make!" (74). For Byron, however, "There is a time for departure even when there's no certain place to go!" (78).

Kilroy too is caught in limbo on the Camino Real, with no locatable origins. In response to the Gypsy's interrogation of the "date and place" of his coming into the world, he replies "Both unknown" (111). He identifies himself as a "Traveler" in response to her request for an address (111), and his parents are "Anonymous" (112). He insists that he is "a free *agent*" (49, emphasis added), in possession of the *agency* that allows him to control the construction of self. His identity is unstable and slippery, as he claims to "like situations [he] can get out of" (112). Kilroy does possess a history of images, however, and performs a "triumphant, eccentric dance" in which he pantomimes "his history as fighter, traveler, and lover" (106), the series of past roles that make up his present self. History is a malleable fiction, a performance that can be manipulated, just as the virginity of the Gypsy's daughter, Esmeralda, is regularly restored with the new full moon for the "fertility rites" that follow. Esmeralda is trapped in her role, and her attempted escape occurs simultaneously with Kilroy's attempted escape from the Officers who want to make him a "patsy." Their identities merge in empathy as Esmeralda cries out "They've got you! They've got me!" (53). When the Gypsy later proposes that Kilroy "sign something" (112) and get "some kind of shot" (113) — arbitrary gestures divorced from original meaning that are a rehearsed part of the process — to fulfill his destiny as her daughter's "chosen hero," Kilroy tells her that doesn't know what's going on. The Gypsy can only answer "Who does? The Camino Real is a funny paper read backward!" (114), a series of distorted images. Nothing here is known or certain, and we are "Not even [sure] of our existence.... [T]he perch we hold is unstable!" (96).

On the Camino Real, authenticity merges with image, and it is a place of contradictions.[6] The play's search for authenticity can be seen in Kilroy's desire for "sincerity" from Esmeralda, in contrast to surrounding images of Hollywood myth — the romantic images of "television" and the "Screen Secrets" fan magazine she reads (108, 121, 136). When Esmeralda is excited over her ability to express human emotion and shed a tear, the Gypsy answers her with the reprimand that she has been watching too much television (136), warning her not to confuse image with reality. Esmeralda is satisfied to believe that Kilroy is sincere "For a while" (131), and he too seems comfortable with the temporary arrangement, this lack of stability, responding that "Everything's for a while" (132). Yet he disdains Esmeralda's malleable performance of virginity, complaining that it lacks sincerity, and wants her to "talk" to him honestly. His desire for conversation, however, rests in performance, roles that are familiar, a script for romance: "That's the way we do things in the States. A little vino, some records on the Victrola, some quiet conversation — and then if both parties are in the mood for romance..." (122). When Esmeralda starts talking, her incredible knowledge and interest in socio-political matters is daunting for Kilroy, and he rejects her discourse, prompting her to revert to performance once again: "What sort of talk do you want?" (123). He is fixated on the loss of his one "real-true woman" the wife he left behind, but even she is an image inspired by Hollywood myth, "a platinum blond the same as Jean Harlow" (121).

At the end of the play, Kilroy collapses while attempting to fight off the "Streetcleaners," the harbingers of death on the Camino Real. As an "unidentified vagrant" with "no legal claimants" (148–9) — no fixed identity — his dead body is given over to the State for scientific dissection. But once the Medical Instructor opens up his chest and extracts a heart "of pure gold and as big as the head of a baby" (150), La Madrecita de los Perditos commands him to "Rise, ghost! Go! Go bird!" (150), and Kilroy is resurrected. Williams says in the opening directions that "a phoenix painted on silk" should be softly lighted now and then in the play, "since resurrections are so much a part of its meaning" (1). Kilroy must be resurrected, as hope in the play depends on malleability and movement:

KILROY: Hopeful?
JACQUES: Always!
OFFICER: Keep moving! [45].

Kilroy the phoenix then "snatches the golden sphere from the Medical Instructor," refusing to give up his heart of gold, his essence, to the oppressive State (152), and even though he realizes that he "had one true woman, which [he] can't go back to," he has now "found another," Esmeralda, and can go forward (155). Esmeralda, however, is unaware of his ghostly presence, and Kilroy retreats in despair.[7] Yet the fountain that has been dried up from the beginning of the play suddenly "begins to flow" (158), begins to show signs of movement and flux. Kilroy too decides "uncertainly" that he "was thinking of— going *on*" from the Camino Real (159), and Quixote too is going on, but is not sure as to where (159). The inscription on the wall that had changed from " Kilroy is Coming" to "Kilroy is Here" (24), continues to mark movement and the passage of time as Kilroy replaces "is" with "was" (160). Gutman, finally, reveals the play as a performance, "a pageant" (160), and takes a bow as the "Curtain Line" is spoken by Quixote: "The violets in the mountains have broken the rocks!" (161). Endurance and forward motion have triumphed, and Kilroy's resurrection confirms his status as a "free agent" who is able to control his own destiny.

Like Kilroy, Hoss in *The Tooth of Crime* is a fugitive who dreams of living "outside the fucking law altogether" (213); he sees himself as "a mover" (218) and needs to wander. Yet he craves authenticity, and laments the ubiquitousness of image in "The Game" of rock 'n' roll performance culture that is his world, a Darwinian staging of competition and survival of the fittest where the winners know how to manipulate image. He wants to believe in an individual essence, a style that "can't be taught or copied or stolen or sold" (249), and the line from Stéphane Mallarmé that gives the play its title ("in your heart of stone there is dwelling/A heart that the tooth of no crime can wound") signifies this yearning for a core of identity and Truth. On the other hand, Crow, a killer "Gypsy" who does manage to live outside the laws of the game, is free from roots, from essence and stability, precisely because "There ain't no heart to a Gypsy" (221).

Hoss's search for authenticity, however, people "just livin' their life" outside the game (219), relies to some extent on image, on myths of the uncontaminated American West: "What about the country. Ain't there any farmers left, ranchers, cowboys, open space?" (219). The core that he craves can't be located, and even his what he considers his own genuine walk was "copped from Keith Moon" (228) and later copied from him by Crow. Hoss objects to Crow's appropriation of his style, feeling that his identity and individuality have been stolen, and orders Crow to "Stop walkin' like that! That's not the way you walk! That's the way I walk!" (232). His assistant Becky, however, is aware of the freedom associated with play, movement, and image, and knows that "the only way to be an individual is inside the game. You're it. You're on top. You're free" (219).

Hoss sees his image in contrast to his essence or authenticity, as he believes that his fame keeps him "insulated from what's really happening" (207). His experience is framed through the myths of "John Wayne, Robert Mitchum and Kirk Douglas" (224), and his sense that he is "pushed and pulled around from one image to another. Nothin' takes a solid form. Nothin's sure and final" (243) disorients him. Crow, on the other hand, has no problem with the image that is "his survival kit" (249). He is the postmodern quintessence of style for style's sake or, as Bottoms puts it, he presents "a style-oriented attitude to the world which functions as an end in itself" (103). In a sense, Hoss and Crow mirror Austin and Lee in *True West*. While both Hoss and Austin crave a stable authenticity, Crow and Lee know that reality is a malleable fiction, and they are able to use this knowledge to survive in the postmodern world by controlling the multiplicity of contradictory images. Bottoms writes that "Crow knows what Hoss has not registered; that the past is not a set of concrete facts, but a conceptual history which can be rewritten at will by whomever has the power to do so. In this world of language games, reality itself is a reinventable fiction" (109).

The language in *Tooth* is highly overdetermined, reflecting the fluidity inherent in identity and history. Becky tells Hoss that he "ain't *playin'* with a full deck" (219, emphasis added), pointing not only to the metaphor that relates card games to sanity (a *stable* mental state), but also to *Tooth*'s world of "the game" itself and the playfulness/instability of image. Similarly, Crow's attention to the (possible) origins of the term "gyped" simultaneously highlights the fluidity of language: "'Gyped'—coming from 'Gypsy'" (233). References to "charts" (to signify maps, celebrity ratings, or astrological readings), and "stars" (celebrities or astrological signs) are layered and imprecise, taking on several meanings at once. There is no consensus of language, and the characters speak playfully in various pop-culture dialects that make it difficult to locate a fixed meaning, highlighting the instability of representation.

The play begins with Hoss singing the lyrics to "The Way Things Are," a song about the "confusion" between representation and truth:

> You may think every picture you see is a true history of
> the way things used to be or the way things are
> While you're ridin' in your radio or walkin' through the late
> late show ain't it a drag to know you just don't know
> you just don't know
> So here's another illusion to add to your confusion
> Of the way things are.
> [...]
> Now everything I do goes down in doubt
> But sometimes in the blackest night I can see a little light
> That's the only thing that keeps me rockin'—keeps me rockin'
> So here's another fantasy
> About the way things seem to be to me [204].

Questioning not only historical narratives of the past, but also "pictures" of present reality, Hoss's lyrics set the stage for a play that challenges knowledge of the world and of the self, destabilizing any certainty regarding both history and identity and privileging doubt. Being and seeming are collapsed, just as in the case of Hoss's Creole friend who "was black" to the white kids "even though he looked white" (223). Even Hoss's own narrative is "a fantasy" based on subjective appearance, the way things "seem to be" to him. The "little light" that keeps him "rockin'," however, could either be his belief in a core of authenticity or, conversely, his hope that he can thrive in this game of image and performance. Either way, the hope is "little," and both possibilities prove futile for Hoss in the end.

Ultimately, Hoss finds authenticity, stability, and a release from image only in death; his suicide is his "original" gesture that "can't be copied" (249),[8] as he decides that authenticity can only be found in the reality of the body outside representation. Once he was able to "shift his personality," but now he is "stuck" in his image (223). At the end of Act I, just before Crow arrives, Hoss tries to convince himself that "The road's what counts. Just look at the road. Don't worry about where it's goin'" (225), yet he feels "so trapped. So fucking unsure" (225). Hoss wants to be a mover, but in order to find the authenticity he craves and escape the game he must stop moving. There is no survival outside the game. His only agency lies in self-destruction, but it is an ironic victory, if a victory at all. For Crow, Hoss was just a "loser" (250) in the game, too static to keep on playing.

Crow survives and wins because he knows that the only reality lies in performance, and freedom is the ability to invent and reinvent oneself, to manipulate image. "Crow's Song," in contrast to Hoss's opening lyric, privileges movement and role-playing in a world of uncertainty:

> What he doesn't know — the four winds blow
> Just the same for him as me
> We're clutchin' at the straw and no one knows the law
> That keeps us lost at sea
>
> But I believe in my mask — The man I made up is me
> And I believe in my dance — And my destiny [232].

Crow knows that both he and Hoss are steeped in "just the same" doubt and uncertainty, but Crow is comfortable with the uncertainty; he revels in it, as it is what frees him and gives him power. He "believe[s] in [his] mask," and there is no distinction between role and essence, creation and creator: "The man I made up is me." The key to Crow's power is the fact that his image bends to his will, he "made up" his own identity with the fragments of image. It is his "dance," remaining in motion and constant flux, that enables him to survive while Hoss does not. Crow's destiny is to survive and go on. He is free because he can manipulate his image and "Never show his true face" (235). Control over representation of the self points to freedom, and Crow tried to warn Hoss that he needed to "get the image in line" (240). While on one level *The Tooth of Crime* can certainly be seen as a critique of the surface reality of a postmodern society steeped in image and lacking substance, on another level the play locates individual freedom in accepting "Crow's sense that identity is no more than a fragmented composite of surface images" (Bottoms 111) and possessing the power to arrange and rearrange the composite.

Just as Williams, in his Production Notes to *The Glass Menagerie*, called for a "new, plastic theatre which must take the place of the exhausted theatre of realistic conventions if the theatre is to resume vitality as a part of our culture" (1:131), Shepard presents identity and history as "plastic" in this play, artificial yet ultimately malleable.

In several of Williams's and Shepard's plays, characters strive for individual freedom though the search for authenticity, origins, a stable self, but ultimately realize that freedom occurs in movement and change. Blanche's plea for "rest" in *A Streetcar Named Desire* (1:335) is met with her ultimate confinement, while Eunice insists that Stella has "got to keep on going" (1:406). Once again, as Byron says in *Camino Real*, "*Make voyages!—Attempt them!—* there's nothing else..." (78). Like Williams's characters, Shepard's too are caught in a "terrible binary of hope and hopelessness" (Roudané, *Sam Shepard* 2), but know they must keep moving, keep changing, to maintain freedom. Playing on the doubleness of the term "forge"— both moving forward and constructing or shaping—Dodge in *Buried Child* sums up the notion of the self in process that characterizes much of Shepard's work: "There's nothing to figure out. You just forge ahead" (78).

NOTES

This essay grew out of an earlier, much shorter version that was published as "'You just forge ahead': Image, Authenticity, and Freedom in the Plays of Tennessee Williams and Sam Shepard" (*South Atlantic Review* 70:4, Fall 2005): 73–93.

1. For a discussion of the influence of blues music on Williams's plays, see Nick Moschovakis, "Tennessee Williams's American Blues: From the Early Manuscripts Through *Menagerie*," in *The Tennessee Williams Annual Review* 7 (2005): 14–36.

2. *The Day on Which a Man Dies* was published by New Directions in a volume of Williams's previously unpublished later plays, *The Travelling Companion and Other Plays*, ed. Annette J. Saddik, in Spring 2008.

3. Both Williams and Shepard have mentioned Samuel Beckett in particular as an influence. In a 1965 interview with John Gruen, Williams said that he admired Beckett, and in 1969 he asserted that Beckett and Albee were his favorite playwrights (Devlin, 120, 137). His later plays, especially *The Two-Character Play/Out Cry*, clearly offer a nod in Beckett's direction. Shepard too has repeatedly praised Beckett's work in his interviews, especially during the 1970s, and continued to do so in a 2002 interview with Matthew Roudané (*The Cambridge Companion to Sam Shepard*, ed. Roudané, 73). Beckett's paradox of stasis and movement, going on when you can't go on any longer, is philosophically tied to similar contradictions in Williams and Shepard. Tilden in Shepard's *Buried Child*, for example, knows that "you gotta talk or you'll die" (78), echoing the simultaneous pleas for silence and dialogue in Beckett's *Endgame*. Similarly, both playwrights have claimed strong Brechtian influences. In 1974, Shepard said that Brecht was his "favorite playwright," as he was able to achieve the impact Shepard strives for in his plays, one that he finds in the nature of music: "when you can play a note and there's a response immediately—you don't have to build up to it through seven scenes" (Marranca 202). *Operation Sidewinder* is one example of a play that is Brechtian in its treatment of characters who create alienation-effect and interrupt any realistic illusion of the action by bursting into song. Similarly, Williams called Brecht's *Mother Courage* "the greatest of modern plays in my opinion" (Day 118), and the script of *The Glass Menagerie*, with its alienation device of "a screen on which were projected magic-lantern slides bearing images or titles" (1:132), along with its episodic scenes and device of character/narrator owes a great debt to Brecht.

4. For a discussion of the various versions of *The Two-Character Play/Out Cry*, see Felicia Hardison Londré, "The Two-Character Out Cry and Break Out," in *The Undiscovered Country: The Later Plays of Tennessee Williams*.

5. I am indebted to Mr. Thomas Keith at New Directions Publishing for bringing this connection to my attention.

6. We see this from the beginning of the play, as the "Survivor" dies early on in the action (23–24).

7. Despite his continuous praise for *Camino Real*, Williams was aware of some of its inconsistencies, calling it a "mutilated play" in a 1965 interview with John Gruen. He told Gruen that *Camino* had his "best writing in it," but that "there were things in it that didn't quite seem rational, even in the terms of the wildness of the play. There were puzzling dichotomies. After his death, Kilroy snatches the gold heart from his own body and he rushes to a pawnbroker with it. The pawnbroker can *see* him, which is odd. Since he is dead. The pawnbroker can *see* him and accepts the gold heart and gives him all kinds of ... all kinds of things that would appeal to a gypsy's daughter. And he rushes to the gypsy's daughter with them, and he cries up to her. And the gypsy's daughter thinks it is just a cat!" (Devlin 118).

8. While *The Tooth of Crime* ends with a suicide, Williams's *In the Bar of a Tokyo Hotel* begins with Miriam's observation that Tokyo has "a very impressive suicide rate," while in America there is "no suicide rate," but rather "an explosion of vitality which is world-wide," or, as the Barman puts it, "many cowboys exported" (7:3). America is seen as the land of image, of Hollywood roles that are indistinguishable from the performance of life or "vitality" in contrast to death. Mark claims that "an artist has to lay his life of the line" (7:22) and, like Hoss battling with Crow, battles with his art: "In the beginning, a new style of work can be stronger than you, but you learn to control it. It has to be controlled" (7:21). The images that he tries to "hold" (7:15), however, won't be stabilized, and wind up controlling him. He loses the battle at the end of the play, falling down dead.

WORKS CITED

Bigsby, C.W.E. *Modern American Drama*. Cambridge: Cambridge UP, 1992.
Bigsby, Christopher. "Born Injured: The Theatre of Sam Shepard." In *The Cambridge Companion to Sam Shepard*. Ed. Matthew C. Roudané. Cambridge: Cambridge UP, 2002.

Bottoms, Stephen J. *The Theatre of Sam Shepard: States of Crisis.* Cambridge: Cambridge UP, 1998.

Day, Christine R. and Bob Woods. *Where I Live: Selected Essays by Tennessee Williams.* New York: New Directions, 1978.

Devlin, Albert. *Conversations with Tennessee Williams.* Jackson, MS: University Press of Mississippi, 1986.

Kolin, Philip, ed. *The Undiscovered Country: The Later Plays of Tennessee Williams.* New York: Peter Lang, 2002.

Londré, Felicia Hardison. "The Two-Character Out Cry and Break Out." In *The Undiscovered Country: The Later Plays of Tennessee Williams,* ed. Philip C. Kolin. New York: Peter Lang, 2002.

Marranca, Bonnie, ed. *American Dreams: The Imagination of Sam Shepard* (New York: Performing Arts Journal Publications, 1981).

Moschovakis, Nick. "Tennessee Williams's American Blues: From the Early Manuscripts Through *Menagerie.*" *The Tennessee Williams Annual Review* 7 (2005): 14–36.

Roudané, Matthew, ed. *The Cambridge Companion to Sam Shepard.* Cambridge: Cambridge UP, 2002.

Roudané, Matthew C., ed. *The Cambridge Companion to Tennessee Williams.* Cambridge: Cambridge UP, 1997.

Saddik, Annette J. *The Politics of Reputation: The Critical Reception of Tennessee Williams' Later Plays.* Madison, NJ: Fairleigh Dickinson UP, 1999.

Shepard, Sam. *Action.* In *Fool For Love and Other Plays.* Introduction by Ross Wetzsteon. New York: Bantam Books, 1984.

_____. *Angel City.* In *Fool For Love and Other Plays.* Introduction by Ross Wetzsteon. New York: Bantam Books, 1984.

_____. *Buried Child.* In *Sam Shepard: Seven Plays.* Introduction by Richard Gilman. New York: Bantam, 1984.

_____. *La Turista.* In *Sam Shepard: Seven Plays.* Introduction by Richard Gilman. New York: Bantam, 1984.

_____. *Operation Sidewinder.* In *The Unseen Hand.* New York: Vintage, 1996.

_____. *The Mad Dog Blues.* In *The Unseen Hand.* New York: Vintage, 1996.

_____. *The Tooth of Crime.* In *Sam Shepard: Seven Plays.* Introduction by Richard Gilman. New York: Bantam, 1984.

_____. *True West.* In *Sam Shepard: Seven Plays.* Introduction by Richard Gilman. New York: Bantam, 1984.

Shewey, Don. *Sam Shepard.* New York: Da Capo Press, 1997.

Smith, Michael. "The Good Scene: Off Off Broadway." *Tulane Drama Review* 10: 4 (Summer 1966): 159–76.

Williams, Megan. "Nowhere Man and the Twentieth-Century Cowboy: Images of Identity and American History in Sam Shepard's *True West.*" *Modern Drama* 40 (Spring 1997): 57–73.

Williams, Tennessee. *Camino Real.* New York: New Directions, 1953.

_____. *The Theatre of Tennessee Williams,* 8 vols. New York: New Directions, 1971–92.

Sons of the South: An Examination of the Interstices in the Works of August Wilson and Tennessee Williams

Sandra G. Shannon

August Wilson was known to raise a few eyebrows during his career, especially when he would repeatedly proclaim his ignorance of plays authored by a list of fellow distinguished playwrights. When pressed, he went a step further to call it a "blessing" not to have read or attended play performances of some of the most recognized names among leading dramatists of the 20th century: "I consider it a blessing that when I started writing plays in earnest, in 1979, I hadn't read Chekhov. I hadn't read Ibsen, and I hadn't read Tennessee Williams, Arthur Miller or O'Neill" (*Telegraph News* 20 September 2007). In a 1987 interview, an unapologetic forty-two-year-old August Wilson told David Savran "I very purposefully didn't read them" (Savran 288–305). If taken quite literally, the playwright's admission that he had not "read" works by leading playwrights of the 20th century certainly baffles the imagination just as much as it fuels curiosity.

To be sure, there is little to be gained by scrutinizing Wilson's reading choices, but far more worthy of investigation is the obviously calculated politics of resistance that surrounds his series of disclaimers. In one sense, Wilson, the self-avowed "race man" and disciple of the Black Arts movement, found it necessary to construct himself in sharp contrast to fellow European and American dramatists. Essentially rejecting the notion of American pluralism, he drew fire from conservative critics, famously represented by *New Republic* drama critic Robert Brustein, who dismissed Wilson's cultural nationalist aesthetic as "a reverse form of the old politics of division" (101). But derisive charges such as this seemed only to embolden Wilson's position that "the majority of black Americans have rejected the idea of giving up who they are — in essence becoming someone else — in order to advance in American society" (Shannon 213). This thinking was at the center of his politics and greatly impacted his writing.

Despite initial impressions, August Wilson did not entirely close himself off from his literary ancestors. He also blurred the lines by openly aligning himself with a continuum that comprised the names of many of the same dramatists whose works he admittedly avoided. He told an audience at the 1996 conference of the Theatre Communications Group,

> In one guise, the ground I stand on has been pioneered by the Greek dramatist — by Euripides, Aeschylus and Sophocles — by William Shakespeare, by Shaw, Ibsen and Chekhov, Eugene

O'Neill, Arthur Miller, Tennessee Williams. In another guise, the ground that I stand on has been pioneered by my grandfather, by Nat Turner, by Denmark Vesey, Martin Delaney, Marcus Garvey and the Honorable Elijah Muhammad [*Ground* 11].

Wilson's double consciousness was often the source of much misunderstanding and debate within the largely white American theatre community. Believed by some to be hypocritical and by others as an artist whose plays "represent the culmination of political, social, and aesthetic objectives presaged by the Harlem Renaissance in the twenties and the Black Arts Movement of the sixties" (Harrison 316), he positioned himself at the cultural crossroads of America as an African American cultural nationalist and as a major *American* playwright.

The tension that surrounds Wilson's essentialist principles of identity construction and that informs his plays is largely due to his efforts to negotiate the historical binaries that exist between being African and being American. This familiar debate still informs much of the critical discourse generated by a number of cultural critics who have passionately argued the wisdom — indeed, the necessity — of both positions. Increasingly, however, in the face of a changing racial dynamics in 21st century America, many critics and scholars of African American literature have since modified their views, responding to the need to forge a space — albeit a guarded space — for examining the common ground or the interstices that exist between *American* writers of various racial and ethnic backgrounds. What has *not* been modified, however, in their less hard-lined positions, is the passionately upheld belief that, in the process of examining commonalities, differences must not minimized, subsumed or overlooked.

Wahneema Lubiana cautions against African Americanists who favor a complete collapse of cultural and racial differences in engaging African American texts. In an essay "Mapping the Interstices between Afro-American Cultural Discourse and Cultural Studies: A Prolegomenon" (1996), she admonishes this group by urging them

to try to make sure the world does not simplify Afro-American cultural production, docs not again rewrite Afro-American history or meta-commentary, does not leave us out of the discussion of ourselves. It is our imperative and that of scholars of minority discourses in general to complicate this "new" discovery of other "Americans." Otherwise our various groups' cultural productions will become simply new colonies for theoretical appropriation and exploitation [651].

In his essay "Writing, 'Race,' and the Difference It Makes," Henry Louis Gates espouses a similar counterdiscourse against American pluralism and urges African Americanists to keep in the forefront of their work a focus upon "how attitudes toward racial differences generate and structure literary texts by us *and* about us" (158). In an essay written in 1997 in reaction to the firestorm that erupted around Wilson's charges of disproportionately underfunded black theatres, Benny Sato Ambush advised a cautious lowering of racial barriers, concluding that "the road to fruitful cross-cultural/racial understanding, bridge building, and synthesis must begin with acknowledging and empowering differences" (585). Post colonialist critic Homi Bhaba is also aware of the potential for polarization that comes with often unilateral or imbalanced attention to cultural diversity. In his essay, "Cultural Diversity and Cultural Differences" (1988), he proposes the creation of "the Third Space of enunciation" to allow the "articulation of cultural difference." He reminds us in this same essay that "by exploring this hybridity, this 'Third Space,' we may elude the politics of polarity" (271).

At this historical moment in cultural studies, Bhaba's virtual "third space' — with all of the attendant precautions — provides for critics and scholars of various backgrounds an uncontested site for examining the work of August Wilson through the lens of an Americanist aesthetic. Such space not only allows them to tease out the American voice in Wilson's plays without charges of cultural heresy, but, more importantly, it also compels them to come to grips with the profound implications of Wilson's conscious and sustained efforts to portray his characters as "Africans in America." Accordingly, this uncontested space opens the way for a type of unchartered discourse and inspires the rigorous examination of the subtle and often unconscious intertextual relationships that do indeed emerge in Wilson's plays when examined alongside dramatic texts authored by fellow *American* playwrights.

By extension, the uncontested space that Bhaba imagines prompts a new set of critical inquiries that redefine "influence" over and beyond the act of reading. Even as Wilson seems to close himself off from other dramatists' works, one can detect the unmistakable imprint of some of these same unread artists on many of his plays. In order to draw attention to a different type of influence at work in Wilson's plays — influence that I contend is defined by confluence, radicalization, and subversion — let us, for a moment, set aside, but not discount, the playwright's claims.

Among America's most influential dramatists of the 20th century — Eugene O'Neill, Arthur Miller, Lorraine Hansberry, Lillian Helman, Edward Albee, and Tennessee Williams — it is Williams whose fiercely nontraditional and experimental playwriting style typifies the common ground shared between him and the late playwright August Wilson. Likewise, the tough aesthetic positions they each adapted to stretch the boundaries of convention in American theatre reveal an unmistakable kinship of creative consciousness. Beyond mere coincidence, the prevalence of such Wilson-Williams resemblances command attention on several levels that include both playwrights' challenge to traditional notions of realism onstage; their tendencies as poets toward lyrical expression, cadenced rhythms, and use of metaphor; their love-hate relationship with the South as central metaphor and site of memory; and a parade of restless and tortured men and women choosing between primal needs and individual quests to find meaning in their existence. While acknowledging Jordan Y. Miller's assertion that "comparisons are misleading, and in the final analysis, irrelevant" (7) and while heeding the matter-of-fact opinion of Wilson's former director, Lloyd Richards that "all comparisons are unfair" (Shannon, "Hansberry to Wilson"131), efforts to juxtapose these two Titans of twentieth century American theatre, yield fascinating new dimensions that are far from inconsequential.

While distinct issues such as race, racism, and cultural history cannot and should not be collapsed for the sake of finding common ground between Wilson and Williams, further study of their oeuvres reveals a number of additional parallels surfacing between the two. This study, however, draws attention to a relatively small number of commonalities, the purpose of which is to argue that both men worked in the similar vein of American theatre while writing plays that clearly portrayed cultural differences and the separate ideologies of both Pulitzer Prize winning American dramatists whose intersecting roots have wound their way from Pittsburgh, Pennsylvania's Hill District and from southern locales in and around Clarksdale, Mississippi only to intersect on the common ground of American theatre.

One may well ask "How could August Wilson *not* know the plays of Tennessee Williams?" Like every major playwright in the late 20th century, Tennessee Williams was an unavoidable influence even when the denial of such influence exists. Thomas Lanier Williams (1911–1983) was a favorite Son of the South, author of over fifty one-act and thirty full-length plays, and — like Wilson — the recipient of two Pulitzer Prizes in Drama and winner of numerous New York Drama Critics Awards. At one point he was dubbed "the most admired playwright in America" (1). Many of his now-classic plays continue to resonate with contemporary audiences and are kept alive through continual performances, an impressive body of scholarship, and a huge following. Likewise, his passionate yet troubled protagonists continue to capture the imagination of audiences worldwide with lines so timeless that have been emblazoned into the American lexicon.

August Wilson stands shoulder to shoulder with Tennessee Williams with an equally impressive list of accomplishments in American theatre and just as noteworthy parallels in the trajectories of their careers. Moreover, although their plays highlight issues of concern for two distinct cultural communities, at the same time, their work has what some critics of popular culture refer to as "crossover appeal" — that is, their work speaks to the human condition, thus allowing audiences to transcend cultural specificity in order to see reflections of themselves on stage or in the dramatic text.

While both, at one time or another, wore the mantle of "America's favorite playwright," August Wilson and Tennessee Williams garnered their share of accolades during their lifetime. Williams received Pulitzer Prizes twice for his plays (*Streetcar Named Desire*, 1947 and *Cat on a Hot Tin Roof*, 1955). Similarly, Wilson welcomed repeat Pulitzer Prizes in 1987 and in 1990 for *Fences* and *The Piano Lesson*, respectively. Moreover, both men have to their credit a list of New York Drama Critics Awards, national commendations, and a host of other awards that underscore the critical acclaim of their work. As a result of both the popular appeal and the critical acclaim of their plays, many of their now-classic plays have achieved immortality, remaining popular both inside and outside of the United States. Performances of their plays are routinely done in various languages before keenly interested international audiences.

Although Williams and Wilson enjoyed the validation, prestige, and popularity that came with their copious awards, when one considers the respective narratives of their early lives, there is little evidence that foreshadows this success. The son of a wayward white German baker and a devoted African American domestic worker, Frederick August Kittel (his name given at birth) grew up essentially fatherless in the Pittsburgh, Pennsylvania low income area known as the Hill District. With little help from her husband, Wilson's mother, Daisy Wilson, waged a valiant effort to keep the Kittel clan together by taking on domestic work to support her six children. Wilson was so moved by his mother's courage, her tenacity, her principles and the many sacrifices she made for the good of her family, that he eventually decided to disavow all things related to his German father and claim his mother's African American heritage. As a means of publicly announcing this allegiance, Frederick Kittel decided to keep his middle name *August* but assume his mother's maiden name, *Wilson*.

For August Wilson, thoughts on his experience within Pittsburgh's educational institutions sparked memories of derision, confinement, and ultimately rejection. Fed up with overt acts of racism from both classmates and from his teachers, he decided to walk away from this environment, effectively ending his formal education at the ninth grade. During his truant months that followed, Wilson turned to the Pittsburgh Public Library to satiate his unquenched and growing intellectual curiosity. Here, he devoured African American literary works by James Baldwin, Richard Wright, and Ralph Ellison. But it was the epiphany he experienced while listening to the lyrics of Bessie Smith's "Nobody Can Bake a Sweet Jelly Roll Like Mine" that further marked the recognition and acceptance of his African American identity. These mirror like reflections of his mother's culture led him to adopt a decidedly Afrocentric mission in his work.

In his early search for artistic voice, Wilson chose to emulate the flamboyant, linguistically daring Welsh poet, Dylan Thomas. Further confirming his reputation among local Hill District residents as an eccentric, he adopted Thomas's trademark tweed jacket and tie and mimicked his habit of smoking a pipe and affecting an accent — all in an effort to imitate his poet hero, the symbol of unadulterated rebellion and a Bohemian who ignored standards, drank profusely, and thumbed his nose at stuffy academicians of this time.

Following his Dylan Thomas phase, the assassination of Malcolm X along with the emergence of the Black Arts, Black Power, and Civil Rights movements stirred the cultural activist yearnings in Wilson and led him to seek company among black cultural nationalists, such as Amiri Baraka and Ed Bullins and among fellow Pittsburgh cohorts Rob Penny, Sala Udin, Chawlie P. Williams, Nick Flournoy, Maisha Baton, and Claude Purdy. As Co-founder of Pittsburgh's Black Horizons Theatre, he created a venue "to raise consciousness and politicize the black community" (Pointsett 74). He did so by reading, directing, and staging the works of his fellow playwrights "in the struggle" whom he considered to best articulate the spirit of revolution. "I had read Ed Bullins and Baraka and black playwrights of the sixties," he admitted to interviewer Vera Sheppard" (103).

August Wilson and Tennessee Williams shared a deep disregard for the strait jacket effect of traditional realism. Their sentiments are acknowledged in C. W. E. Bigsby's assurance that "Williams was never interested in realism" (35) and in Mary Bogumil's observation that Wilson's unrestrained approach to playwriting led him to "question the assumptions that the tradition [realism] was founded upon" (11). Instead of mimetic, photographic depictions of reality, Wilson and Williams significantly modified twentieth century realism as we know it to investigate the human condition and to plumb the debts of despair as never before. While Wilson was compelled to complicate his understanding of *the real* to underscore the lingering influence of slavery within African American culture of today and to show evidence of its hidden presence within the African American psyche, Williams was similarly compelled to stretch beyond the boundaries of classic realism but toward conveying the exotic and perverted personalities of a declining southern culture.

August Wilson negotiated the limitations associated with realism on the stage by complicating his familiar naturalistic settings with metaphysical and supernatural elements and an occasional use of magical realism. On one level, the narratives that unfold in *Gem of the Ocean*, *Joe Turner's Come and Gone*, and *The Piano Lesson*, for example, invite audiences into the daily lives of Wilson's characters through a series of unremarkable familiar sights, sounds, gestures, and rituals that keep each work grounded within the realm of the real. For the most part, characters in these plays go about their daily business changing sheets, preparing and eating meals, cleaning houses, pressing hair, hauling wood, peddling watermelons, pots and pans; growing a vegetable garden; collecting "dog poop" for profit, playing the guitar or the piano, or just enjoying a drink of liquor. We have seen the likes of many of them in our mind's eye.

On another level, such time-specific rituals and recognizable aspects of local color that they inspire in plays, such as *Gem of the Ocean*, *Joe Turner's Come and Gone*, and *The Piano Lesson*, are commingled with the paranormal to complicate illusions of reality. As one baffled observer so aptly put it, "Wilson's elemental efforts remind you of a large man trying to squeeze into a suit two sizes too small. Every now and then, you hear the fabric ripping" (Richards B1, B12). In one instance, a character in *Gem of the Ocean* (2006) holds in his hand a paper boat; in the next, that paper boat is transformed into his lifeline as the repentant Citizen Barlow realizes that he has been teleported to a painful site of his repressed memory called the City of Bones where the remains of thousands of his ancestors lay beneath the Atlantic Ocean. In one instance, a long lost father stands with his daughter at the entrance of a boarding house on the trail of his estranged wife and his child's mother. Yet, in another, this same brooding, enigmatic guest lies sprawled out on the boarding house floor as if in a trance, prompted by "blood's memory," [1] to vividly remember animated bones washed ashore and similar images from the Middle Passage that lay repressed in him.

A gust of wind rippling through billowing white curtains followed closely by the sound of a few melodious notes from an unmanned piano were ominous signs that the Kennedy Center's 1989 production of *The Piano Lesson* would be anything but conventional. From this opening scene on through the play's conclusion, Wilson, with the help of the play's director Lloyd Richards, blurred the lines of reality by conjuring up supernatural elements on stage midst visible reminders of the natural world. They did so fully expecting that the play's audience would willingly suspend their disbelief for the duration of the play. This blurring of reality and introduction of the supernatural in *The Piano Lesson* required audiences and readers alike to suspend disbelief of the legendary Ghost of the Yellow Dog that had so fascinated Mississippi locals that the mythology surrounding the burnt boxcar and relative who perished in it had become the stuff of popular folklore. Moreover, Sutter's pesky ghost, like Toni Morrison's reincarnated vigilante daughter, floats in and out of the naturalistic set much to the horror of unsuspecting intruders. Cued by Berneice and daughter Mareatha's screams at the actual sight of Sutter's ghost along with a detailed pretext that explains possible motivations for the white man's attachment to the piano and his subsequent death by drowning in a well, those who experience the play are asked to accept the play's supernatural premise based upon the "realities" that Wilson constructs. Boy Willie's acknowledgement certainly helps in this endeavor as he reveals rather matter-of-factly, "The Ghosts of the Yellow Dog got Sutter.... Everybody say the Ghosts of the Yellow Dog pushed him" (*Piano Lesson*, I.1.4–5).

Just as Wilson was compelled to redefine and, in some instances, blur boundaries between the real and the imagined, so too was Tennessee Williams moved to redefine obsolete and restrictive conventions of the stage during his time. Thus, Williams set about renegotiating traditional western parameters of staging the well made play to convey the exotic and perverted personalities of a declining Southern culture. He did so by coming up with his own subversive response to the strait jacket effect of realism; he called this liberating experimental approach "plastic theatre." Very much as Wilson was to do some forty years later, Williams achieved "unusual freedom of convention" by "rooting his poetic plays in concrete imagery and allusion — like songs, brand names such as Celotex and Life Saver, proper names, and amounts of money" (Bigsby 36). He was prone to transform, as if by magic, many otherwise ordinary stage props into symbols that were used to depict the inner struggles of his lead characters.

The memory play posed the greatest challenge to both Wilson and Williams, but this form also afforded them the greatest artistic freedom. Williams introduced the genre to the American stage with his first popular success, *The Glass Menagerie* (1945). Told in retrospect by a pensive narrator who reminisces about events that led him to abandon an overbearing mother and a reclusive, physically handicapped sister, the play's basic conflict takes its cue from the collisions that take place when heretofore repressed memories dissolve in the face of stark reality. The challenge for Williams was to capture and use stage machinery to convey the state of psychological denial that both Amanda and Laura Wingfield experience. While Amanda's obsessive recollections about "gentlemen callers" show her to be stuck in time and increasingly delusional, Amanda Wingfield slides further into self loathing and alienation. To draw attention to their troubled inner state of mind, Williams turns to several expressionistic strategies. Laura's chronic case of fragility is projected onto her collection of glass figurines, while her mother projects the splendor of her lost youth onto her carefully preserved gowns. Williams defended these choices in the play's Production Notes:

> When a play employs unconventional techniques, it is not, or certainly shouldn't be, trying to escape its responsibility of dealing with reality, or interpreting experience, but is actually or should be attempting to find a closer approach, a more penetrating and vivid expression of things as they are [xix].

August Wilson defied conventions of realism by introducing to the stage different strategies for examining the present through the lens of the past — what critic Harry Elam refers to as "the past as present." According to critic Elam, "Wilson's cycle suggests that African Americans need to "embrace the legacy of slavery, celebrate the African retentions that remain within African American cultural practices, and acknowledge the psychological scars that still endure" (xix). For Wilson, staging his characters' "blood's memory" became a tour de force requiring more than the conventional set could offer. For Wilson, the challenge in staging the nomadic Herald Loomis of *Joe Turner's Come and Gone* was getting audiences to visualize his inner turmoil. He did so by vividly recreating his nightmarish, surrealistic scenes depicting the horrors of the Middle Passage and by revealing a cultural continuum in a string of characters who possess historical memory and who serve as repositories of the African American past, such as Doaker Charles (*The Piano Lesson*); Aunt Ester (*Gem of the Ocean*); Old Joe (*Radio Golf*); and Holloway in *Two Trains Running*.

Like the artist formerly known as Frederick August Wilson, Thomas Lanier Williams's solution to the circumstances of his early life was to change his name. While August Wilson's renaming himself was tantamount to turning his back on the cultural heritage of his estranged white German father, Tennessee Williams's had more ulterior motives. While visiting his grandparents in Memphis in 1939, he sent several of his short plays postmarked with their address to a contest for young writers sponsored by the Group Theatre. Also, in an effort to circumvent contest guidelines, he misrepresented both his age and his name. Although 27 years old at the time, he indicated that he was 23. Although he still went by the name of Thomas Williams, for this contest, he dubbed himself "Tennessee." He ultimately won the contest under false pretense and kept the catchy pen name for the rest of his life.

The lives of August Wilson and Tennessee Williams may be described in terms of a number of dualities that required constant negotiation throughout their lives and throughout their playwriting careers. In addition to the most obvious duality of Wilson's mixed European and African American parentage, he was faced with what might be termed "triple consciousness"—that is, the constant awareness of his existence as one part European, one part African and one part American in a predominantly white society. Understandably, then, the aesthetic that informed his plays owes much to his need to navigate within these blurred dimensions while also remaining grounded in a culture that has direct links to Africa. For example, the restless, newly released Herald Loomis in Wilson's *Joe Turner's Come and Gone* (1988) must negotiate dual landscapes stretched before him. One contains horrible reminders of his slave past; the other is cut off from every memory of that slave experience. For Loomis, the tension that results when he unwittingly suppresses one landscape emerges in the form of recurring nightmares and troubling visions of the Middle Passage: "I done seen bones rise up out the water," he tells the resident conjure man. "Rise up and walk across the water. Bones walking on top of the water" (*Joe Turner*, I. 4. 53). In *The Piano Lesson* (1990), Wilson's characters debated the recurring questions, What should we do with our legacy? and How best should we put it to us? What is at stake during the heated exchanges between the dueling siblings in the play is whether to remain complacent in merely revering a 125-year-old family heirloom or whether to capitalize on the money it will bring if sold. In *Radio Golf* (2005), Harmon Wilkes must negotiate between the profit-driven corporate world and a community of his elders who stand in the way of plans to demolish a longtime family home place. Harmon eventually backs away from any plans to erect a Borders Bookstore and a Starbucks coffee shop in the site occupied by a family house with ties to his own cultural past.

Like August Wilson, for much of his adult life, Tennessee Williams functioned at the crossroads by situating himself in between competing worlds. In each of Williams's plays is a constant conflict between a host of antithetical forces—between the Old South and the

New South; between the real and the imagined; between the past and the present, and between gay and straight. Williams's *Streetcar Named Desire* (1947) — more so than any of his other plays — contains evidence of each of these binaries that, interestingly, reflect some of the same issues that impacted the author's life. Blanche DuBois personifies an Old South that collides with what Kenneth Holditch calls "the soulless quality of the so-called 'New South,' the land of the Snopeses and Kowalskis, in which there is no place for a Blanche DuBois who yearns for music and poetry and art" (x). Refusing to concede to a decaying Old South, Blanche recreates its past glory in her imagination and lives within her own make believe world.

The most pervasive form of schizophrenia with which Williams had to contend did not involve race or culture. Instead, much of the tension that Williams experienced in his life and that found expression in his plays was, in some way, linked to his homosexuality. Taunted by his father Cornelius Williams, who chastised his young son for his noticeably effeminate ways, Williams went to great lengths to deflect his father's suspicions of his homosexuality. *Cat on a Hot Tin Roof* (1954) draws much of its conflict from Williams own combative father-son relationship in this regard. Wealthy southern landowner Big Daddy Pollitt loves his alcoholic son Brick, yet refuses to acknowledge and accept his homosexuality. Like Cornelius Williams, Big Daddy placed great stock in a son who does not step up to take the mantle of his inheritance.

Like Tennessee Williams, August Wilson was a poet at heart, and poetry lent itself well to the lyrical quality of their writing. Enamored by the sound of words and quite adept at using metaphors to convey their multilayered meaning, Wilson published a few short, obtuse verses in the 1960s and 1970s in several African American literary venues such as *Negro Digest*. But his early poetry, more often than not, privileged words over meaning. He confessed in a 1991 interview: "I was writing obscure poetry certainly first. It actually took me from '65 to '73 before I could actually write a poem that I felt was written in my own voice" (Shannon, *Dramatic Vision*, 202). The touch of the poet may be seen at every turn in Wilson's plays. It emerges in *Fences* in the eloquent and long suffering Rose Maxson, who in an often recited angry speech explains why she has remained married for 18 years to her domineering tyrant of a husband Troy. It surfaces in the wisdom that Bynum Walker shares with the naïve, guitar-playing country boy Jeremy Furlow on what a good woman has to offer beyond the physical: "When you grab hold of a woman, you got something there. You got a whole world there. You got a way of life kicking up under your hand" (*Joe Turner*, 1. 3. 45). Poetry, according to Wilson, is "the bedrock of my playwriting. Primarily not so much in the language as it is in the approach to the thinking — thinking as a poet, one thinks differently than one thinks as a playwright" (Shannon, *Dramatic Vision*, 202).

Williams, too, boasted a touch of the poet, having whetted his appetite for poetry after reading works by a list of his favorite authors whose verse was in the tradition of American poets, French symbolists, and English Romantics. An avid reader, Williams took to his grandfather's library coming across several books of poetry that captured his attention. The verse of Wordsworth, Baudelaire, Dickinson, Whitman, Crane, Yeats, Cummings, and Dylan Thomas both fascinated and inspired him. Matthew Roudane observed that "Williams emerged as the poet of the heart" and that " he worked assiduously in creating poetic stage moments, moments in which social fact, psychological collapse, and eroticized encounter form a still point in which imagination, itself, becomes the last refuge for his fated characters" (3). Much like Williams, Tom Wingfield, the dutiful yet increasingly frustrated son in Williams's *The Glass Menagerie* is a closet poet whose aspirations run counter to the money-groveling he is forced to be a part of in order to eek a living for his mother, his sister, and himself. All comes full circle when, in retrospect, he divulges that he was "fired for writing a poem on the lid of a shoe-box" (I. 7. 96). He leaves permanently for Saint Louis shortly thereafter.

Wilson's confessed disregard for Williams's plays can easily overshadow the fact that the two were surprisingly *conversant* in ways that did not require knowledge of each other's work. For example, both may be justifiably classified as "sons of the South"—not just in terms of time spent in this region of the United States, but also in terms of how the South becomes a large part of—and dominated, to some extent—their creative imagination. Wilson learned of the Deep South through the fascinating tales told to him by his mother Daisy Wilson about his grandmother's migration from the tobacco fields of North Carolina to the steel mills of Pittsburgh, Pennsylvania. Williams, on the other hand, was born in the south and spent a portion of his boyhood in the heart of the Mississippi Delta region, settling in several small southern towns before eventually leaving the south altogether in 1918, but not until he had internalized southern ideals and mores.

Although Wilson claimed the hilly terrain of Pittsburgh, Pennsylvania, as his home, his ancestral roots find their way to the Deep South where his maternal grandmother labored in the tobacco fields of North Carolina. Much like hundreds of others who grew weary of the Jim Crow politics so prevalent in the South, she gave up on working the land and migrated North. The South depicted in Wilson's plays, with its many guitar-carrying and brogan-wearing country boys, its cotton and tobacco fields, and its farm mules, is the site of conflicting emotions that range from blissful nostalgia to outright disdain. Wilson's epic renderings of working class African Americans are comparable to Tennessee Williams's lyrical depictions of the economic and psychological decline of the antebellum southern plantation class. In just as many ways, the two men are clearly part of a larger continuum of American playwrights.

Like Tennessee Williams's, August Wilson's relationship to the South was one that is best characterized by bittersweet ambiguity. On one hand, Wilson acknowledged the southern landscape as the site of unforgettable pain and anguish for African Americans, many of whom were slaves or who were the relatives of former slaves. On the other, he would often argue passionately that African American made a major error in trading their land in the South to pursue the empty promise of a better life up north:

> We came to the North, and we're still victims of discrimination and oppression in the North. The real reason that the people left was a search for jobs, because the agriculture, cotton agriculture in particular, could no longer support us. But the move to the cities has not been a good move. Today ... we still don't have jobs. The last time black in America were working was during the Second World War, when there was a need for labor, and it did not matter what color you were [Moyers 167].

This aversion to the South functions as an undercurrent in each of Wilson's plays. As I have argued elsewhere,

> Levee's potential to self-destruct because of his severed ties with the South is also evident in his futile attempts to replace Ma Rainey's "old jug band music" with his jazzed-up arrangements. He scowls at his colleagues, and repeatedly taunts them with insults stemming from his deep-seated loathing of anything related to life in the South. He condescendingly proclaims "Now we gonna dance it [Ma's brand of music] ... but we ain't gonna countrify it. This ain't no barn dance" [Shannon, "Transplant," 664].

Molly Cunningham of *Joe Turner's Come and Gone* is also forthright in letting her potential suitor know, "Molly ain't going South" (II. 1. 66). But just as determined as Levee is to exorcise the southern flavor from Ma's music and just as adamant as Molly is about not returning to the South, Boy Willie is determined to go back to capitalize on the benefits of landownership. Unlike his accomplice Lymon, he has no intentions of being blinded by the false allure of the North.

Notwithstanding race, class, or culture, the roots of August Wilson and Tennessee Williams converge and run deep in the South. No doubt, the southern landscape that inspired some of William's most memorable characters is not the same setting that Wilson's disoriented former slaves occupy in his plays. Wilson knew well the South's legacy of slavery and Jim Crow ethics; of heart wrenching tales of separation, migration, and reunion; of horrific lynchings and savage beatings; and of bestial labor and rampant sexual abuse. Williams, on the other hand, was intimately familiar with the southern caste tradition, of its conflict with the American middle class Protestant culture, of its hypocritical standards or respectability, and of its aura of pretense and puritanical ardor.

August Wilson's dramatic renderings of what the south meant for African Americans inhabitants from the early 1900s to the present in the United States capture a place where memory is lost, where families have been uprooted and displaced, where lives remain in constant upheaval, and where individuals have lost all sense of hope and direction; in the often-repeated Wilson's words, they have "lost their song." In a lyrical introduction to his play, *Joe Turner's Come and Gone* (1988), Wilson described the human "leftovers" of this southern wasteland: "From the deep and the near South the sons and daughters of newly freed African slaves wander into to the city. Isolated, cut off from memory, having forgotten the names of gods and only guessing at their faces, they arrive dazed and stunned, their heart kicking in their chest with a song worth singing ("The Play," *Joe Turner's Come and Gone*). In his Pulitzer Prize winning play, *Fences* (1986), he is equally cynical in his regard for the south and just as sympathetic to the dire circumstances faced by the tides of displaced southern refugees who fled poverty and death in the south only to be met with indifference in the north:

> For the immigrants of Europe, a dream dared and won true. The descendants of African slaves were offered no such welcome or participation. They came from places called the Carolinas and the Virginias, Georgia, Alabama, Mississippi, and Tennessee. They came strong, eager, searching. The city rejected them and they fled and settled along the riverbanks and under bridges in shallow, ramshackle houses made of sticks and tarpaper [xvii].

The constant movement of Wilson's characters both to and from the South attests to their willingness to be deceived by the lure of the north and their determination to escape the painful memories of the past. For both Williams and Wilson, the South was a hotbed of contention, but both captured its ever-present lure — albeit a lure that is often tempered by bittersweet consequences.

Native son Tennessee Williams was devoted to the South and to capturing the nuances of this region in his characters' speech, their actions, and in their manners. According to Kenneth Holditch and Richard Leavitt, "No writer of this century more than Williams, who was strongly influenced by his Mississippi youth and his many years of residence in New Orleans and Key West, has been as markedly southern in his choice of settings, characters, plots, and themes (Holditch and Leavitt x). For Williams, the South afforded the appropriate exotic backdrop for working out on stage the sexual tensions and neuroses of a declining ruling class. Amanda Wingfield of his classic play *The Glass Menagerie* (1945) and Blanche DuBois of *Streetcar Named Desire* (1947) are classic heroines in this regard. These one-time southern belles desperately seek a return to the antebellum south of their girlhood innocence while many of Wilson's characters go to great lengths to escape the psychological hold it has on them.

The conflict of both *Menagerie* and *Streetcar* has as much to do with their frustration at not being able to return to their mythic south as it does with the gradual understanding that they cannot recapture their previous youth. But for the lack of money, Blanche DuBois would have, no doubt, remained at Bell Reve; however, she, too, was under the spell of the south: "Well, Stella — you're going to reproach me, I know that you're bound to reproach me — but before you do — take into consideration — you left! I stayed and struggled! You came to New Orleans and looked out for yourself. I stayed at Belle Reve and tried to hold it together!" (*Streetcar*, I. 25). For much of *The Glass Menagerie*, Amanda Wingfield wages a fierce battle against *realities* of both a declining south and her impending old age. She boasts before Laura, "Now just look at your mother! ... This is the dress in which I led the cotillion. Won the cake-walk twice at Sunset Hill, wore one Spring to the Governor's Ball in Jackson! See how I sashayed around the ballroom, Laura. I wore it on Sundays for my gentlemen callers!" (*Glass Menagerie*).

The south to which Wilson was intimately connected and the South that he indirectly inherited from his mother and maternal grandmother became the same South that he felt compelled to question, subvert, and reconfigure in his ten-play cycle. By varying degrees, each play demonstrates Wilson's attempts to rewrite the narrative of the South for African Americans, placing them in the position of subjects and giving them a sense of agency in their destinies. In Wilson's sweeping revision, the South occupies a bitter sweet position. In most instances his characters risk all to leave its depressing legacy behind them. In other rare instances, the South becomes the acknowledged home of African Americans who consider it offering their best chance of claiming at least a portion of the American Dream through land ownership.

As true Sons of the South, Williams and Wilson fiercely advocated the importance of land ownership. For Wilson, especially considering the massive relocation and shifting of the African American population during the early part of the 20th century, the acts of selling, losing and being duped out of one's legal rights to land ownership were rampant. He often expressed deep regret over the amount of land that often illegally slipped through the hands of African Americans who had focused their sights, instead, on a better life in the North. *The Piano Lesson*'s Boy Willie is perhaps Wilson's most passionate spokesperson for this cause: "Now I want to get Sutter's land with that piano. I get Sutter's land and I can go down and cash in the crop and get my seed. As long as I got the land and the seed then I'm alright. I can always get me a little something else. Cause that land give back to you" (I. 2. 51).

Like Wilson, Williams knew well the value of land — especially land in the South. As Kenneth Holditch notes, "Tennessee shared that southern obsession with the importance of property" (Holditch and Leavitt 27). For proud southern regionalist writers, such as Tennessee Williams, Walker Percy, William Faulkner, and Eudora Welty, retention of land was the last line of defense against a South in decline. Williams's battered and compromised heroine Blanche DuBois epitomizes the tragic consequences that befall those who do not hold onto the family homestead. "Yes, accuse me! Sit there and stare at me, thinking *I* let the place go! *I* let the place go? Where were *you*! In bed with your — Polack! (I. 1. 27).

In addition to layers of undiscovered intertextual relationships within their work, several striking commonalities exist in the personal lives of these men. For a period of time, both grew up in essentially female-headed households, and both saw very little of their emotionally and, all too often, physically distant biological fathers. Although Cornelius Williams, Tennessee's father, came from an upper-class Tennessee family, the traveling commercial salesman was a verbally abusive alcoholic whose love was never evident to young Tennessee. What little time the two spent together was marred by Cornelius's tendency to belittle his son, whom he suspected was gay; he took delight in penning the name "Miss Nancy" to belittle his noticeably effeminate son. Understandably, then, for Tennessee, this father-son relationship became a source of alienation, fear, and rejection. The overbearing patriarch, Cornelius

Williams, struck fear in the lives of his wife Edwina and the Williams children, frequently insulting and bullying them. As such, one may note a clear correlation between the unchecked egos of the domineering and often unreasonable Big Daddy and Stanley Kowalski.

August Wilson, too, felt the sting of neglect from his white German father, Frederick Kittel, a baker by trade who floated in and out of their Pittsburgh family home paying little attention to Daisy Wilson Kittel, his African American wife, and their six children. As John Lahr writes in *The New Yorker,* "The only father-son experience Wilson remembers was being taken downtown by Fritz in a blizzard to get a pair of Gene Autry cowboy boots" (53). The fourth of six children, the young boy who was little more than his father's namesake, Frederick August Kittel (later known as August Wilson), grew to dislike his absentee father and, out of growing disdain for him, decided to mold himself according to the rituals, ideas, and manners embraced by his African American mother. The father-son disconnect repeated itself later, when Wilson's mother divorced Kittel and remarried his stepfather David Bedford, who often sparred with Wilson and tried to push him to play sports against his will.

While Williams's angst against Cornelius found expression in crude, domineering, and uncompromising characters such as Big Daddy Pollit (*Cat on a Hot Tin Roof*) and Stanley Kowalski (*Streetcar Named Desire*), August Wilson projected his fervent desire for father-son reconciliation onto characters such as Troy and Cory Maxson (*Fences*), James and Booster Becker (*Jitney*), and the fatherless and fateful warrior King (*King Hedley II*). Unfortunately, in each instance, that reconciliation does not occur during their fathers' lifetime. For Cory, Booster, and King, respectively, the closest they come to father-son reconciliation occurs posthumously following the tragic demise of a father who keels over during batting practice, who perishes in a factory mishap, and who is gunned down during a gambling dispute.

Even more so than the strained and sometimes acrimonious relationships that Williams and Wilson endured with their biological fathers, their close working relationships with two well known directors had a major impact on the style and substance of their plays. For all of the successes that August Wilson achieved in numerous collaboration with longtime director Lloyd Richards and for all of the critical acclaim that Williams enjoyed while working with Elia Kazan, both playwrights were faced with the potential to be overshadowed in the creative process. Indeed both walked a fine line between trusting and yielding to the advice of their surrogates and giving up too much of their authorial rights of ownership.

According to Williams scholar Brenda Murphy, "The relationship between Williams and Kazan was based on a mutual affection, trust, and admiration that supported their freedom of experiment artistically." She went on to add, however, "It also contained destructive elements that strained the relationship as time went on, and resulted in its eventual dissolution" (6). Interestingly, Williams himself vacillated between maintaining a respectable amount of control over his scripts and, at one time, actively seeking out Kazan to take the lead. Critics were quick to pounce on what they perceived to be an unhealthy interdependency between playwright and director. As Murphy notes,

> After Williams published a note with the *Cat* [*Cat on a Hot Tin Roof*] script explaining that he had felt pressure from Kazan to make changes in the play he hadn't been sure of, most critics in the fifties tended to describe Kazan's involvement in the script's development as an intrusion of commercial values into the artist's domain and Williams's acceptance of it as caving in to the desire for success [4].

August Wilson and director Lloyd Richards created dramatic art together while using what Murphy describes as a "symphony model"—that is, an arrangement where the director assumes the role of "conductor, merely interpreting the playwright's fixed text" (xii). When one considers the role that Lloyd Richards played in bringing Wilson's plays to the stage, this term has clear limitations. What disqualifies this otherwise appropriate description for both the Wilson/Richards as well as the Williams/Kazan collaborative models is the qualifying word *merely*. As was the case with the latter professional partnership, Lloyd Richards far exceeded traditional parameters for a director's role. This was made clear during a 1990 interview at his Yale School of Drama office. He responded at length to my question, "Where do you draw the line between the playwright's intent and your own ideas on how the play should be staged?"

> I don't draw the line. I consider my responsibility to be to fulfill the intent of the playwright in his work, which does not mean necessarily that I literally do that because sometimes the playwright is not totally conscious of everything that exists in his work. You know, he sees it one way or sees in on one level, but there's a little bit more to an individual, a character, to a situation, to what really has been the deepest provocation of what the playwright is writing about. So my contributions are in discovering what he has to say, illuminating that, and enhancing that [Shannon, "From Hansberry to Wilson," 125].

From the 1984 opening of *Ma Rainey's Black Bottom* to the end of the 1996 run of *Seven Guitars*, the Wilson/Richards team appeared to forge an invincible bond that extended beyond a purely business arrangement. Certainly Wilson saw in Richards a surrogate father figure. He became for the relatively naïve playwright a respected figure who showed him the ropes in navigating the shrewd business world of theatre and introduced him to the industry's elite and power brokers. Also, race was a unifying factor in their relationship as African American men. They shared particular insight on the culture from this vantage. As I point out in "Subtle Imposition: The Lloyd Richards-August Wilson Formula,"

> One factor which is often underplayed when describing this successful duo is the common ground they share as black men in a traditionally white-controlled industry. Certainly their ten-year relationship has been prolific yet not without an occasional brush with green-eyed demons of professional envy of sheer racism. At such times, Richards, in his characteristic wisdom and candor, extends the jurisdiction of his subtle imposition to counsel Wilson on the politics of surviving as a black man in a predominantly white business [Shannon, "Subtle Imposition," 192].[2]

As news of Richards illness increased, he quietly moved off to the periphery of Wilson's career, later to be replaced by Marion McClinton and finally Kenny Leon, but not until he had used his extraordinary talents and his enormous stature within the American theatre community to solidify Wilson's reputation as a major American playwright.

As theatre scholars continue to respectfully explore possible interstices and latent intertextual connections that exist between writers of different cultures, they stand to open up a whole new realm of previously unpopular critical discourse. August Wilson and Tennessee Williams have left us a classic body of work that continues to gain increasing importance in teaching us what makes us *all* Americans in the 21st century.

NOTES

1. August Wilson coined the phrase "blood's memory" to suggest that, despite surface-level differences, Africans in America are kindred in their collective memories of a slave past. As Elam notes, "Wilson constructs blood memory on and through his dramas not as a biological essence but as a symbolic representation that dramaturgically blurs the lines between the figurative and the real" (*Past as Present in the Drama of August Wilson*, xviii).

2. Shannon, Sandra G. "From Lorraine Hansberry to August Wilson: An Interview with Lloyd Richards." 14:1 (1991), pp. 125, 131, Callaloo ©The Johns Hopkins University Press. Reprinted with permission of The Johns Hopkins University Press.

WORKS CITED

Ambush, Benny Sato. "Culture Wars." *African American Review* 31.4 (Winter 1997): 579–586.

"August Wilson: An Interview." By Vera Sheppard. *Conversations with August Wilson.* Eds. Jackson R. Bryer and Mary C. Hartig. Jackson: University Press of Mississippi, 2006. 101–117. Mississippi: University Press of Mississippi, 2006.

"August Wilson." *Obituary. Telegraph News* (20 September 2007). On-line. Internet. Telegraph.Co.UK: (www.telegraph.co.uk/news/index.jhtml).

"August Wilson: Playwright." By Bill Moyers. In *A World of Ideas,* 167–80. New York: Doubleday, 1989.

Bhaba, Homi. "Cultural Diversity and Cultural Differences," In *African American Literary Criticism: 1773 to 2000.* New York: Twayne, 1999.

Bigsby, C.W.E. "Tennessee Williams: The Theatricalising Self." *Modern American Drama, 1945–2000.* New York: Cambridge University Press, 2000.

Bogumil, Mary L. *Understanding August Wilson.* South Carolina University Press, 1999.

Brustein, Robert. "Subsidized Separatism," *American Theatre* (October 1996): 26+.

Conversations with August Wilson. Ed. Jackson R. Bryer and Mary C. Hartig. Jackson: University Press of Mississippi, 2006.

Critical Essays on Tennessee Williams. Ed. Robert A. Martin. New York: G. K. Hall, 1997.

Elam, Harry. *The Past as Present in the Drama of August Wilson.* Ann Arbor: University of Michigan Press, 2004.

Gates, Henry Louis. "Writing, 'Race,' and the Difference It Makes," *The Critical Tradition: Classic Texts and Contemporary Trends,* 2nd Edition, Ed. David H. Richter. Boston: Bedford, 1998.

Griffin, Alice. *Understanding August Wilson.* South Carolina University Press, 1995.

"Introduction" In *The Cambridge Companion to Tennessee Williams.* Ed. Matthew C. Roundane. Massachusetts: Cambridge University Press, 1997.

Harrison, Paul Carter. "The Blues Poetics." In *Three Plays by August Wilson.* Pittsburgh: University of Pittsburgh Press, 1991.

Kenneth Holditch and Richard Leavitt. *Tennessee Williams and the South.* Jackson: Mississippi UP, 2002.

Lahr, John. "Been Here and Gone: How August Wilson Brought a Century of Black American Culture to the Stage." *New Yorker,* April 16, 2001, 50–65.

Miller, Jordan Y. Introduction. *Twentieth Century Interpretations of a Streetcar Named Desire: A Collection of Critical Essay.* Ed. Jordan Y. Miller. New Jersey: Prentice-Hall, 1971.

Murphy, Brenda. *Tennessee Williams and Elia Kazan: A Collaboration in Theatre.* New York: Cambridge University Press, 1992.

Pointsett, Alex. "August Wilson: Hottest New Playwright." *Ebony,* November 1987.

Richards, David. "The Tortured Spirit of *Joe Turner.*" *Washington Post,* 9 October 1987, B1, B12.

Savran, David. "August Wilson*" In Their Own Words: Contemporary American Playwrights.* New York: Theatre Communications Group, 1988. Also in *Conversations with August Wilson.* Eds. Jackson Bryer and Mary Hartig. University Press of Mississippi, 2006.

Shannon, Shannon. "The Transplant that Did Not Take: August Wilson's Views on the Great Migration." *African American Review* 31.4 (Winter 1997): 659–666.

_____. *The Dramatic Vision of August Wilson.* Washington, DC: Howard UP, 1995.

_____. "From Lorraine Hansberry to August Wilson: An Interview with Lloyd Richards." *Callaloo* 14.1 (1991): 124–135.

_____. "Subtle Imposition: The Lloyd Richards-August Wilson Formula." *August Wilson: A Casebook.* New York: Garland, 1994.

Wahneema Lubiano, "Mapping the Interstices between Afro-American Cultural Discourse and Cultural Studies: A Prolegomenon." In *African American Literary Theory.* Edited by Winston Napier. New York: New York UP, 2000.

Williams, Tennessee. *The Glass Menagerie.* New York: New Directions, 1945.

_____. Production Notes. *The Glass Menagerie.* New York: Random House, 1945.

_____. *Cat on a Hot Tin Roof.* New York: New Directions, 1955.

_____. *A Streetcar Named Desire.* New York: New American Library, 1947.

Wilson, August. *The Ground on Which I Stand.* New York: Theatre Communications Group, 2001.

_____. *Fences.* New York: Plume, 1986.

_____. *Joe Turner's Come and Gone.* New York: Plume, 1988.

_____. *The Piano Lesson.* New York: Plume, 1990.

Williams, Mamet, and the Artist *In Extremis*

Brenda Murphy

Tennessee Williams and David Mamet are usually thought of as polar opposites in the field of American drama, Williams's romantic poetry of the theatre at the other end of the spectrum from the hypermasculine hyperrealism of Mamet. Yet Mamet's references to Williams over the years have been uniformly admiring, if brief and cryptic. In an "epitaph" for Williams that was first published in *Rolling Stone* shortly after his death in 1983, Mamet called his plays "the greatest dramatic poetry in the American language" ("Epitaph" 102). In a 1988 interview he said he was "very interested in the work of Tennessee" (Kane 73) early in his career. Speaking of the general state of American civilization in the same interview, he said: "Nothing lasts forever. We had a good time. We had Tennessee Williams. We had the hula hoop. We had the Edsel. All kinds of good stuff. The Constitution. To name but a few. Shelley Winters. Now we have got to pay the piper" (Kane 81). In 1997, when Charlie Rose asked him who his influences were, Mamet mentioned Beckett, Pinter, Terence Rattigan, "Tennessee Williams, of course," and Arthur Miller (Kane 189).

Although Williams clearly looms large on David Mamet's cultural landscape, his influence on Mamet's work seems less clear. In Mamet's earliest plays, before he had been so thoroughly identified with "Mametspeak" and established the tough-guy persona that became his cultural marker, Williams's influence is directly evident. "Prologue: American Twilight," for example, the opening piece in "The Blue Hour" (1979) is reminiscent of Tom's opening monologue in *The Glass Menagerie* in tone and rhythm, and is directly indebted to *A Streetcar Named Desire*:

> **Man**: In great American cities at *l'heure bleu* airborne dust particles cause buildings to appear lightly outlined in black. The people hurry home. They take a taxi or they walk or crush into the elevated trains or subways; or they go into the library where it is open and sit down and read a magazine and wait a bit so that the crush of travelers will dissipate.
>
> This is the Blue Hour
> The sky is blue and people feel blue.
>
> When they look up they will see a light or "powder" blue is in the Western sky where, meanwhile, in the East the sky is midnight blue; and this shade creeps up to the zenith and beyond, and changes powder blue to midnight and, eventually to black, whereat the buildings lose their outlines and become as stageflats in the glow of incandescent lamps. This is the Blue Hour — the American twilight as it falls today in the cities [*Blue Hour* 137].

136

The echoes from *Streetcar*'s opening stage directions are unmistakable.[1] Mamet did not engage in this kind of writing for very long, however, and the presence of Williams is less direct in his work after 1980.

Mamet's epitaph provides some clues about the direction that Williams's influence took in the 1980s. It begins with the observation that "the theater is a beautiful life but a harsh business" ("Epitaph" 101). Playwriting, Mamet wrote, is "a young man's game, for it is easily tolerated only by the inspired and naive — by those bursting with the joy of discovery and completely, unselfconsciously generous of that gift" (101). Mamet suggests that the public who were compelled to pay attention by the "generosity and superfluity of life" (101) in Williams's early writing, were obliged "to consider him already dead" 101) when his life and view of life became less immediately accessible to them. In later years, "his continued being and the fact of his later work disturbed our illusion" (101). Noting that Americans "are a kind people living in a cruel time," Mamet suggests that "we don't know how to show our love. This inability was the subject of his plays" (102). The epitaph ends with honest sentiment: "We thank him and we wish him, with love, the best we could have done and did not while he was alive. We wish him what he wished us: the peace that we are all seeking" (102). The elegy positions Williams sympathetically as the protagonist of his own life-long drama about the artist. As Mamet describes it, Williams's relationship with the American theater and with his audience is paradigmatic for Mamet and his generation of the plight of the artist that Williams dramatizes in his plays, particularly the ones written after 1960. This was a subject that also preoccupied Mamet at the beginning of his career.

Mamet's keen awareness of, and in some sense response to, Williams's dramatization of the artist is clear in his early plays, written at about the same time as his elegy. While Williams's later plays focus on the plight of the older artist and the struggle to keep working in the face of diminishing creative powers, an unappreciative public, a hostile critical establishment, and the brutal economics of the American art business, Mamet's plays understandably focus on the interaction between older artists who find themselves in this situation and younger artists who are placed in a mentor relationship with them, much as he, as a young playwright, was with respect to the writer of the "greatest American poetry of the American language." This article will focus on the treatment of the artist in three of Williams's later plays, *Gnädiges Fräulein* (1966), *In the Bar of a Tokyo Hotel* (1969), and *Clothes for a Summer Hotel* (1980), in relation to Mamet's own early treatments of the artist in *Squirrels* (1974) and *A Life in the Theatre* (1977).

In the plays after 1960, Williams often represents artists *in extremis*, at the end of their careers, misunderstood and rejected by an unfeeling public or by those close to them, suffering in "desperate circumstances," as Blanche DuBois would put it, but tenacious and determined to pursue their art, no matter what environment may surround them. The most histrionic of Williams's characters, the Gnädiges Fräulein, is depicted simultaneously as a clown (*Gnädiges* 243) and a "Saint under torture" (245). An artist with a gift for singing, she has, through the accident of a fatal grab for attention in performance, catching the fish that was intended for a trained seal in her own jaws, degenerated through the artistic hierarchy of performance from performing before the crowned heads of Europe down through hustling drinks as a "B-girl," and finally arrived at the extreme low point, competing with the "cocaloony" birds for the waste fish on a dock in the Florida Keys for the privilege of living in the "dormitory" of Molly's flophouse. An artistic career does not get more desperate than that. The Gnädiges Fräulein is Promethean in her suffering, however. Birds attack her and peck out her eyes as she performs her act of catching the fish in her jaws with a tenacity that is absurd and also heroic. The spectacle of the blood-soaked bandage that covers her eyes suggests the final condition of Oedipus or Gloucester. As her astonishingly callous and exploitative landlady says, "her scroll has been charged with so much punishment lately I thought her spirit was vanquished" (242). Nevertheless, she sings on request, and her drive to perform by catching the fish is undaunted. As the play ends, the boat whistle sounds, and she "*assumes the starting position of a competitive runner*" and "*starts a wild, blind dash for the fish-docks*" (262). As Allean Hale notes, the biographical connection of the Gnädiges Fräulein's condition to the perceived state of Williams's career has been made by critics since the play's first performance (Hale, *Gnädiges Fräulein* 43). If Gnädiges Fräulein is a self-portrait, however, she is also a hyperbolic but powerful representation of the existential condition of the aging artist, the victim of cruel suffering inflicted by indifferent audiences, callous critics, and their own mistaken selling out of their art to please these people. No one wants to hear the Gnädiges Fräulein sing now, just as no one seemed interested in what Williams felt to be the authentic works of his artistic genius in the early 1960s.

In the Bar of a Tokyo Hotel is, according to Williams, about the "usually early and peculiarly humiliating doom of the artist" (Williams, "Tennessee" 36). The play's protagonist Mark, a painter, is clearly *in extremis*, "ravaged" (*Tokyo Hotel* 42) and literally on the verge of collapse, falling to his knees several times in the play, as Williams was known to do during the 1960s. He has reached a watershed in his development as an artist, about to cross a terrifying frontier into a kind of Emersonian transcendental state where his art is at one with the "I." Mark has penetrated, he thinks, to the mystery of color and light. He feels that, as an artist, his life is on the line, and he is terrified of the empty canvases on which he must express his new vision. Mark is loosely based on Jackson Pollock, an artist whom Williams recognized as a fellow sufferer for art and, he felt, a fellow pioneer. He has reached a stage beyond the known techniques. As his wife Miriam says, he's "gone through drip, fling, sopped, stained, saturated, scraped, ripped, cut, skeins of, mounds of heroically enduring color, but now he's arrived at a departure that's a real departure that I doubt he'll return from" (41), crawling naked over the canvas in an attempt to become one with it. Mark's dealer, Leonard, understands the breakthrough he is undergoing, saying he has never seen so much torment expressed before. During the play, Mark is desperately trying to keep his connection to Miriam, who complains about his "tyrannical dependence" (27) and is making plans to escape from him. His death from an apparent heart attack occurs while he is trying to make himself presentable enough so that she will go to lunch with him. More than any other, this play has come to signify the condition of Williams himself as an artist *in extremis*, the portrait of the artist that Mamet painted in his epitaph. John Simon's review was perhaps the most vitriolic in suggesting this, but the substance of the statement was common in the response to the play: "It is a play by a man at the end of, not his talent (that was long ago), but his tether — a man around whom the last props of the dramatic edifice have crumbled and who, in an impotent frenzy, stamps his feet on the few remaining bricks. That someone who was a major American and world dramatist should come to this is a tragedy almost unparalleled in the annals of literature" (Simon 56).

Clothes for a Summer Hotel depicts two artists in Scott and Zelda Fitzgerald, but it is Zelda who is the play's protagonist. In this "ghost play," with its chronological and spatial fragmentation, Scott comes to Highland Hospital, where Zelda will die in a fire while confined to a locked ward, to visit her. The story of their past unfolds in flashback and reminiscence as we witness a middle-aged Zelda in the present locked in the belief that she is about to launch her long-abandoned ballet career. Zelda summarizes her fate as an artist toward the end of the play: "Between the first wail of an infant and the last gasp of the dying — it's all an arranged pattern of — submission to what's been prescribed for us unless we escape into madness or into acts of creation. [...] The latter option was denied me, Scott, by someone not a thousand miles from here. [*She faces Scott.*] Look at what was left me!" (*Clothes* 71). The extreme condition that Zelda faces, and one that Williams feared, is that of the artist who descends into madness because she is denied expression. Nevertheless, she seeks to create art even in her condition as she doggedly practices for a ballet performance that will never take place. Each of the three protagonists in these plays represents a different version of the artist *in extremis*. Despite the fact that they are all on the verge of death, each tenaciously pursues artistic expression in the face of horrendous conditions. It is finally this pursuit that becomes their life in the end. They have nothing but their art.

Mamet's plays *Squirrels* and *A Life in the Theatre* also depict artists *in extremis*. Like the Tennessee Williams Mamet depicted in his epitaph and like the Gnädiges Fräulein and Mark, Arthur in *Squirrels* and Robert in *A Life in the Theatre* are older artists who are somewhat desperately trying to practice their art in the face of diminishing capabilities. *Squirrels* takes place in a writer's office, where "*an old writer*" Arthur is collaborating with "*a young writer*" Edmond (*Squirrels* 5). With many narrative variations, Arthur constantly repeats the same sequence of events, in which a man sits on a park bench watching the squirrels. He clucks to draw a squirrel to him, and as he moves to stroke the squirrel, it bites his hand, and then he grabs the squirrel and squeezes it until it dies. The core story becomes the vehicle for a number of aesthetic disagreements between the collaborators, the main one being that Edmond constantly wants to know the meaning or moral of the story, and Arthur insists that there need not be a meaning or a moral, because "One writes what one feels" (9) and "art is art" (23). The Cleaningwoman, a writer herself who claims to have been Arthur's lover at some point, tells Edmond that Arthur "is dead and dried and hung in the freezer of forgotten dreams"; he is "just jerking himself off, artistically speaking, and has been for years" (25). She advises Edmond to "hit the fuckin' highway quicker than it takes to tell" (25).

Later, Arthur admits that his creative powers are diminishing, confessing to the Cleaningwoman that he may be losing his "ability to generalize" (41). When she tells him, "you still got your old way with an adjective," he responds, "there's more to life than a facility with modifiers. It's possible that I've lost the touch. (*Pause*) Once broken, never mended" (41). As this play was written during the heyday of Structuralist theory, it is no surprise that Arthur is preoccupied with form and formalism. His core squirrel story is like the reduction of a narrative to a series of tropes performed by a member of the Prague School, which of course empties the narrative of the "meaning" that Edmond is always looking to supply. In a parody of such operations on the text, early in the play, Arthur suggests that, "for the purpose of simplicity ... we can divide these four figures into two distinctive units ... one unit can consist of two men ... the second unit shall consist of the remaining man and the squirrel" (11). Later, Arthur holds forth:

> Form Form Form. Form and the use of tools. Precision, restraint, control. (*Ed enters.*) Substance. Meaning. The meaning of a thing. What it *means*. The *why* of it. Walking. Beckoning. Biting [...] being bitten [...] the *acts* of biting and of being bitten. Hoping and hoping. (*Perhaps*) Strangling and being strangled. And the acts of *perceiving* those acts [...] The contract between the oppressed and the oppressor. And who is who [...] and *why* [44].

These are all the things that Edmond wants him to think about, and that he refuses to entertain while they are writing. When Edmond threatens to leave Arthur because he is not happy writing the same story about squirrels all the time, Arthur insists that he is not fixated on squirrels, and that if it's the squirrels Edmond objects to, they can move on to another animal: "Can you truly feel that I'm limited? When you've been in the business as long as I you will not feel that way" (46). To keep Edmond from leaving, Arthur pretends to be able to write about something else, and dictates a passage the Cleaningwoman has left in the waste-basket. In their final scene, they are writing about geese, but it is Edmond who is doing the writing. In his one attempt at a creative contribution, Arthur has the character say, "I almost saw a squirrel today that looked like a small dog" (49), a steal from the Cleaningwoman who had said the same thing about a horse. Even here he is still unable to write about anything but squirrels.

A Life in the Theatre depicts the relationship between an older actor, Robert, and a young actor, John, during a Season of performances in a repertory theater. Its 26 scenes were originally set in a variety of locations, but Mamet got the idea from Gregory Mosher, the play's original director, to set all of them in a theater. Some of the scenes recreate the performances of the actors in the less than stellar plays the repertory company is performing; some show the actors rehearsing on the empty stage; most are set in their shared dressing room, where their relationship progresses throughout the Season. Robert tries to play the role of mentor to John, calling on the privilege of his seniority and his greater experience in the theater to give advice and make sententious speeches about the theater and the art of acting. Much of Mamet's dialogue is seemingly banal and superficial, the daily interchange of two actors who share a dressing room and strike up a casual friendship that includes going out for meals after the show. Beneath the superficiality, there is a good deal more going on, of course. The struggle for dominance that is characteristic of Mamet's male characters emerges, as does the sense that Robert is in a depressed and increasingly desperate state of mind beneath the avuncular confidence he displays toward John. The sense of unease begins with a sigh as he says, "Another day" (*Life* 27) in Scene 7. In Scene 10, he rails against the critics, "the motherfucking leeches. The sots ... The bloody boors ... Why can they not leave us alone?" (39). In Scene 20, unaware of John's presence, he says, "Oh God, oh God, oh God, oh God, oh God" (65). In Scene 23, he is reduced to tears when John makes it clear he doesn't want him around while he rehearses a speech from *Henry V.* In Scene 24, during a performance, he loses track of where he is in the play, insisting on repeating a scene they've already done. In Scene 25, he cuts his wrist with a razor in what is an apparent attempt at suicide, but denies it and keeps repeating to John that he is tired. Robert is clearly a troubled and probably deeply depressed man, who is on the verge of losing his memory, and thus the one thing that sustains him, his career in the theater. The play ends with his summing up of his life — "Ephemeris, ephemeris. *(Pause.)* 'An actor's life for me'" (86) — followed by his farewell to an empty theater: "You know, and I speak, I am sure not for myself alone, but on behalf of all of us [...] *(composes himself)* [...] All of us here, when I say that these [...] *these* moments make it all [...] they make it all worth-while.... Each to his own home. Goodnight. Goodnight. Goodnight" (86).

Where Williams *dramatizes* the suffering of his characters, presenting us with personages who are inherently histrionic, Mamet conceals the human desperation beneath a surface banality and seemingly evasive dialogue that reveals as it conceals. As Annette Saddik has shown, Williams was experimenting with a much more plastic and visual form of drama when he wrote these plays, a version of the Artaudian theatre of cruelty which penetrates to "the inexpressible tragedy and underlying metaphysical cruelty of a cosmic pain beyond language, the primal screams that defy rational comprehension and embrace the pre-logical utterances of unadulterated nature" (Saddik 18). Allean Hale has also noted the influence of Nō, and, perhaps most interestingly, of Andy Warhol's pop aesthetic on *The Gnädiges Fräulein* (Hale, *Gnädiges Fräulein* 45). Williams wrote that the style of the two plays in *Slapstick Tragedy, The Mutilated* and *The Gnädiges Fräulein,* "is kin to vaudeville, burlesque, and slapstick, with a dash of pop art thrown in" ("Slapstick" 95). Mamet's plays are by contrast almost purely dialogic. As is typical of Mamet's plays, little attention is paid to setting or environment.

Squirrels takes place in "*a writer's office*" (*Squirrels* 5); *Life in the Theatre* in "*various spots around a theatre*" (*Life* n.p.). Mamet's focus is on the interaction between the two characters, attempts by the older artists to remain "in the game" by demonstrating their superior knowledge and creative power to the younger artists, attempts that ironically reveal the decline of their artistry and serve as the vehicle for the ascendancy of the younger men to dominance in the relationship and the rejection of their claims to mentorship. As different as they are, all of the plays focus on the effect that the artist's human relationships have on his diminishing capacity as an artist.

The Gnädiges Fräulein is surrounded by exploitative people who make her suffering worse. Molly the landlady is a monstrous figure who deprives her of all dignity as she imposes the conditions for survival in the nightmare world into which she has descended. In an allegorical reading of the play, she and the society columnist for the *Cocaloony Gazette*, Polly, become the caricature of an unfeeling audience for the performance of the Gnädiges Fräulein. The cocaloonies who deal out the Gnädiges Fräulein's "punishment" are like the critics and the press, who, Williams felt, pursued him like harpies. Her beloved fellow performer, Toivo, the Viennese Dandy who threw her "an insincere smile with a very slight insincere bow that broke her heart every time she received it from him ... couldn't stand her because she adored him," but lived off her performances (256). Nevertheless, through the transfiguration of memory, she remembers the smile as sincere and takes her fellow boarder Indian Joe for Toivo. Joe is just as exploitative as Toivo, ignoring the Gnädiges Fräulein, but eating the fish that she gives him. In the last straits of degradation, the Gnädiges Fräulein, the artist, like Prometheus, is existentially alone, but she is still tortured by the people who surround her, people who have no thought for her well-being, but seek only a moment's entertainment or what profit they can take from exploiting her all but extinguished talent.

In *In the Bar of a Tokyo Hotel*, both Miriam and Leonard see Mark essentially as a commodity to be exploited. Although Leonard is more sympathetic to him and more appreciative of the process he is going through as he breaks through to new artistic technique, his interest is essentially commercial. He wants to preserve Mark's value as his "most lucrative property" (*Tokyo* 11). Believing that Mark is psychotic, Miriam frankly plans to dump him on Leonard and consign him to an asylum, claiming her need to escape from his infantile dependence and put some space between them. She has planned carefully for her escape by securing a letter of credit from his bank and placing two hundred "of his best paintings before he discovered color with spray guns" (38) in storage under her name. While Leonard tries to argue Miriam out of her "desertion" (36) and "abandonment" (37) of Mark, she is determined to get away from him, and no longer "live my life with my feet in blocks of cement" (40). Miriam's callous self-interest seems complete, but it is mirrored in Mark's self-absorption: "After the work, so little is left of me. To give to another person" (28). Miriam speaks of clipping flowers outside his studio and hearing him talk to the work as if it were another person in the studio, saying that she felt excluded; when Mark says that "the work of a painter is lonely," she replies "so is clipping flowers" (28). Mark, on the other hand, ascribes the flower clipping to a desire for castration.

A key to their relationship is suggested by Miriam's statement that they are not two people, but two sides of one, "an artist inhabiting the body of a compulsive" (read sex addict). When Mark replies, "Bitch!," Miriam says, "remember that you're denouncing a side of yourself, denied by you" (30). Allean Hale suggests that this is an allusion to the yin and yang of sexuality in the Taoist tradition (Hale, "*In the Bar*" 151). Whether or not there is a specific allusion, the play represents a symbiotic relationship between the two. Mark may be dependent on Miriam in an infantile way, but she is more dependent on him that she admits or knows.

Her immediate response to his death is "released!" (50), but her final lines are "I have no plans. I have nowhere to go" (53), as she wrenches the bracelets that signified her desire to attract men from her arms and flings them to her feet. She had not realized that her life was lived *in relation* to Mark's. A few minutes earlier, she has spoken of living her life in "the circle of light ... it's our existence and our protection" (51), saying that Mark made the mistake of deliberately moving out of its protective circle, thinking "that he could create his own circle of light" (53). What she did not understand was that her circle of light revolved around Mark; without him to play off of, her existence has no meaning to her. As Williams put it, "there remains, unconsciously, a love for him that can only be expressed in her ... feeling when the artist is dead" (Williams, "Tennessee" 36).

In *Clothes for a Summer Hotel*, Williams suggests that Scott's notorious appropriation of Zelda's life — "I had to discourage her attempt to compete with my success as a writer.... So much of Zelda's material was mine and she put it into her novel" (*Clothes* 5) — and the deprivation of her natural form of expression as an artist, is the cause of Zelda's mental decline. In a flashback to an early scene in their marriage, when Zelda demands "What about *my* work?" (35), Scott replies, "your work is the work that all young Southern ladies dream of performing some day. Living well with a devoted husband and a beautiful child" (36). Turning the screw of Scott's defensively sexist attitude, Williams has one of the physicians at the hospital attest to the power of Zelda's talent: "I like to read important writing, and I feel that your wife's novel *Save Me the Waltz* — I'm sure you won't mind my saying that there are passages in it that have a lyrical imagery that moves me, sometimes, more than your own" (55). What's more, he says, Zelda "has sometimes struck a sort of fire in her work that — I'm sorry to say this to you, but I never quite found anything in yours, even yours, that was — equal to it" (55). Scott's predatory attitude toward Zelda is made clear from the beginning of the play, as Scott tries to romanticize their marriage, and Zelda strikes out at him, "*What was important to you was to absorb and devour!*" (11). Alluding to Hemingway's description of her in *A Moveable Feast*, Zelda tells Scott that she has the eyes of a hawk, "which is a bird of nature as predatory as a husband who appropriates your life as material for his writing" (12).

As deeply disturbing as Scott's appropriation of Zelda's life for his work is the creation of an identity that she had to inhabit. Having tried and failed to break out of her marriage through her affair with Edouard, the French aviator, Zelda says she "must resume the part created for me. Mrs. F. Scott Fitzgerald" (44). Did she love Scott? "Belonging to, is it love? *Ça depend.* If he makes of me a monument with his carefully arranged words, is that my life, my recompense for madness. There is none" (44). At the end of the play, Zelda rejects Scott's version of her identity, crying: "*I'm not your book! Anymore! I can't be your book anymore! Write yourself a new book!*" (77). As Thomas Adler has pointed out, this theme has a particular resonance with Williams's identity as an artist, since his use of his sister's Rose's life and his creation of her identity in a series of characters is parallel with Fitzgerald's use of Zelda (Adler 183–84). Although Williams may have been deeply motivated to write this play because of his guilt about his sister, he suggests that Fitzgerald's guilt is far greater. His theft of Zelda's identity and her life is compounded by the destruction of her creative capacity, which is death to any artist. It is clear that Zelda fed Scott's art, which was, as Hemingway says in the play, "Zelda and Zelda and more Zelda" (64). Williams also has Hemingway say that Scott wanted to appropriate Zelda's gender, since "duality of gender can serve some writers well" (64), a suggestion parallel to the notion that Mark and Miriam are "one person." Although Zelda is by far the more exploited party in this relationship, there is a suggestion of symbiosis here as well. However undesired it may have been, Scott did create an identity for Zelda, that of the glamorous Mrs. F. Scott Fitzgerald and the source for the characters in his books. It was an identity she inhabited, the source of her fame. She didn't find out what she had lost by it until it was too late.

Both *Squirrels* and *A Life in the Theatre* present what purports to be a mentorship relationship, in which the older artist tries to teach the younger one, passing on the knowledge gained from a lifetime of practicing his art. Both plays, however, reveal a cruel displacement of the older artist as the younger artist finally rebels against his assumption of authority and rejects the lessons he is trying to impart. In *Squirrels*, Edmond begins as a kind of apprentice to Arthur, taking his dictation, making neutral sounds like "Mmmmmm," and asking an occasional question. Arthur encourages him by telling him he is "doing quite well" (*Squirrels* 10), and Edmond apologizes when he interrupts with an idea. As he becomes increasingly tired of the squirrel scenario, however, Edmond tries to intervene in the narrative, first asking if he can "try one," which begins with a romantic description of a "small and peaceful park" where men "would labor over each and every flower" (18), a speech that prompts Arthur to ask if he is daft. He becomes increasingly insistent on his interventions, however, trying to bring human emotions and motivations into the story. Arthur ignores him, and finally exerts control by ending the session and pulling the schoolboy bully trick of making Edmond give him his lunch to eat. In their second session, it is Edmond who is offering a narrative about a man and woman meeting in the park, but Arthur insistently brings it back to the squirrel narrative. When Arthur asks Edmond, "Have you learned nothing working here?," Edmond says, "No" (33). Arthur insists on his role as mentor, saying that he is trying to teach Edmond something about writing: "Some Johnnie-Come-Lately [...] and I try to make him happy [...] comes in here and I nurture him beneath my wing, give him the benefit of my experience, my expertise, my [...] uh [...] (46).

When Edmond finally tells him he is unhappy because he is "sick of the squirrels" and Arthur is "very overbearing" (46), Arthur gives in, and in order to keep Edmond with him, reads him the Cleaningwoman's fragment about moonlight on the ocean that he finds in the waste basket, ending: "now type that up, you sonofabitch, and get out of here. I'll see you tomorrow in the morning" (47). In the following scene with the Cleaningwoman, Edmond is very happy as he tells her they are writing about geese, calling it "forward motion" (47). Edmond, however, begins to take on Arthur's aesthetic stance, questioning his own earlier insistence on meaning, and saying that artistic development is difficult to perceive, and perhaps that perception is not crucial to the artist. In a string of theoretical gibberish and clichéd phrases about art, he arrives at the notion that "a period of [...] work [...] untempered by harassing elements of [...] introspective examination can be beneficial ... that is, it is potentially not the least valuable aspect of this hiatic (non-introspective) period that it becomes, eventually, instructive. To the creator" (48). He ends with a position that is identical with Arthur's, but, because he is a young man of his generation, it is obfuscated with confused "theoretical" thinking. He says that, "because I did the work and didn't worry those elements once only philosophic and ideal about which I wasted so much thoughts [sic] have become osmosed into my being as technique and are behind me" (48). He declares that there is strength in technique, and, echoing Arthur, that "the true employment of inspiration is in formal endeavors where the inspiration can take form" (48).

To prove to the Cleaningwoman that they have been working, Edmond quotes a poetic passage, saying "I wrote that" (48). But the passage is actually a collaboration among Edmond, Arthur, and the Cleaningwoman. It is cut down from the lines that Arthur plagiarized from the Cleaningwoman's discarded fragment, with the addition of a line about geese. In the final scene between Edmond and Arthur, the two have completely reversed roles, as Edmond goes on about "Geese Geese Geese. Close in formation. Promoting order" (48), and Arthur, after his futile attempt to start a new story with a reference to squirrels, is told to type up the lines about the geese. In a sense, Arthur's mentorship has succeeded. He has turned Edmond into the same kind of writer he is. But in the process, Edmond has assumed ascendancy in their relationship. It is he who makes the claim to creativity; it is he who assumes an overbearing attitude toward Arthur, and Arthur who is reduced to mere amanuensis. The passage they end up with is ridiculously banal: "Geese geese geese. Flying over park and lake. Over sand and water. Over sea and shore, young and old, lion and tiger. Searching searching searching. Searching to be free" (49). Nevertheless, the scene ends with a long pause in which they "*look at each other with satisfaction*" (49). The symbiosis has achieved a balance. In shaping his "Johnnie-Come-Lately" pupil into the formalist writer he would like to be, Arthur has achieved the goal of his mentorship, an aesthetic dominance over the next generation. By asserting his control over the subject matter, and inserting "meaning" into the composition through the motive of "searching to be free," Edmond has achieved dominance in the relationship with Arthur, the young man taking power away from the older one.

Interestingly, it is the Cleaningwoman who has the last word. Throughout the play, it is her narratives that show the most imagination and vitality. She writes a story about sex with an immediate autobiographical connection; a Western story about Black Bart and the Kid; the romantic passage about the moonlight, the desert, and ocean that Arthur plagiarizes; a Civil War story; and an adventure story involving the Royal Canadian Mounted Police. All of these things are bad, but they have great energy and imagination, two things that Arthur and Edmond clearly lack. The play ends with her squirrel poem:

> Squirrels. (Squirrels.)
> Gatherers of nuts.
> Harbingers of autumn.
> Clucking and strangling.
> Strangling and being strangled.
> Rushing to your logical conclusion.
> Searching to be free [50].

What the Cleaningwoman does is to endow a meaning to the squirrel story that Arthur has insisted is meaningless. In "Rushing to your logical conclusion/Searching to be free," the Cleaningwoman articulates two of the fundamental human preoccupations that are articulated in literature, the teleological awareness of fate or inevitable death that informs the tragic and the naturalistic, and the vital desire for freedom from constraint and the dominance of the older generation that informs comedy. Of course the line "searching to be free" is one that comes from Edmond's lines about the geese. Is this collaboration, intertextuality, signifying, or simple plagiarism? In any case, the point is made that all of these writers depend on each other's work in order to write their own. In the end, the Cleaningwoman tosses this poem into the wastebasket before she nods to the audience. After seeing a performance of the play, Mamet added the line, "or words to that effect" (Collins 3D), emphasizing the arbitrariness of the language and the contingency of the work of art.

In his introduction to *A Life in the Theatre*, Mamet speaks of advice that he heard from Sanford Meisner while he was a student at the Neighborhood Playhouse as his inspiration for the play:

> When you go into the professional world, at a stock theater somewhere, backstage, you will meet an older actor — someone who has been around awhile.
> He will tell you tales and anecdotes about life in the theater.
> He will speak to you about your performance and the performances of others, and he will generalize to you, based on his experience and his intuitions, about the laws of the stage. Ignore this man [Mamet, "Regarding" 105].

Of course, in assuming the role of mentor on the strength of his experience in the theater, Meisner was doing exactly what he was telling his students to ignore, and Mamet, his student, was not ignoring it. Mamet also wrote of his time as a very young man working in the Off Broadway theater, when older actors in the company performing *The Fantasticks* "were more than nice to my incredibly green self" (Mamet, "Memories" 33). The ambiguity in these statements is reflected in the relationship between Robert and John. Robert is clearly a lonely man, who, in his mature years, is far from the pinnacle of success in his career. In John, he befriends a young actor who benefits from his knowledge, but he also fulfills his own emotional need to feel that he is influencing, as he puts it, "young people in the theatre [...] tomorrow's leaders" (6). Robert gives John tips about fencing, coaches him through a movement workout, and tries to offer literary insights about the plays they are rehearsing. His most intense teaching, however, is reserved for John's instruction about the acting profession. "We must support each other, John. This is the wondrous thing *about* the theatre, this potential" (24). He insists on etiquette in the dressing room, declaring, "one generation sows the seeds. It instructs the preceding [...] that is to say, the *following* generation [...] from the quality of its actions" (57). He insists that "there must be law, there must be a reason, there must be tradition" (57) in the theater and in society at large.

John is at first grateful for the attention from the older actor. His attitude toward Robert is respectful, attentive, even tender. He praises his work, and is shyly pleased to be asked out for a meal. He lights Robert's cigarette, cleans some stray make-up from his face, and in a scene that David Radavich calls "the most penetrating stage metaphor of homosexual interconnection in all of Mamet's work" (Radavich 73), even pins the broken zipper of his fly in the midst of escalating double entendres, ending with Robert's line, "Oh, fuck you. Will you stick it in?" (34). The tension in the relationship begins to emerge in Scene 6 as Robert shows some jealousy of a "friend" with whom John makes a date to meet after he and Robert have dinner together, and in Scene 8, as John rebels somewhat against Robert's dominance of the dressing room and his suggestion that John "do less" in a scene they have together. This rebellion ends in the zipper-pinning incident, however, reestablishing Robert's dominance, as he stands on a chair while John performs this service.

In Scene 17, John, finally fed up with Robert's pronouncements about the theater, responds to a voluble meditation on greasepaint with the words, "Would you please shut up?" (55), prompting Robert's lessons on etiquette, to which John responds guardedly. In Scene 22, Robert's professional unease erupts, as he remarks that John has been praised too much in the reviews. The scene ends with a rupture as Robert calls John a "fucking TWIT" (70) and John tells him not to use his towels anymore. This scene is followed by the turning point in their relationship, when John, who has landed a better acting job, is rehearsing *Henry V* while Robert eavesdrops. Mamet has written of this turning point as "the moment of the recognition of mortality, at which moment the younger generation recognizes and accepts its responsibilities, and the older generation begins to retire" (Mamet, "'Sad Comedy'" 7). John has been rather guarded throughout the play, speaking little, and responding with monosyllables or clipped neutral phrases to most of what Robert says. Peter Evans, who played John in the first New York production in 1978, said that John's attitude toward Robert is ambiguous. "John is very *careful*; he wants to learn as much as he can. We talked about my respect for Robert, a senior member of the company, one whose approval I needed" (Loney 78). In this scene, Robert lays a claim on John, reminding him that what happens on stage is part of his life, "which is one reason I'm so gratified (if I may presume), and I recognize that it may be a presumption to see you [...] to see the *young* of the Theatre [...] (And it's *not* unlike one's children) [...] following in the footpaths of [...] following in the footsteps of [...] those who have gone before" (72). John responds to this naked plea for recognition and affection by merely saying goodnight, and then Robert breaks down in tears when John catches him watching him rehearse from another part of the theater. Like an insecure lover, Robert pleads, "You're not angry with me are you?" (74), and, later, when it is clear that he still hasn't left the theater, John says "(*sotto voce*) Shit" (75). In the following scene, when Robert forgets where he is in the play and keeps insisting on John's cue for an earlier scene, John whispers, "We've done that one, Robert" (79), and when Robert keeps insisting, he simply walks off the stage.

John's engagement with the older actor ends with its usefulness. The symbiosis of the mentor relationship, with the green young actor seeking the tips about the profession which the older man can give him and the older actor seeking a disciple to keep his work alive in the theater, is no longer balanced. Robert's human needs have become too pressing, his instruction more annoying than helpful. Now that he is losing his competence as an actor, Robert is now an encumbrance holding back John's career. In the final scene, Mamet makes it clear that the roles have been reversed. In the first scene, John had not been eating well because he was nervous. In the last scene, it is Robert who isn't eating. John is going out after the show, not with him but with "some people" (84). Robert has become the subservient one, lighting John's cigarette, and lending him money for his evening out. It is not that John is cruel, but he has the callousness of the young and the ego of the artist, now confident in his talent. He is intent on his career, and Robert serves no further purpose for him. Robert's plight is pathetic in the final scene, his treasured "life in the theatre" a romantic notion that covers the reality of a cutthroat business that "eats the orange and throws the peel away," as Willy Loman says, like any other. The play implies that the valued commodities in the theater are talent and youth. Robert never had much of the first, and he's lost the second. It's John's turn now, and he will never be Robert's child. Mamet's theater is indeed "A beautiful life but a harsh business" ("Epitaph" 101).

Coming full circle, Williams added a coda to his treatment of the aging artist when he published *The Travelling Companion* in the magazine *Christopher Street* in 1981. This brief one-act pares the symbiotic relationship between the aging writer, called simply Vieux, and his younger "companion," Beau, down to its basic dynamics. Vieux is a famous, wealthy, and hypochondriacal artist who cannot bear to be without human companionship. He has hired Beau to accompany him on a trip to New York, but there is a misunderstanding between them about the extent of Beau's duties. He resists sharing a double bed with Vieux and threatens to leave if he does not get a separate room. In the course of the play, Vieux learns that Beau is anxious to get back to San Francisco, where his lover is being exploited by the manager of an escort service, and that he is a musician, who has had to hock his guitar. Vieux insists that he would have redeemed the guitar if he had known about it, providing Beau with the medium of artistic expression through which he achieves his identity as an artist, however minor.

In the end, however, Beau presents him with a moral dilemma: "You can't just walk in a place and take over another person's life and take him away like you bought something at a market" (*Travelling* 40). For Vieux, the issue is that, "being unable to go on alone and having no way to go back to — where would I go back to? To me as difficult as reversing the ways the earth turns" (40). The play ends with the delivery of a cot and Beau saying, "(*finally and softly*) — If you got me a new guitar tomorrow, I might stay on a while longer [...]" (40). Thus Williams suggests, even in this purely economic transaction, a possibility for a symbiotic human relationship that is balanced and productive. Supplied with their basic needs, both men will be able to practice their art, and, with the addition of the cot, no one will be exploited unduly. In its treatment of human relations, it is as harshly unsentimental as a David Mamet play, but it makes, in its way, a positive statement about the survival of art and the artist.

Once a relationship is cut off from love, passion, or other emotion, Williams suggests, there is a possibility for human symbiosis in which art can flourish. But it comes at a cost.

NOTE

1. "*The sky that shows around the dim white building is a peculiarly tender blue, almost a turquoise, which invests the scene with a kind of lyricism and gracefully attenuates the atmosphere of decay.... In this part of New Orleans you are practically always just around the corner, or a few doors down the street, from a tinny piano being played with the infatuated fluency of brown fingers. This 'blue' piano expressed the spirit of the life which goes on here*" (*Streetcar* 243).

WORKS CITED

Adler, Thomas P. "When Ghosts Supplant Memories: Tennessee Williams' *Clothes for a Summer Hotel*" in *Critical Essays on Tennessee Williams*. New York: G. K. Hall, 1997. 175–87.

Collins, William B. "Mamet's Tag Line for His Play on Words." Philadelphia *Inquirer* 29 January 1990: 3D.

Hale, Allean. "*The Gnädiges Fräulein*: Tennessee Williams's Clown Show" in *The Undiscovered Country: The Later Plays of Tennessee Williams*. Ed. Philip C. Kolin. New York: Peter Lang, 2002. 40–53.

_____. "*In the Bar of a Tokyo Hotel*: Breaking the Code." In *Magical Muse: Millennial Essays on Tennessee Williams*. Ed. Ralph F. Voss. Tuscaloosa: University of Alabama Press, 2002. 147–62.

Kane, Leslie. Ed. *David Mamet in Conversation*. Ann Arbor, Michigan, 2001.

Loney, Glenn. "Peter Evans and Ellis Rabb Give Life to the Theater." *After Dark* (February 1978): 76–78.

Mamet, David. *The Blue Hour: City Sketches* in *Goldberg Street: Short Plays & Monologues*. New York: Grove, 1985.

_____. "Epitaph for Tennessee Williams" in *Writing in Restaurants*. New York: Viking, 1986. 101–02.

_____. *A Life in the Theatre: A Play*. New York: Grove, 1977.

_____. "Memories of Off Broadway" in *Make-Believe Town: Essays and Remembrances*. Boston: Little, Brown, 1996.

_____. "A 'Sad Comedy' About Actors." *New York Times* 16 October 1977: Sec. 2, 7.

_____. *Squirrels*. New York: Samuel French, 1974.

_____. "Regarding a Life in the Theater" in *Writing in Restaurants*. New York: Viking, 1986. 103–06.

Radavich, David. "Man among Men: David Mamet's Homosocial Order" in *David Mamet*. Ed. Harold Bloom. Philadelphia: Chelsea House, 2004. 69–81.

Saddik, Annette J. "'The Inexpressible Regret of All Her Regrets': Tennessee Williams's Later Plays as Artaudian Theatre of Cruelty" in *The Undiscovered Country: The Later Plays of Tennessee Williams*. Ed. Philip C. Kolin. New York: Peter Lang, 2002. 5–25.

Simon, John. "The Eighth Descent of Tennessee." *New York* 26 May 1969: 56.

Williams, Tennessee. *Clothes for a Summer Hotel*. New York: New Directions, 1980.

_____. *The Gnädiges Fräulein* in *The Theatre of Tennessee Williams*. Vol. 7. New York: New Directions, 1981.

_____. *In the Bar of a Tokyo Hotel* in *The Theatre of Tennessee Williams*. Vol. 7. New York: New Directions, 1981.

_____. *Slapstick Tragedy*. Esquire 64.2 (1965): 92.

_____. *A Streetcar Named Desire* in *The Theatre of Tennessee Williams*. Vol. 1. New York: New Directions, 1971.

_____. "Tennessee Williams Talks about His Play 'In the Bar of a Tokyo Hotel.'" *New York Times* 14 May 1969: 36.

_____. *The Travelling Companion*. *Christopher Street* 5.10 Issue 58 (November 1981): 32–40.

The Symbiosis of Desire and Death: Beth Henley Rewrites Tennessee Williams

Verna A. Foster

Tennessee Williams was writing his last plays as Beth Henley was writing her first ones. *Am I Blue, Crimes of the Heart, The Miss Firecracker Contest*, and *The Wake of Jamey Foster*, written in the 1970s and 1980s, appear to be influenced by Williams's earlier, better-known plays such as *The Glass Menagerie, A Streetcar Named Desire*, and *Cat on a Hot Tin Roof*. But it is actually his later, less realistic, more grotesque and absurdist plays written in the 1960s and 1970s that share greater dramaturgical similarities with Henley's work. Henley never mentions and most likely had little knowledge of Williams's late plays such as *The Mutilated, The Gnädiges Fräulein, In the Bar of a Tokyo Hotel*, and *A Lovely Sunday for Creve Coeur* because they had limited critical and theatrical success when they first appeared. Equally, Williams could not have known much about Henley's work since her first play to be produced in New York, *Crimes of the Heart*, was staged there only three years before his death. Yet the similarities clearly exist.

It is not, in any case, necessary to claim any very direct influence of late Williams on early Henley (or vice-versa) to account for the similarities between Williams's late work and Henley's plays. There is another, actually more interesting, explanation in terms of the dramaturgy of the two playwrights. This explanation, I would suggest, is fourfold. While both dramatists are to some extent writing out of a Southern Gothic tradition, more specifically and importantly, Williams's earlier plays are variously inscribed in exaggerated and more literal form both in his own late works and in many of Beth Henley's plays. In other words, both dramatists are influenced by the early Williams. Further, both regarded Chekhov as a mentor, though they draw on his plays in different ways, and both were influenced by the Theatre of the Absurd. Williams's turn to the grotesque in his later plays was due in part to the influence of absurdist dramatists such as Beckett, Pinter, and the early Albee, while the much younger Henley was influenced by her admiration for Beckett from the beginning of her career.[1] A comparison of Henley's plays with both Williams's earlier and later work illuminates not only Henley's experimental dramaturgy but also Williams's own experimentation and his critically vexed dramatic trajectory. Even more interesting from the point of view of Williams scholars than the perhaps inevitable influence of the outstanding dramatist of his generation on a talented successor is how the dramatic styles of Henley and the early Williams converge in Williams's own later plays.

148

Before I examine Williams's and Henley's redaction of Williams's early dramaturgy in detail, it is worthwhile briefly rehearsing the historical evidence for Henley's knowledge of Williams's plays and their influence on her own. As a child Henley herself had a small part in a production of *Summer and Smoke* (Plunka 8). Henley's mother, who acted at the Jackson Little Theatre and the New Stage Theatre in Mississippi, played Laura in *The Glass Menagerie* and Blanche in *A Streetcar Named Desire*. Henley watched her mother limping around grocery stores preparing to play Laura and helped her practice her lines for both plays, in the process learning almost the whole of *Streetcar* (Dellasega 252). She also attended rehearsals of her mother's plays (Betsko and Koenig 215). Henley herself has expressed her admiration for Williams, commenting that he is "great" (Jones 181, qtd. in Watson 202). And she explicitly connects her work with that of her predecessor in the Introduction to her *Collected Plays*, volume two, where she says that her earlier plays set in Mississippi and New Orleans "seem to have an amber quality to them; they search to make sense of observations made long ago. To nick a term from Tennessee Williams, they are memory plays" (vi). As Gary Richards comments, the "nick[ed]" term "testifies to Williams's influence on Henley" (48) and shows that "she is self-consciously positioning herself within a particular regional literary production and linking herself to the most central of its figures" (49). Along with numerous other parallels between the two dramatists, which I will discuss below, Henley's reliance on Williams to explain her own work reinforces the propriety and indeed the desirability of an intertextual study of their plays.

While several critics have linked Beth Henley with Tennessee Williams for one reason or another, the references are generally very brief.[2] There are, in fact, numerous parallels, historical as well as dramaturgical, between Williams and Henley, beginning with the fact that both have been seen as "Southern" or "Southern Gothic" writers with all that that rubric implies about geographical specificity, eccentric characters, grotesque humor, and the possibility of creating particularly poetic or comic effects out of reality-based Southern idioms. Both Williams and Henley have commented on the dramatic usefulness of Southern speech to their work. Williams explained his fondness for Southern heroines: "They have the tendency to gild the lily, and they speak in a rather florid style which seems to suit me because I write out of emotion, and I get carried away by the emotion" (Devlin 99). And Henley similarly remarked early in her career, "I like to write about the South because you can get away with making things more poetic. The style can just be stronger" (Jones 183).[3] Henley, as several critics have been at pains to emphasize, is no longer a "Southern" writer. Her plays of the 1990s take place in Wyoming, Los Angeles, and Wisconsin. However, the parallels between Williams and Henley go well beyond their "Southernness."

Both dramatists looked to Chekhov as their chief inspiration and mentor. Williams repeatedly referred to the influence of Chekhov on his work: "I believe that the chief influence on me, as a playwright, was Chekhov" (Devlin 114; also 85, 331). Henley too has said that Chekhov was "Definitely an inspiration" on her work (Dellasega 258) and that she likes "how he doesn't judge people as much as just shows ... the comic and tragic parts of [them]" (Jones 182, qtd. in Hargrove 54). Williams in his earlier plays draws on Chekhovian techniques to create his tragicomic effects (Foster, *Name and Nature* 153). Henley, too, draws on Chekhovian techniques, but she tends to distort and exaggerate them. Rather than creating the tragicomedy ascribed to her by several critics, Henley's adaptation of Chekhovian dramaturgy produces a kind of black comedy infused with the absurd. In this respect her plays are more like Williams's later works, in which he too pushed the Chekhovian tragicomic techniques of his earlier plays towards the absurd and the grotesque.

In his later plays from the 1960s on, as amply demonstrated in Philip C. Kolin's collection of essays *The Undiscovered Country: The Later Plays of Tennessee Williams*, Williams adapts techniques from the Theatre of the Absurd. In doing so, he is both experimenting with a new dramatic form and also drawing out the implications of the grotesque elements in his own realistic earlier plays. Since Beckett was as much the dramatic norm as Chekhov in Henley's earlier years, the younger dramatist draws on absurdist as well as Chekhovian techniques from the beginning of her career, to a lesser extent in *Crimes of the Heart*, her most realistic play, but in all of the others. All of Henley's plays thus share with Williams's later work an absurdist vision of human experience that resonates with and likely derives from the combined influences of Chekhov, absurdist drama, the Southern grotesque, and, one should emphasize, from Williams's own experiments with dramatic technique that occur even in his early work.

Apart from these broad correspondences between Williams and Henley, their plays share many technical and thematic similarities. Both dramatists combine realism with grotesque exaggerations in the staging of their plays. Both write plays set in the South that mix laughter and pain and feature "Southern belles," overpowering mothers, dissatisfied artists, unhappy marriages, and characters with disabilities. Both make use of significant offstage characters (Big Daddy, absent for much of *Cat on a Hot Tin Roof*, foreshadows Old Granddaddy in *Crimes of the Heart*, who controls the lives of Henley's three sisters). Both make extensive expressionist or symbolic use of animals and animal imagery — ranging from the glass unicorn and the eponymous iguana in Williams's plays to the horse struck by lightning in *Crimes of the Heart* and the metaphorical snapping turtle that lets go only when it thunders in *The Debutante Ball*.[4]

For the remainder of this essay I wish to demonstrate more specifically, first, how Williams's earlier plays, especially *The Glass Menagerie* and *A Streetcar Named Desire* (which, we recall, Henley had learned almost by heart) are inscribed in Henley's drama and, second, the dramaturgical similarities between Henley's plays and Williams's later work. Rather than surveying all of Henley's and Williams's drama, I will concentrate on two plays by each dramatist that it seems to me best illustrate both the influence of Williams's early plays on Henley's drama and the ultimate convergence of the two playwrights' dramatic styles.

The plays by Henley are *The Miss Firecracker Contest* (first produced in 1980) and *The Debutante Ball* (first produced in 1985). Both plays, like *A Streetcar Named Desire*, have a Southern setting: Brookhaven and Hattiesburg, Mississippi, respectively. Both deal with families that have suffered deaths and loss. In each the central character is a woman with a troubled past, who suffers from guilt or lacks self-esteem, and has engaged in compensatory but inappropriate sexual liaisons. As Williams pairs and contrasts Blanche with her sister, Stella, Henley pairs Carnelle in *The Miss Firecracker Contest* with her cousin, Elain, and Teddy in *The Debutante Ball* with her half-sister, Bliss. Like *The Glass Menagerie*, each of Henley's plays depicts an overbearing mother, the deceased Ronelle in *The Miss Firecracker Contest* and Jen in *The Debutante Ball*, while the earlier play presents an unfulfilled artist, Delmount, who is, like Tom, in a dead end job, and the later one spotlights a "gentleman caller" who disappoints.

Among Williams's later plays I will discuss *The Mutilated* (first produced in 1966), which is set in New Orleans and focuses on two aging and lonely women, and *A Lovely Sunday for Creve Coeur* (first produced in its two-act form in 1979), a play that has often been seen as a revision of *A Streetcar Named Desire*. Both Henley and the later Williams render the themes and relationships of Williams's earlier plays less realistically and with more emphasis on the grotesque — in the sense of the comically ugly and the sadly horrible. Chekhovian tragicomedy gives way to a darker humor that, paradoxically or perhaps concomitantly, offers in Henley's plays a degree of hope, if only for a "moment" (*Crimes* 63), and in Williams's late plays some slight assurance that his characters, like Beckett's, will be able to "go on."

One theme that occurs throughout the work of both dramatists and in the four plays I am discussing in particular is the search of desperate, existentially lonely people for love or something like it (often just a sexual encounter to keep off the darkness) in a dramatic environment that is at once a specific social space and an absurd universe. According to Lyle Leverich, Williams "once said that desire is rooted in a longing for companionship, a release from the loneliness that haunts every individual" (347). The loneliness of both Williams's characters and Henley's may be explained in both psychosexual and metaphysical terms.[5] And the sexual consolation they seek to give or receive is often connected with death. The central characters/searchers who carry this theme are often (almost always in Henley) women, and often, too, they are damaged in some way either mentally or physically, or they seek out those who are damaged. Blanche Dubois may be seen as the paradigm for later heroines such as Carnelle and Elain in *The Miss Firecracker Contest* and Teddy and Bliss in *The Debutante Ball* as well as for Celeste and Trinket in *The Mutilated* and Dotty and to an extent Helena in *A Lovely Sunday for Creve Coeur*. It is in their handling of such figures and the motifs of desire and death attached to them that Henley and Williams most clearly converge in rewriting Williams's early tragicomedy in terms of the absurd and the grotesque.

Testifying to Henley's creative reimagining and assimilation rather than slavish imitation of Williams, in *The Miss Firecracker Contest* the Blanche figure is split between Carnelle and Elain and in *The Debutante Ball* between Teddy and Bliss. The secondary heroines, Elain and Bliss, reflect Blanche's "Southern belle" qualities — her beauty, her pale elegance, her charm, and her dramatic turns of phrase — as well as her selfishness, her drinking, and her need for admiration and love. Strikingly, each arrives on the scene with luggage in an image reminiscent of Blanche's first appearance in her "*white suit*" (245), valise in hand, at the beginning of *Streetcar*. Elain wears "*elegant pastels*" (*Firecracker* 154) and Bliss White (one wonders if there is an unconscious — or conscious — echo of Blanche's name here) has "*white skin*" and "*silky clothes*" (*Debutante* 271). Elain requests "a glass of this delicious looking ice tea" as she is "about ready to drop dead from the heat," and, like Blanche, she "must have a bath" (*Firecracker* 156, 159).[6] Bliss's theatrical comment on seeing her cousin carrying her late father's "doghead cane" — "What in the world possesses you to fraternize with that grotesque piece of memorabilia?" (*Debutante* 274) — is worthy of Blanche's explanation of how her ancestors lost their land to pay for their "epic fornications" (*Streetcar* 284).

Like Blanche, Elain, the former beauty queen, and Bliss, disappointed of her own debutante ball because of the family scandal (her mother, supposedly, murdered her father), are motivated by a need for admiration and love. But Henley, typically, exaggerates and makes literal what Williams leaves implicit. Explaining her decision to return to her unloved but rich husband, Elain says, "I need someone who adores me" (*Firecracker* 194). Bliss describes her own painful need: "I just have this sort of hole inside me. This desperate longing to love and be loved" (*Debutante* 306). While Elain intends to return to her husband after one dangerous sexual fling, Bliss, like Blanche, is more or less destitute. Her mother does not want her and her rich ex-husband (not seen in the play), after her promiscuity with all of his friends, refuses to take her back. Hugely overweight, Bliss's former husband is perhaps a more grotesque version of chunky Mitch, who woos but then rejects Blanche because of her promiscuity. Mitch is Blanche's last (albeit improbable) chance at happiness before she is led off to the asylum on the arm of the doctor, her last "gentleman caller." Bliss, by contrast, finds consolation and a place to live in a loving lesbian relationship with Frances, her stepfather's deaf and awkward niece from the country, though one cannot see this would-be debutante spending long down on the farm any more than one could envision Blanche as a working man's wife. But Henley, more optimistic than Williams in *Streetcar*, allows Bliss a chance of happiness if only temporarily.[7]

The central heroines of *The Miss Firecracker Contest* and *The Debutante Ball*, Carnelle, who wants to win the Miss Firecracker beauty and talent contest, and Teddy, the reluctant debutante, look less like Blanche but share her troubled past, her compensatory sexual liaisons, and also her courage and her wry sense of humor. Trying to escape the "bloodstained pillow-slips" (388) of her dying relatives and her guilt over the death of her young husband, Blanche engaged in numerous "intimacies with strangers" (386). For Blanche, desire is the "opposite" of death (389), though, as the play shows, tragic and comic, life and death are intertwined as one in the fabric of the characters' lives.[8] Carnelle and Teddy similarly use sex as an escape, but their engagements are totally lacking in tragic dignity. Carnelle, unwanted and unattractive as a child, seeks to boost her morale by numerous sexual liaisons, and Teddy, who killed her violent father (though her mother took the blame), tries to assuage her guilt by a liaison with one ugly and disabled stranger.

Carnelle's father abandoned her to the care of her aunt. Her cousin Delmount vividly recalls how Carnelle's head was shaved because of ringworms and even in summer she had to wear a "yellow wool knit cap" that was supposed to look like hair. She "never did gain any self-esteem," Delmount goes on to say. "Had to sleep with every worthless soul in Brookhaven trying to prove she was attractive" (165–66). Carnelle became known locally as "Miss Hot Tamale" (168), a reputation she desperately wants to live down by winning the Miss Firecracker Contest so that she may leave Brookhaven "in a crimson blaze of glory" (163). Carnelle's soubriquet echoes and makes literal Williams's more subtle and expressionistic allusion to Blanche's sexual propensities in the unseen hot tamale vendor's cry of "Red-hot!" (285) in *Streetcar*. As in so many other instances in Henley's plays, what is evocative in Williams becomes exaggerated and grotesquely literal in Henley. But, as we shall see, this same process of grotesque exaggeration is what happens in Williams's own later plays as well.

Carnelle and Teddy (and also Trinket and Celeste in different ways in *The Mutilated*) share in the visual degradation to which Blanche is subjected as well as in her compensatory promiscuity. In the penultimate scene of *Streetcar* the distraught Blanche dresses in a "*soiled and crumpled white satin evening gown*" (391). Stanley describes her clothes as "that worn-out Mardi Gras outfit ... with the crazy crown on" and asks her, "What queen do you think you are?" (398). Blanche is a travesty of her former self. In *The Miss Firecracker Contest*, Carnelle borrows Elain's dress, red in this instance, which looked "*lovely*" on Elain but "*now looks like a whore's gown on Carnelle. It is faded ad ill-fitted and totally askew.*" Carnelle also has a "*torn and broken*" Mardi Gras mask (186), a literalization perhaps of Stanley's reference to Blanche's "Mardi Gras outfit." Where Blanche becomes a travesty of herself, Carnelle becomes a travesty of the younger Elain. At the beginning of *The Debutante Ball* Teddy displays for her mother her elegant "*white debutante's gown*" (269), to which she will be adding a tiara. By the end of the play this gown has become an even more grotesque version of Blanche's soiled white dress. After the disastrous debutante ball, Teddy returns with the dress "*torn and dirty*" (297) and without her tiara. Furthermore, her white fur stole (reminiscent perhaps of Blanche's summer furs) worn by Frances is covered with "*champagne, dirt, and vomit*" (300). Again, Henley doubles and makes Williams's effects more grotesque.

As Blanche holds herself responsible for her husband's suicide because she told him that his homosexuality disgusted her, so Teddy literally killed her violently abusive father because she was afraid that he was going to attack her mother. Blanche has sought to assuage her loneliness and guilt by "intimacies with strangers." There is, however, a lyrical grace in her description of her sexual liaisons: sometimes Blanche would slip outside to the young soldiers who repaired to her lawn, and "...Later the paddy-wagon would gather them up like daisies ... the long way home..." (389), an image that evokes both beauty and death. Much more grotesquely,

Teddy has had an unlikely sexual encounter with a mutilated man she met in an hotel elevator. Horrified by his stump of an arm and disfigured face, Teddy said to him, "You get away from me, you ugly man" (297). Then because she had distressed him and could not take on any more guilt than she already had for the murder of her father, she gave herself to him. The sexual encounter was ludicrous. After they finished, the man commented, "Mm-mm good" (298), as if Teddy were some kind of candy. From this graceless congress Teddy finds herself pregnant. As we shall see, Williams, too, in his own later plays abandons Blanche's lyrical descriptions of sex for the ugly and the ludicrous.

At the end of *The Debutante Ball* Teddy loses her baby to a graphic onstage miscarriage that is part and parcel of Henley's insistent foregrounding of what the women themselves perceive as the normally unseen ugliness of women's bodies beneath the glamour: the body hair, the blood, Jen's psoriasis that is finally visible as she steps into her bath at the end of the play. Blanche's obsession with her appearance ("I won't be looked at in this merciless glare!"; "I haven't put on one ounce in ten years" [251, 255]) and her endless therapeutic bathing are echoed and rendered more grotesque, especially in *The Debutante Ball*, where the offstage bathroom in *Streetcar* is brought on stage by Henley and becomes an important part of the set.

In this onstage bathroom the women in *The Debutante Ball* are constantly plucking, shaving, cleaning, and spraying themselves and putting on "corrective" make-up, convinced that all of this activity makes a difference to the way they are viewed by the men in their lives and to their own self-worth. And apparently it does. Jen's adoring second husband, Hank, tells his wife that her face "sparkles" (286), and Bliss announces, ridiculously, "I see people so much better when I'm wearing mascara" (272). Only Teddy objects to this frenzy of beautifying. She asks Bliss if men know that "a girl's eyelids aren't really colored bright green and her lips aren't really so dark and red and shiny." Bliss replies, "Of course they're aware it's something of an illusion" (273). Bliss accepts the "illusion," just as Blanche prefers "magic" to "realism" (*Streetcar* 385). Teddy, however, more like Laura in *The Glass Menagerie* complaining about her mother's attempt to make her wear "gay deceivers," sees all of the make-up as "a big trick" (273). Disgust with her own body leads her to pile on layers of make-up but also to cut her face and legs, paralleling the various forms of "mutilation" to which women's bodies are subjected in Williams's later plays.

In presenting to the audience's view the ugly underside of Blanche's and Amanda's obsession with beauty, Henley offers a feminist critique of the expectations for beauty that are constantly imposed upon women, not least by women themselves. Where Williams with wry sympathy accepts the behavior of Blanche and Amanda as parts of their personalities, conditioned by their early lifestyles as Southern belles, Henley, while by no means unsympathetic to her female characters' concerns, satirizes, quite savagely in *The Debutante Ball*, the superficiality and destructiveness of conventional codes of beautification.

In their pursuit of beauty all four of Henley's Blanche figures have been influenced by an overbearing mother who seems to derive to some extent from Amanda in *The Glass Menagerie*. In her mothers Henley exaggerates what is grotesque in Williams's depiction of Amanda, whom she revises as Ronelle Williams (again one wonders if the name is, consciously or unconsciously, significant), the deceased mother of Elain and aunt of Carnelle in *The Miss Firecracker Contest*, and as Jen, the mother of Bliss and Teddy in *The Debutante Ball*. Ronelle is Amanda as witch; Jen is Amanda as former "Southern belle," who wants to reproduce in her unwilling daughter a replica of herself. Tom calls Amanda "an ugly — babbling old — *witch*" (164), and Williams conveys her witch-like characteristics (in Tom's eyes) through expressionistic lighting effects: for example, the "*light on her face with its aged but childish features is cruelly sharp, satirical"* [169]). More witch-like in her appearance (with "long, black hairs all over her body" [151]), Ronelle even possessed a spinning wheel. Carnelle's friend, Popeye, pretends to prick her finger on it, reminding the audience of what witches can do to young women in fairy tales. And, in fact, Ronelle, while considered by many to be an "angel" (167), has had a malign influence on the lives of Elain and Carnelle.

The *Debutante Ball* opens with a scene reminiscent of Amanda's inspection of Laura's new finery in *The Glass Menagerie*. Eager to launch her daughter successfully into society in an attempt to reestablish her own social position as well as Teddy's after the murder of her former husband, Jen praises Teddy's appearance and instructs her on how to comport herself at the coming ball. And like Amanda displaying her *"girlish Southern vivacity"* (*Menagerie* 202) to the astonished Jim, Jen, too, at times reenacts her own youthful charm: "*She twirls around smelling the bouquet,*" saying, "They're so beautiful. Like all the untold secrets of the angels" (275). But despite this ostensible charm, Jen is gratuitously cruel, as Amanda is not. The unseen Ronelle especially and Jen are less complex and less sympathetic than Amanda, though we may feel some pity for Jen at the end of the play. Their characterization offers a further example of the way in which Henley assimilates Williams's characters and motifs to her own darkly comic ends.

A similar process of grotesque revision and literalization is apparent in Henley's handling of other central motifs of Williams's plays: gentleman callers who disappoint, frustrated artists, and characters with disabilities. For example, Teddy's "gentleman caller" who should escort her to the ball is not, like Laura's, simply unavailable; he does not exist. Teddy has invented him to appease her mother and makes ridiculous excuses for his non-appearance. Artist figures appear throughout the plays of both Williams and Henley. One such, Delmount Williams in *The Miss Firecracker Contest*, is, like Tom Wingfield (Williams) in *The Glass Menagerie*, a poet in a dead-end job, in his case, picking up dead dogs from the road. This occupation may reflect Tom's revulsion from his job in the shoe warehouse but it is also literally disgusting. Williams's later artists similarly become more damaged or more grotesque. The most striking instance is the bleeding and blinded protagonist of *The Gnädiges Fräulein* who competes for fish with the cocaloony birds. But even in the more realistic play *A Lovely Sunday for Creve Coeur* Blanche's homosexual young poet is revised, ludicrously, as Dotty's musician ex-boyfriend who suffers from premature ejaculation.

Disabled characters occur in significant roles throughout the work of both Williams and Henley. The grotesque in the form of disablement, accident, or disease in both staged characters and in stories told in the plays is a trademark of Henley's drama. In this respect, as in so many others, Henley shares in the dramaturgy of Williams's later plays, in which disability appears as grotesque, rather than his earlier ones that actually demonstrably influenced her work. There is, after all, nothing grotesque about Laura's limp and only minimally so, though the character himself may be larger than life, about Big Daddy's cancer. By contrast, ailments such as Trinket's mastectomy in *The Mutilated*, the Gnädiges Fräulein's gauged-out eyes, and Sophie's schizophrenia in *A Lovely Sunday for Creve Coeur* are presented as darkly comic, pathetically ugly, and horrifying.

Similarly, Lenny's shrunken ovary in *Crimes of the Heart*, Marshael's mouth ulcers in *The Wake of Jamey Foster*, Mac Sam's numerous ailments in *The Miss Firecracker Contest*, Frances's deafness in *The Debutante Ball*, Will's missing eye in *Abundance*, and Sister's schizophrenia in *Control Freaks* are seriocomic and ugly, though more ridiculous than frightening. Even in the relatively realistic *Crimes of the Heart*, the repeated references to Lenny's shrunken ovary render it ridiculous, as Laura's limp never is; the absurdity of Lenny's ailment underscores the cruelty of Old Granddaddy's imposition on her of a disabling lack of self-esteem.[9] The later

Frances is not only deaf, but she also has worked out a comically grotesque pantomime to make herself understood.

Williams and Henley both use disability metaphorically to represent all of us in our various physical and spiritual ailments — for as Celeste comments in *The Mutilated*, "we all have our mutilations, some from birth, some from long before birth, and some from later in life, and some stay with us forever" (87). But disabled characters are not merely peripheral dramatic symbols in Williams's and Henley's plays. Both dramatists present disabled characters in central roles and display an openness to the often painfully embarrassing ways in which disability impinges on their lives: Trinket's sexual shame about her missing breast, Sophie's diarrhea, Will's anxiety that his mail order bride should love him (she does not) despite his glass eye. It is through their grotesque representations of disability that Williams and Henley avoid either sentimentality or the reduction of disability merely to symbol. M. Beth Meszaros cogently makes this point about Henley, and it is equally true of Williams: "The modality of black comedy allows Henley ... to attend to disablement in a fashion that is intellectually honest and aesthetically engaging" (6).

The most fascinating of Henley's grotesquely diseased characters is Mac Sam, the carnival balloon man, in *The Miss Firecracker Contest*. Mac Sam is a walking catalogue of diseases — "TB, alcoholics disease, rotting gut" (202) as well as syphilis contracted from Carnelle that he has not bothered to cure; he repeatedly coughs up blood clots, admiring their "nice pinkish-reddish sorta color" (189); he smokes; and he seems completely contented "rotting away in the July sun" (193) and "taking bets on which part of [him]'ll decay first: the liver, the lungs, the stomach, or the brain" (202). But he also has *"magnetic"* eyes (175) that he uses effectively on Carnelle and even the glamorous Elain, who agrees to an (implicitly death-defying) assignation with him before returning to her stultifying marriage. Mac Sam epitomizes the symbiotic connection between desire and death that Williams so vividly but implicitly evokes through the structure and imagery of *A Streetcar Named Desire* and to which he will return in a more darkly comic way in *The Mutilated.*

Though Blanche says that desire and death are opposites, Williams shows that they are identical as well. The sexuality that seems to Blanche to be an escape from death in the end leads her on a literal and symbolic journey on a streetcar named Desire via Cemeteries to Elysian Fields.[10] As the play draws to its conclusion, the images of death associated with Blanche become relentless: the Tarantula Arms, where she took her "victims" (386), the Mexican woman selling "Flores para los muertos" (388), the rape, the Doctor and the Matron, presented expressionistically as death figures, who come to take Blanche to the asylum. While Blanche is, as Williams says, "broken" (Devlin 81), the dramatist's use of religious imagery at the end of *Streetcar* does introduce a note of ambiguity that relieves the despair of Blanche's destruction. Blanche imagines a purifying death at sea followed by resurrection into heaven: she speaks of being "buried at sea sewn up in a clean white sack and dropped overboard — at noon — in the blaze of summer — and into an ocean as blue as [*chimes again*] my first lover's eyes" (410). The sound of the cathedral chimes supports Blanche's fantasy of grace, but the fantasy ends, for the audience at least, with the appearance of the Doctor and Matron who lead Blanche off to the asylum.

If Mac Sam represents both a more literal and a more exaggerated symbiosis of death and desire than that lyrically evoked by Williams in *Streetcar*, he also offers more hope for a way out of the impasse. In these two respects the character is typical of Henley's reworkings of Williams's themes. Mac Sam may be a walking emblem of death, but he is also a carnival balloon man. Balloons are joyful things whose natural tendency is to float upwards. Larry G. Mapp comments on Mac Sam's religious significance. While pointing out that religious references in Henley's plays are usually used only as expletives (40), Mapp suggests that Mac Sam "seems almost Christ-like as he takes on the diseased condition of human life and bears it uncomplainingly" (36).

Throughout the second act of *The Miss Firecracker Contest* Mac Sam helps and supports Carnelle. He wishes her well in the contest (178), takes care of her unwanted frog (184), repeatedly tells her she is beautiful (185, 197, 202), stops Delmount from fighting (188), praises Carnelle's performance (195), and admires the way she can "take it on the chin" (202) when she comes in last in the contest. Most strikingly, in a life that does not seem to promise much hope, Mac Sam offers Carnelle the possibility of "eternal grace" (202). The phrase stays with her as she decides, despite her disappointment, to join Delmount and Popeye on the roof to watch the gold and red lights of the fireworks display — which are to be associated perhaps with Mac Sam's colored balloons and certainly with Carnelle's own earlier desire to go out in a "blaze of glory" (204). Mac Sam seems to be instrumental in enabling Carnelle, unlike Blanche, but like many of Williams's characters in his later plays, to "go on." Mac Sam may be a death figure, but like the even more explicitly symbolic Jack in Black in *The Mutilated*, he is sexy and benign.

In *The Debutante Ball* Teddy's unseen mutilated man who impregnates her can, like Mac Sam, also be seen as an emblem of both death and life. Discovering that she is pregnant, Teddy decides to delay her planned suicide until after the baby is born. By the time she miscarries, she has become reconciled to life. Like Carnelle, Teddy ultimately has hope. She tells her mother, "that ole snapping turtle's gonna let loose ... and these arms will want to hold onto somebody and have their arms holding onto me." Teddy, too, will go on, though in Jen's response, which is the last line of the play, Henley emphasizes the ambiguous fragility of Teddy's hope: "Well. I hope so. I, well I ... Yes. Good. Yes" (315). Like Williams, Henley writes unsentimental uncertainty into the endings of her plays, and the happiness her characters and those in Williams's later plays achieve will be for "this one moment" (*Crimes* 63) or "for a while" (81) as the chorus sings in *The Mutilated*.

The stylistic and thematic similarities between Williams's late and Henley's dramatic styles occur in large part because both playwrights are building on and carrying further dramatic possibilities already inherent in the early Williams. Despite their ostensible realism, plays such as *The Glass Menagerie* and *A Streetcar Named Desire* display the experimentation (with expressionism especially and with a mild form of the grotesque) that was to characterize Williams's work throughout his career. *A Lovely Sunday for Creve Coeur*, sometimes regarded dismissively as a parody of *A Streetcar Named Desire*, can be better understood as an absurdist and Henley-style revision of the earlier play. This is so because Williams's own dramatic trajectory took him in a more complex way to where Henley began. That trajectory included his experimental and often undervalued plays of the 1960s such as *In the Bar of a Tokyo Hotel*, *The Two-Character Play*, and his double-bill *Slapstick Tragedy*, comprising *The Mutilated* and *The Gnädiges Fräulein*.

In *The Mutilated* two middle-aged women, on-and-off friends, living in the French Quarter of New Orleans, seek to ward off the darkness of loneliness or death itself one Christmas Eve and Christmas Day through drink and through sexual liaisons; they ultimately find solace in their friendship with one another. Trinket and Celeste are necessarily less recognizable as versions of Blanche Dubois than Henley's Carnelle, Elain, Teddy, and Bliss, because they are middle-aged women. But they too share Blanche's obsession with her appearance, her drinking habit, and her desperate need for a man. Celeste sometimes even sounds like Blanche: "Bless you, Henry, you old sweet thing, you!" (83).

Trinket, despite having some money, lives in a room in a run-down hotel; normally she helps to support Celeste, a part-time shoplifter and prostitute. At the beginning of the play, however, they are at odds because in the midst of an earlier quarrel Celeste threatened to expose the secret of Trinket's mastectomy, about which Trinket is morbidly sensitive. On Christmas Eve Trinket succeeds in paying for a degrading sexual liaison with a drunken sailor that nonetheless makes her feel superior to Celeste, who is by herself in the cold, congratulating herself, in turn, on her two breasts. At the end of the play the women are reconciled and experience a comforting vision of the Virgin Mary. Throughout the play a chorus of the characters sings carols about the possibility of some kind of temporary consolation for the "mutilated" (81), "the lost," "the solitary" (102). At the end the carolers are joined by "Jack in Black," a sexy death figure, clad "*in a black cowboy's suit*" studded with "*diamond-like brilliants*" (121), who benignly concludes by singing, "The bell has stopped because I smile,/ It means forget me for a while" (130).

A Lovely Sunday for Creve Coeur, too, ends with an ambiguous hope that moderate happiness may be possible. Dotty, not quite a Southern belle but possessed, supposedly, of a "Southern belle complex" (186), is a less grotesque and more workaday version of Blanche than Trinket and Celeste, though she too suffers her own "mutilations" of plumpness and nerves. Dotty, a schoolteacher, lives with Bodey, a large, eccentric German-American woman, who wants Dotty to marry her fat twin brother, Buddy. Dotty's colleague, Helena, another, albeit attenuated, Blanche figure, wants Dotty to live in elegant spinsterhood with her in an up-market apartment. Dotty, disappointed of the man she had, unrealistically, hoped to marry, finally settles for Buddy, whom she goes off to meet at Creve Coeur amusement park as the play ends.

It is understandable why Dotty's trajectory in *A Lovely Sunday for Creve Coeur* has been read as a comic, even parodic, revision of Blanche's journey in *A Streetcar Named Desire* (Thompson 196, Saddik 129–30). Both Blanche and Dotty journey, in effect, from "belle reve" to "creve coeur," but while Blanche's streetcar takes her via "Cemeteries" to "Elysian Fields," the one Dotty is about to take as the play ends goes only to an amusement park. However, rather than being a parody of *Streetcar*, *A Lovely Sunday for Creve Coeur* is really a different kind of play, one in which Williams's mix of realistic and absurdist techniques underscores what is comically grotesque, and thus absurd, rather than what is painful in his heroine's experience of love, loss, loneliness, and disappointment. In this respect Williams's play is as much akin to Henley's black comedies as it is to his own earlier works. Dotty is more resilient than Blanche. Like Teddy, she finally rejects despair, managing to "*discharge her sense of defeat*" with a gesture against "*the way of the world.*" Like Carnelle, she is able to take it on the chin, give up her dream, and "go on" (*Lovely Sunday* 199).[11]

In Williams's later plays in general as in Henley's drama there is a more exaggerated and literal use of the expressionist techniques that characterized his earlier work: an emphasis on jarring visual and aural effects, more extreme characterizations, particularly in the grotesque representation of disability, more overt symbolism, especially in figuring the relationship between desire and death. Such effects push the plays of both dramatists towards the absurd. In *The Mutilated*, for example, repeatedly a "*cold wind whines*" or "*howls*" (84, 86, 87). These stylized sound effects are more like the precise and comically sinister sounds called for in Beckett's radio play *All That Fall* than they are like the romantic aural effects (storms and so forth) that evoke psychological states in Williams's earlier plays. Visual effects are similarly exaggerated. "*[F]lashes of bluish-white light*" accompany Celeste and Trinket's fight over the drunken sailor, and Celeste, cartoonishly, charges Trinket "*like a bull*" when she steals her bag (109–10).[12]

A Lovely Sunday for Creve Coeur, too, is full of garish colors and loud sounds that assault the audience's eyes and ears. Bodey's apartment features a purple carpet, orange drapes, "violent yellow daisies" on the lampshades, and "exploding" roses on the wallpaper (172); the audience's ears are assailed by slamming drawers, Bodey's screeching hearing aid, Helena's unpleasant laughter (*"like a cawing crow"* [189]), and Sophie's wailing and moaning. In fact, in his use of this kind of exaggeration, Williams goes beyond what Henley is doing in her earlier plays, which remain grounded in realism, and approaches the more schematic strangeness of later works of the 1990s such as *Revelers* and *Impossible Marriage*.

The characters in *The Mutilated* and *A Lovely Sunday for Creve Coeur* also are larger than life. Sometimes they are grotesques like Celeste with her large bosom and low-cut dress or Sophie with her dribbling, wailing, and moaning. Sometimes Williams presents them as allegorical figures like Jack in Black or sometimes as both, even in the partially naturalistic context of *A Lovely Sunday for Creve Coeur*: Bodey Bodenhafer, large-bodied and wearing a paper flower at her ear, is the nurturing, life-affirming cow who wants Dotty to produce little children with her brother, Buddy; Helena Brookmire, who looks like a *"predatory bird"* (136) and hisses her words, is the slimy snake who wants Dotty to live with her in a kind of spinsterish "death" (173).

Disabled characters especially are presented as grotesque in the manner of Henleyesque black comedy. In *The Mutilated* Trinket herself invests her mastectomy with horror, Celeste uses it to blackmail her, and Slim, her one-night stand, finds it disgusting. In *A Lovely Sunday for Creve Coeur* Bodey's deafness is rendered grotesque by the large paper flower she wears to cover her hearing aid, and the schizophrenic Sophie looks like a "religieuse *in a state of sorrowful vision*" (154). Even the artist figures who appear or are referred to in these late plays are grotesquely afflicted: the pathetic fake Bird Girl with feathers glued onto her body in *The Mutilated* or Sarah Bernhardt with her wooden leg in Celeste's song as well as Dotty's former musician boyfriend who suffered from premature ejaculation.

One of the chief themes of *The Mutilated* and *A Lovely Sunday for Creve Coeur* is the same struggle between and ultimate fusion of life and death that is played out as Chekhovian tragicomedy in *Streetcar*. In his late plays Williams renders the terms of this struggle in more grotesque and exaggerated forms, producing a broadly symbolic and expressionist rendition of the theme in *The Mutilated* and an allegorized though still somewhat naturalistic version in *A Lovely Sunday for Creve Coeur*. The humor in both plays is darker than it is in *Streetcar*, though the endings are lighter. The grotesque exaggerations, the relish with which both plays engage in dark comedy, and the temporary or ambiguous hopefulness of their endings emphasize how far Williams's later work has come from his earlier Chekhovian tragicomedy and how close it has come to the darkly comic vision and quirkier manner of Beth Henley.

The *Mutilated* contains many images of death, beginning with Celeste's dour and proper brother, who is an undertaker. Death and life are symbiotically connected as they are in *Streetcar*, though in more overtly contrasting and grotesque ways. For example, a man at the bar Trinket enters has just died while telling a joke. Despite finding a dead cockroach in the cookie tin, Celeste is hungry enough to have no compunction in eating "after a cockroach" (125) — she jokes that one does that in all the best restaurants. And Jack in Black, representing death but also magnetic and compassionate, could be a symbolic abstraction of Mac Sam. In *A Lovely Sunday for Creve Coeur*, too, death and life are inextricable. Dotty, like Blanche and Trinket, thinks that life without a man is a *"death* time" (*Mutilated* 117). Though marriage with Buddy is not what she wants, Dotty chooses even this attenuated form of life over the sterility of spinsterish card parties with Helena despite the danger, as she has comically observed, of being "asphyxiated gradually by cheap cigars" (133).

In an interview with Ira J. Bilowit in 1979 Williams emphasized that Dotty, unlike Blanche (but like Henley's heroines), goes on at the end of the play: "She goes right on to Creve Coeur" (Devlin 316). Trinket and Celeste, too, in *The Mutilated* share in this resilience. Celeste says that as long as one has longings, satisfaction is possible: "Give up is something I never even think of. I'll go on" (94). And Trinket too says, "*I have absolutely no intention of giving up*" (100). Their determination to go on receives a kind of blessing, less ephemeral than the cathedral chimes at the end of *Streetcar*, through the choric carols that are sung throughout the play and the final religious vision that the two women share.

Both Williams and Henley write about the mutilated, and as Celeste reminds us, we are all "mutilated" in our own ways. Like the people living in the Silver Dollar Hotel, too, we are all transients, "only passing through," as Blanche puts it in *Streetcar* (413). Nonetheless, a fragile happiness may be possible. Such happiness may come from a brief encounter with another, as the carolers sing in *The Mutilated*, and though he may not stay, "It may be softer where he was" (82), and this encounter will constitute a "miracle"—"The dark held back a little while" (119). When the lover Trinket desired to ward off her darkness proves to be a "*scorpion*" (126), she finds her Christmas miracle instead in forgiveness and renewed friendship with Celeste. This miracle is finally authenticated, however ambiguously, by the two women's shared experience of the presence of Mary in the room with them, as, like Carnelle with Popeye and Delmount at the fireworks display, they share a moment of "eternal grace" (*Firecracker* 202, 203). And in *A Lovely Sunday for Creve Coeur*, though Dotty's hoped-for gentleman caller, "the long-delayed but always expected something that we live for" (*Menagerie* 145), turns out to be Buddy, she decides to grasp such happiness as she can have.

Williams in his late plays and Henley throughout her career invest less in the tragic dimension of life than Williams does in his earlier work. They concentrate instead on what is absurd and, therefore, comic in human existence in all its dimensions: the grotesque, the ugly, the disturbing, the sadly funny, the ridiculous, even the mean. The result is that the plays in which their styles converge are not tragicomedies but dark comedies. The grotesque elements in the plays prevent the tragic experience of life that may lie just below the surface from making itself felt. That is why Williams's late plays, like Henley's plays, however dark and ugly some of the events portrayed in them may be, can offer more hope that the characters will "go on" than Williams's earlier more lyrical, Chekhovian tragicomedies in which the tragic is inextricably involved in the laughter. Blanche and Laura possess a tragic radiance at the ends of their respective tragicomedies. But it is the characters who are deprived of dignity and even rendered ludicrous in their sufferings, characters like Carnelle and Teddy and Trinket and Celeste and Dotty, who have a better chance at finding happiness for "this one moment" or "for a while." The vision of human existence is darker but also more accommodating for the mutilated.

NOTES

1. Williams expressed admiration for these dramatists (Devlin 95, 99, 120, 137); Henley found reading *Waiting for Godot* in high school an inspiring experience (Plunka 9).

2. For example, among theatre reviewers John Simon, Frank Rich, and Megan Rosenfeld and among academic critics, Billy J. Harbin, Kimball King, Janet V. Haedicke, Charles S. Watson, and Gene A. Plunka have made connections or noted parallels. King connects Williams and Henley as Southern dramatists (647); Haedicke links Carnelle's sexuality with Blanche's (208); Watson notes that Henley's women often resemble Blanche (202). Plunka cites the comments by Simon, Rich, and Rosenfeld (3, 25, 205 n. 51). Only Gary Richards, however, has offered an extended comparison in his incisive discussion of *Control Freaks* as a parody and feminist revision of *The Glass Menagerie* (52–55).

3. Commenting a few years later on the Western frontier language of *Abundance*, Henley again remarked,

"You can be more poetic, use stranger twists of phrase, which is what I always liked about the South" (Hoffmann 5, qtd. in Plunka 125).

    4. Henley's use of animal imagery is noted in Betsko and Koenig, 216.

    5. See Foster, *The Name and Nature of Tragicomedy*, 155; Bigsby,38. Plunka argues that Henley "can best be perceived as a dramatist who delineates a deeply rooted existential despair" (5); he quotes Henley's comment in an interview published in Betsko and Koenig: "What is amazing to me is the existential madness we — everyone — are born into" (221; qtd. in Plunka 43). See also Hargrove, 59–61; Kachur 18–22, Kullman 21–22.

    6. Harbin notes that Elain's dialogue often echoes Blanche's lyricism (91).

    7. Henley has remarked, "But I do feel that all my plays are extremely optimistic" (Betsko and Koenig 216, qtd. in Watson 202).

    8. For an extensive discussion of *Streetcar* as tragicomedy see Foster, *The Name and Nature of Tragicomedy* (149–58).

    9. Plunka, citing Rosenfeld, offers a more extensive comparison of Lenny and Laura (205, n. 51).

    10. On the symbolism of *Streetcar* see Quirino.

    11. For a full discussion of *A Lovely Sunday for Creve Coeur*, including a stylistic and thematic comparison with *Streetcar*, see Foster, "Waiting for Buddy."

    12. Dorff discusses Williams's use of cartoon imagery in his later plays.

WORKS CITED

Betsko, Kathleen and Rachel Koenig. *Interviews with Contemporary Women Playwrights*. New York: William Morrow and Company, Inc., 1987.

Bigsby, C.W.E. *Modern American Drama, 1945–2000*. Cambridge: Cambridge University Press, 2000.

Dellasega, Mary. "Beth Henley." In Philip C. Kolin and Colby H. Kullman, ed. *Speaking on Stage: Interviews with Contemporary American Playwrights*. Tuscaloosa and London: University of Alabama Press, 1996. 250–59.

Devlin, Albert J. *Conversations with Tennessee Williams*. Jackson and London: University Press of Mississippi, 1986.

Dorff, Linda. "Theatricalist Cartoons: Tennessee Williams's Late 'Outrageous Plays.'" *Tennessee Williams Annual Review*, 2 (1999): 13–33.

Foster, Verna A. *The Name and Nature of Tragicomedy*. Aldershot and Burlington, VT: Ashgate, 2004.

_____. "Waiting for Buddy, or Just Going On in *A Lovely Sunday for Creve Coeur*." In Philip C. Kolin, ed. *The Undiscovered Country: The Late Plays of Tennessee Williams*. New York: Peter Lang, 2002. 155–67.

Haedicke, Janet V. "Margins in the Mainstream: Contemporary Women Playwrights." In William W. Demastes, ed. *Realism and the American Dramatic Tradition*. Tuscaloosa and London: University of Alabama Press, 1996.

Harbin, Billy J. "Familial Bonds in the Plays of Beth Henley." *Southern Quarterly*, 25:3 (1987): 81–94.

Henley, Beth. *Crimes of the Heart. Collected Plays Volume I 1980–1989*. Lyme, NH: Smith and Kraus, 2000.

_____. *The Debutante Ball. Collected Plays Volume I 1980–1989*. Lyme, NH: Smith and Kraus, 2000.

_____. Introduction. *Collected Plays Volume II 1990–1999*. Lyme, NH: Smith and Kraus,2000.

_____. *The Miss Firecracker Contest. Collected Plays Volume I 1980–1989*. Lyme, NH: Smith and Kraus, 2000.

Hoffman, Roy. "Brash New South Is Still a Stranger to Its Dramatists." *New York Times*. 2 July 1989. 2: 5.

Jones, John Griffin, ed. "Beth Henley." *Mississippi Writers Talking: Interviews with Eudora Welty, Shelby Foote, Elizabeth Spencer, Barry Hannah, Beth Henley*. Jackson: University Press of Mississippi, 1982. 169–90.

Kachur, Barbara. "Women Playwrights on Broadway: Henley, Howe, Norman, and Wasserstein." In Bruce King, ed. *Contemporary American Theatre*. New York: St. Martin's Press, 1991. 15–39.

King, Kimball. "Tennessee Williams: A Southern Writer." *Mississippi Quarterly*, 48 (Fall 1995): 627–47.

Kolin, Philip C., ed. *The Undiscovered Country: The Late Plays of Tennessee Williams*. New York: Peter Lang, 2002.

Kullman, Colby H. "Beth Henley's Marginalized Heroines." *Studies in American Drama, 1945–Present*, 8: 1 (1993): 21–28.

Leverich, Lyle. *Tom: The Unknown Tennessee Williams*. New York: Crown Publishers, Inc., 1995.

Mapp, Larry G. "Lessons from the Past: Loss and Redemption in the Early Plays of Beth Henley." *Beth Henley: A Casebook*, ed. Julia A. Fesmire. New York and London: Routledge, 2002. 32–41.

Meszaros, M. Beth. "'Enlightened by Our Afflictions': Portrayals of Disability in the Comic Theatre of Beth Henley and Martin McDonagh." *Disability Studies Quarterly*, 23: 3–4 (Summer/Fall 2003). www.dsq-sds.org/2003 summfall toc.html

Plunka, Gene A. *The Plays of Beth Henley*. Jefferson, NC and London: McFarland & Company, Inc., 2005.

Quirino, Leonard. "The Cards Indicate a Voyage on *A Streetcar Named Desire*." In Jac Tharpe, ed. *Tennessee Williams: A Tribute*. Jackson, MI: University Press of Mississippi, 1977. 77–96.

Rich, Frank. "Stage: *Lucky Spot* by Beth Henley." *New York Times*. 29 April 1987. C: 22.

Richards, Gary. "Moving Beyond Mississippi: Beth Henley and the Anxieties of Postsouthernness." In *Beth Henley: A Casebook*, ed. Julia A. Fesmire. New York and London: Routledge, 2002. 42–63.

Rosenfeld, Megan. "Beth Henley's World of Southern Discomfort." *The Washington Post*. 12 December 1986. C1: 10.

Saddik, Annette J. *The Politics of Reputation: The Critical Reception of Tennessee Williams' Later Plays*. Madison, N.J.: Fairleigh Dickinson University Press, 1999.

Simon, John. "Sisterhood Is Beautiful." *New York*. 12 January 1981, 42.

Thompson Judith J. *Tennessee Williams' Plays: Memory, Myth, and Symbol*. New York: Peter Lang, 1987.

Watson, Charles S. *The History of Southern Drama*. Lexington: University Press of Kentucky, 1997.

Williams, Tennessee. *The Glass Menagerie. The Theatre of Tennessee Williams*. Vol. 1. New York: New Directions, 1971.

_____. *A Lovely Sunday for Creve Coeur. The Theatre of Tennessee Williams*. Vol. 8. New York: New Directions, 1992.

_____. *The Mutilated. The Theatre of Tennessee Williams*. Vol. 7. New York: New Directions, 1994.

_____. *A Streetcar Named Desire. The Theatre of Tennessee Williams*. Vol. 1. New York: New Directions, 1971.

"Period of Adjustment": Marriage in Williams and Christopher Durang

John M. Clum

As to emotional dangers, one should always try to avoid crazy people, especially in marriage or live in situations, but in everyday life as well.
— *Christopher Durang,* The Marriage of Bette and Boo

The human heart would never pass the drunk test.
—*Tennessee Williams,* Period of Adjustment

When asked who his favorite playwrights are, Christopher Durang responded:

Oddly, if I had to choose one, it would probably be Tennessee Williams. Even though I don't write like him, I so admire and am taken by the psychology of his characters. I find them touching, sometimes funny, sometimes tragic. Some of his dialogue is stunning. I think *Glass Menagerie* and *Streetcar* are both very great plays [http://www.christopherdurang.com/Q&A3.htm].

Echoes of Tennessee Williams's work can be heard in Christopher Durang's plays, not only in the parodies of Williams's plays (*For Whom the Southern Belle Tolls* [1994] and *Desire, Desire, Desire* [1987]), but more particularly in his autobiographical play, *The Marriage of Bette and Boo* (1985). In these works, we see two responses to Williams's work, particularly the early semi-autobiographical play *The Glass Menagerie*: a parodic queering of the play in *For Whom the Southern Belle Tolls*, and a use of the play as model in *The Marriage of Bette and Boo*. The latter is, like Williams's *Period of Adjustment* (1960), a critique of marriage and a satire on the values of suburban Americans.

One does not initially think of marriage as the focus of Williams's *The Glass Menagerie*, but the action hinges on Amanda's hapless efforts to provide a husband for her daughter. Without a husband to support her, Laura will become, in her mother's words, one of those "little birdlike women without any nest — eating the crust of humility all their life!" (156). Amanda's own economic situation is the result of an unhappy marriage and a disappearing husband. Marriage in Williams's early plays is an economic necessity, not the living out of an ideal of love and companionship. Yet marriage has not provided economic security for Amanda. Indeed, if her stories of past courtship have any semblance of truth, she could have made a "good marriage" in an economic sense, but chose to marry the man for whom she felt the greatest desire. Nor is marriage of any kind a likely outcome for her dysfunctional daughter.

Even Maggie, in *Cat on a Hot Tin Roof*, filled with desire for her feckless alcoholic husband, knows he and she need his family's fortune. Williams is always skeptical of whether sexual desire can be contained within marriage or whether a lifelong intimate connection between two people is possible. The pathos-filled ending of *The Glass Menagerie* left the members of the Wingfield family without partners. In his unsuccessful comedy, *Period of Adjustment* (1960), resonant, like *The Glass Menagerie*, with echoes of his mother, Williams tries to offer a comic vision of marriage. To some extent, *Period of Adjustment* is a reworking of themes from the earlier play, centering on Williams's favorite conundrum: whether social misfits can negotiate some sort of working relationship. As comedy must, *Period of Adjustment* works toward some sort of connection for its two married couples. I'm not sure how familiar Christopher Durang is with Williams's *Period of Adjustment*, but this minor comedy also came to mind as I considered Durang's use of Williams's work.

The autobiographical dimension of *The Glass Menagerie* has been discussed many times by the playwright and his biographers. Like that play's matriarch, Isabel Haverstick, the heroine of *Period of Adjustment*, bears many similarities to Williams's mother, Edwina. Williams's biographer, Lyle Leverich, wrote of Edwina: "Militantly forthright and possessed of puritanical opinions, Edwina was frequently disliked for the very thing for which her son was esteemed: a mastery of words. She not merely talked—and talked—she had the ability to overcome friend and adversary alike, usually leaving them limp and defenseless under the sheer weight of words."[1] On Edwina's sexual relations with her husband, Leverich notes: "She continued to resist his fumbling advances, leaving him frustrated and angry. As young as he was at the time, Tennessee remembered hearing his mother's crying protests in her bedroom" (p. 42). Isabel, too, has been raised by staunch Christian parents and has become an exaggerated version of certain stereotypical qualities of southern women of an earlier generation: prim, garrulous and a bit delicate, though tougher than she seems. She has lost her nursing job because she fainted in the operating room. She needs a husband to support her but, like Edwina Williams, Isabel has a horror of sexual relations and is, to put it mildly, garrulous.[2] She marries George, whom she met when she was a nurse-in-training at a veteran's hospital and he was a patient suffering from what we would now call post traumatic stress disorder which manifested itself in uncontrollable shaking. Like many of Williams' women, Isabel feelings for George were sexual, but she was also attracted to his weakness: "So *handsome?*. And so *afflicted?* So afflicted and *handsome?* (32). He was attracted to her because he mistook her back rubs (which she was required to give) as signs of sexual interest: "I DIDN'T TOUCH YOUR BODY EXCEPT AS A NURSE HIRED TO DO IT" (p. 51). As they leave St. Louis in the used hearse he has purchased (can there be a Williams play without some image of death?), George tells Isabel that his self-consciousness about his shaking led to his quitting his job. So the marriage begins with no money and only George's impractical dream of raising longhorn cattle for television westerns. Isabel is terrified of poverty and horrified at her husband's crude, drunken sexual overtures on their wedding night at the Old Man River Motel:

> [He] Threw off his clothes and sat down in front of the heater as if I were not even present ... Continuing drinking ... Then began the courtship and, oh, what a courtship it was, such tenderness, romance! I finally screamed. I locked myself in the bathroom and didn't come out until he had gotten to bed and then I slept in a chair [33].

So Isabel is left with the two central problems faced by Williams's heroines: looming poverty and a sexual standoff.

The action of *Period of Adjustment* takes places at the suburban Memphis home of George's army buddy, Ralph, whose wife has just left him after he quit his job working for her father. Ralph married Dorothea despite her homeliness because her father was wealthy and seemed to be at death's door. But the rich and mean have a way of hanging on and Ralph feels trapped working for his father-in-law and married to the boss's homely daughter. To compound his misery, he is sure his wife is turning their son into a sissy (echoes of Williams's father). Ralph and Dorothea's home is one of a row of identical Spanish style bungalows which have been built over a cavern. The homes are slowly sinking as the living death of conformity and spiritual emptiness overtake the neighborhood. Can a marriage, founded literally on shaky ground, thrive?

Williams works his way toward an unconvincing denouement in which the two couples find a way to begin again on building their marriages. Ralph comes to appreciate his wife and she respects his decision to free them of her parents' domination. George learns the need for tenderness with his wife and Isabel realizes, as many of Williams's women have before her, that she will need to take care of her husband. The men are victims of the wars they had to fight (World War II and Korea), as Ralph points out to his in-laws: "We both of us died in two wars, repeatedly died in two wars and were buried in suburbs named High Point" (Williams: 1982, p. 85). Isabel realizes that George's bullishness is a result of a sexual fear all men share: "Inside or outside, they've all got a nervous tremor of some kind, sweetheart.... The whole world's a big hospital, a big neurological ward and I am a student nurse in it" (Williams: 1982, p. 93). In this dysfunctional world, nothing is more terrifying than marriage:

> ISABEL: What an awful, frightening thing it is!
> GEORGE: What?
> ISABEL: Two people living together, two, two — different worlds! — attempting — existence — together! [Williams: 1982, p. 90].

Williams's picture of what keeps these husbands and wives apart is more convincing than his reconciliation of what seems irreconcilable. It is one thing to get these couples into bed, another to imagine them happy over time. This is a typical problem with Williams's supposedly happy marital resolutions (Stella and Stanley, Brick and Maggie). They are built on sex and lies, but not on love. The marriage bed is still sinking into a cavern as the middle-class suburban society seems to offer no sustenance for the spirit or the imagination. *Period of Adjustment* was not a success as a play or a film (very poorly cast), but a 2006 critically acclaimed London revival shows that the play was underrated in 1960.[3]

Durang's best play, *The Marriage of Bette and Boo*, has direct links to Williams's *The Glass Menagerie* and similarities to *Period of Adjustment*. There are, of course, major differences between these writers. Durang's style is different from Williams's in many ways. He is less interested in the specific social and physical settings of his work. For Williams physical settings are both real and metaphorical. More than anything else, they define the trap in which his central character is placed. *Period of Adjustment* takes place in a very specific neighborhood, albeit one with metaphorical resonances that underscore the play's social satire. Suburbia is sinking into a black hole and marriages are always on shaky ground. Durang's world is mental: the black holes are in his characters' psyches. Settings are not specific and seldom carry metaphorical weight. Except for a few props and pieces of furniture, Durang's plays take place on a bare stage. They are almost totally dependent on language. Their setting is the theater itself or, perhaps, the inside of Durang's head. *The Marriage of Bette and Boo* takes place somewhere in suburban America, but its characters seem cut off from any meaningful relationship, positive or negative, with their geographical surroundings or their community.

In Williams's world, one sees the norm from which his characters diverge, though that norm is seldom presented in positive terms. Tom describes Jim in *The Glass Menagerie* as "an emissary from a world of reality that we were somehow set apart from" (145), though Jim has his own illusions. Ralph's successful in-laws, the McGillicuddys, in *Period of Adjustment* are rooted in the world of money, possessions and acceptance of too little: "I gave you a fatherly talk. I told you that monotony was a part of life" (78). There are no "normal" characters in Durang's major plays. Even the representatives of social and moral order (the priests) and mental well being (psychiatrists) are shown to be out of touch or demented (see, for instance, his *Beyond Therapy*). Though Williams moved toward the absurd in some of his later work, he never seemed as comfortable with Ionesco-infused linguistic chaos as Durang is in his best work. Yet the two share a world in which people in relationships cannot easily connect in a positive way, in which women are stronger and more articulate than men, though often less moored to reality, and in which aspects of the author's own life are always close to the surface. If the world in *Period of Adjustment* is a "big neurological ward," it is a psychiatric intensive care ward in Durang's plays.

More than any playwright since George Bernard Shaw, Durang's published collections of plays offer both script and commentary. Alongside the voices of his characters we hear the voice of Christopher Durang, spelling out the relationship between playwright and play. For even more information, one can go to Durang's website, where he has provided lengthy answers to the questions most frequently asked by high school and college students. The only issue on which he is somewhat guarded is his sexual orientation.

Though Durang has expressed his admiration for Williams's plays, in the introduction to *For Whom the Southern Belle Tolls*, he mixes his respect for Williams's first successful play with irritation at pathologically shy Laura of *The Glass Menagerie*:

> And though I as a child always felt sympathy for Laura, as an adult I started to find Laura's sensitivity frustrating. I mean, how hard was typing class really ... as an adult I felt restless with her little hobby. Did she actually spend hours and hours staring at them [her glass animals]? Couldn't she try to function in the world just one little bit? Why didn't she go out bowling or make prank phone calls or get drunk on a good bottle of bourbon? [Durang: 1995, p. 10].

For Whom the Southern Belle Tolls is Durang's second parody of *The Glass Menagerie*. At Yale Drama School, he and fellow playwright Albert Innaurato penned and performed a seven minute spoof of a dialogue between Amanda and Laura which they performed in outlandishly inappropriate costumes: "we didn't dress as women, we dressed as priests" (Durang: 1995, p. 10). Durang includes Italian filmmaker Federico Fellini among his favorite playwrights: "his playfulness and the way he casually included his Italian Catholic roots influenced me" (http://www.christopherdurang.com/Q&A3.htm), and this early parody demonstrates the mix of psychological realism and the surreal that will dominate Durang's major work. Playing Williams in priests' garb is certainly Fellini-esque: the Italian master's work is filled with grotesque, often comic, priests and nuns. It also underscores the fact that from the beginning that Durang's Catholic education and his disillusionment with Catholicism have been central to his work. In Durang's plays, Catholicism offers a structure for thought and feeling, particularly feelings of guilt, but it does not offer comfort: "I felt that the church I had grown up with had gotten stuck in rules, and that some of the rules were illogical, and some had misled people and caused them psychological pain" (Durang: 1995, p. 414). Durang's focus is on the church teachings that maim people in their intimate personal relationships, particularly those pertaining to sexuality, marriage and birth control. We see this played out most literally in *Sister Mary Ignatius Explains It All for You*. Durang's nun moves from being a relatively benign exponent of traditional Catholic doctrine who hands out cookies to her protégé to a fanatical murderess when confronted by former students who defy the church's teachings on sex. The only one who earns her approval is the unhappily married Aloysius:

SISTER: And you're married?

ALOYSIUS: Yes.

SISTER: And you don't use birth control?

ALOYSIUS: No.

SISTER: But you only have two children. Why is that? You're not spilling your seed like Onan, are you? That's a sin, you know.

ALOYSIUS: No. It's just chance that we haven't had more.

...

SISTER: Well, I'm very pleased then.

ALOYSIUS: I am an alcoholic. And recently I've started to hit my wife. And I keep thinking about suicide.

SISTER: Within bounds, all those things are venial sins. At least one of my students turned out well [Durang: 1995, p. 401].

Yet Durang's religious pessimism goes beyond criticism of the Catholic Church. God may exist, but is hardly beneficent:

MATT: I don't think God punishes people for specific things.

BETTE: That's good.

MATT: I think He punishes people in general for no reason [Durang: 1997, p. 364].

And, as the man in Durang's *Laughing Wild* makes clear, those who claim their good fortune is from God may have their priorities confused:

I remember when everyone won Tonys for *Dreamgirls*, and they all got up there thanking God for letting them win this award, and I was thinking to myself: God is silent on the holocaust, but He involves himself in the Tony awards? [394].

Two men performing Amanda and Laura in priests' costumes demonstrates Durang's love of absurd connections and his disinterest in poetic realism, the dominant theatrical mode of the first half of the twentieth century in the United States. Fluidity of gender is being suggested ironically by costumes representative of an organization devoted to maintaining traditional notions of gender and sexuality.

Despite the influence of religion in Williams's upbringing and his later conversion to Catholicism, Williams's plays are almost completely secular. Organized religion appears as an instrument of sexual repression in *Summer and Smoke*, as another agent of greed and mendacity in *Cat on a Hot Tin Roof*, and lost faith in *The Night of the Iguana*. Though he frequently uses Christian imagery in his work, Williams's religion is based on the flesh, not the spirit; on illusion, not faith; on the pleasures of this world, not a longing for the next. "Sometimes there's God so quickly" (356), Blanche DuBois exclaims when she thinks she has found a kind man to support her and take care of her. This is less a statement of faith than a sigh of relief.

Durang's next assault on *The Glass Menagerie*, the one-act "For Whom the Southern Belle Tolls" (1993) both parodies and queers Williams's play. In this clever spoof, Williams's crippled, agoraphobic Laura becomes Lawrence, who suffers from a variety of real and imagined malaises: asthma, eczema, and the delusion that he is crippled. Lawrence's only subjects for conversation are his ailments and his collection of glass swizzle sticks which he describes in absurd detail: "This one is called Stringbean because it's long and thin" (13). His mother, Amanda, has far less patience than Williams's counterpart: "YOU IDIOT CHILD! DO I HAVE TO LISTEN TO THIS PATHETIC PRATTLING THE REST OF MY LIFE? (Durang: 1995, p. 26).

Lawrence's brother, Tom, plays out the gay subtext of Williams's original.[4] Durang's Tom goes to movies like "Humpy Bus Boys" and brings home sailors to share his bed. His mother won't allow him to escape until he has taken care of his brother: "But don't leave us until you fulfill your duties here, Tom. Help brother find a wife, or a job, or a doctor. Or consider euthanasia. But don't leave me here all alone, saddled with him" (Durang: 1995, p. 23). The "feminine caller" Tom brings home to court his brother is a deaf lesbian who has "two clocks to punch," her job and her girlfriend, Betty. At the final curtain, Amanda and Lawrence are together, wishing for more swizzle sticks.

"For Whom the Southern Belle Tolls" is a spoof that tells us more about Durang than about Williams. On his website Questions and Answers, Durang describes himself as an icon-oclast: "A dictionary meaning says: 'A person who attacks or ridicules traditional or vener-ated institutions or ideas regarded by him as erroneous or based on superstition.' I think this is less true of me now that I am older, but not it's not gone entirely" (www.christopherdu rang.com).

Durang is not merely spoofing Williams's work. He is satirizing Williams's cautious approach to sex and sexuality in this play and, more important, questioning Williams's basic point of view toward his characters. Switching Laura's gender heightens the potential risibility of her dysfunction and queering the play serves to underscore the queerness at the heart of Williams's work. On a more fundamental level, *The Glass Menagerie* elicits our sympathy for its three misfits. The Wingfields do not fit into conventional economy or conventional patterns of behavior. All three are trapped in fantasy worlds. Tom's restlessness is the opposite of Laura's neurotic stasis, but it is a sign that he will never fit into a conventional domestic pattern.

Durang's parody pokes fun at Williams's unconditional love for his misfits and their illu-sions. Durang is far too clear-eyed to see such dreaminess as in any way positive. While Durang's plays are often about people who are victims of illusions, he does not romanticize illusion as Williams or Eugene O'Neill do. If anything, he wants to expose the muddled thinking that traps his characters. Though Durang shares William's penchant for creating damaged people, he does not seem to be in the least interested in sentimentalizing them.

Nor is he interested in the mystification of sexuality that Williams needed to practice in the commercial theater of 1945. *The Glass Menagerie* is an oddly chaste play for Williams, who would profit from the reputation of being the most candidly sexual playwright of his time. Laura's long standing crush on Jim O'Connor only makes her more frightened of being in the same room with him, and Jim's kiss has more to do with the impression he wants to make than of any sexual desire. Durang, a generation older than Williams, presents his char-acters as sexual beings and can only see Tom's guarded sexuality and sentimental lament for his sister as absurd: "So I'll leave them both dimly lit in my memory. For nowadays the world is lit by lightning; and when we get those colored lights going, it feels like I'm on LSD. Or some other drug. Or maybe it's the trick of memory, or the memory of some trick" (Durang: 1995, p. 25). Williams's Tom finds food for his imagination in the movie palace, which in Williams's short stories is a site of homosexual activity.[5] Durang's Amanda observes of her cineaste son: "He only seems to meet men at the movies" (14).

"For Whom the Southern Belle Tolls" shows one side of Christopher Durang: the clever prankster who loves to play theatrical games with literary masterpieces and B movies. This camp aspect of Durang's work can descend into good-natured chaos as it does in his other Williams parody, "Desire, Desire, Desire," written to be a companion piece to his parody of *The Glass Menagerie*. "Desire, Desire, Desire" moves, like the more famous "An Actor's Night-mare," though a series of plays, in this case classics by Williams, O'Neill, Beckett and even-tually even the less classic *Harvey* ("From the Pulitzer Prize winning play by Mary Chase, *That was a lean year*." Durang: 1995, p. 192). It's all a bit scattershot and nowhere near as focused or funny as "For Whom the Southern Belle Tolls."

If his Tom spends a lot of time at the movies, all Durang's characters seem to be filled with memories of B movies, television shows and books from Dostoevsky to that camp expose of Joan Crawford's maternal behavior, *Mommie Dearest*. Durang is one of the first generation of American children raised in front of the television set, but who also took literature and film seriously. Cultural references abound, but his plays can give one a sense of being trapped in a theatrical Trivia game. One wonders what the current, much less culturally literate generation makes of Durang's work. In Durang's best work, the cleverness is linked to a dark satiric vision: in the weaker plays, it can get tedious.

Durang's best and favorite play, *The Marriage of Bette and Boo*, is, like *The Glass Menagerie*, a memory play telling, as the playwright puts it, "the rather sad story of my parents' marriage and a bit about my place in it" (Durang: 1997, p.369). Resemblances to Williams's play don't end there.

The Marriage of Bette and Boo is narrated by their son, Matt, the only one of Bette's five children who survives childbirth. Williams's narrator, Tom, sees the play's action through the haze of memory, offering "truth in the pleasant guise of illusion" (Williams: 1971, p. 144). Williams uses his own given name for his narrator as a way of linking the play's action to his own life. Durang played Matt in the New York production of his play, "a head-on way of dealing with the 'author's voice' nature of the part" (Durang: 1997, 372). Durang's Matt is more rational than sentimental. He wants to understand the memories he presents. He begins, "If one looks hard enough, one can usually see the order that lies beneath the surface" (Durang: 1997, p. 315). Understanding is what he is after, and as the play progresses, we learn that what Matt wants to understand is why the people around him don't change, why their repetition of mistakes only ends at the moment of their death. His parents seem caught in an endless cycle. His mother, Bette, has four stillborn babies. Like Durang's parents, Bette and her husband Boo have Rh negative blood incompatibility. The death of Bette's babies places her in a cycle of depression and exacerbates her husband's drinking problem which leads her to nag him incessantly. When she finally divorces him, she marries another alcoholic. Matt's paternal grandfather also has a drinking problem and is cruel to his wife and daughter-in-law. His mother has one sister trapped in an unhappy marriage to a constantly absent husband and another so riddled with Catholic guilt that she has nervous breakdowns. Toward the end of the play, Matt asks his paternal grandfather why he was so cruel to his wife. When the old man asks him why he wants to know, Matt responds:

> Because I see all of you do the same thing over and over, for years and years, and you never change. And my fear is that I can see all of you but not see myself; and maybe I'm doing something similar, but I just can't see it. What I mean to say is: did you all *intend* to live your lives the way you did? [361].

His grandfather dismisses the question and him, but such questions are never answered in the play. By this time, Matt has reached a state of Hamlet-like uncertainty:

> Having intelligence allows one to analyze problems and to make sense of one's life. This is difficult to achieve but with perseverance and persistence it is possible ... not even to get out of bed in the morning. To sleep. To sleep, perchance to dream, to take the phone off the hook and simply be unreachable. That is less *dramatic* than suicide, but more *reversible*.
> "I can't make sense out of these things anymore" [Durang: 1997, p. 361].

Matt's mental state is an echo of the depression Durang experienced as an undergraduate at Harvard:

> Harvard was a wonderful, valuable experience — but it was also a time when I grew up a lot, went though a pretty bad depression, found out I didn't like academic work anymore, didn't do well in my classes in the middle two years, but pulled myself out of the slump my final year.

My depression was caused by the negative side of my family upbringing—I come from an alcoholic home, and there was lots of struggle and arguing and no problems ever seemed to get solved. I had trouble feeling not hopeless about life [http://www.christopherdurang.com/Q&A1. htm].

As Matt narrates the play, he is attempting to write a term paper on Thomas Hardy whose point of view toward his characters is similar to Matt's: "The sadness in Hardy—his lack of belief that a benevolent God watches over human destiny, his sense of the waste and frustration of the average human life, his forceful irony in the face of moral and metaphysical questions" (326) are all part of Matt's response to his family's experience. Yet the conflation of Matt's own past and his writing of an essay on Hardy is one expression of his growing confusion and his inability to make sense of his experience:

Now the fact of the matter is that Boo isn't really an alcoholic at all, but drinks simply because Bette is such a terrible, unending nag. Or, perhaps, Boo *is* an alcoholic, and Bette is a terrible unending nag in *reaction* to his drinking too much, and also because he isn't "there" for her, any more than Clym Yeobright is really there for Eustacia Vye in *The Return of the Native*, although admittedly Eustacia Vye is very neurotic, but then so is Bette also [333].

Like Durang at Harvard, who was for two years incapable of completing his term papers on time, Matt is unable to see his life or work constructively. Matt's situation in *The Marriage of Bette and Boo* echoes Daisy's in Durang's previous full-length play, *Baby with the Bathwater* (1983). A victim of nightmarish child rearing by parents with no sense of reality (they didn't even notice that he was male) and lots of chemicals, Daisy takes thirteen years to get through his first two years of college. His depression has given him writer's block and he can't get past the first sentence of the term papers he has been assigned: "I have this enormous desire to feel absolutely nothing" (Durang: 1997, p. 295). Clearly Durang believes that nurture, particularly horrific nurturing, has a greater influence on our behavior than nature. But, like Daisy's psychiatrist, he also feels that one must fight his way past the damage parents cause: "I mean we know you had a rough start but PULL YOURSELF TOGETHER!" (Durang: 1997, p. 297).

Williams's *The Glass Menagerie* chronicles the period before he, trapped in an awful job with no outlet for his fertile imagination, had a major breakdown: "He was suffering an inverted hysteria with a full range of neurological symptoms: nervous exhaustion, arrhythmic heartbeat, immobilizing indecision, self-conscious blushing, shyness and a gamut of unnamable fears" (Leverich: 1995, p. 169). Like his Tom, Williams moved on, but was haunted by the memory of the frail creature he left behind, his sister Rose. He became the bard of the misfits. While Durang at this stage of his career writes out a series of variations on his family problems, he believes that people can change, can overcome their weaknesses. He doesn't romanticize his characters' dysfunction. At the end of *Baby with the Bathwater*, Daisy, now with the gender appropriate name Alexander Nevsky (Daisy is obviously a fan of Eisenstein and Prokofiev) and his wife are learning to treat their baby in an appropriate, loving way that is quite different from the bizarre rearing he received. At the end of *The Marriage of Bette and Boo*, Matt is asking the right questions which may free him from his family's cycle of destructive repetition.

Matt's confusion is also reflected in the play's structure, which is dependent on Durang's/ Matt's organization of events. Though framed by Tom's narration, *The Glass Menagerie* is presented in traditional linear form. There is no attempt on Williams's part to capture the sometimes random sequence of memories explores by modernist novelists like James Joyce, Virginia Woolf, or William Faulkner or the fragmentation of time we see in the plays of Thornton

Wilder, though his use of an onstage narrator comes out of the latter's *Our Town*. While Williams has forsaken the traditional three act structure for a series of ten to fifteen minute scenes, there is nothing radical about his dramaturgy. Durang's *The Marriage of Bette and Boo* is comprised of thirty-three short scenes that jump back and forth in time.

The first act is basically linear with one intervention, a scene between Matt and his father that takes place twenty years after the events of Act One. Matt's parents have divorced and Boo, his father, says: "I miss your mother, Skip. Nobody should be alone. Do you have any problems you want to talk over. Your old man could help out" (Durang: 1997, p. 324). Boo laments the loss of an ideal of marriage, not the reality. Everything in the play suggests that Bette and Boo were lonely in their marriage, that marriage does not bring happiness or even companionship. Since we see the entire play through Matt's eyes, we also know that his father's advice or example would be of little use to Matt. This father-son scene is repeated in a more elaborate form, still out of chronological order, in Act II, where it is linked to a more guilt provoking dinner with his mother, "You know, you're the only one of my children that lived. How long can you stay?" (Durang: 1997, p. 343).

Here Matt also imagines a dialogue with his mother in which she is rational about her relations with the men in her life: "I realize that Boo and I must take responsibility for our own actions.... One has no choice but to accept facts. And I realize that you must live your own life, and I must live mine" (Durang: 1997, p. 343). This is wishful thinking, for Bette has none of the practicality of Williams's Amanda Wingfield who, for all her illusions about the past, is primarily concerned with economic survival: "I mean that as soon as Laura has got somebody to take care of her, married, a home of her own, independent — why, then you'll be free to go wherever you please, on land, on sea, whichever way the wind blows you!" (Williams: 1971, p. 175). The repetition of the father-son dinner reminds the audience that this is a play about repetitive patterns and their effect on our narrator. During the second act, Durang repeatedly abandons linear time and his narrator on occasion begins a scene with "Back into chronology again."

Each act of *The Marriage of Bette and Boo* has a nightmare family holiday. If Thanksgiving and Christmas are supposed to be celebrations of family, Durang's holidays become something quite different. Matt tells the audience that holidays were invented by "a sadistic Englishman" so that "everyone would feel disappointed that their lives had fallen so short of their expectations" (339). For Matt's family, the holidays are more elaborate replays of smaller family hostilities. The Thanksgiving dinner that ends Act I has Bette screaming at a drunken Boo for trying to vacuum the gravy that he has caused to be spilled as the extended family beat a hasty retreat. The lights dim with Boo unconscious on the floor, Bette obsessing over the gravy and Matt looking "exhausted and trapped" (357). The Christmas celebration that opens Act II has Boo's father making cruel jokes about Bette's miscarriages, then pouring his drink in her lap as she screams hysterically.

Williams's *Period of Adjustment* takes place on Christmas Eve and here, too, the family is imperiled. A large Christmas tree dominates the small living room and Ralph's gifts for his wife (a fur coat that has taken all of his savings) and gifts for their son are in place under it, but Ralph's wife has left with their son: "I quit my job so my wife quit me" (21). This seems to be a Catholic household, but religion plays not part. There is a statue of the Infant of Prague on the bed table which Isabel sees as a mirror of her loneliness: "Little boy Jesus, so lonesome on your birthday. I know how you feel exactly" (67). For Ralph, the Infant is merely a good luck charm that hasn't worked. In Durang's *Laughing Wild*, the man dreams he is the Infant of Prague appearing on Sally Jesse Rafael's television talk show to voice Catholic doctrine on sexuality: "The divine is impractical. That's why it's divine" (412). Ultimately Christmas for

Williams becomes a time of reconciliation, a move from the turbulent "period of adjustment" to understanding and physical union. In *The Marriage of Bette and Boo*, the holiday only underscores the lack of understanding and insensitivity characters can show for one another.

Unlike Williams, Durang is not interested in the economic circumstances of his characters who appear to be middle class and affluent. Their traps are psychological or products of their spiritual and cultural education. Bette may be one of the two least bright girls in her elementary school class, but she seems to have married well, and Boo's alcoholism doesn't lead to destitution. Bette's mistaken ideas about family come from an odd mix of Catholicism and popular culture. She is obsessed with *Skippy*, one of those sentimental thirties movies with a child star, and wants to name her son after the title character. Some of her pronouncements make no sense at all: "I want a marriage and a family and a home and I'm going to have them, and if you won't help me, Boo, I'll have them without you" (Durang: 1997, p. 332).

If Tennessee Williams's women seem to live in a dream world, they are very down to earth about their material circumstances. Bette doesn't have that sort of reality check. Williams's Amanda uses the phone to sell magazine subscriptions. Bette calls elementary school friends in the middle of the night. Yet traits of the women in *The Glass Menagerie* are shared by Bette and her siblings. Neurotic, guilt-ridden Emily is much like Laura and Bette shares Amanda's (and her counterpart Edwina Williams's) garrulousness: "She'd talk and talk like it was a sickness. There was no way of shutting her up" (357), the same barrage of talk Isabel fires in *Period of Adjustment*.

At Bette and Boo's wedding, Bette's sister Joan was to sing Schubert's *"Lachen und Weinen"* accompanied by her father and sister, Emily. However, Emily, in a typical moment of panic and confusion, has forgotten the music. *Lachen und Weinen*—laughing and crying or, as a Durang character in *Laughing Wild* puts it: "Laughing wild amid severest woe" (Durang: 1997, p. 383). In his afterword to *The Marriage of Bette and Boo*, Durang explains, "watching repetitive suffering is very irritating and upsetting, and transforming one's view of it into some combination of sad and funny seems as sensible a thing to do as any" (369). "Sensible" seems an odd word to use in the context of this play which Durang admits some audiences find "too angry." There's always a pain in the laughter.

Williams in his best moments also combines comedy and pathos. Williams's Amanda and Isabel are in unhappy circumstances—loneliness, disappointment, anxiety—but also funny in their ornate rhetoric and social pretensions. Humor is a way for Blanche DuBois and Maggie Pollitt to cope with their desperation. Yet Williams never takes his characters to the extremes of absurdity we find in Durang's play. Even at the moment of death, Durang's Bette natters on about a dead parakeet she had as a young woman, Mrs. Wright: "And I called her Mrs. Wright because she lived in a Frank Lloyd Wright birdcage, I think. Actually it was a male parakeet but I liked the name better" (Durang: 1997, p. 366). When she and her husband look back on their unhappy marriage, the bizarre disconnection and irony remind one of Beckett:

BETTE: Do you remember when you tried to vacuum the gravy?
BOO: No.
BETTE: Well, you did. It was very funny. Not at the time, of course. And how you used to keep bottles hidden in the cellar. And all the dead babies.
BOO: *(Smiles. Happy.)* Yes, we had some good times [366].

Boo, now addled with some neurological disorder, is so eager to see his marriage as the central and best fact of his life that he denies all its unhappiness. Bette now lives totally in the past. Bette's death is a quiet moment of resolution. Matt's final speech to the audience is not the tear-jerking expression of loss and guilt Tom voices in *The Glass Menagerie*. It echoes lovingly Bette's childlike view of experience:

> Bette passed into death and is with God. She is in heaven where she has been reunited with the four dead babies and where she waits for Boo, and for Bonnie Wilson, and Emily, and Pooh Bear and Eeyore, and Kanga and Roo; and for me [368].

Laughing and crying. A eulogy to a mother that captures the tragedy in her life as well as her silliness. We find the same mixture at the end of *Period of Adjustment*. Both couples face an uncertain economic future and some question of whether husbands and wives can really support one another through their anxieties. At the same time, Williams wants us to see the humor in these characters — even the humor in living over a cavern. Isabel says: I don't think a married couple can go through life without laughs any more than they can without tears" (29).

The reconciliation Williams has offered is, typically, sexual. George and Isabel's marriage is about to be consummated and Ralph is back in bed with the wife he claims is unattractive. Williams believes in his Big Mama's dictum that the problems in a marriage and their solutions occur in bed. Yet this ending is unconvincing because we see no evidence that there is any foundation for the two marriages Williams depicts, either in emotional affinity or even that *sine qua non*, sexual desire. The bond seems to be fear of loneliness, but the characters have already expressed the fact that they still feel lonely even in their marriage. The basic problem is that Williams is trying to present something he really doesn't believe in — lasting, happy heterosexual marriage — yet he is writing for Broadway success in a genre alien to him: domestic comedy. By the time Durang wrote *The Marriage of Bette and Boo*, Broadway was dead as a site for domestic comedy and traditional generic conventions no longer pertained. Durang's skepticism about marriage could be fully played out.

It is not clear in Durang's play why people get married. Father Donnally lashes out at a retreat for married couples:

> I get so *sick* of these people coming to me after they're married, and they've just gotten to know one another *after* the ceremony, and they've discovered that they have nothing in common and they hate one another. And they want me to come up with a solution. What can I do? There's no solution to a problem like that [353].

This is the point at which we begin *Period of Adjustment*, but Williams's play is based on the premise that if the two couples could just get into bed, everything will be all right.

In the final scene of *The Marriage of Bette and Boo*, husband and wife are divorced, but Boo sits in Bette's hospital room as if they are still married. There is still an insoluble bond between this husband and wife, but is it love or simply habit? Boo has said: "Nobody should be alone" (Durang: 1997, p. 324) and that fear of loneliness keeps him at his wife's side. "Till death do us part" is the operative principle here. Both Williams and Durang present marriage as a difficult, almost impossible process. They both wonder whether one can really break through the walls of selfhood and treat one other human being with love, understanding and compassion. Williams believes that there are moments in sexual union that can approach the mystical but the combination of sexual hunger and Puritan guilt many of his characters experience make even that difficult. Both women in *Period of Adjustment* begin their marriages terrified of sex with their husband. Ralph's wife is quickly cured of her "psychological frigidity" and Isabel at the final curtain will have sex with her husband on her terms:

> GEORGE: Come here!
> ISABEL: No, you come here. It's very nice by the fire [p. 94].

Durang is more skeptical about the mystification of sex. The man in *Laughing Wild* certainly does not accept Williams's view: "And sex itself people say is beautiful — but is it? Maybe you think it is. Terrible viscous discharges erupting in various openings may strike you as the equivalent of the Sistine Chapel ceiling, for all I know. It doesn't strike me that way" (396). Where does that leave marriage? There is no talk in *The Marriage of Bette and Boo* of sex as a pleasurable activity: "But sex is for having babies, right? I mean, it's not just for marriage" (350).

Durang's characters are as uncomfortable in what could be called "normal society" as those of Tennessee Williams, but they, like Matt, are plagued with doubts and questions. They find little solace in the illusions that keep Williams's characters going. The ideal of marriage, policed by the Catholic church, seems impossible to realize in Durang's plays. Williams, writing in the conservative nineteen-forties and nineteen-fifties, tries to celebrate marriage, but at best it is a kind of compromise. The critique of marriage we see in the work of both writers stems in part from the experience of their parents and from their own positions outside of the conventional system of compulsory heterosexuality. *Period of Adjustment* ranks as one of Williams's minor works because the conventional comedy of marriage did not allow the kind of passionate exploration of characters outside of conventional morality that was his forte. Durang's *The Marriage of Bette and Boo* is considered his best play because it mixes heartfelt memory with anguished doubts about the possibility of the kind of relationship his parents idealized but could not realize. Humor is a weapon in the arsenals of Williams's best characters, a way of defying their situations. For Durang it is a means of coping with real psychological and spiritual pain: "Laughing wild amidst severest woe." Nowhere is this more necessary than when two people try to connect in a loving way.

NOTES

1. Lyle Leverich, *Tom: The Unknown Tennessee Williams* (New York: Crown, 1995), pp. 47–87.

2. Williams's biographer, Lyle Leverich, says of Edwina: "Militantly forthright and possessed of puritanical opinions, Edwina was frequently disliked for the very thing for which her son was esteemed: a mastery of words. She not merely talked — and talked — she had the ability to overcome friend and adversary alike, usually leaving them limp and defenseless under the sheer weight of words" (*Tom: The Unknown Tennessee Williams*, New York: Crown, 1995, pp. 47–8). On Edwina's sexual relations with her husband, Leverich notes: She continued to resist his fumbling advances, leaving him frustrated and angry. As young as he was at the time, Tennessee remembered hearing his mother's crying protests in her bedroom (p. 42).

3. Produced by the Almeida Theatre, London, February-March, 2006, directed by Michael Attenborough.

4. For a convincing discussion of the ways Williams hints at Tom's gayness, see Michael Paller, *Gentlemen Callers: Tennessee Williams, Homosexuality, and Mid-Twentieth Century Drama* (New York: Palgrave, 2005).

5. See the short stories "Hard Candy" and "The Mysteries of the Joy Rio."

WORKS CITED

Durang, Christopher. *Baby with the Bathwater,* in *Christopher Durang: Full Length Plays, 1975–1995* (New York: Smith and Kraus, 2002).

_____. "Desire, Desire, Desire, in *Christopher Durang: Volume I: 27 Short Plays* (New York: Smith and Kraus, 1996).

_____. "For Whom the Southern Belle Tolls, in *27 Short Plays*.

_____. *Laughing Wild* in *Christopher Durang: Full Length Plays, 1975–1995.*

_____. *The Marriage of Bette and Boo,* in *Christopher Durang: Full Length Plays, 1975–1985.*

_____. "Sister Mary Ignatius Explains It All to You," in *27 Short Plays*.

Leverich, Lyle. *Tom: The Unknown Tennessee Williams* (New York: Crown, 1995).

Williams, Tennessee. *The Glass Menagerie*, in *The Theatre of Tennessee Williams: Volume I* (New York: New Directions, 1971).

_____. *Period of Adjustment*, in *The Theatre of Tennessee Williams, Volume IV* (New York, New Directions, 1972).

"All Truth Is a Scandal": How Tennessee Williams Shaped Tony Kushner's Plays

Kirk Woodward

Tony Kushner has frequently acknowledged Tennessee Williams's influence on his imaginative, energetic, and provocative plays. "I've always loved Williams," Kushner has said. "The first time I read *Streetcar*, I was annihilated. I read as much Williams as I could get my hands on until the late plays started getting embarrassingly bad.... I'm really influenced by Williams" (Savran 297). Kushner expresses a connection with Williams both as a playwright and as a Southern writer: "My favorite playwright is Tennessee Williams," he has said, "and he's a very, very Southern writer, and I'm very much influenced by him" (Verlicky 136). On the other hand, while working on a screenplay about Eugene O'Neill, Kushner seemed to rank O'Neill above Williams: "The more time I spend with him, the more I come to believe that what he did is really unmatchable. Williams and Miller got sort of close. But I don't think any American playwright has done anything that really compares to *Long Day's Journey Into Night*" (Honegger 126).

Nevertheless Kushner's masterwork *Angels in America* demonstrates Williams's influence: characters in the play directly quote both *The Glass Menagerie* ("You're just a Christian martyr"; 67) and *A Streetcar Named Desire* ("I have always depended on the kindness of strangers"; 271). Beyond explicit references, a sampling of the works of the two writers shows resonances between the literal or figurative travels into unknown territory of women like Blanche DuBois and Catherine Holly (*Suddenly Last Summer*) and the British housewife in *Homebody/Kabul*; a questing attitude toward God shared by both writers and expressed by the amusingly and theologically named Prelapsarianov in *Slavs*: "But the Ancient of Days remains evasive, ineffable, in Heaven as on Earth" (169); and something of the frantic off-beat black comedy of numerous later Williams plays in knockabout Kushner works like *Slavs*. In a more general sense Kushner shows the influence of the generous opportunities Williams gives his characters to explain and justify themselves, and the powerful, even tragic sense in which he presents their varied fates.

As a child Tennessee Williams's black nurse, Ozzie, entertained him with stories, and young Williams adored her. To his continuing regret, in a heated moment the boy called her a "nigger." Shortly afterwards she left the family's employ, and Williams always felt — not necessarily correctly — that his use of that horrid word was the reason she left (Leverich 43). Years later, in 1999, the Public Theatre in New York City presented a workshop of a musical,

Caroline, or Change with book and lyrics by Tony Kushner about a boy living in the South who deeply alientates his family's black housekeeper in a dispute over a twenty dollar bill, causing her to leave the family's employ. Between Williams's disastrous insult to his nurse and the opening of Kushner's musical in New York are remarkable developments in the lives of two playwrights. Each grew up in the American South, absorbing its atmosphere and its use of language; each became critically aware of the issue of race, struggled with his sexuality, and found a balm in the magical world of the theatre, which underwent a remarkable transformation in the same period of time, as did the nation as a whole; and the older playwright significantly influenced the younger. Unlike some of the playwrights in this volume, the influence of Williams on Kushner was one-directional; Williams died in 1983 just as Kushner's career began to take off. Nevertheless the two writers share commonalities that may be viewed in terms of contrasts. Both create characters vibrant with life who nevertheless face its most devastating circumstances. Both employ language and theatrical technique that are at the same time convincingly realistic and intensely poetic. Both conduct a search for ancient verities from a modern perspective. Furthermore, in the words of James Fisher who has written extensively on the two playwrights, both "deal centrally and compassionately with complex issues of sexuality from a gay sensibility" (*Living* 6), although Williams did not express his homosexuality publicly until his television interview with David Frost in 1970, when he was fifty-nine, while Kushner began speaking at a much younger age from an acknowledged position as a gay man. In David Izzo's words, "It is Tennessee Williams' spirit and his homosexuality that became Kushner's inspiration for the tone of his plays" (Izzo, 92).

Tony Kushner is perhaps generally thought of as a New York writer, but both he and Tennessee Williams spent significant parts of their childhoods in the American South — Williams primarily in Clarksdale, Mississippi and Kushner (born in 1956) about 375 miles away in Lake Charles, Louisiana. Unlike Williams, Kushner's family — he was one of three children — shared a commitment to the arts; his parents were both trained musicians, and his mother was also an amateur actress. Both Tennessee Williams and Tony Kushner moved north — Williams to St. Louis where his father transferred, and Kushner to New York City in 1974, at the age of eighteen, to attend Columbia University.

Tony Kushner's only play to date produced in New York that takes place in the American South brings Williams's plays to mind in several ways. The plot of that play, the musical *Caroline, or Change* with book and lyrics by Kushner and music by Jeanine Tesori, does not resemble that of a particular Williams play, but Caroline's life story, as described by the Radio in the play, shares the trajectory of Blanche's life in *A Streetcar Named Desire* and of other Williams heroines: they "took a wrong step/slip and fell." The basement in *Caroline* "planted in the swampy soil" recalls the house in Williams's *Period of Adjustment* built over a crevice into which the house is sinking, echoed in *Angels* where Louis refers to "the cracks that separate what we owe to our selves and ... and what we owe to love" (77). Public statuary in a Southern town plays a role in *Caroline* in the statue honoring the Confederate Soldier with its head knocked off, reminiscent of the statue of an angel named Eternity in *The Eccentricities of a Nightingale* with an inscription so faded that it has to be read like Braille, with the fingers.

Kushner affirms the influence of his years in the South on his writing. "You have some affinity for the Southern writers?" Robert Altman asks, and Kushner replies, "I do. Sometimes they make me crazy because they sound too much like the people I grew up with. But I do" (Vorlicky 136). In an interview with Rabbi Norman J. Cohen, Kushner says, "The South is a very good place for writers to grow up. I'm not entirely sure yet why that's so, except that I think that the south has a very lively mix of linguistic traditions, that it has a very ornate, sort of purple relationship to language that the more industrial North has ground out a little bit" (Vorlicky 224–225). A strong case can be made that characteristics of the "ornate, purple" nature of Southern writing are shared by Williams, who is recognized as a Southern writer, and Kushner, who is not. A useful definition may be seen in Robert Heilman's description that "The Southern temper is marked by the coincidence of a sense of the concrete, a sense of the elemental, a sense of the ornamental, a sense of the representative, and a sense of totality" (Hoffman, 48). One might substitute the word "ornate" for Hoffman's use of the word "ornamental" to the extent that his word suggests that elements of Southern writing are superfluous, since in fact, as Hoffman says, "Southern writing is a particularized vocation, preoccupied with images and words. There is less of the abstracting sense, generally, than exists in other literatures" (4). Balancing the concrete nature of Southern writing is the quality that we may describe as ornate — "a sense of the incantatory powers of language, as well as a sense of its gifts of the grotesque and of the riches of the writer's powers" (Hoffman, 4).

The juxtaposition of the paradoxical qualities of the concrete and the ornate, the beautiful and the horrifying, the naturalistic and the poetic, characterize the recognizably Southern use of language that Williams showcased on the American stage, taking the oppositional qualities of Southern writing and extending them into an approach that may be described as gothic, in the sense that it emphasizes the grotesque and the desolate. Many of Williams's later plays (although scorned by Kushner in the quotation above) illustrate this tendency, representative among them *The Gnädiges Fräulein* (1966) with its blind, bloodied, bald title character catching fish intended for a seal, or the corpses sitting in the hotel lobby in *Now The Cat with Jewelled Claws* (1970). But the gothic quality is by no means limited to Williams's later work; *Suddenly Last Summer*, first produced in New York in 1959 and subsequently made into a Hollywood film, features an equally grotesque array of elements including a vivid account of cannibalism.

Kushner's sensibility does not lean toward the gothic as Williams employed it, but he uses the freedom gained through Williams's gothic representations to achieve a freewheeling variety of incident, bringing to mind Hoffman's description of "the Southern writer's ability to go beyond the particulars of an experience and, without losing their concrete values, to use them in a wide-sweeping symbolic gesture or in a suggestion of the past's residing in and influencing the present" (Hoffman 5). That Tony Kushner goes beyond the gothic, shaping it for his own ends, may be seen in his choice of the term "fantasia," a word with rich associations that he uses to characterize *Angels In America* and that may be applied more generally to much of his and Williams's work. A primary meaning of the word fantasia, often encountered in music, is a work that carries out the author's intention without being restricted to norms of form or content. A fantasia may be expected to take liberties with both, subject only to the will of its creator; it is a liminal event, locating itself near the outer borders of experience. Such an approach appealed to Tennessee Williams from early in his career; as Linda Dorff (13) makes clear, "The roots for the late outrageous plays extend back to some of Williams's earliest drama" (Dorff 13), citing *The Case of the Crushed Petunias* (1941) and Kilroy's "patsy outfit" in *Camino Real* which Dorff sees as "parodying not only the actions of other characters in the play, but breaking the fourth wall, and thereby metatheatrically thumbing (or lighting) his nose at the 'serious' American traditions of Broadway realism" (Dorff 14). That Williams intended the result that Kushner labels a fantasia is clear in the description of his intention in the forward to *Camino Real* (1953): "My desire was to give these audiences my own sense of something wild and unrestricted that ran like water in the mountains, or clouds changing shape in a gale, or the continually dissolving and transforming images of a dream," a description that can profitably be applied to any number of Williams works that may otherwise be misread. Williams's taste in the fantasia tends, as previously noted, toward the grotesque, as demonstrated in *The Night of the Iguana* (1961), his last Broadway success, with its mixture of Catholicism, sexuality, animalism, and the looming spiritual world of exorcisms, and the same tendency becomes even more evident in later plays such as *Vieux Carré* (1977), described in a review at the time by Clive Barnes as "incidents, some funny, some poignant, all faintly bizarre, all seen through a glass oddly," or the even more out-of-bounds *The Remarkable Rooming House of Mme. Le Monde* that, as Kolin says, "intensely builds upon many of Williams's chronic fears but also highlights his experiments with anti-mimetic dramaturgy, dramatic allegories, and comic horror" (Kolin 41), although a fantasia like *Something Cloudy, Something Clear* (1981), with its coexistence of present and past, shows a gentler touch.

A comparison of two plays, *Camino Real* and *Hydriotaphia, or The Death of Dr. Browne* by Tony Kushner, helps to clarify the idea of the fantasia. Williams sets the wide-ranging *Camino Real* in the Hispanic world that, as Kolin (35) demonstrates, "allowed Williams to enter the liminal world where his sexual and political anxieties, triggered by conventionalism, could be expressed and eased"—one might say, eased in personal conduct and expressed as fantasia. *Camino* brings the seeker Kilroy into almost a fever dream of a no man's land of a dismal border town governed by the cruel and abusive and populated by figures as varied as Don Quixote and the street cleaners who carry corpses out with the garbage. Although not a financial success in its initial Broadway run, from today's perspective *Camino Real* ranks as one of the most influential plays in American theatre, especially for Kushner—a play that open possibilities not often seen in mainstream Western theatre since Medieval drama and its successors in the Elizabethan age. *Camino Real* corresponds to the definition of a fantasia as an extravagant and unrestrained event. The play mixes individual and allegorical characters, realistic and hallucinatory events, political commentary and extreme romanticism, poetic and literal styles of dialogue, hope and despair. It features a disregard of conventional notions of time and place, a smorgasbord of invented characters and figures from literature, and a pervasive air of living in a nightmare. *Camino Real* also requires a sprawling cast, some thirty-nine roles, unusual in these days of two character, one set plays, and appealing to Kushner, who says "I like big, splashy, juicy plays" (Living Past Hope, 208), a description that perfectly fits *Camino Real*.

Characteristics of a fantasia similar to those of *Camino Real* are evident in Tony Kushner's *Hydriotaphia*. In focusing on a literary character, the author Thomas Browne (born two years after the death of the first Queen Elizabeth), the play follows the example of *Camino Real*, whose characters also include the writers Lord Byron and Casanova. More significantly, while Kushner's play lacks the broad sweep of *Camino Real*, it resembles it in its central situation: a character striving to live and facing death, surrounded by realistic, fanciful, and allegorical characters, in an atmosphere of, in varying degrees, dream, hallucination, or nightmare, an atmosphere increasingly present in Williams's later plays and characteristic of the fantasia. Williams provides a model for Kushner of both theatrical and emotional experimentation that can produce a feeling of dislocation similar to that of surrealism, as in Harper's hallucination in *Angels* when she encounters Prior, a character in the play that she has never met and therefore logically should not be able to talk to, except under the conditions of a dream.

The close relationship between the words fantasia and fantasy suggests that a fantasia embodies a free-ranging act of imagination on the part of its creator, and both Williams and Kushner meet this expectation in their innovations in theatrical presentation. In the introduction to his Memoirs (1975), Williams writes, "My thing is what it always was: to express my world and my experience of it in whatever form seems suitable to the material," precisely the definition of a fantasia. The fact that throughout has career Williams experimented with theatrical form as well as content is not generally known to audiences familiar only with the best known half-dozen or so of his plays, but through this theatrical daring Williams has helped pave the way for Kushner's complex, emotional, and often sprawling dramas.

Williams did not limit his interest in experimentation with theatrical form to the latter part of his career. For example, Tony Kushner has acknowledged his debt to Bertolt Brecht and his Epic Theatre, including writing an adaptation of Brecht's *The Good Person of Setzuan*, but Williams studied with and worked for Brecht's sometime mentor Erwin Piscator at the New School for Social Research in New York City before Kushner's birth, from 1940 through 1942, working on Piscator's epic theatre production of *War and Peace* and attempting to modify his early play *Battle of Angels* to fit the epic theatre approach. Michael Paller in *The Tennessee Williams Encyclopedia* (193) notes that Piscator's concepts may have influenced the production style that Williams suggested for *The Glass Menagerie* (1944), as did the fact that the script originally saw life as a screenplay. In his published production notes for *Menagerie* Williams calls for a "new, plastic theatre which must take the place of the exhausted theatre of realistic conventions if the theatre is to resume vitality as a part of our culture," rejecting "[t]he straight realistic play with its genuine Frigidaire and authentic ice-cubes, its characters who speak exactly as the audience speaks" (xix–xxii). At this significantly early point in his career Williams had already started to campaign for a new freedom of form in theatre, a freedom that clearly connects Williams's concept of "sculptural drama" or "plastic theatre" to the idea of the fantasia as found in Kushner's *Angels*. The original stage directions written by Tennessee Williams for *Glass Menagerie* include such elements of staging as projections using slides, lighting effects such as fades and dissolves that resemble those used in movies, and music scored like films, atypical of the mainstream theatre of the time but appropriate for a fantasia. Williams was in fact an experimental playwright even earlier, from the 1930s onward. Evidence of his experimentation ranges as widely as the hint of science fiction in the early *Stairs to the Roof* (1941), the bold depiction of sexuality in the film *Baby Doll*, the bold departures from Broadway convention in *Cat on a Hot Tin Roof*, *Orpheus Descending*, and *Night of the Iguana*, and on into the wild later plays. (Ironically, film adaptations of Williams's plays tended to ignore the fantastical possiblities of the movies and made his plays more conventional and therefore more acceptable to the American public at large.) Williams's combination of realistic and fantasmagoric elements may be compared to similar devices in many plays of Kushner, who in his notes to *Angels* records an impressive array of theatrical elements including "the appearance and disappearance of [the imaginary] Mr. Lies and the ghosts, the Book hallucination," minimal scenery moved, according to Kushner's request, by actors as well as by stagehands, and as noted, the spectacular crashing of an angel through the ceiling.

Linda Dorff uses the term "outrageous" to describe the elements of the fantasia in the plays of Williams in which he treats the theatre itself, as well as its subject matter, in terms of broad farce that calls into question the entire theatrical establishment, an approach that Dorff calls "meta-mimesis," or the imposition of elements of parody, parable, and farce on top of a familiar dramatic form (Dorff 14). The ideology and dramaturgy of fantasia also falls under Linda Dorff's overarching study of the outrageous valorized in the later plays but clearly present earlier. According to Dorff, "The outrageous late plays are bawdy, over-the-top farces that appropriate systems of metadrama and the aesthetics of the cartoon to parody the state of contemporary theater" (Dorff 13). Kushner's appropriation of the same approach is emblemized by the spectacular appearance of the Angel, an event that both heightens the theatrical nature of the play and calls the "reality" of its events into question, and equally in the second scene of *Only We Who Guard The Mystery Shall Be Unhappy* in which a playwright named

Tony Kushner discusses with Laura Bush the preceding scene in which she attempted to read Dostoyevsky's story of the Grand Inquisitor to a group of dead Iraqi children protected by, once again, an angel, thereby bringing his own theater, as well as the theater itself, into a new and startling context.

The concept of the fantasia helps distinguish the influence on Tony Kushner of Tennessee Williams and Eugene O'Neill, a resolute theatrical experimenter. Like Williams many of O'Neill's best known plays today (in particular *Long Day's Journey Into Night* and *The Iceman Cometh*) are conventionally structured. More to the point are his experiments with form contained in such plays as *Strange Interlude*, *The Great God Brown*, and *Dynamo*. However, O'Neill's experimentation has a deliberate, rather than a surrealistic, quality, whereas, as Richard Kramer notes, "In *Camino Real* and many later plays, for example, Williams consciously exploits non-realistic styles like expressionism, surrealism, and absurdism, which he explicitly calls on playwrights to use in their search for truth" (Kramer, par. 1) and the same may be said of Kushner. Williams provides an example for Kushner of both theatrical and emotional experimentation marking the fantasia style that can produce a feeling of dislocation similar to that of surrealism, as in Harper's hallucination in *Angels* when she encounters Prior, a character in the play that she has never met and therefore logically should not be able to talk to.

The association of content and form in the idea of the fantasia suggests that in order to create significant art, daring in the one must be matched by daring in the other. A concentration on theatrical innovation at the expense of a radicalization of content is a decadent activity — the triumph of presentation over meaning. Through the demanding nature of the content of their plays, both Williams and Kushner resist the temptation toward formalism. Williams suggests an approach to content embraced by Kushner that may be characterized by a remark of the exuberant and beleaguered poetess Sabbatha Veyne Duff-Collick in the Williams short story "Sabbatha and Solitude" who proclaims "All truth is a scandal ... and all art is an indiscretion!" (512). Like any form of communication, scandal requires two parties, the sender and the receiver, the one who provides the grounds for scandalized feelings and the one who chooses to feel scandalized. The relationship is complex; on the one hand, the provocation of scandal may be either inadvertant or deliberate, and on the other hand, the person scandalized may be essentially liberal, even progressive, on issues other than those considered "scandalous." It is also possible to distinguish degrees of scandal, although of course such distinctions are subjective. Tennessee Williams enjoyed provoking scandalized feelings among the straight, the puritanical, and the unaware. As Williams aptly put it in his *Memoirs*, "I know how to be outrageous" (239).

The atmosphere of torrid sexuality both characterized his plays and separated them from those of any other major playwright, and led to his being considered a scandalous figure in many circles. Such feelings did not deter him either from living his own kind of life or from writing plays that emphasized sex, and this fact alone would make him influential among many of Tony Kushner's generation. The plays of Tennessee Williams and Tony Kushner, like their lifestyles, privelige, court, broadcast, and seek scandal — scandal is polyvalent in their canons. Williams's *Memoirs* demonstrated that he had not lost his power to shock. The film director John Waters writes, "Why was 'Memoirs' reviewed so badly when it first came out? 'The love that previously dared not speak its name has now grown hoarse from screaming it,' Robert Brustein wrote, two years later, in *The New York Times*. Today, few critics would be so blatantly homophobic, but Tennessee did love to bait his enemies.... In fact, the day Tennessee showed up at Doubleday Bookshop in Manhattan and signed more than 800 copies became known as 'The Great Fifth Avenue Bookstore Riot'" (Waters, par. 6).

The exuberance Williams felt in provoking scandal is clear in his Letters, for example in the letter of July 25, 1941 to his buddy Paul Bigelow: "My cumulated sexual potency is sufficient to blast the Atlantic fleet out of Brooklyn. Perhaps I shall when I get back to NY—I have had three affairs since I left and been trade in them all..." (Williams, 326). The spirit of these letters transfers easily to the more public statements of Tony Kushner about his own homosexuality. But the spirit of the letters is also reincarnated in the plays of Tennessee Williams, and the same may be said for the plays of Tony Kushner.

But beyond the "scandal" of his lifestyle and plays, Williams identifies a deeper source of scandal—the overwhelming truth, as he sees it, that the world is always battering away at the sensitive of heart and spirit, a theme found throughout his work from beginning to end, as typified in the way Stanley destroys Blanche's relationship with Mitch and her mental health, rapes her, and causes her to be removed to a mental hospital without punishment for his brutality. Williams is a model of the artist willing to create and risk scandal for the sake of observed truth. As he presents the triumph of the strong over the weak, he finds it scandalous. He also recoils from it, identifying with society's victims and transmuting their struggles into art. When Blanche says, "I don't want realism. I want magic! Yes, yes, magic! I try to give that to people. I misrepresent things to them. I don't tell truth, I tell what ought to be truth" (117), the truth of destructive power that she tries so desperately to "misrepresent" in order to mitigage its effects clearly links the themes of fantasia ("magic") and scandal.

Tennessee Williams and Tony Kushner share a sense of the outrageous both in their personal writings and in their plays, resulting in a profound radicalization of outlook, a refusal to accept society in its current form combined with a determination to expose the scandal that results from attitudes that condemn homosexuality as such. This sense of scandal takes different but related forms in the works of the two writers. That homosexuality is explicit both in Tony Kushner's work and in his writing about himself, illustrates the enormous distance that has been traveled between Tennessee William's career and Tony Kushner's. Through most of his life, unlike Kushner, Williams felt compelled to disguise or play down his homosexuality in public. The fact of his gayness became common knowledge in his personal circle, assumed within the theatrical community, and the subject of speculation in the larger world; but until roughly the last decade of his life, particularly with the publication of his *Memoirs*, Williams refused to acknowledge his homosexuality publicly as he did privately in his letters. Such an indescretion, he felt, would be too great. However, many nevertheless identified his homosexuality as a scandal, as Gore Vidal makes clear: "For thirty years he was regularly denounced as a sick, immoral, vicious fag. *Time* magazine, as usual, led the attack. From *The Glass Menagerie* up until *The Night of the Iguana*, each of his works was smeared in language that often bordered on madness. 'Fetid swamp' was *Time* critic Louis Kronenberger's preferred phrase for Tennessee's mind and art" (xxiii). Paller confirms that an awareness of Williams's homosexuality lay behind much of the sense of scandal that Williams provoked, as demonstrated in Howard Taubman's (1961) and Stanley Kauffmann's (1966) articles in the *New York Times* generally perceived as suggesting that homosexuals should write only about gay characters (Fisher 68). These reviewers may be and have been challenged at many points, but they cannot be said to have misunderstood Williams. "I cannot write any sort of story," he told Gore Vidal, "unless there is at least one character in it for whom I have physical desire" (Vidal xxiii).

The result is the popular conception of Williams's plays as "dripping with sex"—hot, steamy, putting the subject of sexuality very much up for discussion, a subject unacceptable to more puritanical tastes. Williams felt he had to be cautions about public discussions of his homosexuality, but when he came out of the closet in the 1970s, particularly in his *Memoirs* in 1975, retrospectively so did the plays he had written from the 1940s on, because Williams had made the sexuality of his characters so central to his plays. But if Williams did not publicly confirm his own homosexuality until late in his life, from the beginning he freely acknowledged his gay predecessors, in particular the poet Hart Crane, and he wrote more openly about homosexuality in his poems and short stories than in the plays that made his reputation, from the early story "One Arm" to the outrageous Sabbatha Veyne Duff-Collick, accompanied on her wanderings by her flamboyant and openly gay attendant. Many of both Williams's short stories and poems are told in the first person, and male sexuality is a frequent subject, for example in "Hard Candy" and "The Mysteries of the Joy Rio," stories in which sexual encounters take place in a former opera house, now a movie theatre, a representation of the closeted and yet significant sexuality in theatre and films of the time. Though Williams did not trumpet his homosexuality, he engaged the subject in his plays to an extent that sets him apart from the playwrights of his time and prepared the way for Kushner and other playwrights of the future, making himself to some extent a notorious figure, caused in part by the fact that Williams unquestionably presents homosexuality — and sexuality in multiple forms — without embarrassment, although, possibly reflecting his own reserve, in Williams's more famous plays the overtly homosexual characters themselves are usually spoken about rather than seen. Blanche DuBois's gay husband Allan is dead when *A Streetcar Named Desire* begins, but his offstage suicide is the initiating incident for the events of the play, as is the destruction of Sebastian, the poet, at the hands of the boys he desired in *Suddenly Last Summer*, and the death of Brick's homosexual best friend Skipper in *Cat on a Hot Tin Roof*.

Tony Kushner's representations of homosexuality both acknowledge and go beyond those of Williams. Kushner emphasizes his role as a member of the gay community, and affirms the importance of Tennessee Williams as a trail-blazer in this regard. When Michael Lowenthal asks Kushner, "As the [gay rights] movement has progressed, how has this affected the trajectory of gay writing for the theatre, from somebody like Tennessee Williams, who was very gay but it's all in subtext...." Kushner replies, "I'm part of a progress that's been made. Tennessee wasn't out, but he sort of outed sexuality in general without outing himself, which would have been virtually impossible [at the time]" (Vorlicky 153). Later in that same interview, Kushner adds, "It's very important if you're a gay playwright to have Tennessee Williams, to have *Streetcar Named Desire*, or even something completely unobtainable like Shakespeare. You need to define yourself against that, and you also need to know that it is possible for human beings to make something of that kind of beauty, even though you yourself will almost certainly fail in doing it" (155).

Nevertheless, whether such characters are present on stage or vivid in the imagination, an underlying cause of the sense of scandal Williams provoked, and an essential factor in his influence on Tony Kushner, is that he does not treat homosexuality as a separate kind of life, but presents it in the continuum of human experience. As James Fisher says, "No gay dramatist seems to directly follow Williams, who, as Delma Eugene Presley writes, 'made serious efforts to explore the subjects of reconciliation and redemption' in their work. Before Williams, only Eugene O'Neill faced such questions and, of course, not in the area of sexuality; after Williams, only Kushner, who deals with sexuality centrally" (Essays 16–17). Kushner, like Williams, dramatizes issues of homosexuality as part of the fabric of life. Impartiality itself may provoke scandal. Those who consider homosexuality a special form of malady or evil will find little comfort in Williams, but he also does not indulge in special pleading. Notably, when Williams did put gay characters onstage in *Small Craft Warnings* in 1972, ten years before the first production of a play by Tony Kushner, neither of those characters — Quentin, a screenwriter, and Bobby, a boy he has just picked up — are presented as "positive gay role models," and Quentin speaks openly about the desperation of the gay life as he has experienced it. The fact that Williams persevered through years of concealment and rumors and was able nevertheless to bring sexuality into focus as a center of his plays, that he raised the subject of homosexuality repeatedly in his plays, poems, and stories, and that he ultimately could affirm his identity as a gay man to the public, may have been scandalous for others but could only have been liberating for Tony Kushner as he struggled with his own sexual identity throughout adolescence: "I grew up very, very closeted, and I'm sure that the disguise of theatre, the doubleness, and all that slightly tawdry stuff interested me" (Savran 293).

By 1980, Williams himself could say that "Fortunately, this falsely moral sort of censorship has now collapsed. You might say that the sky is the limit — or the taste of the artists involved" (Phillips 35). However, the center of scandal has shifted rather than disappeared. *Angels in America* demonstrates how Kushner has taken advantage of the freedom Williams won to expand the range of the scandalous in his art by focusing on society rather than on the individual. Kushner, a socialist schooled in economic theory, has created a sense of scandal grounded specifically in the political. Aware that his own homosexuality may scandalize others, he nevertheless turns the focus of scandal outward, accusing society of truly serious indiscretions. Many of Kushner's works turn on actual and disastrous political events: *A Bright Room Called Day* depicts the descent of Germany into Nazism, combined with explicit comments about the Reagan administration; *Slavs* dramatizes the collapse of Soviet communism; *Home Body/Kabul* centers around events in the Middle East; *G. David Schine in Hell* revisits Roy Cohn and the McCarthy era; *Only We Who Guard The Mystery Shall Be Unhappy* tackles the Bush administration including the deaths of Iraqui children. But in making this point about Tony Kushner's political orientation (which it must be remembered is by no means the only feature of his writing), Tennessee Williams's political commitment must not be overlooked. This essay mentioned earlier the connection between Williams and Epic Theatre, typically a thoroughly politicized form. While the dialectic element in Brecht's plays unquestionably plays a major role in Kushner's work, Williams also engages political subjects, for example, the themes of prison conditions in *Not About Nightingales*, political oppression in *Camino Real*, racism in *Sweet Bird of Youth*, and the entire political environment of the 1960s and 1970s in *The Red Devil Battery Sign*. In a broader sense the scandal of oppression of the weak by society is ever-present in Williams's oeuvre.

It may in fact be argued that Williams has exercised a significant influence on Kushner in the realm of the political by his refusal to withdraw sympathy from his characters. Williams may on occasion look at his creations from above, so to speak, as he does with the two ladies in the short comedy "A Perfect Analysis Delivered by a Parrot," and his more gothic works frequently create a distancing effect, a fact that has grievously alienated a number of reviewers of Williams's later plays. Williams nevertheless insists on empathy with his characters, seeing them from the inside and allowing them emotional space in action and dialogue. The world may not care for his damaged and vulnerable characters, but Williams does. One sees these traits in Kushner's work as well. They are strongly at work in the last scenes of *Perestroika*, the second part of *Angels In America*, where the social and political energy of the play nevertheless allows individual characteristics to dominate the ending. From a strictly Marxist or Brechtian point of view, in Janelle Reinelt's words, "The replacement of class analysis by other identity categories, while useful and strategic in terms of contemporary exigencies, leaves the play with no other foundation for social change than the individual subject, dependent on an atomized agency" (Geis and Kruger 243). But the replacement of the political by the personal at the end of *Perestroika* may also suggest that as Brecht influenced Williams's presentation of characters, so Williams passed that influence along in his own manner to

Kushner who absorbed and extended it, proving that dialectic does not have to be didactic. Kushner himself says, "People want to see me as being a sort of flat propagandist. But I don't think that I am. I think my plays aren't like that" (Honegger 127).

Kushner's art, while like Williams's thoroughly grounded in character, finds scandal in historical as well as in personal events. Permeating all of *Angels* is the scandal of the indifference to the AIDS crisis of the Reagan administration, personified in its central characters, a gay man suffering from AIDS, his partner struggling with his desire to escape from the relationship, and a powerful political figure (Roy Cohn) dying of AIDS and unable to admit his homosexuality even to himself. Kushner has described his selection of Cohn as a character in several ways, but one of the most significant is that Cohn embodies in himself so many forms of scandal. His political influence; his manipulation of the government, particularily the Department of Justice, for his own ends; and his admitted subversion of the rule of law in the way he influenced the judge in the Rosenberg case, all are distressing in themselves and point to a deeper scandal: a pervasive corruption in the national government of which Cohn is representative but by no means unique. Cohn may be seen in many ways as a descendant of Williams's character of Big Daddy in *Cat on a Hot Tin Roof*. The two share a number of significant traits. Both believe that their personal power enables them to bluff their way through any situation, so Big Daddy dismisses the implications of Brick's relationship with Skipper, just as Roy tells Joe to find a law he can break. Both use language in an extravagantly vulgar way, and both want to be a strong father to their real or chosen "son," just as Roy Cohn says, "I've had many fathers, I owe my life to them, powerful, powerful men. Walter Winchell, Edgar Hoover. Joe McCarthy most of all. He valued me because I am a good lawyer, but he loved me because I was and am a good son" (62). Both Big Daddy and Cohn revere power. There are hints that Big Daddy himself may have had homosexual experiences in his youth, as in his reference to the gay couple that took him in. And both "fathers" are doomed by disease, yet both will go down fighting passionately against their fates. The most significant difference between the two characters is that Cohn is an inveterate liar, while Big Daddy, as Shackelford precisely puts it, "declares the 'truth' no matter how harsh and how painful the world where we live — society — might find it" (114) — the truth that leads to scandal, but that ultimately must be told.

The fact, both dramatic and historical, that Cohn, dying of AIDS, refuses to acknowledge in any way that he is gay, reveals another scandal: the way society makes it difficult for people, many of them from an earlier generation, to acknowledge their complete selves. Cohn, a character roughly Tennessee Williams's age (Cohn died three years after Williams), embodies the difficulty Tennessee Williams also faced — and ultimately overcame — in openly acknowledging his homosexuality. Cohn flatly refuses to identify himself as homosexual, a category he identifies as consisting of the weak and powerless, just as he refuses to acknowledge the nature of the disease, AIDS, that is killing him, the ravaging illness often referred to at that time as "the gay disease." Notably, although Kushner does not soften Cohn's personality in any way — quite the contrary — he by no means turns him into a caricature, and in fact, as Atsushi Fujita points out, actually presents him as forgivable (112). It may reflect one of the most important aspects of Williams's legacy to Kushner that although perhaps most frequently characterized as a "political" playwright, Kushner does not present his gay characters reductively as arguments for a position, but as individuals with their own complexities of character.

Kushner presents Roy Cohn as he does in part because of the personality of the actual historical figure. But there are other parallels between *Cat* and *Angels* that indicate the similarities may not be merely coincidental. W. Douglas Powers has the inspired idea of relating *Angels* to *Cat on a Hot Tin Roof* using the concept of midrash, that is, the illumination of "scripture" (as Powers refers to *Cat*—that is, canonical literature) in "paraphrase; prophecy; or parable or allegorical reading" (Powers 121), and on this reading of the plays relates them by asserting that "Midrash as paraphrase is Kushner's primary methodology, although he first recognizes the allegory inherent in Williams's text, enhancing it through midrashic paraphrase." Powers notes parallels between Joe and Harper Pitt in *Angels* and Brick and Maggie in *Cat*, both in the nature of their relationships, with the growing awareness of the homosexuality of the male in each pair, and in such details as that "Joe's conservative Republican ideals are not unlike the notion Brick holds regarding homosexuality" and in the passive, detached attitude that both Joe and Brick take toward making love with their wives. In both plays the wives, Maggie and Harper, create false reports about pregnancies in order to disguise the truth about the possible or definite sexual orientation of their husbands. The parallels between the plays suggest that Kushner has read Williams with attention.

If "all truth is a scandal," then the determination of both Tennessee Williams and Tony Kushner to tell the truth must inevitably lead to scandal. Tony Kushner has received criticism, as Williams did, both for his plays and for his proclamation of his gay identity, as well as for his political stands. Unquestionably the candid presentation of homosexuality and of political issues has much to do with this sense of scandal, but there may also be a deeper cause for the offence that both playwrights have caused. Often unacknowledged in the criticism received by both playwrights is a significant fact that demonstrates the influence of Tennessee Williams's career on Tony Kushner's: the oppressed characters in Williams's plays are frequently trapped within overpowering circumstances, but they resist their fates, they struggle against them, and even if they lose their fights, as they frequently do, they do not passively endure their defeats. Laura in *The Glass Menagerie* risks the pain that comes when she allows an outsider into her isolated world; she is crushed, but she has tried. Blanche in *Streetcar* is crushed by her collision by Stanley's brute sensuality, but she does resist and she loses the struggle only at the cost of her sanity. The Princess in *Sweet Bird of Youth* fights in numerous ways the aging process that is robbing her of her career.

These examples can be multiplied, but the point is that the ability of a character like Belize, the gay black nurse in *Angels*, to stand up to the bullying of Roy Cohn has its forerunner in the determination of many of Tennessee Williams's characters to confront the limitation of their own lives, a determination demonstrated, for example, by the self-examinations conducted by the bar full of mixed character types in *Small Craft Warnings*. Belize himself, in fact, could easily be a character from a Tennessee Williams short story. Neither writer presents their characters as passive, giving in to their fates. They fight; they resist. Their refusal to respond passively to their circumstances may cause society the most discomfort of all. Revelation of character can lay the foundation for a revolution in attitudes.

Tennessee Williams gives Tony Kushner and his generation the gift to be able to understand characters of any sexuality as individuals, not just as members of groups, but as shaped by similar powerful forces. If we are members of a community of suffering, Williams demonstrates, we are still members of a community. Tony Kushner champions advances in the human condition in ways that Williams did not, but Williams opened the way for Kushner's drama as a Southern and a gay writer and as a theatrical innovator, and his effect on the younger playwright accordingly has been a profound act of liberation.

Works Cited

Barnes, Clive. "Stage: 'Vieux Carre' by Williams Is Haunting." *The New York Times*, May 12, 1977.
Dorff, Linda. "Theatricalist Cartoons: Tennessee Williams's Late, 'Outrageous' Plays." *The Tennessee Williams Annual Review* 2, 1999.

Fisher, James. "The Angels of Fructification: Tennessee Williams, Tony Kushner, and Images of Homosexuality on the American Stage." *The Mississippi Quarterly* 49.1, December 1995.

_____. *Living Past Hope: The Theatre of Tony Kushner*. New York: Routledge, 2002.

_____, ed. *Tony Kushner: New Essays on the Art and Politics of the Plays*. Jefferson, North Carolina: McFarland & Company, Inc., Publishers, 2006.

Fugita, Atsushi. "Queer Politics to Fabulous Politics in *Angels in America*: Pinklisting and Forgiving Roy Cohn" in *Tony Kushner: New Essays on the Art and Politics of the Plays*.

Geis, Deborah R. and Kruger, Steven F., editors. *Approaches to Millennium: Essays on Angels in America*. Ann Arbor: The University of Michigan Press, 1997.

Heilman, Robert B. "The Southern Temper" in *South: Modern Southern Literature in its Cultural Setting*, edited by Louis D. Rubin, Jr. and Robert D. Jacobs. Garden City, New York: Doubleday, 1961.

Hoffman, Frederick J. *The Art of Southern Fiction, A Study of Some Modern Novelists*, Carbondale and Edwardsville: Southern Illinois University Press, Feffer & Simons, Inc., 1967.

Honegger, Gitta. "Romantic Pragmatist." *Theater*, 37:3, 2007.

Izzo, David Garrett. "Then and Now: W. H. Auden, Christopher Isherwood, Tony Kushner, and Fascist Creep" in *Tony Kushner: New Essays on the Art and Politics of the Plays*, James Fisher, ed.

Kolin, Philip, ed. *The Tennessee Williams Encyclopedia*. Westport, Connecticut: Greenwood Press, 2004.

_____. "Compañero Tenn: The Hispanic Presence in the Plays of Tennessee Williams." *The Tennessee Williams Annual Review* 2 (1999): 35–52.

_____. "*The Remarkable Rooming House of Mme. Le Monde*: Tennessee Williams's Little Shop of Comic Horrors." *The Tennessee Williams Annual Review* 4 (2001): 39–48.

Kramer, Richard. "The Sculptural Drama": Tennessee Williams's Plastic Theatre. *The Tennessee Williams Annual Review* Number 5 (2002): 14 pars. Dec. 2007 <http://www.tennesseewilliamsstudies.org/archives/2002/3kramer.htm>.

Kushner, Tony. *Angels In America, a Gay Fantasia on national Themes*. New York: Theatre Communications Group, 1995.

_____. *Caroline, or Change*. New York: Theatre Communications Group, 2004.

_____. *Death and Taxes: Hydriotaphia & Other Plays*. New York: Theatre Communications Group, 2000.

_____. *Only We Who Guard The Mystery Shall Be Unhappy*. (Scene 1) The Nation, March 24, 2003.

_____. *Only We Who Guard The Mystery Shall Be Unhappy*. (Scene 2) Salon.com. August 4, 2004.

_____. *Plays by Tony Kushner*. (*A Bright Room Called Day, The Illusion, Slavs*). New York: Broadway Play Publishing Inc., 1992.

Leverich, Lyle. *Tom: The Unknown Tennessee Williams*. New York: Crown Publishers Inc., 1995.

Nelson, Benjamin. *Tennessee Williams The Man And His Work*. New York: Ivan Obolensky, Inc., 1961.

Paller, Michael. *Gentlemen Callers: Tennessee Williams, Homosexuality, and Mid-Twentieth Century Drama*. New York: Palgrave Macmillan, 2005.

Philips, S.J., Gene D. *The Films of Tennessee Williams*. New Brunswick, NJ: Associated University Presses, 1980.

Powers, W. Douglas. "Lifted Above Tennessee Williams's *Hot Tin Roof*: Tony Kushyner's *Angels in America* as Midrash" South Atlantic Review, Vol. 70, No. 4, Fall 2005

Savran, David. *Communists, Cowboys, and Queers: The Politics of Masculinity in the Work of Arthur Miller and Tennessee Williams*. Minneapolis: University of Minnesota Press, 1992.

_____. "Tony Kushner," in *Speaking on Stage. Interviews with Contemporary American Playwrights*. Edited by Philip C. Kolin and Colby H. Kullman. Tuscaloosa: U of Alabama P, 1996, 291–313.

Shackleford, Dean. "The Truth That Must Be Told." *The Tennessee Williams Annual Review*, Premier Issue, 1998.

Vidal, Gore. Introduction to *Tennessee Williams Collected Stories*. New York: New Directions, 1985.

Vorlicky, Robert. *Tony Kushner in Conversation*. Ann Arbor: The University of Michigan Press, 1998.

Williams, Tennessee. *Camino Real*. Dramatists Play Service Inc., 1953, 5–6.

_____. *Letters, Vol. 1—1920–1945*. New York: New Directions, 2000.

_____. *A Streetcar Named Desire*. New York: New Directions, 1947.

_____. *Memoirs*. Garden City, New York: Doubleday and Company, 1975.

_____. *The Glass Menagerie*. New York: New Directions, 1999.

Twilight in Tennessee: The Similar Styles of Anna Deavere Smith and Tennessee Williams

Harvey Young

> When I think of theater I think of the playwrights as having the most impact.
> Eugene O'Neill, Arthur Miller and Tennessee Williams.
> Those are the people I think of, when I think of theater.
> — *Actor/Film Director Rob Reiner*

In 1998, *Time* magazine sponsored a public roundtable discussion, involving film director Rob Reiner, actress Anna Deavere Smith, and singer/songwriter Sheryl Crow among others, to identify the individuals who had "the most impact in [artistic] culture over the last 100 years" (*Time*). The purpose of this seemingly self-defeating and potentially never-ending conversation (which was given a one hour time limit) was to draw attention to the magazine's special issue, *Time 100*, a *fin de siècle* retrospective of the most pivotal figures of the preceding century. It is conceivable that the roundtable was arranged to demonstrate the difficult task of selecting only twenty people in *Time 100*'s "artists and entertainers" category and, as a result, to insulate the *Time* editorial staff from criticisms over their selections — such as the inclusion of master puppeteer Jim Henson and fictional cartoon character Bart Simpson and the exclusion of every playwright and theatre director. The discussion, moderated by television journalist Charlie Rose, began with the panelists being invited to identify particularly influential individuals who worked within select media. After several minutes of introductions and opening discussion, Rose steered the conversation toward the theatre. Reiner located 20th century theatrical achievement in the work of select playwrights: O'Neill, Miller, Williams, and Shaw. Smith, after a few moments, challenged Reiner's investment in playwrights by spotlighting directors and actors whose contributions to theatre, in her opinion, were equally, if not more, lasting. She proceeded to cite Bertolt Brecht and Peter Brook among others.

I am intrigued by Anna Deavere Smith's intervention. While her response is justifiably corrective — reminding panelists that there are more position players in the theatre than just the playwright, it also suggests that the actress may believe that actors and directors have played the most instrumental roles in the shaping of contemporary theatre. Although Smith creates allowances for "spillage from the last century," the vanguard of late 19th century European realist and naturalistic writers such as Henrik Ibsen and Anton Chekhov, who inspired a range of 20th century theatre practitioners, her comments suggest that playwrights like Miller, O'Neill, and Williams built upon the innovations of others and were not innovators themselves (Time). In contrast, Brecht and Brook were revolutionary forces who did something entirely new. Both physicalized the theatre. Brecht transformed it into a tool for social activism. Despite the fact that the performer has asserted in numerous interviews her indebtedness to Shakespeare and her memories of watching performances of Arthur Miller plays with "awe-filled intensity," she, through her intervention, spotlights, as meaningful and worthy of recognition, the type of work that she herself does (Smith, Oh 192).

In this essay, which appears within a larger collection of writings pairing Tennessee Williams with other canonical figures within the American Theatre, I identify four traits shared by Smith and the esteemed playwright. I do this with the aim of revealing the similarities of the two artists, who often are thought, within contemporary academic discourse, to champion opposing theatrical styles: a lyrical or poetic realism versus investigative, documentary theatre. Fiction *vs.* Fact. I contend that both dramatists challenge conventional theatrical realism through their incorporation of poststructuralist elements, including fragmented narratives premised upon a series of monologues. Both are theatre personalities as well as theatre practitioners whose auteur status shrouds their later works. Their plays can be understood as travelogues which grant the spectator a privileged glimpse into their nomadic but social lives. Furthermore, their plays take taboo topics — the subjects about which we speak in hushed tones and whispers — and center them onstage.

Despite the fact that there is little direct evidence to support the contention that the playwright's works inspired or directly impacted Smith's dramaturgy, the solo performer, as both a student and teacher of theatre, had to have been familiar with the body of Williams' plays and may have been influenced by them. It is unlikely that Smith, who has referred to her classroom engagements with Shakespeare, Chekhov, Ibsen, and Miller among others, would not have been exposed, at length, to the unique theatre of Tennessee Williams. It is important to note that I am not contending that Anna Deavere Smith patterned her dramaturgical style in the manner of Williams. There are other more influential figures, such as Studs Terkel and Adrienne Kennedy in addition to Brecht and Brook whose process not only resembles but also predates Smith. In drawing the connection between Smith and Williams, I do not seek to read those moments when Smith behaves like or sounds like the playwright. Such an approach would deny Smith's original contributions to the theatre. Instead, I propose that we flip the equation, accept Smith's style as distinctively her own, and consider those moments when Williams behaves and sounds like Smith. What happens when we read Tennessee Williams through a contemporary, critical lens — the type used to analyze Smith's dramaturgy — with the aim of locating those moments when his poststructuralist and social activist voice appears?

On the Road

Before *Fires in the Mirror* and *Twilight, Los Angeles 1992* brought national attention to her performance work, Anna Deavere Smith had spent a decade developing her signature approach to making theatre. Commissioned by organizations, universities, and, occasionally, corporations which were seeking avenues toward approaching and then engaging with potentially divisive issues involving their members/staff/employees, Smith would interview dozens of people, record their voices, make note of their physical expressions and bodily comportment, and compile their voices into a single theatrical narrative that she herself would perform before those whom she interviewed. The motivating factor for her commission consistently was a desire to facilitate dialogue on a particular issue or "problem" among disparate members of a common community. As Sandra L. Richards writes, in "Caught in the Act of Social Definition," "Issuing a commission to Anna Smith most often constitutes an intervention into a volatile situation that a community is struggling to understand and ameliorate" (46). The drama of Smith's quasi-therapeutic theatre existed not only in the content of her informants' accounts but also in Smith's skillful juxtaposition of narratives which placed privileged (onstage) voices in conversation with one another. Her audience, often consisting of the informants themselves, were made privy to a direct address to which they rarely were given access. Through Smith, a president of an organization could listen to the expressed opinions of an entry-level employee. The reverse was true; an employee could hear the thoughts of her employer. These fabricated conversations, assembled and stitched together by the solo performance artist, established a democratic theatre in which the people (understood in its most expansive, communistic fashion) could engage with one another.

Although Smith's approach toward constructing performance has adhered to the same basic principles since her early years working for organizations and universities, the significance and, potentially, revolutionary power of her work on a national level was not fully appreciated and, perhaps, realized until *after* she completed and performed her two most famous performance pieces *Fires in the Mirror* and *Twilight, Los Angeles 1992*. *Fires* is the story of the 1991 Crown Heights riot which was prompted by the accidental death of a young black male who was hit by a car belonging to or associated with the Grand Rebbe of Brooklyn's Lubavitcher sect. Allegations that medical emergency teams treated the less seriously injured members of the Rebbe's entourage over the critically injured and dying boy prompted a riot that resulted in the murder of an Australian tourist. *Twilight* is based on the 1992 Los Angeles riot, which was sparked by the acquittal of police officers who were charged with using excessive force in their detention of a motorist, Glen "Rodney" King. The arrest and "beating" by the police was videotaped by an observer. The video, frequently played on television news, gave the impression that the officers were guilty. When the jury reached a different conclusion, riots ensued and targeted shopkeepers and passing motorists among others. In the aftermath of each civil disturbance, Smith entered the communities and interviewed the leading and supporting players in the social drama. Her resulting plays, *Fires* and *Twilight*, catapulted her to the highest echelon of American theatre practitioners and won her numerous accolades, including a 1996 MacArthur "genius" award.

Anna Deavere Smith operates in a manner similar to Augusto Boal's "spect-actor." Within the Brazilian director's theatre for social change, the "spect-actor" is the idealized audience member who, awakened by the social drama presented onstage, reacts within the space of the theatre (Boal 120, Patterson 37). Rather than sitting complacently on her seat, she feels compelled — by the urgency of the issues of the play — to go onto the stage and to become a part of the drama with the aim of helping it to achieve a satisfactory resolution. Similarly, Anna Deavere Smith does not remain still. A witness to social dramas, riots, civil unrest, and the pageantry of the press among others, she desires to be involved, to assume a role within these real life spectacles, and to work toward resolution. Unlike the "spect-actor," Smith does not propose an answer or even a possible solution. In both *Fires* and *Twilight*, the performer does not offer a way for everyone to "get along." What she does within her dramaturgy is to create a play out of social performances. She takes the already theatrical — riots, etc. — and puts them onstage before an audience who, through their exposure to Smith's enactments, might become "spect-actors" themselves. In support of this possible outcome, Smith and/or the theatres that produce her work often schedule talk-backs immediately following her performances. These post-show discussions enable spectators to find their activist voices.

The activism espoused by Smith is not radical in any conventional sense. She does not seek to create civil unrest. She does not strive to initiate public protests. Smith wants her audience not only to listen to one another, as mediated through her own body, but also to hear what is being said. If individuals and, by extension, larger groups with antagonistic relationships are put into conversation, then each person (and group) would soon realize that their differences are not as extreme nor as insurmountable as they once imagined. For example, if the teenaged black male's words could be heard by the police officer, then racial profiling and, at times, the overaggressive treatment of "suspects" or "suspicious persons" during police stops might end. Conversely, if the police officer's perspective could be understood by teenage youths, then the perception that the police, as both a social organization and a group of individuated figures, are racist could be minimized.

Although Smith's theatre has the potential (the capacity) to create or spur social change, it does not compel audience action. There is room for societal complicity and spectatorial indifference. While the juxtaposition of perspectives can help the viewer to see how misperceptions can develop into dominating stereotypes, the performer avoids inserting her own subjectivity, her "voice," into the staged conversation. As a result, an announced and repeated stereotype within the drama is never challenged directly by the performance artist. To an extent, her structuring of the play and the privileging of accounts which seem to respond to discriminatory or controversial statements could be understood as accomplishing this aim. However, the success of these responses depends upon a spectator's identification with the individuated speaker (as presented by Smith) or interpretation of the (imagined) aims of the playwright. It remains possible for a person, who shares certain prejudicial beliefs, to encounter them within the "play," to listen to and not agree with the contradictory perspective, and to leave the theatre feeling as though her beliefs have been validated by a character within the performance, if not the performance piece itself. Fueling the likelihood of this possibility is that the original and, arguably, the intended audience for Smith's pieces are the informants themselves. While the doubling of the theatrical narrative does create the opportunity for the informants to hear themselves and, perhaps, to see who they are, it also enables them to realize, at times, how right they are and how wrong everyone else is. An example appears in a public conversation that Smith had with Henry Louis Gates, Jr., and Diane Wood Middlebrook at the Djerassi Resident Artists Program Salon when she recalled the reactions of one of her informants who attended a production of *Fires*: "The brother of the young Hasidic scholar who was killed in retaliation for the death of the boy accused me of 'intellectual dishonesty.'" The young man was upset by Smith's decision to give the last word, the final monologue, to the father of the boy who was killed rather than himself or his own father.

The young man's reaction to *Fires* highlights a feature often overlooked or underexamined in critical explorations of Smith's theatre. Within academic accounts of Smith's plays, especially *Fires* and *Twilight*, the frequently stated assumption is that the plays develop organically and that they are unedited, transcriptions of everyday life and transpositions of those daily scenes onto the stage. The goal of such readings is to emphasize the performer's status as the *bearer* of the words of others and, simultaneously, to minimize her role as transcriber, editor, and, most importantly, the person who transforms a real-life person into a character. These efforts to downplay Smith's subjectivity in the process of creating the performance event appears designed to spotlight her virtuoso abilities. She almost seems to disappear and leave only the characters whom she plays. Performance scholar Richard Schechner likens Smith, an African-American woman, to a shaman. In his article "Acting as Incorporation," he writes:

She does not "act" the people you see and listen to in *Fires in the Mirror*. She "incorporates" them. Her way of working is less like that of a conventional Euro-American actor and more like that of African, Native American, and Asian ritualists. Smith works by means of deep mimesis, a process opposite to that of "pretend." To incorporate means to be possessed by, to open oneself up thoroughly and deeply to another being [63].

Schechner's deliberate use of the word "incorporate," especially when coupled with his identification of Smith's "deep mimesis," appears designed to give the impression of *becoming* without actually using the problematic word. For Schechner, Smith's acting style bears similarities with other modes of performance in which the subjectivity of the performer gets replaced or possessed by another (Emigh 22). Smith in interviews seems to encourage such readings by frequently repeating a phrase of advice spoken to her by her grandfather: "If you say a word often enough, it becomes you" (Thompson 133).[1] William H. Sun and Faye C. Fei write, "She has the courage to prove in this self-created Pirandellian predicament that she, the actress, can be as true as, or even truer than, her skeptical and critical characters who are watching her perform them" (Sun 18). Undergirding all of these accounts is a sense of *urgency*. The "real" either possesses or rushes forth through her body and presents itself directly to the assembled audience. The theatrical experience, based upon politically relevant issues happening *now*, proves immediate and renders those real-life events proximate. Although Smith does not bring "the riots" into your living room, she brings them with her or, more accurately, through her to a city near you. This analytical reading does two things. It pre-emptively challenges any assertion that the theatre of Smith is a theatre of impersonation. Implied in references to ritual, possession, and incorporation is that something real, really important, and potentially transformative (for the artist, and, perhaps, society) is happening. It also minimizes dismissals, anchored in anti-theatrical prejudice, which assert that the arts is not the place to stage a politically efficacious conversation. Although I do not want to dispel the sense of "magic" associated with an evening with Smith, I believe that it is important to remember that her performances are scripted, edited, and staged for an audience. The fingerprints of Smith appear everywhere on her pieces.

Despite the fact that she identifies primarily as an actress, Anna Deavere Smith functions as the playwright within her various performance works. She is the person who does due diligence and researches the social events which will comprise the narrative of her plays. She identifies her various informants and arranges to spend time with them — in person or via the telephone (Martin 46). She records their voices and, when possible, their mannerisms and continually replays them throughout her rehearsal process (Richards 41). She edits them and, equally importantly, determines where she wants to situate them within her evolving narrative. The juxtaposition of informants can add tension or comic relief to the performance piece. What Smith does not do — with the notable exception of the inclusion of her voice as interviewer — is to allow herself long monologues *as herself*. The fact that Smith does not "own" — did not create — the words which she speaks, has led at least one well-known artist to deny her the label of "playwright." Performance artist and playwright Dael Orlandersmith, referring to Smith, in a 2002 interview, contrasted Smith with her black, female theatre contemporaries: "Anna is somewhat different. Anna is a sociologist, and what she does is documentary in theater. It is valid, and it is needed. But when you talk about Kia Corthron, Suzan-Lori Parks, and myself— we are writing characters." To Orlandersmith and likely many others, Anna Deavere Smith is a performance ethnographer who does a valuable service by investigating social issues and by mirroring society to itself but her work is not tantamount to creating characters and writing dialogue.

In "Performing Race," Janelle Reinelt offers an unintended refutation to assertions that

Smith should not be considered to be a playwright when she challenges the commonly held belief, even by the performer herself, that Smith performs "verbatim" the words of others. Comparing the filmed version of *Fires* with the published script, Reinelt writes:

> Although critics often describe Smith's stage transcriptions as "verbatim," stressing her ability to capture the rhythm and verbal style of people (indeed the video includes a statement at the beginning that "these portraits are based on verbatim excerpts from interviews conducted by Anna Deavere Smith"), a comparison of the video of *Fires in the Mirror* to the published script reveals that she does not quite perform "verbatim" texts. She does vary the occasional word, or engage in some repetition — which, of course, does alter rhythm. I point this out not to detract from Smith's enormous accomplishment, but rather to underscore the critical rhetoric with which she has been constructed to be the bearer of truth, accuracy, and validity [610].

While a skeptic could dismiss Reinelt's analysis for spotlighting the rare exceptions within a Smith performance, I believe that these moments reveal the constructed nature of the performance piece. Presumably implemented to aid Smith's ability to memorize and recall a succession of monologues, these inserted repetitions create a rhythmic, lyrical dimension to the plays which are not present within the informant's transcripts. These words belong to Smith, as playwright, and impact the manner in which the performance is understood by the assembled audience. They, in particular, add an unexpectedly poetic quality to the urban accounts of her informants. Smith creates a composition out of these speech fragments and, like a composer, finds harmonies in their arrangement. Naomi Matsuoka, in an article comparing the styles of Smith and writer Murakami Haruki, notes that the performer's "editing is polyphonic, as individual voices are heard distinctly, and yet they form an indispensable part of the chorus" (312).

It is this feature of Smith's dramaturgy, the melodious tension between individual elements which stand on their own and, at the same time, blend together within the larger piece, that has led several scholars to identify the performer as a poststructuralist playwright. Debby Thompson, in "Is Race a Trope," asserts that Smith's "post-structuralist acting practices arose out of her frustration with acting based in "psychological realism." She observes:

> Smith ... is determined to encourage "other-oriented" rather than "self-based" approaches to acting. Instead of "finding the character with ourselves" (as Uta Hagen puts it), actors should look for the character outside of themselves. Instead of building a character from the inside out, actors should build from the outside in [131].

Dorinne Kondo, a cultural critic and a dramaturg of the original production of *Twilight*, writes, in "(Re)Visions of Race," "Smith's plays refuse linear narrative structure and refuse to enshrine a central protagonist, instead according careful attention to each character. This nonlinear, decentered structure contests conventions of the well-made play, with its throughline, its positing of a central protagonist who embarks on a journey characterized by a narrative arc" (98). For each author, Smith, through her embrace of a poststructuralist style, establishes a democratic space — shared, equally subjective — and theatrical presence for minoritized groups.

The persona of Anna Deavere Smith looms large within her plays. This exists, in part, because she is the one person who performs all of the monologues. To see *Fires* is to see Smith mediating the voices of Hasidic Jews and black Brooklynites. To see *Twilight* is to see Smith mediating the voices of a Korean store owner, a white truck driver, and an array of other Los Angelenos. To see *House Arrest* is to see Smith mediating the voices of former presidents and current members of the national press. In short, Smith's virtuoso performance proves as much of a draw — if not more — than the subject matter of her pieces. A person goes to the theatre not to see a story about racial tension but rather to watch a play about racial tension *as presented* by Anna Deavere Smith. Indeed, the narrative, which was pieced together by Smith, offers numerous moments in which the artist surfaces as herself before submerging into her next character. There are occasions when Smith allows her voice as interviewer to enter the play and to ask the featured informant a question. More rarely, the informant, as played by Smith, calls attention to Smith's presence within the interview by directly addressing her. This in turn re-establishes her *as Smith* onstage.

The presence of Smith in the performance heightens the authentic feel of her plays. Audience members are aware that Smith met with each person whose voice she presents onstage. Her proximity to the informant in "real life" adds to the reality factor of the play by collapsing the distance that separates the audience member from the actual informant. For example, the fact that Smith met with former president William (Bill) Jefferson Clinton and then, at some later moment in time, performed as Clinton before an audience member appears to collapse the distance between the spectator and the former president because now that person knows someone who knows Clinton. The world seems smaller. The experience being spoken appears more immediate. In Smith's performances, she introduces audience members to scores of people with whom she interacted personally. Taken together, the various narratives that comprise Smith's plays function as travelogues which document the movements and experiences of the actress/playwright. Audiences *go with* Smith as she visits the offices of politicians, the homes of grieving parents, and the White House among other places. Sitting still, the audience travels with her — and this experience of vicarious adventure combined with the thrill of meeting new and, at times, famous people provide the drama in an evening with the performer.

When Smith lectures on the corporation and university circuit, she always performs but in a manner different than in her full-length stage shows. Rather than downplaying her subjectivity and foregrounding the words of others, Smith continually centers and recenters herself. This approach, in part, is born out of necessity as she often gets hired to talk about *her* efforts to spur a public dialogue on social issues. In order to satisfy the demands of her audience, she introduces (or frames) various excerpts from her plays and then proceeds to perform them. In the framing, she reminds her audience that she, often, sat before the informants, listened to their stories, and, as a result of that past experience, can share their voices with the assembled spectators. While the framing offers an efficient way for the performer to introduce her style and then to proceed to perform, the consistency with which she uses this approach can create the misleading impression of "self-indulgence" and "monumental egotism" (Kalb 14).[2] It is easy to see how this perception can exist. One cannot say, "Homi Bhabha and I were talking about mimicry," as Smith did in her talk at the Djerassi Salon, without sounding immodest (Middlebrook 192). However, the reality is that the artist has unparalleled access to the famous, infamous, and lesser known and her conversations with them not only inspire her performance work but also influences the way in which she critically reads her own artistry.

Smith is a light-complexioned, black woman. Several scholars have hypothesized that her success as a performer who can convincingly play various types of people may anchor itself in her physical appearance (Richards 46; Sun 131). On the one hand, her illegibility as a black woman, when accompanied by a specific vocal dialect, costume, and physical gesture, promotes many possible readings and interpretations of Smith's performing body. Could a darker complexioned actress be as convincing or as persuasive as Smith in playing a Korean shopkeeper, a Latino retiree, or a white socialite? On the other hand, Smith's status as black and female, a double minority, grants her the opportunity to play a variety of types without her performance appearing oppressive or dominating and to speak convincingly about social justice and "racial grief."[3] Could a white male play as many roles without his privilege of whiteness and maleness interrupting and, possibly, silencing the voices of the featured informants?

Smith's own comments point not only to her awareness of her centrality within her performance pieces but also to how critics and audiences read her body. In a 1992 interview with Carol Martin, the performer contests the interviewer's description of her work as "hypernaturalistic mimesis" when she declared,

> I don't believe that when I play someone in my work, that I "am" the character. I want the audience to experience the gap, because I know if they experience the gap, they will appreciate my reach for the other. This reach is what moves them, not a mush of me and the other, not a presumption that I can play everything and everybody [Kondo 96].

The following year, Smith, in an article entitled "Not So Special Vehicles," wrote "Largely because of my race and gender, I am political without opening my mouth. My presence is political. The way I negotiate my presence becomes political. If I tried to deny my politicalness, I would be even *more* political" (87). With her body, especially because of its blackness, being always already political, Smith realizes that standing onstage, centered before an audience, is an act that will elicit political readings. The fact that her body engages with controversial subject matter amplifies its charge. In short, she realizes that her presence not only frames the words of her informants but also alters the manner in which it will be read. Her body enhances the racial, gender and class tension that rests at the heart of her plays. It is the "gap" between the upper-middleclass, black, female, educated Smith and her various informants that provides the subplot to her performance pieces.

In Reverse Gear

Tennessee Williams died in 1983, a year after Anna Deavere Smith began performing and a decade before she developed *Fires* and *Twilight* (Time; Richards 35). There is not any direct evidence to suggest that Williams met or influenced Smith. Although the performance artist has referred to having studied the works of Shakespeare, Chekhov, Miller and others, she tends to identify artists of color as being her primary influences and personal role models: Paul Robeson, James Baldwin, and Adrienne Kennedy (Richards 40). While Williams' style certainly echoes in Smith's dramaturgy, it is not clear whether the similarities are directly attributable to the playwright or were mediated by other artists, such as Adrienne Kennedy. Could Smith have modeled herself in the fashion of Kennedy who, in turn, was influenced by Tennessee Williams? Is this the *slippage*, those oblique influences and references, to which Smith referred in the *Time* roundtable? Rather than seeking to find Williams voice within the work of Smith and then to declare it his (and, by contrast, not hers), I want to concentrate on those moments in which attributes which are deemed as distinctive aspects of Smith's dramaturgy surface within the work of Williams. This is done not with the aim of asserting that Williams did these things *first* but to demonstrate how an analysis of contemporary performance styles can offer new insight into the performance traditions that preceded them.

The characters within Williams' plays and short stories have been taken from everyday life. Thinly veiled depictions of real-life people, his characters, similar to Anna Deavere Smith's staged informant's, reveal the playwright's impressionistic view of society. They are multidimensional figures who reside within a stratified (often by class) social environment and who offer the spectator the sobering opportunity to view life from their perspective and to vicariously stand-in their shoes. Unlike Smith, who relies upon direct address to create a sense of spatial intimacy with the performed informant, Williams blends "fourth wall" realism with the jarring nature of direct address. Beginning with "fourth wall" realism, the playwright establishes the spectator as an outside observer who looks into the lives of the characters of a play. As the play progresses, Williams reveals that the primary motivation for his characters is often psychological — something that cannot be seen — which then prompts a desire within the spectator for monologues. When the playwright gives his characters a monologue — such as Catherine's in *Suddenly, Last Summer,* he transforms his audience's engagement with them from sympathetic to empathetic identification.

To be clear, the characters, although predicated upon actual figures whom Williams knew, speak not in their own voices (i.e. sharing the sentiments held by the people themselves) but in a manner consistent with the demands of the dramatic narrative and, therefore, the dramatist. Whereas Rodney King spoke the words uttered by Smith in *Twilight,* Blanche's poetic voice in *A Streetcar Named Desire* belongs entirely to the playwright. Nevertheless, Williams, according to several individuals who knew him well, did succeed in capturing the likeness and mannerism of those figures whom he scripted into his theatrical universe. Dakin Williams, the playwright's brother and the trustee/guardian of his literary estate, noted, "My mother was the 'spitting image' of Amanda [in the *Glass Menagerie*], so much so that my brother, after he became a success, felt obligated to give her fifty percent of the profits of the play" (Bray). Williams' mother, Edwina, observed, "The old man Nonno, in *The Night of the Iguana,* is a particularly true picture of father" (225). The playwright's inclusion of real-life figures went beyond his immediate relations. Allean Hale, in his article "Early Williams: The Making of a Playwright," notes that Williams' fraternity brothers at the University of Missouri were the inspiration for the character Mitch in *A Streetcar Named Desire* and Jim O'Connor in *Glass Menagerie* and that the character Big Daddy in *Cat on a Hot Tin Roof* was based on Jordan Massee, Sr., a Georgia plantation owner and the father of a dear friend. Supporting this latter reading, Kenneth Holditch and Richard Freeman Leavitt in their book *Tennessee Williams and the South* not only cite the opening lines — "To Big Daddy" — of a letter to Massee by Williams but also offer visual evidence. They present two pictures — side by side — of Massee, a large, rotund figure wearing a white suit and suspenders, and of actor Burt Ives, who played the role in the original Broadway cast, and appears in exactly the same manner and seems nearly identical to Massee (27).

The presence of these differently, geographically-situated individuals within Williams' dramas invite a consideration of his plays as travelogues. Similar to Smith, who criss-crossed the nation to record the voices and her impressions of individuals with the aim of bringing them to the stage, the playwright traveled the globe and introduced his audience to events, places, and people who actually exist somewhere within the world. Among Williams biographers, there is a wide consensus that the playwright's wanderlust inspired the encounters that appear within his plays. Hale notes that his time in Acapulco informed his selection and depiction of the city in *Night of the Iguana.* In his article "Sentiment and Humor in Equal Measure: Comic Forms in *Rose Tattoo,*" Philip Kolin contends, "While in Sicily, Williams must have soaked up enough local culture to write knowledgeably about the folklore, language, and characters of the region and create the Dionysian elements he claimed to capture in the play" (215). His brother Dakin locates the playwright's "romantic" vision of the South in the stories that he heard and to which he closely listened as a youth. Williams recalls, "he was always listening to those stories [of Mississippi Delta folk]. He had big ears, and that's what people did — they didn't have television or radio — they sat on verandas and told stories" (Bray). It is conceivable that Tennessee Williams may have been thinking about the various people who inspired his characters and, in turn, prompted his plays when he, in his autobiography *Memoirs*, wrote, "I would guess that chance acquaintances or strangers have usually been kinder to me than friends — which does not speak too well for me" (cited in Hayman x–xi).

Williams' tendency to create theatrical mirror images of people and places that he knew has prompted scholars to analyze the playwright's dramas with the aim of better understanding the dramatist himself. Were the characters and, perhaps, the plays themselves reflections of Williams? Donald Pease in his article "Reflections on the Moon Lake: The Presences of the Playwright" contends that Williams, in his later life, consciously scripted forewords for the published versions of his plays with the aim of giving the impression that they were autobiographical. Pease writes, "It seems that Williams placed these forewords at the beginning of the plays so that his plays might be seen not only to originate in and transform but also to replace his individual life" (830). Ronald Hayman, identifying the playwright's homosexual and/or colonialist "guilt" in his characterization of Sebastian's spectacular murder at the hands of Mexican youths in *Suddenly, Last Summer*, observes, "This was most ferocious image Tennessee had yet found to express the guilt he felt at eating luxuriously in cities where the natives were starving, and at paying boys to make love when they were too poverty-stricken to say no" (174–175). Dakin Williams, referring to his brother's late career plays, asserted, "Every play he wrote on drugs was a dramatic self-portrait; they always concerned two people, like the brother and sister in *Out Cry*, a wonderful play. *In the Bar of a Tokyo Hotel* [reveals that] both characters are sides of himself" (Bray). Considering that the plays were fictional creations which were populated with recognizable people whom the playwright knew and identifiable places where he lived, it logically follows that they were reflective of the playwright to some degree.

Certainly, the presence of sexuality, especially homosexuality, within his plays appear to anchor themselves in the many admonitions he received in his youth about not behaving like a "sissy" and his later, public homosexual relationships and affairs.[4] In one of the earliest critical reviews of the playwright, John Gassner, a former professor of Williams, identifies the treatment of homosexuality as a trait that is particular to his dramaturgy. Writing for *The English Journal* in 1948 about Williams' first plays (many of which were published in *27 Wagons Full of Cotton*), Gassner observes, "He was developing a precise naturalism, compounded of compassion and sharp observation and filled with some of those unsavory details that Boston had found offensive but that Williams considered a necessary part of the truth to which he had dedicated himself" (388). It is these "unsavory" details which would surface within the majority of his major works, including *Cat on a Hit Tin Roof*, *Glass Menagerie*, and *Suddenly, Last Summer*. What is particularly interesting about Williams' commitment to presenting the "truth" of sexuality and sexual relationship within his plays is that he demanded their inclusion during a period rife with censorship. Although it was Arthur Miller's *A View from the Bridge* that weakened theatrical censorship in Great Britain in the 1950s, Tennessee Williams' plays were the immediate beneficiaries of the lifting of the ban (Darlington 143). When Hollywood film censors threatened to edit out the rape scene in *A Streetcar Named Desire* (1951), Williams wrote a forceful letter to Joseph Breen, Head of the Production Code, about the importance and truthfulness of the scene (Devlin 187).

Without oversimplifying the theatrical activism of Williams and Smith, we can locate, in part, their concentration on issues of sexuality and race in their own varying, minoritized status as gay, black, and/or female. Williams placed a spotlight on queerness and undermined heteronormative assumptions by depicting numerous characters tormented by their own sexuality. He made sexuality a part of the national conversation — which was enhanced by the numerous theatre and film stars who lined up to perform a Williams role: Jessica Tandy, Marlon Brando, Paul Newman, Richard Burton, Elizabeth Taylor, Vivien Leigh, Uta Hagen, and Katherine Hepburn among others. Although the playwright was less expressly political than Smith, I suspect that his theatre may have been more actively political. Unlike Smith who sought to find one-dimensional representations of ideological positions and then introduce the gamut of perspectives to her audience, Williams privileged complicated and, indeed, conflicted characters who appear more relatable and, perhaps, more "real" than the actual informants performed by Smith.

David Savran, in *Communists, Cowboys, and Queers*, persuasively argues for not only a poststructuralist reading of Tennessee Williams but also a determination of Williams as a poststructuralist playwright. He contends that there are "two modes of address or interpellation" in the playwright's works, including both his plays and his short stories (159). The first mode "calls upon a spectator to be attentive to what characters 'said or did,' to plot, narrative continuity, and anecdote, to the larger structures of desire and meaning that impel Williams' theatre" (159). This approach, according to the author, appears primarily within his plays and develop alongside dominating, hetero-normative relationships. In *A Streetcar Named Desire*, the plot, the sexual relationships that we actually see onstage occur between men and women: Stanley and Stella, Mitch and Blanche, and Stanley and Blanche. Savran continues:

> The second mode of address, which is more likely to be evoked through diegetic prose, stage directions, or visual images, is far more unstable and perilous. It is the force that pulverizes plot by drawing the reader or spectator's attention to a detail, an image, a metaphor, or a charged moment of silence [159].

This approach, which the author identifies as "camp," enables and, indeed, ennobles queer readings of Williams' writings, especially his short stories. Returning to *Streetcar*, we can think of the non-normative activities which emerge through Blanche's various monologues: the homosexuality of her young lover and her romantic/physical activities at Belle Reve and the Flamingo Hotel. Ultimately, Savran contends that these modes of address create a space for difference within the playwright's work. Beyond merely creating a theatrical presence for sexual (gender) difference onstage, Williams scripts a critique of societal norms and values which vilify it. Furthermore, he depicts heteronormativity as a social problem which is responsible for the establishment of sexual anxieties.

Anna Deavere Smith and Tennessee Williams make strange bedfellows. In establishing a relationship between the two writers, I seek not to overlook nor minimize their differences. Instead, I am interested in locating those places where their styles appear similar and their politics seem in concert. Reflecting upon the two figures, it is clear that both embrace a poststructuralist formula to create a space and presence for the minoritized within their narratives. Within their fabricated, theatrical worlds, they situate characters who are based upon real-life individuals, whom the playwrights actually met and, in some cases, came to know, and, in so doing, blur the lines between artifice and the everyday. As authors whose travels define or, at least, support their creative work, their presence looms over all of their projects. It is Smith — not the subject matter of her pieces — that attracts her audiences. As evidence of this, the published version of *House Arrest* interweaves the artist's own autobiographical narrative with the stories of those whom she interviewed. Similarly, the photograph of Smith on the cover of her acclaimed book *Talk to Me* suggests that the titular pronoun refers to the performer herself. Although Tennessee Williams became a drug-addicted caricature of himself, especially in his later years, his iconic status remains.

NOTES

This article benefited from conversations with Erika Rankin, Eric Senne, and Lisa Tibbetts, students in my summer 2007 American Theatre seminar at Northwestern University, along with Timothy Mitchell.

1. Despite citing her grandfather's statement within dozens of interviews, Smith frequently — at times, within the same interviews — asserts that she never "becomes" her characters even within performance.

2. In his article, Kalb suggests that "self-indulgence" and "monumental egotism" are common traits of solo performance artists but does *not* assert that these descriptors apply to Smith. In fact, she exists as one of the exceptions for the author. See Kalb.

3. See Anne Anlin Cheng's *The Melancholy of Race: Psychoanalysis, Assimilation, and Hidden Grief.*

4. The concern over Williams "becoming" homosexual appears in the majority of his biographies but the word "sissy" appears most frequently in the reflections of his mother and brother in their respective published interviews on the playwright. See Robert Bray. See Edwina Williams and Lucy Freeman.

WORKS CITED

Boal, Augusto. *Theatre of the Oppressed.* Trans. Charles A. McBride and Maria-Odilia Leal McBride. New York: Theatre Communications Group, 1985.

Bray, Robert. "An Interview with Dakin Williams." *The Mississippi Quarterly* 48.4 (1995): 776–89.

Cheng, Anne Anlin. *The Melancholy of Race: Psychoanalysis, Assimilation, and Hidden Grief* Oxford: Oxford University Press, 2001.

Darlington, W.A. "London Report: 'A View from the Bridge' Big Hit." *New York Times* November 11, 1956.

Devlin, Alberto and Nancy Marie Patterson Tischler, eds. *The Selected Letters of Tennessee Williams, Vol. 2: 1945–1957* New York: New Directions Publishing Co: 2004.

Emigh, John. *Masked Performance: The Play of Self and Other in Ritual and Theatre.* Philadelphia: University of Pennsylvania Press, 1996.

Gassner, John. "Tennessee Williams: Dramatist of Frustration." *The English Journal* 37.8 (1948): 387–93.

Hale, Allean. "Early Williams: The Making of a Playwright." *The Cambridge Companion to Tennessee Williams.* Ed. Matthew C. Roodane. Cambridge: Cambridge University Press, 1997. 11–28.

Hayman, Ronald. *Tennessee Williams: Everyone Else Is Audience.* New Haven: Yale University Press, 1993.

Holdritch, Kenneth and Richard Freeman Leavitt. *Tennessee Williams and the South.* Jackson: University Press of Mississippi, 2002.

Kalb, Jonathan. "Documentary Solo Performance: The Politics of the Mirrored Self." *Theater* 31.3 (2001): 13–29.

Kentucky Educational Television. "Black Women Playwrights: Interviews: Dael Orlandersmith." 2007. website. September 2007. <http://www.ket.org/content/americanshorts/poof/orlandersmith.htm>.

Kolin, Philip C. "Sentiment and Humor in Equal Measure: Comic Forms in *the Rose Tattoo.*" *Tennessee Williams: A Tribute.* Ed. Jac Tharpe. Jackson, MS: University of Mississippi Press, 1971. 214–31.

Kondo, Dorinne. "(Re)Visions of Race: Contemporary Race Theory and the Cultural Politics of Racial Crossover in Documentary Theatre." *Theatre Journal* 52 (2000): 81–107.

Martin, Carol. "Anna Deavere Smith: The Word Becomes You. An Interview." *The Drama Review* 37.4 (1993): 45–62.

Matsuoka, Naomi. "Murakami Haruki and Anna Deavere Smith: Truth by Interview." *Comparative Literature Studies* 39.4 (2002): 305–13.

Middlebrook, Diane Wood. "The Artful Voyeur: Anna Deavere Smith and Henry Louis Gates, Jr., on Private Life and Public Art." *Transition* 67 (1995): 186–97.

Paterson, Douglas L. "A Role to Play for the Theatre of the Oppressed." *The Drama Review* 38.3 (1994): 37–49.

Pease, Donald. "Reflections on Moon Lake: The Presences of the Playwright." *Tennessee Williams: A Tribute.* Ed. Jac Tharpe. Jackson, MS: University of Mississippi Press, 1971. 829–47.

Reinelt, Janelle. "Performing Race: Anna Deavere Smith's Fires in the Mirror." *Modern Drama* 39.4 (1996): 609–17.

Richards, Sandra L. "Caught in the Act of Social Definition: On the Road with Anna Deavere Smith." *Acting Out: Feminist Performance.* Eds. Lynda Hart and Peggy Phelan. Ann Arbor: University of Michigan Press, 1993. 35–53.

Savran, David. *Communists, Cowboys, and Queers*. Minneapolis: University of Minnesota Press, 1992.

Schechner, Richard. "Anna Deavere Smith: Acting as Incorporation." *The Drama Review* 37.4 (1993): 63–64.

Smith, Anna Deavere. *House Arrest and Piano: Two Plays* New York: Anchor, 2004.

_____. "Not So Special Vehicles." *Performing Arts Journal* 17.2/3 (1995): 77–89.

_____. "Oh, but for a Fool." *The Drama Review* 50.3 (2006): 192–93.

_____. *Talk to Me: Listening between the Lines*. New York: Random House, 2000.

Steiner, George. "Close-up of Britain's Censor." *The New York Times* 1956: SM6.

Sun, William H., and Faye C. Fei. "Masks or Races Re-Visited: A Study of Four Theatrical Works Concerning Cultural Identity." *The Drama Review* 38.4 (1994): 120–32.

Thompson, Debby. ""Is Race a Trope?" Anna Deavere Smith and the Question of Racial Performativity." *African American Review* 37.1 (2003): 127–38.

Time Magazine. "Person of the Century at the Getty in La." 1998. September 2007. <http://www.time.com/time/time100/artists/debate/symp_transcript.html>.

Williams, Edwina Dakin and Lucy Freeman. *Remember Me to Tom* St. Louis: Sunrise Publishing: 1963.

Theatre of the Gut:
Tennessee Williams and
Suzan-Lori Parks

Harry J. Elam, Jr.

In a 1996 interview with dramaturge Shelby Jiggets, Suzan-Lori Parks — then only an up-and-coming playwright not yet a Pulitzer Prize winner or MacArthur Fellow — said in response to Jiggets's question about people who had influenced her work:

> Another writer who has had an influence on me was Tennessee Williams. I remember I read one of his plays I mean, it was the kind of play that people, you know, the cool people, were calling dumb theater, but it was theater that I liked. I'm a big fan of bad theater. Tennessee Williams is not an example of bad theater, but it could be compared to "serious theater."[1]

Perhaps it seems strange even to imagine that Parks, a contemporary African American experimentalist woman writer, could be influenced by this white male modernist playwright. And yet, in this interview with Jiggets's and subsequent interviews, Parks repeatedly posits Williams as a source of inspiration and admiration. After winning the 2001 Pulitzer Prize for *Topdog/Underdog*, Parks was again asked by Elizabeth Farnsworth, on the *NewsHour with Jim Lehrer,* about writers who influenced her craft, to which she immediately replied, "people like, you know, certainly James Baldwin, who was my teacher over at Mount Holyoke College, and Tennessee Williams." (Interestingly, one of the other strong influences in Parks's work is another Southern modernist writer, the novelist William Faulkner.)

Within the content as well as the form of Parks's work we can see the impact of Williams. Both writers push against the constraints of realism and interrogate what constitutes the real. Highly eclectic, Parks like Williams can not easily be pigeonholed in terms of theatrical style. With her early non-linear avant-garde works such as *Imperceptible Mutabilities in the Third Kingdom* (1986) and *The Death of the Last Black Man in the Whole Entire World* (1989), Suzan-Lori Parks burst onto the American stage and critics hailed her as "theatre's vibrant new voice,"[2] an "indigenous theatrical talent" and even, in 1990, as "the most promising playwright of the year."[3] The previous predictions of her promise have proved prescient as she has been awarded a John T. MacArthur Foundation "genius" Fellowship award for 2000 and won the aforementioned 2001 Pulitzer Prize. With its two character, hyper-realistic format, *Topdog* veers decidedly from Parks's previous imaginings of dramatic form and dialogue as do her other more recent stage pieces including *In the Blood* (1998). The prolific Williams moved constantly between naturalism and expressionism and even surrealism. Even his most popular and successful plays, *Glass Menagerie* (1944), *A Streetcar Named Desire* (1947) and *Cat on Hot Tin Roof* (1955), cannot simply be classified under the genre of realism. What these works share with his less-linear, more experimental plays such as *Rose Tattoo* (1950), *Camino Real* (1953), and the later *Red Devil Battery Sign* (1976), is the exploration of the symbolic as well as an appreciation for the power and beauty of language. Parks, as well as Williams, finds poetry in language, and an authority beyond its surface meanings.

In addition, Parks follows Williams in expressing within her dramas a dissatisfaction with the existing social order. Williams maintained that art should serve as a "criticism of things as they exist."[4] Parks believes, as did Williams, in the dynamic power of theatre to function as a form of social critique. For Parks, invariably questions of race, blackness, and racism are subjects. Yet, even as her dramas comment on racial inequalities in America, Parks is never didactic or overt. In her *America Play* (1990), that features a black actor whose job is to portray Abraham Lincoln, Parks resists explicitly discussing the actor's race, but does so only through inference. She refers to him as "the foundling father," "the lesser known," who was "Digger by trade from a family of Diggers."[5] That Digger rhymes with the "N" word is intentional. Williams had no problem using the "N" word in his writing and in creating virulent racist figures. And yet, in his plays as in his life, Williams's relationship to race was complex. Even as his plays feature only peripheral black figures and several racist white ones, Williams spoke out publicly against racism calling it "the most horrible thing." His treatment of race in his plays was perhaps not as overt but nonetheless significant. As with Parks's coded use of "Digger" in *The America Play*, critics such as George W. Crandell have pointed out that Williams employs, "a coded discourse, concealing an implicit but nonetheless discernable African influence and presence."[6] Repeatedly in the work, ethnic male figures — the Polish Stanley Kowalski in *Streetcar*, the Italian Silva Vaccaro in the film *Baby Doll* (1956) — function as surrogates for the black racialized other. Critiques by Crandell, David Savran, and Philip Kolin point out how Williams uses these ethnic men to embody the bestiality, physicality and sensuality associated with black masculinity.[7] In each of these works, the racialized male figure is also highly sexualized, and sex and violence are purposefully linked. Parks is also extremely interested in the relationship between sexuality and race and its social and cultural implications.

In the Jiggets's interview, Parks does not state which play by Williams she read. Yet this play, however objectionable it was to the "cool people," fueled her interest in creating "serious theater." And while Parks does not elaborate on what she means by "serious theater," later in the interview she states: "I write from the gut. I think theater should come from there. Especially because it's life and, you know, you gotta infect people with language — it comes from the gut.... What I think theater or a play should do is provide the opportunity to feel it in your gut."[8] I read this image of infecting people, of reaching them in their "gut" as a particularly "serious" genre of theatre, perhaps we might even consider this statement as a definition of what Parks seeks in serious theatre. In this essay, I will relate this gut wrenching, gut level theater of Parks back to Tennessee Williams. For Williams most certainly in his language and his dramatic expression of reality reached people in their gut. In fact, Williams had difficulties with his own gut in his real life, suffering from depression, alcoholism, and other associated ailments. His gut problems functioned, perhaps, as sign of his own inner turmoil, his internalization of the societal rejection and demonization of his once closeted homosexuality.

As I will discuss in the pages to follow, for Parks as well as Williams, one pathway to the gut in their dramas was through the "gutter," through the depiction and disclosure of dirty little secrets, of sexual indiscretions and transgressions. The revelation and representation of sexual desire in Parks, evidences the legacy of Williams. I will explore how Williams's radical inventiveness finds particular expression in Parks in the expression of sexual desire. Through his work and its acclaim, Williams brought sexuality into much more prominence in the public sphere, even as he kept some aspects of his own desire and his own perspective on sexuality closeted. Parks follows Williams as she eschews sexual taboos and deals extremely forthrightly with carnality and passion. Significantly, for each of these playwrights sex exists in their plays not simply as subject matter but as psychic and dramatic conduit, a lever providing deeper access into the social and cultural mores and motives of the worlds their characters inhabit. Clearly, sex and sexuality operate in Parks and Williams at the gut level.

Two plays that highlight the utility and power of sexuality in Williams and Parks are Williams's Pulitzer Prize winning *Cat on a Hot Tin Roof* (1955) and Parks's *In the Blood* (1999), a tale of a black homeless woman, Hester, and her brood of children. In Williams's *Cat on a Hot Tin Roof*, family secrets, questions of sexual impropriety and deviance lurk behind closed doors. Previously hidden truths are exposed and reverberate loudly as what constitutes the normal and the prurient are called into question. Similarly, in Parks's *In the Blood*, the confession of sexual proclivities compels the audience to contest the purported morality of the social order and to reconsider who is the victimizer and the victim. Form functions as the internal logic of content in these two plays as Williams and Parks challenge heterosexual normativity and the legitimacy of family values. Parks's central figure Hester, and her sexual and racial body politics make for revealing comparison with Williams's family dynamics in *Cat on Hot Tin Roof*. Hester has direct collation with Williams's fierce Maggie, as they provide feminist assertions of self, a questioning of gender roles and sexual agency as well as an interrogation of the meanings of motherhood. Parks's play evidences Williams's legacy as it shows the power and possibility of this homeless, supposedly sexually deviant, and socially outcast, woman struggling against seemingly insurmountable odds. Both plays function as forms of social resistance attacking the status quo and social complacency. At the same time, Hester's blackness provides for an interesting riff on Williams, adding a dynamic that "colors" her interactions and that impacts her fate in ways that do not apply to Williams's Maggie.

Sexual Normalcy

Questions of sexuality and sexual deviance are critical to *Cat on a Hot Tin Roof*. Haunting the connection between Maggie and her husband Brick, centrally impacting the action in *Cat on Hot Tin Roof*, is Brick's previous relationship with the deceased Skipper and the suggestion of homosexuality. As the play begins, we learn that Brick, the one-time football hero, the son of Big Daddy and his preferred heir to the plantation, is a mere shell of his former self. Now the embodied symbol of impotence, unable to find his own way without assistance, Brick hobbles around on crutches, after having unsuccessfully tried to leap track and field hurdles as he did in his youth and breaking his ankle in the process. Yet, the pain eating at his psyche overpowers that in his foot. With his mind wrought by guilt after Skipper's death and the sexual innuendos and suspicions that have plagued him, Brick drinks heavily and refuses the sexual advances of his wife, Maggie, blaming her, at least in part, for Skipper's demise. In response to Maggie and others who would label his bond with Skipper as abnormal or queer, Brick defensively proclaims that what they shared was "a clean true thing ... too rare to be normal."[9] Thus, he declares that space beyond the normal in which he and Skipper united is a virtue not a matter of social deviance.

Before and after Skipper's death, the unique linkage of these two male friends, Skipper and Brick threatened Maggie. In what René Girard's refers to a "triangular desire,"[10] Maggie mediated between Skipper and Brick with the intention of challenging the men's closeness and so — the audience discovers through retrospective structural revelations — she enticed Skipper, in attempt to save her relationship with Brick. She entered into a tryst with Skipper that precipitated his death. Provoked by her words and his own troubled conscience, Skipper sleeps with Maggie in attempt to prove his heteronormativity, to disprove his love for Brick, but in the end he only confirms his desire for Brick and undoes his own psychological stability. Talking with Brick in the play's first act, Maggie admits her responsibility for Skipper's unfortunate end. "In this way, I destroyed him, by telling him the truth that he and his world which he was born and raised in, yours and his world, had told him could not be told?" (*Cat on a Hot Tin Roof,* 1, 45). Maggie expresses culpability in Skipper's death in order to breathe new life into her own relationship with her husband. However, they exist together in a seemingly loveless marriage, maintaining only the facade of normalcy in order to placate the dying Big Daddy and hopefully to earn his favor and inheritance.

In the Blood also centrally considers questions of sexual normalcy and familial inheritance. In the first scene, the central figure Hester La Negrita kneels on the ground and awkwardly sketches the letter "A" with chalk on the cement as her eldest son Jabber attempts to teach her the alphabet. She is illiterate. Moreover, she is an unwed welfare mother of five children, each with different fathers. Hester appears to be a blight on the normal social order, a welfare queen who lives parasitically off the sweat and toil of others. Parks terms *In the Blood* one of her two "Red Letter Plays," and along with *Fucking A,* this work repeats and revises ideas from Nathaniel Hawthorne's *Scarlet Letter.* Like her namesake Hester Prynn of *The Scarlet Letter,* Hester La Negrita has been ostracized from society because of her sexual transgression. From the outset of Hawthorne's novel as she exits from prison, Hester Prynn is publicly humiliated and exorcised from the community and forced to sew onto her clothing the scarlet letter "A" publicly announcing her adultery. After Hester La Negrita scribbles her "A" on the ground, she asks Jabber to read the word "slut," which has been scrawled on the wall under the bridge where Hester and her illegitimate children live. This writing on the wall publicly marks her as deviant, as an agent of sexual license with a disregard for normal propriety. One issue in the play is how do the five children inherit or continue the condition of the mother? What legacy do they have from their fathers, who pay no child support? Ultimately, Hester kills her son Jabber in an act that resonates culturally, socially and politically, as this infanticide symbolically strikes out against the tyranny of a national order which not only restricts the roles of women and people of color, but also preordains how one's offspring will function within this system.

With *In the Blood,* Parks challenges the status quo and undermines principles of conventional morality by depicting her Hester as not simply a ward of the system, but exploited by it. The chorus of characters in the play's prologue hurls insults at her and ridicules her as she passes by:

> SHE KNOWS SHES A NO COUNT
> SHIFTLESS
> HOPELESS
> BAD NEWS
> BURDEN TO SOCIETY
> HUSSY
> SLUT[11]

This chorus, consisting of the other characters in the play, attempts to place the onus for Hester's impoverished condition on her own moral indiscretions and welfare dependency. And yet, what Parks shows throughout the play is that the answer is not that simple. The singular, yet representative figures of the Doctor, Reverend and Welfare Lady all take advantage of her to satisfy their own prurient sexual desires. Thus, Parks like Williams finds contradiction and even hypocrisy in the principals of social normalcy.

Juxtaposing images of homosexuality to heteronormativity in *Cat on a Hot Tin Roof*, Williams subjects normalcy to serious interrogation and contestation. Tennessee Williams explicitly embeds homosexuality in the history of the plantation and its legacy of inheritance. As Williams explains in the "Notes for the Designer," the bed/sitting room that serves as the locale for all the action, originally belonged to, and is now haunted by, the spirits of Jack Straw and Peter Ochello, "a pair of old bachelors" who shared "all their lives together" in a relationship that "must have involved a tenderness that was uncommon" ("Notes for the Designer," *Cat on a Hot Tin Roof*). Their homosexual bond of uncommon tenderness directly correlates with the potentially homosexual, but certainly homosocial ties between Brick and Skipper, that Brick defines as "too rare to be normal." These uncommonly close relationships that traditional society in Williams's time of Cold war politics — or even in early 21st century America, when gay marriage is the subject of moral outrage — would condemn as aberrant, Williams presents as the only examples in the play of compassionate companionship. Significantly, three of the four partners are dead as the play begins. So, their unique interconnections exist now only as memory, as trace and taint, conjured and preserved, shaped and misrepresented by other characters. Moreover, their idealized bonds contrast sharply with Williams's representation of the heterosexual marriages in the text: Brick and Maggie subsist in a sexless, tension-filled union. Brick's father, Big Daddy who inherited the estate from the gay partners Straw and Ochello, has not slept with Big Mama, his wife, in five years and in fact claims that he "has not been able to stand the sight, smell and sound of that woman for forty years now" *Cat on a Hot Tin Roof*, 2. 80). Gooper, Brick's older brother, and his wife Mae are evidently still sleeping together; however, rather than love, it appears that feelings of envy, suspicion, and greed drive their union. While they fulfill the heterosexual mandate to procreate — the dying Big Daddy wants progeny to carry on his legacy — they produce only a brood — they have five children just like Hester in *In the Blood*— of loud and unruly "no-neck monsters" as Maggie calls them and "five same monkeys" as Big Daddy dubs them.

Williams paints compulsory heterosexuality as unfulfilling and even unsightly. Brick describes heterosexual sex with Maggie not as an act of intimacy, but rather just as crude animal behavior, "She and me never got any closer together than two people who just get in bed, which is not much closer than two cats on a — fence humping" (*Cat on a Hot Tin Roof*, 2. 92). Even when he "laid" Big Mama "regular as a piston," Big Daddy admits that he "never even liked it, never did" (*Cat on a Hot Tin Roof*, 2.70). In contrast to this image of legally condoned, conjugal heterosexuality, as David Savran notes, Williams casts homosexual desire "not as masculinity's anathema but as that which always already inheres inside the male subject (like a cancer)." [12] Big Daddy, the embodiment of patriarchal or masculine authority in the play, views the relationships of Straw and Ochello or Brick and Skipper without negative judgment. Rather, when Big Daddy talks with Brick about Skipper, Big Daddy does not condemn this potential homosexual liaison but confides to his son that in his youthfulness he himself "knocked around in his time" and that he "bummed, bummed this country and that he seen all things and understood a lot of them" (*Cat on a Hot Tin Roof*, 2.85). The inference is that Big Daddy might have engaged in homosexual activity or at least understood the inclination and that homosexual encounters are not tangential to one's development into manhood. It is just a stage that he feels Brick must just grow out of and then move on. Conventional notions of sexual normalcy within the play are continually questioned.

Confessional

Notably, Big Daddy's admission of his youthful discretions to Brick function as form of confession, a confession that upsets the conventional ethics of confession associated with Christian orthodoxy. For Big Daddy confesses his past transgressions to Brick not in an attempt to expiate his sins or to beg forgiveness, but rather to exalt in the act of sinning. Even in his now diminished state, the elderly and dying Big Daddy informs Brick of his previous conjugal dalliances with Big Mama in an attempt to remember and to hold onto his claim to virility and hyper masculinity. Big Daddy celebrates that fact that Big Mamma "never got tired of it," and that he "was good in bed." Not satisfied with this pronouncement, he boasts to Brick that he still not only has a desire for other women, but the will and the sexual potency to act on his masculine bravado:

> Well I got a few left in me, a few, and I'm going to pick me a good one to spend 'em on! I'm going to pick me a choice one, I don't care how much she costs, I'll smother her in — minks! Ha ha! I'll strip her naked and smother her in minks and choke her in diamonds! I'll strip her naked and choke her with diamonds and smother her with minks and hump her from hell to breakfast [*Cat on Hot Tin Roof*, 2.72].

Big Daddy seeks to roll around in the gutter even as cancer strikes him in the gut. He suffers from uremia and an insidious cancer which Gooper describes as "a poisoning of the system due to the body's inability to eliminate poisons" (*Cat on a Hot Tin Roof*, 3. 113). His previous sexual excesses, Williams hints, have lead to this condition. His sexual perversions have perverted his body, and the disease now eats away at him. Violent and crude, Big Daddy's confessed fantasy does not simply objectify his female partner, but brutalizes her, overpowers her, snuffs and silences her in service of his own pleasure. As the economist Thorstein Veblen might argue, the minks and diamonds, given in excess, are not a gift or sign of Big Daddy's largess, but a symbol of his own economic potency.[13] With Brick as his audience, Big Daddy's confession functions as what Joseph Roach terms "surrogacy," a performance that stands in for what was, for his lack — as Big Daddy on the verge of losing control of his house and his health asserts his power.[14] He does not ask Brick for forgiveness, he does not want to be cleansed, but rather seeks to enlist Brick himself into his masturbatory tale of perversion. Big Daddy seeks for Brick to act as witness and accomplice, and thus provides sanction for his assertion of virility.

Similarly, Maggie confesses her tryst with Skipper to Brick, not in attempt at forgiveness, but rather out of her need to convert and enlist him in her own desire. She reveals to Brick, "Skipper and I made love, if love you could call it, because it made both of us feel a bit closer to you" (*Cat on a Hot Tin Roof*, 1.42). For Skipper and Maggie, attempted sex with each other only served as surrogate for their unfulfilled desire for Brick. Now, Maggie performs another act of surrogacy: confessing as an act of intimacy and sharing stands in for the intimacy that she and Brick lack in their own relationship. Maggie plans through confession to reinvigorate their bond. "But Brick?!—*Skipper is dead! I'm alive*" (*Cat on a Hot Tin Roof*, 1.45)! Moreover, if she is complicit in Skipper's death as she acknowledges to Brick, then he must be equally culpable. After all Brick reports that he hung up on Skipper after Skipper confessed to Brick his "deeper" feelings. Maggie's revelation, then, is an attempt to remove the barriers between them by implicitly calling on Brick to admit his own responsibility for his friend's decline. "I'm honest!— Give me credit for that, will you *please*," she entreats him. As with Big Daddy, Maggie does not express remorse nor ask for forgiveness, but rather she asks Brick for acceptance.

What is equally significant about these confessions is where they take place. Williams places them in the Straw/Ochello bedroom, haunted by those ghosts, Brick and Maggie, Brick and Big Daddy converse on and around the bed on which, as Bricks laments "That pair of old sisters slept" and "where both of them died" (*Cat on a Hot Tin Roof*, 2. 87). As such, it is the site of complex confluence of past memories, of love, of illicit consummation, and of death. The confessions within this space figuratively raise the dead, as the past profoundly impacts on the present, and the happiness of Ochello and Straw's "immoral" union challenges the morality on display within these unhappy characters.

As David Savran notes, the space which the Straw/Ochello bedroom metonymically represents is "the closet." Eve Sedgwick in her now classic book, *The Epistemology of the Closet*, notes that the closet has functioned in modern America as a critical element within gay subjectivity. "Even at an individual level, there are remarkably few of even the most openly gay people who are not deliberately in the closet with someone personally, economically or institutionally important to them." [15] Thus, the closet served as a strategic hiding place within which one could negotiate one's identity. Given the outside institutional pressures against the "love that dared not speak its name," the closet offered protection. Yet within *Cat*'s closet, the idea of secrecy is constantly compromised. Mae and Gooper eavesdrop in order to glean evidence against Brick and Maggie in the service of their own cause. "The walls have ears in this place," Big Daddy cautions Brick during their conversation (*Cat on a Hot Tin Roof*, 2.63). The porous nature of this closet complicates the intimacy of the confessions, for they are at once private and public. In his presentation of the tensions between the public and private, the personal and political, Williams critiques the Cold War politics of his day and the environment of suspicion and fear that kept homosexuality in the closet. Critics such as John Bak and Bruce McConachie, discuss in detail these Cold War dynamics and how they operate in *Cat on Hot Tin Roof*. The specters outside the room listening at the door, Mae and Groper represent forces of social conformity, the type of McCarthyist tribunal that rationalized as patriotic the crimes of eavesdropping and informing on your friends and neighbors.[16] Big Daddy rails against such abuses, "I can't stand sneakin' and spyin', it makes me sick" (*Cat on a Hot Tin Roof*, 2.62). Mae with her five no-necks, and a sixth on the way, represents vindictive and dangerous social mores and fertility run amuck. This "moral majority" Williams questions and protests.

As David Savran observes, with the play's adherence to neoclassic unities, the room also serves as a "modern analogue to what Roland Barthes calls the Racinian Antechamber: a space between."[17] It is liminal space, between and betwixt, and as such is a space of great destructive and creative potential. An ineffectual priest, Revered Tooker transgresses the space and interrupts the conversation of Big Daddy and Brick in an attempt to find the men's bathroom. His violation of this space emphasizes how the closet is not by any means impervious to threat and can be violated. At the same time, the fact that he has lost his way to the bathroom humorously points to how wrong-headed religion can be on such questions of intimacy. The confessions in the closet that reach beyond the closet question sexual propriety in a world order that Williams suggests needs to be questioned.

Parks's *In the Blood* draws directly on this notion of confession challenging the social status quo, and troubling the line between the public and the private. At various moments in Parks's play, characters step forward and share with the audience their stories of sexual relations with Hester. As with the closet confessions in *Cat on Hot Tin Roof*, these moments are at once public and private. The characters speak directly to the audience without any form of mediation. Parks, in Brechtian style, numbers and announces each of these five confessions and gives each of them a title. By speaking openly to the audience, they attempt to enlist the audience in the story. The spectators become the social arbiters and social conscience. At the same time as they are delivered publicly, the confessions are extremely personal and intimate. The Welfare Lady, the Doctor, the Reverend, Amiga Gringa, and Chili all reveal the most confidential details of their sexual misuse of Hester. As with the confessions in *Cat on a Hot Tin Roof,* none of these characters declares their guilt and ask for forgiveness. Rather, they boldly and unashamedly exalt in the sexual fetishes and past practices. In fact, they accuse Hester in the process of enabling their trysts through her loose, and even wanton, sexuality. Just as Gooper and Mae report back to Big Mamma, and indirectly Big Daddy, on what they believe to be Brick's sexual deviance in *Cat on a Hot Tin Roof,* Welfare and the others detail to the audience what they construe as Hester's licentiousness. Parks contrasts the supposed moral righteousness of these characters, their disdain for the impoverished, and purportedly parasitic Hester, with the hypocrisy of their sexual proclivities, their fetishized desires, and their evident exploitation of Hester La Negrita. Implicit in these confessed rationalizations of their indiscretions with Hester is Parks's critique of the establishment, the "moral majority" and its claims to an ethical higher ground.

Parks, following and expanding on Williams in these confessions, critiques conventional representations of sex and sexuality, and questions what is normative in sexual desire. Her open discussion of sexual perversity operates, as with Celine Parreñas-Shimizu in *The Hyper Sexuality of Race,* as "a political critic of the normal." [18] Williams's Blanche in *A Streetcar Named Desire* constitutes another hypersexual figure, an outcast for her sexual improprieties with young boys. Through Blanche's desperate desire to transcend the mundane, to revive a mythical past, Williams provides a "political critic of the normal." In Parks's play, the other characters cite Hester as outside social norms, dirty, living in the gutter. These characters hurl insults and abuse at Hester, just as Mitch and Stanley ridicule and excoriate Blanche for her indiscretions. Paradoxically, with *In the Blood,* the characters' confessed complaints only serve to indict themselves. The Reverend, the Doctor, and the Welfare Lady all use Hester for masturbatory, self-gratifying and self-indulgent fulfillment of their missionary desires. They justify their exploitation of Hester through the narcissistic celebration of their own charity towards her, the "erotics of benevolence." In each case, they use her disadvantage to their sexual advantage.

The Doctor, who through his street practice attends to the needs of the underprivileged, presents himself as a picture of liberal exhaustion. He has given so much to the socially destitute and Hester represents "one of my neediest cases for several years now." He expresses his repulsion of her—"At first I wouldn't touch her with gloves on." But this antipathy toward her eventually animates his desire and enables him to interpret her need for medical assistance as sexual need:

> Each time she comes to me
> looking more and more forlorn
> and more in more in need
> of affection [*In the Blood,* 44].

Unable or unwilling to satisfy her medical problems, the Doctor is able to have sex with Hester and projects on to her his own monstrous cravings.

> Sucked me off for what seemed like hours
> But I was very insistent. And held back
> And she understood that I wanted her in the traditional way.
> And she was very giving very motherly very obliging very
> understanding very phenomenal [*In the Blood,* 45].

Perversely, the fact that Hester was initially, for the Doctor, so very marginalized, so beyond the pale of his consideration, even as another human being, now catapults their intercourse for him into the level of the mythic. That he imagines her within the sex act as "very moth-erly" and "very phenomenal" places this relationship in the idealized realm of the symbolic.

This Doctor bears some relation to the figure Doc in Williams's *Small Craft Warnings*, a role that Williams played himself in the 1972 Off Broadway production at the Truck and Warehouse Theatre on East 4th Street in New York. Doc, an alcoholic, like Parks's Doctor, is exhausted by his street practice. In fact, he has lost his license to practice, but proceeds to administer to certain patients anyway. *Small Craft Warnings* focuses in on Doc and the other denizens of Monks Bar, a seedy beachside establishment south of Los Angeles. *Small Craft Warnings,* like other plays Williams wrote during his years of depression and drug and alco-hol abuse in the 1960s and 1970s, such as the one-act play *The Mutilated* (1966), focuses on the gutter, homeless figures, and life on the street. His explorations of these desperate and dissolute souls stuck on the margins of society—figures like Leona, a beautician who lives in a trailer park but repeatedly plays Jascha Heifetz's recording of Tchaikovsky's "Serenade Melan-cholique" at the bar—find self-possession and dignity within these characters. Parks reveals such humanity and determination in her homeless welfare mother, Hester. Williams in his work again pushes against the limits of realism; he allows each character a monologue and voice in telling the story. William Faulkner's *As I Lay Dying* (1930) follows a somewhat sim-ilar narrative pattern, as does Suzan-Lori Parks's novel, *Getting Mother's Body* (2003), that explicitly riffs on Faulkner. Moreover, the moments of character narratives in *Small Craft Warnings* also serve as like those in Parks's *In the Blood* as a form of confession. Williams's original title for the play was just that, *Confessional*.

In the Welfare Lady's confession, Hester's class difference equally becomes a point of attraction. At first, the Welfare Lady reports that her job requires her negotiation and main-tenance of the social borders:

> I walk the line
> Between us and them
> Between our kind and their kind.
> The balance of the system depends on a well
> drawn boundary line
> And all parties respecting that boundary [*In the Blood*, 42].

The social order, the delineation of self from the other, she argues, requires the maintenance of these strict boundaries. And yet, sex facilitates border crossings as she admits that she had arranged for Hester to partake in a *ménage-à-trois* with her husband and her, after her hus-band grew bored with the routines of their lovemaking:

> Hubby did her and me alternately.
> The thrill of it—.
> *(Rest)*
> I was so afraid I'd catch something
> But I was swept away and couldn't stop....
> She let me slap her across the face
> and I crossed the line [*In the Blood*, 62].

The slap constitutes a display of violent authority and sexual power but also privilege and perverse pleasure. For the Welfare Lady it is the act by which she recognizes that she has "crossed the line," from functioning as a mere participant, to becoming a full agent in the activity. And yet, the Welfare Lady protests that her crossing the line was simply a product of being caught up in the emotion of the event. She also argues that inviting Hester over was an effort to satisfy her husband's fantasies more than her own. While she sees her own par-ticipation as unconscious, she maintains that Hester was a willing partner. "She was surprised, but consented (*In the Blood*, 62). The picture Welfare presents is of a woman attempting to rationalize her own sexual difference and sublimate her prurient desires.

Sadomasochistically, the Reverend yokes his selfish sexual desire to Hester's pain. When Hester appeals to him for financial assistance for their baby, he offers no child support, only avoidance. Instead, sexually aroused, attracted by her supplication before him and her destitute circumstances, the Reverend asks her for a blow job. Then, after she reluctantly consents, he offers his confession to the audience where he admits:

> Suffering is an enormous turn on....
> She had that look in her eye that invites liaisons
> Eyes that say red spandex [*In the Blood*, 45].

Rather than encouraging his religious compassion, her suffering and poverty stimulate his prurient sexual urges. Parks with her Reverend, like Williams with the Reverend Tooker in *Cat on a Hot Tin Roof*, offers a biting critique of the hypocrisy often present in conventional religion and its platforms of morality, and in the economics of faith. The Reverend dodges Hester's solicitations for financial aid or "backing" for their child, by claiming that he himself must wait for his own backers. "Do you know what a 'Backer' is? ... It's a person who backs you.... My backers are building me a church" (*In the Blood*, 44). In a scene similar to the encounter between the Baron Doctor and the Venus Hottentot in Parks's *Venus*, where the Baron Doctor turns his back to the Venus on the bed and masturbates, the Reverend turns his back to her and pleasures himself sitting on a rock while Hester reveals her vision of an eclipse that has engulfed her like the hands of fate. His arousal, like that of the Baron Doctor's, removes him from and denigrates Hester's fetishized difference, even as it demonstrates his perverted response to her suffering. "That's how we like our poor. At arm's length" (*In the Blood*, 44). She embodies for him "poverty erotica." And yet at the same time he blames and loathes her:

> In all my days in the gutter I never hurt anyone.
> And now hate I have for her
> and her hunger
> and the *hate* I have for her hunger [*In the Blood*, 79].

The Reverend, who escaped from the gutter, sees Hester as attempting to drag him back into it, and despises her as a result. Confession functions as mechanisms not for self-critique, but self exoneration and for fortifying the other characters conviction of Hester's guilt.

Hester, Brick, and the Personal as Political

In Hester, Parks creates a character who has much in common with Williams's Brick. For Hester, much like Brick, becomes a screen onto which others project their own desires. Brick faces equally selfish demands. Big Daddy wants Brick to be his heir and imagines him bearing him a grandson. The vindictive Mae and Gooper hope to expose Brick's homosexuality and thereby assure his disinheritance and their own ascension. Maggie envisions Brick rediscovering the sexual ease that he expressed in their youth. "Your indifference made you wonderful at lovemaking—*strange*—but true," she tells him. Similarly in *In the Blood*, the Doctor, Welfare, and the Reverend all exploit Hester's impoverished status to their own ends. As with Big Daddy's and Maggie's sexual propositions of Brick, Hester's involvement with the Doctor, or the Reverend or the Welfare Lady, are about economics and power. In the last section of the play, Hester's long-lost love, Chilli, Jabber's father, returns in search of the innocent girl he remembers from their naïve first sexual explorations of youth. Within this fantasy, he, like the others, patronizes her to serve his own interests. He intends to make her his wife, but only if she conforms to his prenuptial conditions. "You would be mine and I would by yrs and all that. But I would still retain the rights to my manhood" (*In the Blood*, 93). Chilli seeks a relationship but only on his terms. He is not in search of mutual love, but rather self-accentuation. "I would rule the roost. I would call the shots. The whole roost and every single shot" (*In the Blood*, 93).

In response to these ways that others seek to define and mold them, both Brick and Hester attempt to escape. For Brick, escape comes through alcohol. He drinks in excess until he hears the "click" in his head that makes him "peaceful" (*Cat on a Hot Tin Roof*, 2.73). Hester fantasizes a different life for her children and herself where she has "a leg up," enough food, clothing, and money. Not unlike Big Daddy, Hester has pain in her gut that requires treatment. Yet while his pain comes from excessive acting out, hers is due to a lack of nourishment. She goes without food in order to try and make sure her children are sufficiently fed. In the face of a world of hypocrisy that surrounds them, Brick and Hester cling to an idealized view of what relationships can be. Brick wants to remember and keep his relationship with Skipper unsullied. He pleads with Maggie, "One has one great good thing in his life. One great good thing which is true!— I had friendship with Skipper" (*Cat on a Hot Tin Roof*, 1.44). His alliterative excess "great" and good" serve as his way of solidifying in his own mind what others have questioned and so protecting this relationship from threat. Hester romanticizes a love that will sweep her off her feet, a wedding in a white dress and matching white shoes. In fact, she has kept a pair of unsullied white shoes for just this occasion, and when Chilli returns, this dream almost becomes a reality. In a vivid scene filled with pathos and possibilities, Parks has Hester put on these white shoes, after Chilli dresses her in the wedding dress that he just happens to be carrying in a basket. Hester's chance at happiness appears almost palpable until the image is smashed and left unfilled when Chilli discovers that rather than just the one child that he fathered, Hester has four others. Hester is left desperate and psychically alone. However, Brick, cornered by Maggie's proclamation of her false pregnancy, comes to understand that he can no longer afford to be alone and must act with her to consummate their union and potentially bring forth that heir. For both Hester and Brick the responsibility for and possibilities of reproduction have profound personal consequences.

Through both Brick and Hester, Williams and Parks reveal the personal as political. Brick's psychological angst around issues of sexuality and reproduction reflect larger social issues of tolerance. Brick, however, is the exponent of intolerance, while Hester is the object of its abuse. The chorus of other characters ostracize Hester for her purported sexual deviance, but Brick himself rails against "queers" and "ducking sissies" and protests those who would see his relationship with Skipper in such terms. Brick also fervently rants against mendacity. But, as critics such as Jon Bak and Foster Hirsch have pointed out, mendacity functions as a "pseudonym for 'homosexuality' and its sociopolitical component 'homophobia.'"[19] As Big Daddy indicates, the problem Brick sees with mendacity is actually with himself. Brick's homophobia is a defense against what he does not want to see or even refuses to see in himself. John Bak maintains, "For at the heart of Brick's reticence to name his relationship with Skipper is his inability to understand what homosexuality is, or how it is precisely defined or even vaguely knowable — an epistemology mire for which Williams holds his Cold War society ultimately responsible."[20] Brick's problem with homosexuality is that he can not situate it in relation to himself or know what homosexuality means in possibly more palatable terms. It is only "queer." As Bak argues, this is more than an existential problem, it is socio-political one that Williams associates with the Cold War climate and culture of witch hunts and fears. Brick gives voice to such prejudicial suspicions and Williams, through his representation, calls such attitudes into question.

While Williams shows Brick as both the voice and the embodiment of Cold War anxiety and homophobia, Parks draws Hester as the agent and object of abusive racialized sexuality. Hester as a poor black woman is objectified and, as Perreñas-Shimizu calls hypersexualized,[21] she is over-determined by sex and sexual ascriptions. Moreover, with Hester these sexual representations are equally racialized. The sexual exploitation of Hester reaffirms the historic stereotype of black woman as sexual temptress, a Jezebel, as an object of desire, subject to the abuse of the white master in slavery. Yet, not unlike Parks's title character Venus in her exploration of the sad history of the Venus Hottentot, *Venus* (1995), Hester is not simply a sexual victim. Her figure is not solely defined by her sexual subjugation. Like Venus, she is not simply a desired object, but a desiring subject with a degree of agency even within her oppressive circumstances. Hester chooses not to tell on and turn into the Welfare authorities any of the fathers of her children. As with Parks's Venus, Hester's situation allows for few options other than to use her body in an attempt to change her socio-economic circumstances. However, Hester finds no sense of self, no freedom in these acts. Sex does not liberate her from but only further imprisons her in the system.

With Parks, Hester literalizes and intensifies the dynamics of Brick's angst. While Brick has a "gut" reaction to the mendacity in the world, Hester actually has a real pain in her gut. As Brick feels the social threat of association with homosexuality, Hester faces the active threat of being sterilized by the Doctor "taking out her women's parts." The Doctor and Welfare conspire to prevent Hester from having any future children, and stop her from becoming a further burden on society. They will render her "spay." The notion of spaying her is purposefully dehumanizing. Even as they would have sex with her, they still would deny her civil rights or individual choice. Rather, her fertility constitutes a social blight that they must curtail, not unlike what they would do to a feral cat. Parks's representation of forced sterilization has a firm basis in contemporary reality as the United States government since the 1930s, has systematically carried out racialized sterilization efforts as a method supposedly of population control. These efforts have impacted predominantly poor women of color, and disproportionately African American women. In 1972, the federal government funded some 100,000 to 200,000 sterilizations.[22] According to a 1970 National Fertility Study conducted by Princeton University's Office of Population Control, 43 percent of the women sterilized by federally subsidized programs were black.[23] With Parks's Hester, elements of race, class, and gender intersect with questions of sexuality and the politics of reproduction. The fact that she is poor and black is implicitly and explicitly responsible for exploitative measures enacted on her.

Maternal

Hester is not merely a victim of racism, but a woman fighting to remain boldly outside the conventional definitions of womanhood. And in her presentation of Hester, Parks creates a character that, borrowing her own phrase of "reps and revs," repeats and revises not Brick, of course, but Williams's Maggie. A determined survivor, Maggie's past has informed her present. Born into poverty, she determines never to return to this life and to do whatever necessary to maintain her new comfortable life in luxury. Hester equally resolves not to live within society's expectations. While society does not condone children out of wedlock, she chooses to have five children. All the codes that society poses as normative — illiterate and unemployed, she lives outside on the street under a bridge — Hester fails to observe and, rather, charts a different path. Maggie defines herself as the ultimate feline, a cat situated on a hot tin roof. She understands the precarious nature of her own situation, and this only fuels her determination. She is willing to manipulate people and circumstances to enable her own success. In this way, her self assertion and resolve stand juxtaposed to the genteel images and expectations of white women at this time, particularly southern white women caught in the codes and expectations of domesticity. Each woman, then, strikes out in what might seem unusual or unconventional ways toward positions of feminist self definition.

Yet, even as Maggie and Hester strive to remain outside of social conventions and of womanhood, they also in ways desire and even conform to more traditional images of motherhood. Hester defines herself as a mother. When Amiga Gringa prods her to sell one of her children, she replies, "My kids is mine. I got rid of 'em what do I got? Nothing" (*In the Blood*, 28). Hester sees herself in relation to her children. They are her possessions and she will do anything to ensure their survival. For Maggie her survival depends on having a child, becoming a mother. In order to inherit the plantation she must bear Brick's child. Motherhood for her, then, represents a site not simply of conformity then, but a space of possibility. Patricia Hill Collins writes, "Viewing motherhood as a symbol of power can catalyze Black women to take actions they otherwise might not have considered."[24] For both Maggie and Hester, motherhood represents power and compels them to take daring actions.

Both women present alternative constructions of gendered resistance and racialized sexuality. C.W. E. Bigsby calls Maggie one the most "powerful and original characters in American drama" whose "whole being is a resistance movement, a denial, a refusal."[25] Bigsby's notion of resistance I find particularly significant as Maggie employs non-traditional means to rebel against the status quo. Maggie uses sexuality as resistance in her pursuit of Brick, in her seduction of Skipper, in her quest for Big Daddy's inheritance. Hester attempts to traffic in sexuality as an act of political revolt against the status quo, and as means for advancement beyond her economic station in life. In order to convince the Reverend finally to commit to paying child support, she consents to giving him a blow job. Ultimately, this attempt to pleasure the Reverend does not lead him to fulfill his paternal duties. More pointedly, Hester's bowing down submissively to the Reverend's sexual demands points to the racialization of sexuality. As a black woman she is drawn within certain hypersexual expectations. In fact, acts of sexual subversion are always racialized and dependent on how one negotiates these racial lines. The recourses to economic power the white Maggie seeks are not available to the black welfare queen Hester. Parks in this play complicates the relationship between race and sexuality, as do both the Reverend and Welfare Lady who exploit Hester and are also black. Yet, this intraracial abuse does not change, but only serves to intensify the ways in which race is indexed to poverty, to sexual deviance, and thus separates Hester's plight further from that of Maggie.

The final method in which each woman comes to confront motherhood ultimately underlines their shared feminist resistance and also their racial difference. In the climactic moments of *Cat on a Hot Tin Roof*, Maggie announces to the disgruntled Mae and Gooper, the thrilled Big Mama, and the startled Brick that she is pregnant. Then, in the final scene after she has calculatedly emptied Brick's liquor cabinet of its supplies, she announces in to him her intention for them to sleep together and make her premature pronouncement a reality: "And so tonight we're going to make the lie true, and when that's done, I'll bring the liquor back here and we'll get drunk together" (*Cat on Hot tin Roof*, 3.123). The dynamics of power have shifted. Maggie is now in control. She now assumes the normative role of masculine authority, directing the action.

While Maggie imaginatively brings an heir to life, Hester ends the life of Chilli's heir, her son Jabber. Feeling the overwhelming pressure of the hand of fate coming down on her after Chilli's departure, the desperate Hester tries one final time to exhort money from the Reverend. He, however, refuses. He beats and insults her and tells her "You'll get nothing from me!" and calls her a "common slut" (*In the Blood*, 103). Jabber overhears and childishly repeats the word that his mother does not want to hear, "slut." Blinded by her desire to resist this and other pejorative labels, and overwhelmed by her inability to control her own destiny, Hester picks up a club and bludgeons her son to death. With her hands covered in her son's blood, the crazed, grief-stricken Hester writes the letter "A," the letter that Jabber taught her, on the ground and then moves to cradle her son. Philip Kolin writes, "In this tragic tableau, blood is part of a sacrificial ritual where Hester is both murderer and loving mother. Presented as a bloody Pieta, she evokes the Blessed Virgin Mary cast as a welfare mother pushed beyond the limits of pain."[26] While this picture evokes the Virgin, the infanticide recalls that of other black mothers in history and literature, the slave Margaret Garner, Sethe in Toni Morrison *Beloved*, who killed their children as act of violent love saving them from the horrors of life in a racist world. Moreover, Hester kills her son Jabber in an act of indirection and transference. Rather than vent her frustrations and rage at the men who have betrayed and abandoned her or the social system that exploits her, Hester murders the one thing that she loves most, one of her children, the ones for whom she has gone without and was determined to protect.

Still in the final scenes of resolution of the play, Hester is able to voice a cry of resistance as she stands accused and damned by the very system that has used and abused her. A chorus that includes the Doctor who wants to sterilize her after they had sex, the Welfare Lady that uses her for a threesome with her husband, the Reverend who asks her for a quick blow job, all stand over her chanting as she sits alone in her prison cell: "She is the Animal, No skills, 'cept one, cant read, cant write.... That's why things are bad like they are cause of girls like that" (*In the Blood*, 50). Their hypocrisy is glaringly evident. Hester, at first, seems consigned to submit to their charges and admit her crime of giving birth to her brood, her wards of the state. But, then, she realizes that having children represents her ultimate act of self-definition and defiance against the social order that would restrict her rights of reproduction:

> No
> I shoulda had a hundred
> A hundred
> I shoulda had a hundred-thousand
> A hundred-thousand a whole *army*...
> Spitting em out:
> Bad mannered Bad mouthed Bad Bad *Bastards*! [*In the Blood*, 107].

Hester, about to be rendered spay, voices the tension between population control and reproductive rights and, in so doing, defies the notion that only certain people, white and privileged like Maggie, should be allowed to have children. As Angela Davis notes, "While women of color are urged at every turn to become permanently infertile, white women enjoying prosperous economic conditions are urged, by the same forces, to reproduce themselves."[27] Hester's is a chant of resistance. She does not express desire for a husband and a conventional family but rather her own production of a excessive disorderly brood of bastards that in their repetitive badness reinforce her opposition to a social system riddled with hypocrisy and determined to limit her freedoms.

Parks's *In the Blood* bears the legacy of Tennessee Williams in its bold and frank discussion of sexual normalcy. In this play, as in Williams's *Cat on a Hot Tin Roof*, the playwright uses the exploration of sexual intimacy as a lens to examine greater social ills. Parks, like Williams, comments on the internal angst of her characters, but at the same time is able to critique without didacticism an intolerant culture that surrounds the play. What complicates these questions for Parks is the dynamic of blackness. But if blackness is, and contexts of racialized sexuality are critical to *In the Blood*, we must also recognize how whiteness figures in *Cat on a Hot Tin Roof*. It informs the social privilege, the family values, and sexual politics of Big Daddy, Brick, and Maggie. The intersections of race and sexuality are spaces that at once unite these playwrights but also serve to separate them.

NOTES

1. Shelby Jiggets, "Interview with Suzan-Lori Parks," *Callaloo*, 19.2 (1996): 309.

2. Kevin Kelly, "The Astonishing Power of 'Last Black Man,'" *Boston Globe* 14 February 1992.

3. Mel Gussow, "Dangers of Becoming a Lost Culture," *New York Times*, 25 September 1990.

4. Tennessee Williams, "Something Wild...," *Where I Live* (New York: New Directions, 1978), 8.

5. Suzan-Lori Parks, "*The America Play*." *The America Play and Other Works* (New York; Theatre Communications Group, 1995), 160.

6. George W. Crandell, "Misrepresentation and Miscegenation: Reading the Racialized Discourse of Tennessee Williams's, *A Streetcar Named Desire*," *Modern Drama*, 40.3 (Fall 1997): 338.

7. See Philip Kolin, *Literature & Film Quarterly*, and David Savran, *Communists, Cowboys, and Queers: The Politics of Masculinity in the Work of Arthur Miller and Tennessee Williams* (Minneapolis: University of Minnesota Press, 1992), 126–131.

8. Shelby Jiggets, "Interview with Suzan-Lori Parks," *Callaloo*, 19.2 (1996): 312.

9. Tennessee Williams, *Cat on a Hot Tin Roof* (New York: Signet Books, 1985; original copyright 1954). Act 2, 89. All other references to this play will be made in the text.

10. See René Girard, "'Triangular' Desire," *Deceit, Desire and the Novel*, trans. Yvonne Freccero (Baltimore: Johns Hopkins, 1965), 1–52.

11. Suzan-Lori Parks, "*In the Blood*." *The Red Letter Plays* (New York: TCG Press, 2001; original copyright 1998), "Prologue," 7. All other references to this play will be made in the text.

12. David Savran, *Communists, Cowboys, and Queers: The Politics of Masculinity in the Work of Arthur Miller and Tennessee Williams* (Minneapolis: U of Minnesota P, 1992), 101.

13. Thorstein Verblen, *Theory of Leisure Class* (New York: Augustus M. Kelley, Publishers, 1970).

14. Joseph Roach, *Cities of the Dead* (New York: Columbia U P, 1996), 4.

15. Eve Sedgwick *Epistemology of the Closet* (Berkeley: U of California P, 1990), 68–69.

16. See John Bak, "'sneakin' and spyin" from Broadway to the Beltway: Cold War Masculinity, Brick, and Homosexual Existentialism," *Theatre Journal*, 56 (2004): 225–49. And Bruce McConachie, *American Theater in the Culture of the Cold War: Producing and Contesting Containment 1947–1962* (Iowa City: U of Iowa P, 2003), 103–25.

17. Savran, 104.

18. Celine Parreñas-Shimizu, *The Hypersexuality of Race: Performing Asian/American Women on Screen and Scene* (Durham NC: Duke U P, 2007), 23.

19. John Back, "'sneakin' and spyin','" 230; Foster Hirsch, *A Portrait of the Artist; The Plays of Tennessee Williams* (Port Washington NY: Associated Faculty P, 1979), 50.

20. John Bak, "'sneakin' and spyin" from Broadway to the Beltway: Cold War Masculinity, Brick and Homosexual Existentialism," *Theatre Journal*, 56 (2004): 227.

21. Parreñas-Shimizu, 23.

22. Angel Davis, "Reproductive Rights," *An Introduction to Women's Studies; Gender in a Transnational World*, second edition, eds. Inderpal Grewal and Caren Kaplan (Boston: McGraw Hill, 2006), 105.

23. Ibid. 105.

24. Patricia Hill Collins, *Black Feminist Thought: Knowledge, Consciousness, and the Politics of Empowerment*, second edition (New York; Routledge, 2000), 194.

25. C.W. Bigsby, *Modern American Drama, 1945–2000* (Cambridge: Cambridge U P, 2000), 57.

26. Philip Kolin, "Parks's *In the Blood*," *The Explicator*, 64.4 (Summer 2006): 254.

27. Angela Davis, "Reproductive Rights," 106.

WORKS CITED

Bak, John. "'sneakin' and spyin'" from Broadway to the Beltway: Cold War Masculinity, Brick, and Homosexual Existentialism," *Theatre Journal*, 56 (2004): 225–49.

Bigsby, C.W. *Modern American Drama, 1945–2000*. Cambridge: Cambridge U P, 2000.

Collins, Patricia Hill. *Black Feminist Thought: Knowledge, Consciousness, and the Politics of Empowerment*. Second Edition. New York; Routledge, 2000.

Crandell, George W. "Misrepresentation and Miscegenation: Reading the Racialized Discourse of Tennessee Williams's *A Streetcar Named Desire*," *Modern Drama*, 40.3 (Fall 1997): 338.

Girard, René. *Deceit, Desire and the Novel*, trans. Yvonne Freccero. Baltimore: Johns Hopkins U P, 1965.

Grewal, Inderpal, and Caren Kaplan. *An Introduction to Women's Studies; Gender in a Transnational World*, Second Edition. Boston: McGraw Hill, 2006.

Gussow, Mel. "Dangers of Becoming a Lost Culture," *New York Times*, 25 September 1990.

Jiggets, Shelby. "Interview with Suzan-Lori Parks," *Callaloo*, 19.2 (1996): 309–17.

Kelly, Kevin. "The Astonishing Power of 'Last Black Man,'" *Boston Globe*, 14 February 1992.

Kolin, Philip. "Parks's *In the Blood*," *The Explicator*, 64.4 (Summer 2006): 254.

_____. *Tennessee Williams: A Guide to Research and Performance*. Westport, Conn.: Greenwood, 1998.

_____. *The Undiscovered Country: The Later Plays of Tennessee Williams*. New York: Peter Lang, 2002.

_____. *Tennessee Williams Encyclopedia*. Westport, Conn.: Greenwood P, 2004.

McConachie, Bruce. *American Theater in the Culture of the Cold War: Producing and Contesting Containment 1947–1962*. Iowa City: U of Iowa P, 2003.

Parreñas-Shimizu, Celine. *The Hypersexuality of Race: Performing Asian/American Women on Screen and Scene*. Durham NC: Duke U P, 2007.

Parks, Suzan-Lori. "*The America Play*." *The America Play and Other Works*. New York: Theatre Communications Group, 1995.

_____. "*In the Blood*," *The Red Letter Plays*. New York: TCG, 2001.

Roach, Joseph. *Cities of the Dead*. New York: Columbia U P, 1996.

Savran, David. *Communists, Cowboys, and Queers: The Politics of Masculinity in the Work of Arthur Miller and Tennessee Williams*. Minneapolis: U of Minnesota P, 1992.

Sedgwick, Eve. *Epistemology of the Closet*. Berkeley: U of California P, 1990.

Verblen, Thorstein. *Theory of Leisure Class*. New York: Augustus M. Kelley, 1970.

Williams, Tennessee. *Cat on a Hot Tin Roof*. New York: Signet Books, 1985; original copyright 1954.

_____. "Something Wild...,"*Where I Live*. New York: New Directions, 1978.

Swimming to Chekhovia: Edward Albee on Tennessee Williams — An Interview

David A. Crespy

The following is an interview with Edward Albee, conducted at his Montauk, New York, home, 25 July 2007. It reveals how and why Williams played an essential role in Albee's works.

Crespy: You have said in many interviews that theatre didn't get serious until around the end of the second world war with Tennessee Williams and the late O'Neill.

Albee: Interesting American plays were written before then. One of the most interesting was written around 1904. I wish I could remember what it was called. It was written by someone named Percy or something. I'll think of the name of it. Strange, strange play about an artificial person created by somebody else. Wonderful, wonderful play. Percy Mackaye, perhaps. 1904. There were a couple of interesting plays in that period. And we had some experimental plays in the United States, we had Elmer Rice's *Adding Machine*. And we had a really wonderful play by a woman playwright — a very strange wonderful play.

Crespy: *Machinal*. Sophie Treadwell.

Albee: Sophie Treadwell, yes. Sophie Treadwell — she was a very interesting playwright. And then we got into the thirties and we starting having some what I felt were very second-rate people, though highly, highly regarded — Maxwell Anderson, Robert Sherwood. Those people. And O'Neill of course was writing and Lillian Hellman was beginning to write. I don't think any of them were ... Sherwood or Anderson or Hellman ... were major figures. And O'Neill wrote some interesting plays. I think what's interesting for me with O'Neill is that I find his early plays and his late plays the most interesting. I find the middle period unhappily derivative. And it wasn't until the Second World War that we began to understand what was happening in Europe in the theatre, but at least people like Arthur [Miller] and Tennessee [Williams] were starting to write. We had the agitprop theatre in the thirties — Odets being as good as the best of those, but these were basically socially-useful but not terribly valuable plays. Politically leftist, but not valuable. I don't think anyone can say that there were many great American Plays written before the Second War. After that Arthur starts writing, Tennessee Williams starts writing...

Crespy: What was it about Tennessee's writing that in some ways sets him apart — what was he doing that was so different?

Albee: I've found that theatre is split around the turn of the century. The Chekhovians and the Ibsonians. And I've always been infinitely more fond of the Chekhovians rather than the Ibsonians. And it even happened in America! Arthur, an Ibsonian, started writing and Tennessee, a Chekhovian. I'm ignoring Bill Inge here, because at that point, he wasn't an important playwright. And late O'Neill was happening and that was very important. But what took me so much with Tennessee was that he was a Chekhovian in his sensibility.

Crespy: Well, what do you mean by that?

Albee: He was interested in real people, not as symbols, not as metaphors, not carrying the baggage of symbols, but real people. Chekhov did write about the collapse of Russian society, the collapse of the Tsarist society, and his plays were, in a very, very subtle way, as politically and socially valuable as anything that Ibsen did. But Ibsen is doctrinaire and his characters were created for their social usefulness rather than any individual meaning, and besides the feeling in all of Chekhov's plays is that the people are real as opposed to being symbolic and necessary for the message. The message plays were always problematic for me; one of the critics or somebody used to say that messages should be sent through Western Union. They shouldn't be put on the stage. Ibsen symbolizes things, Chekhov gave you people.

Crespy: What we were talking about, which I thought was interesting, you were talking about Tennessee's Chekhovian qualities in writing characters as real people.

Albee: Right. Where Arthur was working in the Ibsonian fashion creating characters as tools for a message. I mean, everybody who writes a play, if they're any good, writes *about* things. And Tennessee's plays are *about* things. And the plays you've seen of mine are *about* things. O'Neill's plays are *about* things. But some people are directly sociologically involved and others are indirectly involved. As I was saying, Chekhov was certainly writing about the collapse of the Tsarist society. You can't look at the *Cherry Orchard* without realizing what's happening, a whole new class of people taking over from the rich, it's a collapse of that society. But that is seemingly incidental to Chekhov writing real people in real situations — which is why I thought he was so good. Every basically naturalistic area of theatre follows either Chekhov or Ibsen. But at the same time, incidentally, I find this kind of reality is very effective, of course. And Pirandello led the experimental playwrights. America has always been more naturalistic in its enthusiasms for playwriting, and Tennessee and Arthur and O'Neill are fundamentally naturalistic playwrights. But of course there is no such thing as naturalism in the theatre — it's all artifice. And we don't nearly pay terrible much attention to the really avant-garde American writers.

Crespy: Not really. Mac Wellman is a case in point.

Albee: Now some of my plays are fairly experimental and they've never been as popular as the naturalistic ones, but ... well, they're seemingly naturalistic. But that's what was interesting me about Tennessee, that these were real people. And they did not carry the baggage of "look at what I represent."

Crespy: What was your first encounter with Tennessee Williams' work? Do you remember what was the first piece of his that you can remember right now that struck you as being different or interesting?

Albee: Well, it was probably around the same time as the, the late forties, that I encountered *The Iceman Cometh*, the world premiere in 1948 — and I must have seen Tennessee's plays around then. I never remember what I've seen, or when I've seen it.

Crespy: Well, actually, you don't remember it, but at some point William Flanagan said that you were struck by *Suddenly Last Summer*.

Albee: There are qualities to *Suddenly Last Summer* that to my mind ... I didn't see a good production of it ... and the production I saw was unfortunate ... and I haven't bothered to see productions of it since ... and I thought these qualities were taking some of Tennessee's concerns further into almost a surrealist area than some of the other plays. And I don't think that one got as much bothered by other people's corrections as the real Broadway successes. Kazan's rewriting of Tennessee was problematic. Not that Tennessee minded; he knew the rewriting would result in more money. And greater fame. And he wanted it. And then publish earlier versions of the script. *[Albee chuckles]* So you see. Having it both ways.

Crespy: He was a smart business person.

Albee: Yeah. Certainly.

Crespy: He was a professional in the theater.

Albee: There were occasions when Kazan's ideas were better than Tennessee's. But they were not part of his process of creation.

Crespy: Let me go back to *Suddenly Last Summer* for a second. Because there are a number of characters in that ... you know that one of the things I'm writing about are the women in your plays.

Albee: I'm going to stop you there for a second.

Crespy: Okay.

Albee: Because ... *[sighs with a bit of frustration]* I guess Tennessee's women are more important than the men in roles that they play — this is not true with me.

Crespy: I don't think that's true of either one of you, I was just looking for a focus...

Albee: It's much more true with Tennessee.

Crespy: Oh, really?

Albee: Even to the extent that bizarre things happen which shouldn't ... there is a very interesting play by Tennessee called *Orpheus Descending*. Which is always produced incorrectly. It's a play about Orpheus — it's called *Orpheus Descending*. But every production I see, he's barely visible and the play is about the woman,

Crespy: Lady?

Albee: About Lady, and this is a distortion of the play.

Crespy: Because he's the Guy in the Snakeskin Jacket.

Albee: And the play is about him. It's *Orpheus Descending*! Not *Lady Descending*! Or *Lady Rising*! It's not that. And so people tend to emphasize the women in Tennessee's plays in production, to the detriment of the play sometimes. But I do think the women are more important in Tennessee's plays than the men are, generally speaking. And I don't think this is true of my work. So I don't think there is a fair parallel to form there.

Crespy: That's interesting.

Albee: Certainly in *Virginia Woolf,* George is just as important as Martha.

Crespy: Oh, yeah, naturally.

Albee: Naturally. That goes without question. And while there are three women in *Three Tall Women*, look at the other plays. Look, in *Zoo Story* of course, there are two men, and you'll find that the men are just as important as the women.

Crespy: Now you offered a foreword to *Cat on a Hot Tin Roof*— now why was that?

Albee: Well, somebody else had already taken *Streetcar* and I just thought I ought to be involved. And I thought *Cat* had some interesting things. I didn't like the rewrites for the most part.

Crespy: Where Big Daddy is brought back on...

Albee: And I also thought that Tennessee did not hold to the important homosexual element in the play, writing it out. Even going so far as saying once, "that anybody thinks that the homosexuality in this play is important, you're mistaken." Preposterous.

Crespy: Let me read you this quote, which I sent to you earlier, from the stage directions of *Cat on a Hot Tin Roof*: "Some mystery should be left in the revelation of character in a play, just as a great deal of mystery is always left in the revelation of character in life, even in one's own character to himself." He's saying this essentially to avoid the "pat" solution to Brick's relationship with Skipper.

Albee: There is a difference between what he's talking about and contradiction. Ambiguity is one thing; contradiction is another. And I think he's lying to himself if not to his audience.

Crespy: Well, and, you know, it's ... yeah, he essentially says, "even to one's own character to himself."

Albee: Which I think is preposterous.

Crespy: Was he just ... from a generation that wasn't comfortable...

Albee: He was being poetic. By the way, I think that *Glass Menagerie* would be an infinitely better play without the narrator in it.

Crespy: Well, that's what you teach — don't write a "Tom" play.

Albee: That play is not as good as it could have been. But no matter. It started him off, which is very nice. More than *Battle of Angels* ever did.

Crespy: What is it, beside the nature of the Chekhovian nature of Tennessee Williams' plays what else struck you about the characters he created or the language that he wrote or things.

Albee: The fact that Tennessee was capable of elevating language into music at the same time keeping it absolutely believable ... that's naturalistic dialogue ... that's a pretty good trick.

Crespy: That's a pretty good trick.

Albee: He gave his people arias that you believe and revealed character ... that's pretty good.

Crespy: Now at some point he made some historic comment about you, that you were the next important playwright.

Albee: I think his agent told him to stop saying that.

Crespy: But you know, he said it a lot, and he loved your writing. What do you think the connection was for him?

Albee: Probably what I've been talking about — the Chekhov connection, the reality of the characters, the music of the language. All of those things. And also, we both are concerned with failure to a certain extent, characters failing to live their lives fully aware, in a way they should have lived them. The sadness of all that. Yes. A tragic sense of life. It's all they have, actually.

Crespy: I asked people when I told them I was writing this article — what is the one thing that you think that Edward Albee's and Tennessee William's plays have in common, and almost all of them said, "outsiders" — that your plays deal with people who are outside, who don't get the chance...

Albee: Well, they are the people who are interesting — and if you have people who are completely adjusted to society — there's something wrong with them to begin with! *[he chuckles]* They're not participating or they feel too comfortable in their society. And of course, people who have greater intelligence, a greater sensitivity, a greater sense of isolation — these are going to be more interesting people. And we'd rather write about interesting people. You don't write about dull people who've bought into it all.

Crespy: What was your personal experience of Tennessee, your memories that struck you about him?

Albee: Well, we'd see each other at cocktail parties and unfortunately by the time I got to know him at all well he was out of it more often than he was in — he came out to Montauk several times and took a room, a couple of rooms in a place up beyond the town. And he usually brought some pretty boy — usually some nice young kid — unfortunately, he would beat up on him. Tennessee was something of a sadist, but he would swim in my pool, for hours at a time. He loved swimming.

Crespy: Was it was obsessive, or was it something that he did to...?

Albee: I think that was his exercise, and he loved to do it — and it is wonderful form of exercise. He always liked swimming. And we would talk, well, like all writers talk. When I spent time with Beckett, we didn't sit around talking about writing. I didn't spend time talking about writing with Tennessee. That only happens in bad fiction. *[Albee chuckles]* We talk about sex and politics and money ... all the good stuff. *[Albee laughs]* Tennessee knew I liked him, that I admired him a lot. Though I wasn't happy with a lot of his later plays.

Crespy: You liked *Camino Real*, which everyone else beat up.

Albee: Well, I liked *Camino Real* because of the interesting fact ... the irony of the fact that people started complaining before he wrote *Camino Real* that he was writing the same play over and over again, repeating himself, and then he wrote *Camino Real* about as distant from that style as he could possibly get, and what did the same critics say? "Why doesn't he stay with what he knows?" So he got beaten up for doing what they told him to do.

Crespy: Which is what happened to you, with critics expecting you to write *Who's Afraid of Virginia Woolf?* over and over again.

Albee: Of course. Exactly. And I thought *Camino Real* had a lot of interesting stuff in it. Good play.

Crespy: Who writes expressionism, or even attempts to write expressionism?

Albee: Not many people.

Crespy: The last question I have, and this is really ... it's not that I think that the female characters are the only good characters in your work, but there's odd dichotomy between the critics and the actresses who have played the roles in your plays and in Tennessee Williams plays.

Albee: This is because the female characters may tend to seem more extravagant, they seem more theatrical, but you'll find in George in *Who's Afraid of Virginia Woolf* you'll find the spine of the play. In *Delicate Balance*, in Tobias, you'll the find basically the essence of the play. The men may be a little quieter than some of the women, but basically they are even more important than the women who seem more important.

Crespy: Basically the women revolve around them, the men provide an axis.

Albee: Well that may or may not be true, but I just find that the men are quieter, not as flamboyant, and therefore the women get more attention. And I've heard people say "we want to do a production of *Who's Afraid of Virginia Woolf?* and we've got a woman for Martha, let's go and rehearse, and I've said, "Oh no, find me a George, and then I will give you permission." And this true of the other plays, that the male characters are just as important.

Crespy: Well, I'll try to be careful about that in my essay.

Albee: There are two parallels that don't tell us much our work. (a) the focus on the female characters — in my case, they're not more important than any other factor in my plays, and also (b) the fact that both Tennessee and I are both gay. Totally irrelevant.

Crespy: And you've gotten beat up on this.

Albee: Of course. And they're totally wrong. That's to stop people from writing, among other things.

Crespy: It's not the women who have written those articles; it's men like Philip Roth or Stanley Kaufman who are somehow bothered by this or somehow disturbed by this.

Albee: Too bad!

Crespy: Good! That's good. I'm done, that's all I need.

About the Contributors

Philip C. Kolin, professor of English at the University of Southern Mississippi, has published nearly 40 books and 200 articles. His books on Williams include a cultural/theatre history of *Streetcar* in production — *Williams: A Streetcar Named Desire* (2000); the *Tennessee Williams Encyclopedia* (2004); *The Undiscovered Country: The Later Plays of Tennessee Williams* (2002); *Confronting Tennessee Williams's A Streetcar Named Desire: Essays in Critical Pluralism* (1992); and *Tennessee Williams: A Guide to Scholarship and Performance* (1998). Kolin has also written *Understanding Adrienne Kennedy* (2005) and recently edited *Contemporary African American Women Playwrights* (2007). His *Successful Writing at Work* will go into its 9th edition (in 2009). A poet as well, he has published three books of poems and edited (with Susan Swartwout) *Hurricane Blues: Poems About Katrina and Rita* (2006).

Nancy Cho is associate professor of English and director of the American Studies Program at Carleton College. Her published work includes an essay that cross-reads the theatre of Anna Deavere Smith and Chay Yew, and she currently is working on a comparative study of ethnic theatre in the post–Civil Rights era.

John M. Clum is professor of theater studies and English at Duke University. His books include *Still Acting Gay: Male Homosexuality in Modern Drama* (2000) and *Something for the Boys: Musical Theatre and Gay Culture* (1999). He has written extensively on British and American drama and film including a number of essays on Tennessee Williams.

David A. Crespy is a playwright and an associate professor of theatre at the University of Missouri-Columbia, and serves as the artistic director of the Missouri Playwrights Workshop. He has written a book on Edward Albee and his influence on the Off Off Broadway theatre entitled *Off-Off-Broadway Explosion* (2003), and his article on the Albee-Barr-Wilder Playwrights Unit was published in *Theatre History Studies*.

Harry J. Elam, Jr., is the Olive H. Palmer Professor in the Humanities at Stanford University. He is author of *Taking It to the Streets: The Social Protest Theater of Luis Valdez and Amiri Baraka* and *The Past as Present in the Drama of August Wilson*; and co editor of four books, *African American Performance and Theater History: A Critical Reader*, *Colored Contradictions: An Anthology of Contemporary African American Drama*, *The Fire This Time: African American Plays for the New Millennium*, and *Black Cultural Traffic: Crossroads in Performance and Popular Culture*. His articles have appeared in *American Theater*, *American Drama*, *Modern Drama*, *Theatre Journal*, *Text and Performance Quarterly* as well as journals in Belgium, Israel, Poland and Taiwan. He has also written essays published in several critical anthologies.

Verna A. Foster is an associate professor of English at Loyola University Chicago, where she teaches courses in modern drama, Shakespeare, and dramatic theory. She is the author of *The Name and Nature of Tragicomedy* (2004) as well as numerous articles on Renaissance and modern European and American drama, including Tennessee Williams's *A Streetcar Named Desire* in *American Drama* and *A Lovely Sunday for Creve Coeur* in Philip C. Kolin's *The Undiscovered Country: The Late Plays of Tennessee Williams*. Currently, she is working on a book focusing on contemporary women dramatists. She is also the book review editor of *Text & Presentation*.

Michael L. Greenwald, a professor of theatre and English at Texas A&M University, is currently the director of A&M's International Studies Degree Program. He is the author of *Directions by Indirections: John Barton of the Royal Shakespeare Company* (1985) and has written numerous articles about Shakespeare in production. A practicing theater artist, Greenwald has directed or acted in over 80 plays (including Inge's *Picnic* and *The Dark at the Top of the Stairs*) in professional and academic theatre settings. He is also the lead author-editor of *The Longman Anthology of Drama and Theater: A Global Perspective* (2000) and *The Longman Anthology of Modern and Contemporary Drama: A Global Survey* (July 2003); he co-authored *Shakespeare: Script, Stage, Screen* (2006) as well.

Susan Koprince is professor of English at the University of North Dakota, where she teaches courses in modern American fiction and drama. In 2002, she published *Understanding Neil Simon* (2002) and has contributed an essay on Neil Simon to the *Dictionary of Literary Biography* (2003). Her publications on Williams included articles on "Domestic Violence in *A Streetcar Named Desire*" and "Tennessee Williams's Unseen Characters" printed in *Tennessee Williams's Cat on a Hot Tin Roof: Modern Critical Interpretations* (2002).

Tom Mitchell, associate professor of theatre at the University of Illinois Urbana-Champaign, has directed the 21st century premieres of Tennessee Williams's early plays *Candles to the Sun* and *Stairs to the Roof*, as well as productions of *Fugitive Kind* and *Spring Storm*. He has also compiled and directed a staged introduction to these plays, "Caged Hearts: The Early Plays of Tennessee Williams." He convened a symposium on "Tennessee Williams: The Apprentice Plays," and has contributed to the Tennessee Williams/New Orleans Literary Festival Scholars Conference and Washington University's "The Secret Year: Tennessee Williams International Symposium."

Brenda Murphy is Board of Trustees Distinguished Professor of English at the University of Connecticut. She has written numerous articles and books about American drama and theater, including *Tennessee Williams and Elia Kazan: A Collaboration in the Theatre* (1992), *The Provincetown Players and the Culture of Modernity* (2005), *Congressional Theatre: Dramatizing McCarthyism on Stage, Film, and Television* (1999), and as editor, *The Cambridge Companion to American Women Playwrights* (1999) *Twentieth Century American Drama: Critical Concepts in Literary and Cultural Studies* (2006). Her book on David Mamet in the Routledge Modern and Contemporary Dramatists series will be published in 2010.

Annette J. Saddik is an associate professor in the English department at New York City College of Technology (CUNY), and also teaches in the Ph.D. program in theatre at the CUNY Graduate Center. Her area of specialization is twentieth-century drama and performance, particularly the work of Tennessee Williams. She is the author of *Contemporary American*

Drama (2007) and *The Politics of Reputation: The Critical Reception of Tennessee Williams's Later Plays* (1999), and has also edited and introduced a collection of Williams's previously unpublished later plays, *The Traveling Companion and Other Plays* (2008). She has published several essays in *Modern Drama, TDR, Études Théâtrales, The South Atlantic Review, The Tennessee Williams Annual Review, The Undiscovered Country: The Later Plays of Tennessee Williams,* and *The Tennessee Williams Encyclopedia.*

Sandra G. Shannon, professor of drama in the Department of English at Howard University, is one of the nation's leading authorities on the works of Pulitzer Prize winning playwright August Wilson. Her works include *The Dramatic Vision of August Wilson* (1995), and *August Wilson's Fences: A Reference Guide* (2003). She also co-edited the collection *August Wilson and Black Aesthetic* (2004). In addition, Shannon has published numerous chapter length essays on Wilson. Most recently, she published a critical essay and interview with Lynn Nottage in *Contemporary African American Women Playwrights* (2007). Shannon is currently editing *Approaches to Teaching August Wilson* to be published by the Modern Language Association. She now serves as president of the Black Theatre Network and co-editor of *Theatre Topics Journal.*

Arvid F. Sponberg, professor of English and former department chair at Valparaiso University in Indiana, is the author of *Broadway Talks: What Professionals Think About Commercial Theatre in America* (1991) and *A.R. Gurney: A Casebook* (2004). He has taught and published widely about the profession of playwriting in the United States in the twentieth century. In 2007, a Kapfer Family Research Award helped him launch www.chicagotheaterhistoryproject .org

Kirk Woodward is artistic director of the Troupe of Vagabonds theatre company in Bloomfield, New Jersey. The author of over twenty produced plays, he is also a technical writer for the Visiting Nurse Service of New York, a frequent public speaker, and a contributor of reviews and articles to journals and books, including the *Tennessee Williams Encyclopedia.*

Harvey Young is an assistant professor of theatre at Northwestern University with appointments in performance studies and radio/television/film. He is the president of the Black Theatre Association and the author of numerous articles on black theatre/performance, including "The Black Body as Souvenir in *American Lynching*" for *Theatre Journal.* His first book, *Embodying Black Experience,* is forthcoming from the University of Michigan Press.

Index